LIBRARY AND SOCIETY

(IInd REVISED AND ENLARGED EDITION)

Dr. J.K. Khanna

M.A.(Hist.), M.A., Phd. (Pol. Sc.)
M.Lib. Sc., Phd. (Library Science)

Ess Ess Publications
New Delhi-110 002.

First Edition : 1987
Second Revised and Enlarged Edition : 1994

ISBN : 81-7000-373-3

Price : Rs. 1200/-

Printed in India

Published by Sheel Sethi (Mrs.) for M/s Ess Ess Publications.

Ess Ess Publications
4837/24 Ansari Road, Darya Ganj
New Delhi-110 002
Phone : 326 0807

PREFACE TO THE SECOND EDITION

It gives me a great pleasure to write a preface to the second edition of my work " Library And Society " which has been highly appreciated by the students and teachers of Library Science alike. Keeping in view it's popularity, M/s Ess Ess Publications are bringing out it's second revised and enlarged edition.

During the past eight years, Library and Information activities in India have entered a new phase. Individual libraries are coming out of their splendid isolation and endeavouring their level best to share resources, knowledge, bibliographical data, facilities, and other fruits of modern technology, man's ingenuity, and the results of the accumulated wisdom of the past. Forced, motivated, or logic driven by the strains of ever-dwindling financial resources, the libraries/ information centres are opting for resource sharing to provide better services and more facilities to their users without proportionate increase in their expenditures. It is the transmigration of the individualistic philosophy of the library service into a co-operative service.

Enthused by the desire to provide promptly, conveniently, pin-pointedly, economically and with precision, the portion of the current or previous literature that will be useful-

- to a particular user;
- at a particular time;
- for a particular problem or interest;
- and in a form that is useful to him/ her irrespective of:
- where it is generated;
- in what form or language;
- or how it must be located and processed.

A large number of library resource sharing networks like Metropolitan Area Networks such as CALIBNET (Calcutta),DELNET (Delhi),BONET (Bombay), PUNENET (Pune),MALIBNET (Madras), and countrywide ones like ERNET (Educational And Research Institutions), SIRNET (CSIR Laboratories), INFLIBNET (Universities And Research Institutions), and DESINET (Defence Laboratories), and sectoral ones like BTISNET (Biotechnology) and

TIFACLINE (Technology Perse), are under various stages of conceptualisation, design and development. A host of agencies like the NISSAT/ DSIR, Department of Electronics, INSDOC/CSIR, DESIDOC/ DRDO, DBT, NIC, and TIFAC/ DST, are involved.

INSDOC is a premier S & T information organisation of India serving the information needs of the scientific community by providing high quality information services based on recorded human knowledge of the world and through the utilisation of current and emerging information technologies.

INSDOC's activities are organised under eight divisions at its headquarters in Delhi:

1. Database Division (DBD)
2. Translation Services Division (TSD)
3. Data Services Division
4. Computer Services Division
5. Education and Training Division (ETD)
6. Advance Russian Studies in S & T (ARSST)
7. Programme Management Division (PMD)
8. National Science Library

INSDOC has established three regional centres at Bombay, Calcutta and Madras with a view to provide S & T information Services to the R & D community of the country. The regional centre of INSDOC help in mobilising the resources available in the major cities/ regions for supporting the document copy supply services.

NASSDOC is for the social scientists what INSDOC is for the scientists. The services of National Social Science Documentation Centre (NASSDOC) are based on its rich resource collection consisting of : (a) Specifically discipline-oriented reference sources like dictionaries, encyclopedias, directories, bibliographies; (b) ICSSR priced and non priced publications brought out with financial support from ICSSR ; (c) Indian doctoral dissertations; and (d) documents on micro-film/fiche. Information technology input has facilitated creation of machine readable databases, namely, Periodicals in Delhi Libraries,

Doctoral Dissertations in NASSDOC, Research Reports in NASSDOC, etc. Services from international databases and CD-ROM, entitled, Popline, and CD-ROM proto-type , etc., are provided to social scientists, policy makers, and others.

NASSDOC has developed linkages at national and international levels through DELNET, APINESS, etc. It participates in electronic mail network under DELNET programme.

IFLA held its 58th general conference in New Delhi during August 30- September 5, 1992. It was a great occasion which brought together librarians and Information scientists from over 81 countries for the first time in India. The focus of attention of 1324 delegates (398 from India) was the theme ; ," Library and Information Policy Perspectives" being both relevant and topical, it enthused a wild spectrum of professionals.

CONTENTS

LIBRARY AND SOCIETY THROUGH THE AGES : A PROLOGUE

Man and Communication

Man is a social animal and society is the "web of social relationships". Being a social animal, man wants to communicate because of all animals only man is "endowed with the gift of speech".

Man has used various means of communicating his ideas, his beliefs, his faith, his ethos and pathos with his fellow-beings. He communicates by gestures, facial expressions, grunts and cries which can very effectively communicate emotions. Man also commicates by touch, by pictures and visual signs, by mathematical and scientific signs and symbols, by music and dance, and above all, by words—spoken and written.

In the beginning, we are told was word. Without "Word", indeed, there could he no beginning. Prehistorical man groped his tortuous journey to the historic man when he started sharing his experiences and thoughts with his fellow-beings. The spoken word became the unit of language while the written word formed the key-stone of the literature of graphic records at a much later stage.

The spoken word as the unit of language has been the most laudable achievement of *Homo Sapiens* in developing complex societies. Only now we have started realising how deeply relavent commnication is to progress of man.

If speech was the first great step forward in the development of human communication, the second great milestone was invention of writing, By virtue of writing, history could be recorded permanently and in detail, technical discoveries could be handed on, and records of every kind could be kept. There was no longer any barrier to communication between living men or between the past and present.

The third great leap forward came with the invention of printing, by means of which what was written could be reproduced and distributed in quantity, thus, disseminating information and learning among ever widening circles of the community.

Bewildering bursts of progress have accompnied the development of electronic systems of communication—the telegraph and telephone, and especially radio-television and satellites. Recently, the electronic computer has brought yet another revolutionary possibilities. Man can now have whole areas of his physical labour done for him by Robots. His ability to move at terrific speed about the face of earth, and beyond it has increased prodigiously within the past hundred years. Man's conquest of the moon has marked the down of new era in human progress.

Man will soon have previously unimagined opportunities for the storing and dissemination of knowledge and ideas. In the meanwhile one may trace the relationship between library and society from the hoary past, as the library is vital link in the chain of man's communication. The story of library and society through the ages reveals a strong organic relationship between them. The library has been the chief conserver of knowledge and ideas accumulated by man in his struggle to annihilate the physical world leading to his landing on the moon and projected Mars-walking, to relate himself effectively to the society of his fellow being, and to cultivate his mental and spiritual faculities. Through libraries (including museums, of course) the society has preserved its cultural heritage) vital to the education of man and to the exchange of ideas. The processes of social change are interwoven in the facts, ideas, and inventions of man; and each new idea or invention grows out of accumulated and preserved knowledge.

Historical Evolution of Library and Society

The invention of Alphabets played very important part In the establishment of Libraries. We can learn much from these libraries which are the gift given by alphabets.

Man with his tremendous capabilities of intellect, wisdom and mind has been mastering his situations since his very inception. With the development of our thought, growth of our experiences and minuteness of our observations the knowledge has been growing considerably through the ages. But parallel has also been the course of human recording which also grew and developed in relation to man's requirements. In the light of material and the demand of the society at a particular juncture of the human history the man had been developing methods of recording his experiences through the clay-tablets, wax-tablets, papyrus sheets, parchment rolls and through modern books. and other audio-visual equipment.

Mesopotamian Civilization

The Mesopotamian Civilization flashes across our mind when we think of having the glimpses of earliest possible libraries.

Mesopotamia means 'the land between the rivers'. It was the country watered by two great rivers—Tigris and Euphrates—and is modern Iraq. In ancient days its southern most region was known as Sumeria. Babylonia and Akkad, lay in the North-East of Sumer. The highlands of Assyria lay in the North. Various civilizations flourished in the lands of Sumeria, Bobylonia, Akkad and Assyria at different times covering a time span of about 2000 years. The ancient civilization comprising all these civilizations is known as Mesopotamian civiliztion.

The earliest writing literature is in the Sumerian language; their civilization flourished between 4000 and 3000 B.C. Pictography was their original way of writing which ultimately flowered into a phonetic system through the hieroglyph. The Sumerians wrote on wet clay tablets upon which they created impressions by means of an arrow-shaped (three edged) tool of metal. The tool of writing is known as stylus and the impression as cuneiform. The other reading materials which they used are known as prisms, and cylinders. For the preservation and use of their documents, the Sumerians established private, temple and government libraries. The mankind owes its first-ever written book to Sumerians called GILGAMESH which contains a mythical epic poem narrating the tale of creation. The other themes of their writings revolved around their hymns, prayers, rituals, sacred legends and magic formula.

The Babylonians assimilated the Sumerian script to sharpen their own language which became the recognised diplomatic language of the Middle-East. Though a complex system of idographs and syllabic signs, the Babylonian cuneiform system was a superb advance over the primitive pictographic form. One of the Babylonian Kings Hammurabi is famous for his code of laws which he inscribed on a large stone seal. These inscriptions are said to be the second book of the ancient world.

A great part of our knowledge throwing light on the Babylonian civilization is evidenced on the tablets of the library of Borisppa. These tablets in turn were copied and then preserved in the library of Ashurbanipal—an Assyrian king, who reigned from

658-626 B.C. This library was situated in his own palace at Nineveh which became the finest city in Western Asia—a city of vast palaces and imposing temples.

The library of King Ashurbanipal contained tens of thousands of tablets books on a variety of subjects. Strangely enough, these books on clay tablets were arranged subject-wise which we consider the most useful method of arranging books on the shelves at present and the latest one also. Such books were listed and shelved systematically and tagged for identification with a list of the thought-content of each shelve painted or carved on the entrance to serve as a catalogue. This library, it is said, was open to the people.

Ancient Egypt

Historians divide the history of Egypt into the three periods : The Old Kingdom (3000-2000 BC); the Middle Kingdom (2000-1750 BC), and the the New Kingdom (when the Egyptian Kings regained their power after loosing it to Hyksos in 18 century BC).

The Egyptian script is known as hieroglyphic, which means 'sacred' writing. Probably the Egyptian learned the idea of writing from the Summerians before 3000 BC, but their writing is not a copy of cuneiform.

The Egyptian book was made up of papyrus rolls; it was preserved in a metal cylinder with tags displaying the subject of the book.

There were temple libraries and the Egyptian priests used to prepare copies. King Ramesses II founded a library at Thebes in about 1250 B.C. This library is believed to have had 20,000 books and was called "a place of Healing for the Soul". The thought-content of the books reveals that they pertain to official literature as well as religious, philosophical, historical and science. The writing started from the right to the left and the text of books proceeded from top to bottom. Therefore, to read the papyrus, roll was unfolded top downward, The librarians were called the "Keeper" of books and their profession was almost hereditary,

Greece

The history of Greece is not a history of mighty empire but of a new spirit, a new genius with a keen desire to have ideas and perfection. Greece shows her greatness not in size but in spirit,

Greeks obtained the alphabet from the Phoenicians. There were libraries in Greece, including those of Peisistratus—the tyrant of Athens, and Polycrates, the tyrant of Samos. But their true development began during the decades of Plato and Aristotle. Plato himself was a librarian and formed a library at Syracuse. Aristotle (384-322 B.C.) is believed to be the first person to accumulate, preserve and use the culture of past. Aristotle bequethed his library to Theophratus, who willed it to Neleus. This library alongwith that of Apellicon was confiscated by Sulla when he captured Athens in 86 B.C.

The first Public Library in Greece was established in Athens in 330 B.C. But the the most important libraries at ancient Greece were established during the golden period of Hellenic Age in Greek Colonies in Asia Minor, Egypt and Sicily. The greatest of these grew up at Alexandria—a City founded by Alexander the Great in 332 B.C.—, under the blessings of Ptolemics I and II (322-283 BC). When at its zenith, the library possessed about seven lakhs rolls. Ptolemy III established another Library in the Temple of Serapis in some other part of Alexandria. This library is believed to have a collection of about 100,000 carefully selected rolls.

The collections of these two libraries were classified and organised; all the texts were edited, arranged into convenient form and provided with commentaries; and a comprehensive bibliography of Greek literature was compiled by scholar-librarians like Zenodotus, Aristophanes of Byzantium and Callimacus who were poets, critics and grammarians.

The Greeks used papyrus for recording their thoughts. Parchment or the skin of animals, principally those of sheep and goat was also used. Vellum or the skin of lamb or kid was used for expensive writings, while for messages and notes the Greeks used wax-coated wooden tablets. The Greeks fastened together papyrus or parchment leaves as in the modern book. This was known as 'codex' which proved the forerunner of the book. as we know it at present and was further improved by the Romans

Rome

The Roman civilization, centred in Italy, is often considered a kind of bridge. Over this bridge the ideas of the Greeks and the civilizations farther east travelled to Europe. The Romans learned much of philosopby, literature, rhetoric, art and science from the Greeks. Their greatest contributions lay in the fields of Law and governance. The Romans used papyrus, parchment, vellum and wooden tablets coated with wax and the stylus for writing; their book was the roll. Once the Romans were at the zenith of their glory, they found the roll inconvenient to write upon and to read and difficult to refer promptly, hence its supercession by the 'codex' (used by the Greeks to some extent) in which parchment sheets were fastend and bound together as in a book. The use of the codex was a great milestone on the road leading to bookmaking, and providing closeness to the soul of the modern book. Moreover, the use of parchment in codexes greatly enhanced the chances of book survival, use of larger pages providing space for illustrations or for the foot-notes or commentries.

Maintaining of private libraries became a fashion with the Romans' aristocracy when their generals started bringing home, the Grecee libraries as war spoils. The wealthy people collected manuscripts both in Greek and Latin, though, more to make a show of their wealth than for the sake of learning.

Julius Caesar planned a public library which would preserve books and records, serve as a means of instructing the people, and add to the cultural influence already being exerted by the private libraries, bookshops, and schools; and the nucleus of their collections would be the historical and political archives. Unfortunately, Ceaser died and could not realize his novel idea. Nevertheless, one of his friend Asinius Pollio in the reign of Augustus concretized Ceaser's dream by founding the Palatine Library in the Temple of Apollo consisting of both Greek and Latin documents. It is believed that twenty-eight public libraries flourised in Rome in the 2nd century.

As a part of Rome's civilizing process, libraries sprang up up throughout the Empire. There were public libraries in almost every important town and city in Italy, Greece, Asia Minor, Cyprus, and Africa. Worth-mentioning was the one established by the Emperor Trajan (98-117 A.D.) at Timgad in North Africa. Trajan also founded the Ulpian Library in Rome. It had two divisions, one housing the Greek and the other Latin literature. The library founded by Emperor Hadrian (117-138 A.D.) in Athens had a magnificient building and a rich quality of documents. By A.D. 500, the Western Roman Empire declined and with it the development of libraries.

The Chinese, too, had developed a system of writing which comprised pictograms and ideograms They manufactured paper cut of rags, wood pulp and flax even in the 2nd century A.D. They even knew block printing. It can be presumed that they produced considerable literature and possessed libraries to preserve the materials.

Dark Ages

Libraries existed even during the period ranging roughly between 500—1000 A.D.* better known in history as the 'Dark Ages' because of the supremacy of barbarianism, terrorism, religious persecutions and blight. The cultural, political and intellectual progress the Rome had made declined and with it the secular literature that Greece had bequeathed for the generations to come. Consequently, the period witnessed the decay and destruction of libraries. Fortunately, every dark cloud has a silver linning. Constantine the Great, had become the Emperor of both the Eastern and the Western Roman Empire in 324 A.D. He made the Constantinople his capital and made Christianity the state religion. This proved a turning point at least in the history of Europe in respect of cultural, political and religious advancement as Constantinople became the source of civilization to both Eastern and Western Europe

Constantine founded the Imperial Library with emphasis on the collection of Latin works as it was the official language. His successors enhanced the collections by adding Christian and Pagan Works in Latin and Greek; the collections of the library stood at about 1,20,000.

To disseminnte the message of Christianity, many, Christians reached Rome, and despite religious bloody persecutions, established monastries, where they lived as hermits. It was exactly in these monastries that the fragments of the Greco-Roman culture were preserved. Areas were ear-marked for monastery libraries where copies of Bible together with commentaries and religious literature were accumulated and preserved. There was a mush-room growth of Churches and as required each Bishop had a library under his charge. This resulted in the wide-spread growth of libraries which kept the flame of knowledge burning during the dark ages. The monastic collection stored in ecclesiastical libraries were kept in chests and lists were prepared which served catalogues. Books were by and large chained to desks with brass frames and rings : the fundamental reason being that it took years to copy a manuscript. Possession of private libraries was a fashion among the wealthy people towards the close of Middle Ages. Feudalism was reigning supreme and the feudal lords displayed their riches by collecting rare books all over Europe. The most conspicuous events of the period in the history of libraries were the crusades, the rise of universities, and the development of vernacular languages and literature. The Crusaders (Seljuk Turks) captured Constantinople in 1204 A.D. and wroughted fire and destruction over it resulting in the loss of libraries; many manuscripts were dispersed, and from that time Greek Works, including the original texts of Aristotle found their way to Western Europe increasingly. Nevertheles. the 12th Centuary Europe was exposed to the highly developed civilization of the East—new ideas, new literature.

It will be a travesty of facts if one does not touch upon the role of Greek philosophy and science in Perisa. As Greek influence over the cultural and intellectual life of the Romans began after the conquest of Greece, similarly the Arab conquerors of Persia were defeated by the Persian culture. They were introduced to Aristotle's logic. As Bagdad shot into centre for the study of Greek Works. physicians and scholars flocked there to study and to translate Greek medical, scientific. and philosophical works into Arabic. This translation moveme it reached its zenith when "a house of wisdom" was established in 830 A.D. : it was an institution of learning that combined the functions of library, academy, and translation bureau. Medicine, mathematics, and natural sciences were studied as were also the works of Plato, Aristotle, Hippocrates, and Galen which were translated into Arabic. The Arabs had come to know the Chinese way of manufacturing paper and they set-up paper-making factories in Samarkand (Bhagdad) in the eighth century when the Western World was still using parchment and even papyrus. A large number of libraries sprang-up in Baghdad.

Another centre of Arab culture was established in Spain where Muslim rulers patronized scholars and founded libraries which flourished between the tenth and twelfth centuries. In the libraries of Cordova, Toledo, and Seville, the Greek classic translated into Arabic were preserved until they found their way to the new universities of Europe through the scholars of 12th century who rendered them into Latin. With the Muslim Empire in Spain, and the fall of Abbasid Caliphate in Baghdad, the period of Great Arab libraries came to an end. In the 11th Century the library of the Caliph of Cairo contained some 100,50,000 volumes.

Middle Ages

The most significant event of the Middle Ages was the emergence of the universities, almost every city of Europe had a university before 1400 A.D. Influenced by the works of Plato and Aristotle, scholars showed renewed keeness in theology and logic as well as philosophy and astronomy. With universities developed the libraries. But those libraries did not resemble the modern ones. They consisted of only one book case containing hand-written documents chained to the shelves. As the number of students grew, the growth of universities and libraries was the logical outcome. Eventually, every college had a library.

Peoples enthusiasm for learning was accelerated with their exposure to Latin grammar, the development of writing in the language of the masses, and more favourable socio-economic conditions. One of the greatest landmark of the period was the Renaissance Movement. Renaissance means re-birth. The name is usually given to the period around A.D. 1400 when there was a new interest in the art and literature of the ancient Greeks and Romans. It was time when the Europians began to change their outlook on life and to think of themselves. They were no longer satisfied with the feudal organization of society. The absolute faith they had in the Church gave way to questioning and reasoning. Scientific thinking had started.

The questioning of the right of the Catholic Church to control the life of its followers led to the Protestant Movement and Reformation. People hungered after more knowledge. They came to feel that human life is important, that man is worthy of study and respect, that there should be efforts to improve life on this earth. From this interest in human affairs, men passed on to the study of literature and history. Literature and history came to be called the Humanities, which were primarily concerned with understanding the affairs of man in his early earthly life, not with life after death. "Man is the Measure of Everything" is the essence of Humanism.

This main spirit of Humanism found expression in the new art and literature. Renaissance artists took their themes from the Bible but portayed the human form in all its earthly beauty and vigour. The Renaissance writers were also chiefly concerned with man. Scholars left the East in great numbers and came to Italy. The learning of the ancient Greeks thus spread through Italy and in several Italian cities, huge libraries of manuscripts were started. Cosimo de Medici who ruled till 1464 A.D. was a great patron of the Latin classics. He established the library of San Macro and also founded the great Medici Library, at present housed in the Laurentian Library in Florence. His grandson the Lorenzo greatly augumented the Florentine library of Greek and Latin classics.

The zeal for learning generated by the Renaissance brought about a passionate demand for books which couid not be satisfied by handwritten manuscripts. There was an urgent need for the faster medium for disseminating knowledge. Gutenberg laid the foundations of modern era by giving to the mankind the printing machine with moveable types. This gave great impetus to libraries.

Thereafter, equiped with modern paper and machines, the man gave birth to a series of socio-economic and political thoughts backed by Renaissance and Humanism as well as recognition of the rights and values of the common man in the human society through the concept of Democracy i.e. *Socialisation of Education*. Further, the enactment of Library Legislation made provisions for *library services for all.*

The human society cannot survive without being fully familiar with all the past intellectual contributions of man on one side as well as keeping itself up-to-date with the growing and ever adding knowledge in the domains of disciplines i.e. Humanities, Social Sciences, Sciences and Technology. It is an endless process getting complex from compound day by day. The librares are the institutions which the modern man has discovered to overcome this complexity. Therefore, the man has to assimilate and utilize this oceanic knowledge, so essential for the human welfare, at large.

In the context of totality of knowledge our needs are multiple and endless. The destiny of human thought lies in its preservation, organisation and dissemination by way of multiple or multifocal services organised to-day by the libraries. Information Services and Documentation Activities are new horizons in Reference Service laying more stress on the micro-documents and requirements of the specialist reader—the Scientist or Researcher.

Flowering of Libraries in Europe and other countries in Modern Era

Now let us first take up growth of libraries in Europe. In Western Europe, the development of library service has in general followed one or two patterns. In Switzerland and Scandinavian countries, and to a lesser degree in Belgium and Netherlands, library service includes strong state libraries backed up by many small popular libraries. Denmark has probably the best public library service of any country in Europe. The Royal Library in Copenhagen has over two million volumes and more than 2.5 million items of music, maps and prints and it is only one of several large government libraries. In Sweeden there is also an excellent public library in Stockholm and in the university of Lund. Norway and Finland are not as advanced in library service as their Scandinavian neighbours because both suffered considerable library damage during World War II. Switzerland has a complicated system of local, cantonal and national libraries, further confused by the four national languages, but it, neverthelesss, pro ides excellent library service for its whole population.

For those who cannot reach the libraries themselves, there is national package library service available by mail.

In the Southern parts of Europe including Spain, Portugal and the Balkans, a second pattern of library development can be seen. Here, there are few large research libraries.

In Eastern Europe, behind the iron curtain, library service is strictly controlled by the governments and is a prominent part of the political system. A very large Russian Library is the *Lenin State Library* in Moscow, with over 10,65,8000 volumes, (1975) and also in the same city there is Moscow University Library almost as large.

There are library schools at the larger universities, particularly at Moscow, Leningrad and Kharkov. Several library and bibliographic journals are published and there are national, regional and local Library Associations

Australia and Newzealand have good systems including large public and university libraries. In Australia, Public Libraries are under state rather than national control and each of Australian States has a large central library that serves both as a reference collection and as a circulating library in some cases.

Japanese libraries, before 1945, consisted mainly of Government and University collections with the Imperial library in Tokyo with some half million volumes, being the most important. Library history in China is nearly as ancient as that nation itself. In the beginning of the Christian era there was a library of 11,000 volumes in China, and its catalogue in book form has been preserved.

We see, that there are so many libraries in a country, but the award of these libraries goes to the Alhabets, because without alphabets nothing could be possible.

Britain : She has probably the most extensive and the finest library system in the world both in its variety of libraries and their coverage. But Britain's available library system has directly emerged from its library legislation. The Act of 1964 (Public Libraries and Museum Act, 1964) has made the library service a statutory one.

British Museum Library, till recently the National Library of England and Wales was opened to the public in 1759 (now the British Library). It has a valuable collection on Indian history, religion, languages and philosophy. Antnony Panizzi, its librarian from 1856-66 A.D. designed its famous circular reading room and contributed to development of the library code. Next in importance is the Oxford University Library popularly known as the Bodlein Library named after its founder Sir Thomas Bodley in 1602 A.D. The Cambridge University Library established in 1209 A.D., comes third in importance in England. In addition there are special libraries attached to science and technical institutions, BOAC, etc. The British National Bibliography has become the model for bibliographers and librarians all over the world.

The Library of Congress is the National Library of U.S.A. It is housed in James Medison Memorial building of White Marble which was donated to the nation on April, 24, 1980. It has eight reading rooms. It has a collection of more than 200,000,00 books and pamphlets; 350,000,00 handwritten manuscripts; about

400,000,00 maps and atlases; 100,000,00 prints and photographs; 1200 newspapers, 5000,000 sound records, 250,000 motion pictures and more than 300,000.000 micro films. Its shelving space runs to 532 miles. It is considered as the largest library of the world[1].

French libraries were modelled on the Italian pattern. Its national library had its origin in several royal libraries dating from early 15th century. The Library depository provision started in France as early as 1538 A.D. by the order of the king by merit of which one copy of each book printed in France should be presented to the National Library.

The state libraries of Germany were established in Berlin in the year 1661 A.D. and in Munich in 1550 A.D. Germany had two types of libraries in the sixteenth and seventeenth centuries viz., Church Libraries, and University Libraries. The first alphabetical catalogue in Germany was compiled in 1776. It was in Germany that the idea of circulating libraries, popular reading rooms, published library catalogue, inter-library loan, Union Catalogue and children's libraries was floated.

INDIA : Education is no exotic in India. She has been the cradle of one of the earliest and brilliant civilizations. The greatest and wisest of her monarchs found in the promotion of learning their noblest and most beneficient achievements and saw in the foundation of the university the most enduring memorials of their thrones. There is, in fact, "no country where the love of learning had so early an origin or has exercised so lasting an influence. From the simple poet of Vedic age to the Bengali philosopher of the present day, there has been an uninterrupted succession of teachers and scholars"

The well-equipped libraries with vast, choicest collections of manuscripts and other marerials of ancient wisdom attached to the internationally renowned Indian universities like Takshila, Nalanda, Vikramsila, Valabhai, Benaras and Ranchi in ancient India were solely ornanised and functioned with a view to advancing the traditional, philosophical, ecclesiastical and classical education for its own sake.

The libraries in the Medieval and Mughal India were created of, by, and for the elite. This close association of the library with

1. Punjab Kesri, Nov. 30, 1986.

the elite soon brought to it a prestigious status, and it is not surprising that the patronage or possession of library became a symbol of aristocary in the Mughal India. Nevertheless, the benefits of these libraries were confined to Royalty and nobility; the poor had no access to knowledge.

Public library system has not taken roots even in independent India. Only five states viz., Madras, Andhra Pradesh, Mysore, Maharashtra and West Bengal have passed legislation. The Advisory Committee Report, 1958 is a great milestone in the history of iibrary movement in India. It recommended that every state should have a library legislation to ensure a perennial source of income. The ministry followed this up by circulating a model Public Libray Bill to all the State Governments in 1962. Six Five-Year Plans have given a further impetus to the development of public libraries. At present every state has a state library. To stimulate and support the Library Movement in India, the Govt. of India took a laundable step by establishing Raja Rammohan Roy Library Foundation in Calcutta. It aims at vitalizing the State Libraries to work more effectively and setup a nucleus of district libraries so as to disseminate knowledge for the benefit and elevation of the layman.

Our National Library is situated at Calcutta and despite its drawbacks possess fabulous collections. It boasts of 18, 10, 401 books covering 30 miles of shelf space, 19,000 periodicals, 76, 575 maps, more than 4, 26, 444 official documents both Indian and foreign and 3000 of the rarest manuscripts in addition to archival materials. The delivery of Books Act, 1954 as amended in 1956 brings an annual deluge of documents.

Moveover, there are about 148 Universities and institutions deemed to be universities. Each has its own library. The U G.C. has been giving grants to the Universities and Colleges for the development of libraries, staff and documents.

Special libraries have also grown in Information Centres, Associations, and National Councils like INSDOC. SENDOC, DESIDOC, SSDOC, ICMR, ICAR, BARC, NISSAT, etc.

Still much remain to be achieved. One must, however, mention one commendable feature for the growth and development of public libraries in West Bengal. When the government fought the Legislative Assembly election in 1977, they assured in thei *election manifesto* that a public library system will be developed through library legislation. This was for the first time, not only in the history of West Bengal but may be in the entire Indo-Pak sub-continent, that library development was made an issue in a political battle like election. Total number of Government controlled and sponsored public libraries in West Bengal at present is 2,418 viz.. State Central Library 1; District Library 20; Rural Area/Primary Unit Libraries 2,276, other libraries 3. The Government allocated Rs. 5,00,260,000 for improvement, expansion and maintenance of public library service during 1983-84. This expenditure on public library services is the highest in any of the states in India.

Amendments to West Bengal Public Libraries Act have taken place. These amendments (1985) related to the following :

—Nomenclature of District Librarian, State Central Library, Public Library and Sponsored Library.

—Enhanced jurisdiction of W.B. Public Libraries Act over libraries registered under the Society Registration Act.

—Functions of the State Library Council.

—Control of State Government over the Local Library Authorities.

—State Central Library.

—Responsibility and functions of the Director of Library Services.

—Power of Government to frame rules, regulations, etc.

Committee on National Policy on library and Information System

The Government of India, Department of Culture set up a committee in October 1985 to advise them in the formulation of a National Policy on Library and Information System. The committee submitted an interim report to the Minister of Human Resource Development on March 8, 1986. The policy contains recommendations, among other things, on Public Library System, Academic Library System, Special Libraries and Information System, National Library System and Bibliographic Services, Manpower Development, and Professional Status, Modernization of Library and Information Systems, and implementing agencies and financial support.

The salient features of recommendations of this committee are ;

—Provision and promotion of free publc library services in the country.

—Development of school libraries.

—Strengthening of Libraries for distance education.

—Establishment of a National Library and information Systems.

—Preservation of national heritage; and

—Modernisation of library operations.

The basic emphasis of the policy presentation is the extension of library services to the weaker sections of the Indian society living in remote and backward areas, the physically and socially handicapped persons, the children, students of non-formal streams, and linkages among different systems for effecting economy and ensuring optimum services to the public.

Today, we look upon the library as a "social institution". It is a product of society for its cultural advancement. The traditional function of the culture is to enable a group to survive, and this principle implies the conservation of the past. Not only do the libraries conserve our culture, but as agencies of communication they play a vital role in its transmission. Its description as the mind of society"; the "community's intellectual centre," reflects its influence in moulding the l'fe of the community.

Great libraries have rightly been hailed the roots and friuts of great civilizations. Libraries show light to enable people to become better citizens, and to plan for peace and prosperity. Library thus affects society and is an acknowledged social agency with which society must be concerned.

So strong is the communion between library and society that the libraries have tended to prosper.

—In societies of political and cultural maturation which recognise the necessity of collecting, preserving, utilizing, transmitting, and enlarging the body of knowledge;

—during periods of relative peace and tranquility which afford time to plan and pursue cultural and intellectual activities;

—when individuals have both leisure and the means to "cult vate the finer arts and improve the common stock of knowledge";

—in periods of intellectual creativity and scholarly activity, when large and varied collections of materials are required for study and research:

—when there is large social emphasis on self-improvement and a well informed citizenry;

—during revivals of learning which centre around and depend upon accumulation of graphic records and access to them;

—in areas with concentrated population and especially in an urban environment which can provide the leadership, the financial means to support libraries, and the cultural and intellectual interests to stimulate their use;

—when economic prosperity provides sizeable individual and corporate wealth and encourages philanthropic giving:

—in times when, as in recent times, economic growth and national power and status are considered to be dependent upon the wide dissemination and use of information and knowledge which have utilitarian value.[2]

In brief, socio-political and economic conditions play a great role in the growth and development of libraries. Libraries are shaped by society.

Need of this Study

Libraries command respect in our soeicties. They are as ubiquitous as schools. Their value is acknowledged without reservation and considerable amounts of public money and resources are made available for running libraries efficiently and effectlvely to produce material happiness, mental joy and spiritual delight. Yet painfully enough, the library profession as such appears to be largely unaware of and unconcerned with the vitality of library role in moulding and shaping the society.

Epoch-making contributions have been made by the library scientists particularly in the fields of classification and cataloguing. There has also begun some study of users' needs and habits; but as yet no real attempt has been made to analyse and assess the role of library in modern society, hence tne need of present study.

Library power derives primarily from the repository and custodial functions of libraries. Libraries are the store—houses of

2 . J.K. Gates, *Introduction to librarianship* (N.Y., McGraw Hill, 1968).

humanistic, scientific and technological knowledge. They conserve and transmit culture. They underpin education—both individual and formal. A striking characteristic of all underdeveloped nations is their paucity of libraries; and a poor man is almost invariably an uneducated man. They feature vitally in our economic welfare. They are crucially related to our intellectual, artistic and creative activities. They are the vehicles of socio-political change. And as the guardians of the freedom of thought, they are bastions of liberty. Therefore they are distrusted and, very often in history, have been suppressed by dictators, despots and autocrats of every kind[3]. If the world is to remain free from the shadow of authoritarianism and dictatorship, it requires thinking people, cultivated men and women gifted with disciplined minds, high intellect and moral calibre, developed in the climate of freedom of thought and expression, and capable of holding opinions independently arrived at. This remarkable function of training the mind and spirit of man, enabling him to work for the social, cultural, moral, spiritual and material advancement of society is the basis of all library academic pursuits. Ortega y Gasset has observed : "Democratic society is a daughter of books, the triumph of the book written by man over the book revealed by God, over the book of laws dictated by the autocracy.' The library, is then, a forum for mutual understanding, cohesion, mutual cooperation, and mutual tolerance and peaceful co-existence—not as homogenizing institution but as a unifying, living, and dynamically growing force.

One may logically ask : what is a library ? What are its social functions, how it helps in the dissemination of information and the related questions. The answer is attempted in the text to follow.

January 26, 1987. **J. K. KHANNA**

3. James Thompson, *Library power* (Lond., Clive Bingley, 1974).

1

GROWTH AND DEVELOPMENT OF THE LIBRARY CONCEPT

Library is the product of our "cultural maturation"; it is essentially a response to the total communication patterns of modern society. The advent and advance of democracy; the extension of the horizons of education; the intensification of research, and the virtual explosion of knowledge and information have necessitated the services of a well-stocked, well-staffed, well-organized and up-to-date library.

A public library is the nucleus of the community's intellectual attainments; an academic library is the beating-heart of the educational institutions; and a business or special library is the life-blood of government departments and big industrial or commercial organizations as well as professional bodies and learned societies. But library took centuries to become the web of social relationships; the hub of research activities; the crowning glory of education, and an agency for educating the masses in the values of democracy – Justice, Liberty, Equality and Fraternity. This leads one to define the library in historical perspectives. No doubt the practising librarian is more concerned with emerging patterns of modern librarianship, but historical traditions and experiences create values, culturally defined norms, and modes of behaviour that survive even when the original conditions that gave rise to them fade into oblivion. Probably, no where this is more true than in library science.

Evolution of Library Concept

The word 'library', which in English refers to a collection of books gathered for study, research, reference and recreation, is derived from the Latin *liber*, "a book". But the word *libraire* in French does not have the same meaning, being used to denote a bookshop or, by extension, a publisher; the word used in many other countries to signify a collection of books (public or private), is derived from a Latinized Greek word, *bibliotheca* : hence *bibliotheque* in French, *biblioteca* in Italian and Spanish. *Bibliothek* in German, *biblioteka* in Russian. In Japanese, the word is *toshoshitsu*[1]. The use of the word library to denote a building, room, set of rooms in which a collection of books is housed and organised is also common.

Doubtlessly, since times immemorial libraries have preserved man's priceless acquisitions of knowledge, but this definition conveys only one meaning of the library—repository of various forms of recorded information. Nevertheless, it conveys only the custodial function.

More appropriately said, a library houses an organised collection of documents to preserve them and make them available for use Probably, the most important word in this definition is "use", for which libraries have become indispensable in the modern world. As knowledge becomes more extensive, it is increasingly necessary that it be accumulated and processed in a manner that makes it highly accessible to the common man, and to specialists—a scholar writing a book or a scientist conducting a research project. In addition to their vital role in the academic world, libraries serve all branches of business, government, and civil life, supplying information needed by individuals and organizations.

Interpreted as such, the term library can easily he distinguished from an associated word "Archive". An archive is a collection of historic documents and records; unlike a library, whose main emphasis is on accessibility and use of records, an archive is primarily a place for storage and preservation and its records are made available only to a limited class of people, such as government officials or scholars. But the laudable aim of the library—"The aim", as John Powell says, is "of making books more helpful, of getting more people to make more and better use of books as instruments in their attempts to make living richer, more satisfying and more humane"[2].

S.R. Ranganathan, puts the meaning of the word 'Library' in historical perspectives for our better understanding.

1. *New Encyclopaedia Britannica, Macropedia*, v. 10.
2. John Powell "One step nearer librarianship" *LT*, (April 1, 1946) p. 443.

An early meaning, now obsolete, is, that a library is "a place where books are written"[3]. Obviously, in this definition, there is no mention of readers, explicit or implied.

In another sense, the term 'library' is used to denote a place set apart to keep books—a room in a house, or a building. Evidently, the term "Keeper of Books"[4] or one who watches and guards the books to denote a librarian had originated from this definition of library, and it continued to be used for many centuries right up to recent times.

Still another sense in which the term 'library' is frequently used, is "a collection of books"[5] merely a collection as such. Libraries in this sense have been formed at all times by Royalties (Kings), Noblemen and even Commoners. Library came to be regarded "A Symbol of Respectability".[6] But the owners of such libraries were quite jealous to permit others to use them; and in some cases the owners were ignorant enough to use libraries themselves.

Even during the latter half of the fourteenth century, the term 'library' was defined in the Oxford English Dictionary as a place where books were kept for "reading, study, or reference"[7]. By the nineteenth century, the word 'library' denoted "a building, room, or set of rooms containing a collection of books for the use of public or some portion of it, or the members of society". Simply, library came to the regarded as a "public institution"[8] or establishment charged with the care of a collection of books for use. In time, the concepts of circulation and administration of the collection of books were added to the definition.

Taking the thread from the description of the library as a public institution, Ranganathan defines the term as below :

"A library is a public institution or establishment charged with the care of a collection of books and the duty of making them accessible to those who require use of them"[9].

3. S.R. Ranganathan, *Reference Service.* (Asia Publishing House, 1961), p. 61.
4. Ibid.
5. Ibid.
6. Ibid., p. 62.
7. cf. Jean Key Gates, *Introduction to librarianship* (N.Y., McGraw-Hill, 1968)., p. xi.
8. Ibid.
9. Ranganathan, op.cit., p. 63.

Ranganathan's definition ascribes two major functions to libraries. First, "The care of a collection of books". This means protecting the collection from the ravages of the four enemies of books—fire, water, vermin, and human beings. Librarians engineered techniques for the due discharge of this function. Naturally, the spirit dominating in them was janitorship or care-takership. Definitely it was not establishing contact with readers.

The second function assigned by Ranganathan to libraries in his definition "The duty of making them (the books) accessible to those who require the use of them", gave an opportunity for looking upon human beings, at least occasionally, as different from book-thieves. This function is in direct opposition to the age-long tradition of care-taker librarianship. During most part of the nineteenth century, the idea of library as a museum was dominant. A library was considered a place where the books were preserved for study, reading or reference. But with the advance of democracy coupled with the Acts of Compulsory Education in countries like U.K. and U.S.A., the librarians took it as their moral obligation to help the common man across the street from ignorance to knowledge. From a passive stance they assumed an active role in helping man to educate himself. The often unarticulated aims of the total library were social : illiteracy was to be removed, readers were to be told what was best for them to read, and in the process the moral fibre of the nation was to be raised. This was to be done by building large collections, indicating to readers how they might use the books for raising their standards, enlarging their intelligence, deepening their perceptions through the simple process of reading. The librarians began to feel their obligation even answering necessary questions which might help the reader in his pursuit of self-improvement and self-fulfilment But it took practically the whole of the nineteenth century to reconcile Ranganathan's two functions of library.

Modern Concept : Service Agency

The modern libraries are service agencies that welcome users and are organized to facilitate the use of graphic records. Writing in his *Introduction to Library Science*, Pierce Butler stated that "The basic elements of librarianship consist in the accumulation of knowledge by society and its continuous transmission to the living generation so for as these processes are performed through the instrumentality of graphic records"[10]; and that "the fundamental phenomenon of librarianship...is the transmission of the accumulated experience of society to its individual members through the instrumentality of the book"[11]. Probably keeping this in view Richardson defined library as "an institution where books are acquired for use, and it is the use which is the prime motive of the libraries". It was, however, Carl M White who commented that modern librarianship is concerned with assuring the continuance and full use of power to retain, organize, and use the accumulated heritage of all generations of all mankind in all its forms—the written word being only one[12]. A library thus be defined as a collection of graphic, acoustic and holistic materials such as books, periodicals, manuscripts, newspapers, maps, charts, recordings, motion pictures, slides, filmstrips, magnetic tapes, art reproductions, and still pictures, phonographs, records, music scores, and microforms (micro-filmed materials). Public libraries often serve as cultural centres, with facilities for meetings, lectures, concerts, exhibits, and film presentations. As one newscaster sees them; "Today's libraries are much more than books alone. They are also art reproductions, music recordings, language aids, motion pictures, micro-films, meeting rooms for discussion groups ...They are behives of activity...busy humming market places of ideas where the fields of interest are not narrowed to the educational or the cultural, but limitless as the span of man's own consciousness : a veritable treasure chest of facts and follies... a kind of intellectual service station"[13]. This gives the feeling of the modern busy library, though some secondary activities are put at a par with primary functions.

In sum : for centuries together, the physical care of books was the primary function of libraries. So dominant was the conservation function that the early writers on the organization and management of libraries devoted much attention to the custody of books as physical entities, as artefacts. The library

10. Pierce Butler, *Introduction to library science* (Chicago, Univ. Press, 1933), p. 29.
11. Ibid., p. 84.
12. Care M. White, Ed., *Bases of modern librarianship* (N.Y., Macmillan, 1964) pp. 10, 11.
13. cf. Joseph L. Wheeler and Herbert Goldhor, *Practical administration of public libraries* (N Y., Harper, 1962), p. 4.

as a museum fulfilled a social need. Library accumulated and preserved the records of its scholarship against ravages of time and the depredations of men because graphic records were both useful and scarce, as well as highly prized. But the intellectual content of the culture, its scholarship, had to be actively transmitted from generation to generation as well as preserved. Because of this historical necessity the two functions : preservation of books and making them accessible to people who want to read them merely for the pleasure of reading or to satisfy intellectual curiosity had to coalace. Hence, today, we take library as a service agency equipped with documents for 'use' as against collection built up for sale, for display, for the pride of possession or for any of the purposes for which books may be assembled. Now-a-days the librarianship must be treated as salesmanship and library staff has to act as the canvassing agents for their wares converting library as a service agency. As a service agency, the modern library performs vital functions for the elevation of the society to the study of which we may turn.

2

LIBRARY IN MODERN SOCIETY

Library and society are inter-linked and inter-dependent. Society without libraries has no significance, and libraries without society has no origin. Commenting on the role of library in society, J H Shera writes : "The library is a product of our cultural maturation"[1]. It came into existence when societies ceased to be nomadic and started becoming urbanized, and when graphic records became important to the effective operation of organized human relationships. There is no record of when, or how, libraries began, but one can assume, from the scattered and fragmentary evidence that has survived, that early libraries were essentially archival—storage places for the preservation of records that were necessary for the transactions of business or commerce, the administration of the state, and the communication of belief to succeeding generations. Thus, from the very beginning the library has been a product of social organization and a handmaiden of scholarship, and during those centuries when learning was so intensely individualistic it was almost the sole resource of the philosophers, the scholars, the savants, the wisemen and the probers of the unknown[2].

Social Agency

Today, we look upon library as a social agency. The library has been created by actual necessities in modern civilization. It is now a necessary unit in the social fabric. It is a product of society for its cultural advancement. The traditional function of a culture is to enable a group to survive, and this principle implies the conservation of the past. Not only do the libraries conserve our culture, but as agencies of communication they

1. J.H. Shera, *Foundations of education for librarianship* (N.Y., Becker & Hayes, 1972).

2. Ibid.

play an important role in its dissemination. Library is actually the "mind of society"; it reflects the social aspirations. The modern society now expects man to be self-governing, truth-loving, a believer in the unity of means and ends and non-violence He should be well-informed, generous, tolerant, reverant, a champion of freedom of thought and expression, a citizen of the world, imaginative, aware of beauty, and desirous of making the world, safe for democracy, liberalism, parliamentarianism, and humanitarianism. When we expect such magnificient moral, social, cultural and political values of the society in respect of man as individual, we realize the full potentialties of the library as an agency in society which only can deliver the goods. That libraries offer a "principal road to achievement" becomes an axiomatic truth, and libraries take firm roots in the social concepts[3] The descriptions of library as "Mind of Society"; the "House of Wisdom"; the "House of Learning"; the "Community's Intellectual Centre", a "Training School for Democracy", project its influence in moulding the life of the community. To serve as a vehicle of social progress, the library plays a vital role to

1. assemble, organize, preserve, socialize, and serve all expressed thought embodied as manuscripts, books, periodicals, their constituent documents, however minute, and every other similar document produced as a means for communication; and by this means to
2. help in the transmission of knowledge of the earlier generations to the later ones; and by this means to
3. help in cumulation and further building up of knowledge from generation to generation; and in a similar way to
4. help in the contemporary development of knowledge, by the unintended and purposeless repetition of effort and the consequent wastage in the research potential of humanity; and further to
5. conserve the research time of humanity by the separation of literature search from positive search[4].

One may examine the role of library in modern society in its endeavour to work for social progress.

3. A K. Mukherjee, *Librarianship : Its philosophy and history* (Asia, 1966).

4. Ranganathan, op. cit., p. 171.

Social Functions

1. Continuing Education

Library and education are sister services : Education bereft of library service sounds like staging Hamlet without the Prince of Denmark.

Education implies discipline and cultivation of the intellect; "an intellect able to operate well in all fields"[5]. It enables the individual to know himself, the vicissitudes of life about him; and learn the levels of the true, the good, and the beautiful with which to measure "the stream compounded of, sense perceptions, feelings, hopes, desires, mental activities, adjusting thoughts to thoughts, which form our life"[6]. Of course, the importance of formal education imparted through a social, a college, or a university can hardly be over-exaggerated, yet education does not end with one's formal education. As Carroll V. Newsom has aptly remarked, "All education is really self-education .. Learning cannot be passive, one who would develop the powers of his mind must seek deliberately 'to match his wits' with problems provided by his natural and man made environments. He must accept the wisdom inherent in the statement "One learns to think by learning"[7]. It is now being increasingly realized that self-education permeates the entire life of the individual from cradle to the grave. Informal education cultivates in individual the virtues of self-help, self-confidence, self reliance, and initiative. And the most appropriate agency of continuing education for people of all ages is the public library. It serves as a centre for arousing and stimulating intellectual curiosity and the desire to learn among people by offering materials and programmes to satisfy their desire for knowledge. If the society has an obligation to feed, clothe and house the people comfortably, it has a similar moral obligation to educate them and to feed them with mental food through educational institutions and libraries, respectively. This twin obligation is the *sine qua non* of a modern society, which flourishes when it nourishes the belly, brawn and brain of its entire

5. Robert Maynared Hutchins, *The higher learning in America* (Yale Univ. Press, 1936), p. 63.

6. Alfred North Whitehead, *The Aims of education* (Lond., Williams and Norgate, 1947), p. 6.

7. *A University President speaks* out (N. Y., Harper, 1961) pp. 1–2.

populace. Education and library are, therefore, two most important factors of social metamorphosis.

The frenzy of enthusiasm for continuing education marked a transition from the individual centred to the community-centred library It enthused Alvin Johnson to hail public library as a people's university. The impelling need of self-education makes the library serve not merely the aristocrats, the rich or powerful, but each in the measure of his intelligence quotient and field of interest. In communities where there is no flow of appropriate reading materials and no stimulus to write, literacy in itself may have little significance. Therefore, the library, if it is to achieve its fullest role in society, is not passively to make books available when needed by a potential reader, but actively to stimulate the use of books. The wisdom and patience of teachers must be supplemented when the students have left their schools by liberal provision of means such as public libraries provide for the self-education of those whose ambitions and interests, having been stimulated, are active forces in the development of the individuals and of society[8].

2. *Stimulation of Reading*

As a social agency, the most important function and a continuing activity of the libraries is the stimulation of reading and guidance of the reader in choosing his/her book in the form of planned reading programmes, book talks and reviews, book lists and specialized bibliographies, displays and exhibits, browsing areas, open access, and teaching the use of specific library tools. Libraries can do their best work for children and in adult education programmes. But the biggest contribution which libraries could make is to get people into libraries. As James Thompson[9] succinctly comments : Most libraries are monumental and intimidating in appearance : their services are hedged about with restrictions and prohibitions of every sort—fines; notices demanding silence in a lending library. They indulge in ridiculously complicated cataloguing and classification systems; they do not offer helpful signs and guides; and too often library staffs are brusque and officious. No disadvantaged reader would comfortably go near a presentday library.

8. UNESCO. *Access to Librarles*, (1952), p. 7.

9. James Thompson, *Library* power (Lond., Clive Bingley, 1974).

Therefore, to promote the use of library and to participate in teaching and research progammes as well as to become a nucleus of intellectual gravity of the community it serves, the library staff has to interpret the materials which includes the—

1. Provision of information pin-pointedly, exhaustively and expeditiously;
2. Answering factual and complex reference questions by literature searching;
3. Compiling bibliographies and making annotations or abstracts or preparing indexes wherever necessary;
4. Maintaining information and other files;
5. Borrowing and lending materials on inter-library loan, and finally
6. Giving instructions in the use of the library by conducting formal classes only by giving instructions to individuals or groups in the use of library materials.

The aim of the library must be to sell itself, go out and promote its services. Library must encourage reading at all levels and for different purposes : reading for education, reading for information, reading for seeking status, reading for emotional release, reading for self-realization—attaining Moksha or spiritual emancipation. Library must inculcate in the minds of individuals that reading is of far greater significance for the creation of intellectual, moral, aesthetic, social and political values, and in the context of reading, a book represents a social relationship between writer and reader, and the library has the clearest view of this relationship being a social agency. On the basis of this unique position the library can hope to analyse the present in order to plan for the future.

In stimulation of reading habits among public, the public library plays a vital role. With its network of branches, distribution points, book-mobiles and with its new responsibility towards children, neo-literates, and other less favoured individuals as readers, the public library penetrates into the country's remotest corners and reaches every reader.

In the social context, librarys role in never passive; it is ever dynamic. Although the library is primarily an institution designed to serve the reader, its contemporary position in society suggests an active initiation of ideas rather than a passive provision of books (Nitecki's). The more dynamic a society, more accelerated is the rate of social change which brings in its wake an up-surge for reading, an increased demand for knowledge and information. Society is the determining factor in such cases.

Society, Education and Reading derive their strength from research, which is our next point of discussion and an important function of modern library.

3. Research

Research is the life-blood of modern society, as our economic standard of living, our culture, and our age of progress depend upon it.

Research is an endeavour, to discover, develop, and verify knowledge. It is an intellectual act that begins with the asking of question and progresses through the critical exmination of evidence that is both relevant and reliable, to the revelation of truth that is generalization and universal. Its goal is the pursuit of truth, a goal that can never be attained, but which must always to be attainable.

Research, whether it endeavours to formulate new principles or theories and generalizations or concepts without concern for their application, requires an awareness of the state of existing knowledge and a free flow of information. It is at this point that library enters into ihe research process and helps in its advancement.

The purpose of research is to expand the horizons of knowledge for our socio-economic advancement which in turn depends upon the progress in scientific and technological fields. Inherent in research are unpredictable demands for information which would further its direction or lead it into more fruitful paths.

The development of modern research is a natural effect of newly developing social forces. The two fundamental factors leading to this are : (1) Increase in population pressure; and (2) rise in the standard of life. Population pressure has gone beyond the capacity of natural and near-natural commodities to maintain the people. The result of this is (1) the intensification of the production of natural commodities; and (2) the production of artificial commodities. These have to be based on the continuous improvement of technology; and in its turn, this has to be based upon continuous research on large-scale—development research, pragmatic research, applied research, and pure or fundamental research. But the bed-rock of research is information. And it is the function of national, university, research and special libraries to disseminate information pin-pointedly, exhaustively and expeditiously.

By and large, the library offers many types of specialized services to help in the advancement of research in society. The basic services are :—

(a) Identifying, accumulating, processing for use needed and pertinent materials speedily;

(b) Preparing and circulating lists of latest additions;

(c) Evaluating and interpreting new documents and providing to the right users requisite information contained in them in the form of reviews, abstracts, tables of contents, and photo-copies of excerpts;

(d) Maintaining highly specialized reference files and indexes;

(e) Conducting literature searches;

(f) Providing accurate, factual and relevant information to inquirers;

(g) Preparing bibliographies;

(h) Translating publications wholly or in part;

(i) Providing cheap and rapid means of photo-copying;

(j) Providing quick reference and referral services;

(k) Extending the limitations of its own resources by inter-library loans, cooperative acquisitions and through such methods of bibliographical cooperation as union lists, and catalogues and the exchanging of catalogues and bibliographies[10]

4. Citadel of Individualism

Libraries, in Shera's view, are the stronghold of individualism. "To the library men come seeking truth, each in his own way and for his own ends In the library the patron is not told what to think or when to think it, but in his search each must discover for himself the thoughts and opinions of others and try to

10. J.K. Gates, op. cit., For details, see the chapters on University libraries, and Special libraries.

understand them, to appreciate them for what they are, even though he may not share them"[11].

Needless to comment that library is a 'sanctuary' of independent thinking—the one surving hope of intellectual freedom as also a means of securing and safeguarding it. Of course, the freedom of enquiry and expression derives not only from library services; the library being only one among institutions that embrace this principle. Nonetheless, it is in a most strategic position. because the books, as contrasted with mass media, are "the private forum of the mind"[12]. Whatever else may happen there can be "no final abridgement of intellectual freedom"[13], so long as individuals, privately and voluntarily, can choose their readings from libraries to seek and grasp the truth in the way they like best. It is essential to encourage dissent which is so vital a factor for a healthy intellectual environment. In fact, the growth and development of knowledge and achievement in action are the products of "both conflict and cooperation, both a struggle among beliefs and a sharing of beliefs"[14]. These are the terms on which those within the democratic society have lived and worked effectively in the past; these are the only terms which will ensure the safety and vitality of the democratic society in the future[15]. The library, is, then, a forum for mutual understanding, for mutual cohesion, for mutual cooperation, and for mutual tolerance and peaceful co-existence—not as a homogenizing institution but as a unifiying, living, and dynamically growing force.

S.R. Ranganathan records some more social functions of the library :—

1. To increase the economic resources of humanity to the extent necessary to maintain the ever increasing population, in comfort and free from want of any kind, and also
2 To help in the elevating, self-dependent use of leisure with the aid of freely served books, pictures, sound records, and other graphic materials; and

11. Shera, op. cit.
12. F.A. Sharr, "Silent upon a peak in Darien", *Library Association Records*, v. 72, no. 1, p. 2.
13. Ibid.
14 B.C. Swank, "Six Items for Exports; international values in American Librarianship". *LJ* (v. 88, Feb. 1963), p. 715.
15. Ibid.

3. To help in increasing the opportunity for the spiritual awakening of one and all of the members of humanity[16].

One may validly argue that many of basic social functions performed by libraries today viz ; educational, research, informational, civil responsibility, aesthetic appreciation and recreational, are also served by other agencies and groups. But it must firmly be asserted that library is the only agency devoted solely to the purpose of collecting, processing, making readily accessible, and securing the widest and most effective use of the records of human civilizations by the society of which it is an integral part. Since the library is intertwined in purposes and functions with society's needs, any piece or item of recorded material is a potential library acquisition function and no part of the social structure, irrespective of its development is outside the scope of library's generic concern. L R. McColvin has rightly recorded that today we have reached the stage where we advocate universal library provision, not merely because the masses have the right to equality of opportunity in respect of access to knowledge, but also because we firmly believe that mankind will not be able to exercise wisely their rights and powers unless they do intend enjoying such access to the mine of knowledge. And Shera projects the library's role in society as a disseminator of information He characterizes the present age as being largely concerned with the utilization of applied science in the design of society, and writes that we are, therefore, very much depended upon the successful communication of information. The dissemination of information is, thus, one of the most basic of social activities, and one of the most essential. The value of such a service is indisputable.

5. *Changing Dimensions*

Library is the only effective repository of our cultural heritage. It has aptly been referred to as a "live depository of the cultural past that anticipates the future"[17]. Conservation of knowledge is basic and fundamental to the library. Even today, Shera comments, there are librarians who still regard custody of the books as a material object as the supreme expression of the

16. Ranganathan op. cit.

17. Ralph W. Conant, "Sociological and institutional changes in American life—" *ALA Bull.* (v. 58, 1964), p. 994.

librarian's art, and this veneration of the 'rare book room or the bibliographic museum' has projected the librarian as being somebody who is more concerned with preservation than with use. It is painful that "a social function as important as the conservation of the cultural heritage should lead to the excesses of bibliomania". He sees it as understandable that conservation for immediate and practical use should have merged into conservation for its own sake. With the passage of time, the purpose of conservation became blurred and indistinct.[18]

Library collections must be carefully built and conserved, but for the use and benefit of the community, present and future : not for their own sake, not for prestige, and not in any way for the satisfaction of librarians themselves. Custody of archival materials should be secure, but not prohibitive. To be "a live depository of the cultural past that anticipates the future is not enough. The documents must be used to the largest possible extent and with least trouble : they must be used as tools for expanding the horizons of knowledge rather than guarded as treasure-troves.

Free library service for all is another changing dimension. For centuries, the library was "a nest in which to hatch scholars"[19] The sons of nobles, and rich alone had access to libraries, while those whose means did not permit them to purchase books were too often deprived of them. Even the 19th century was for long swayed by the concept that people beloning to the lower strata of society had no right to education; hence no right to books : library was created of, by and for the elite. But old thinking started changing and by the later half of the mid nineteenth century those who believed that education could save the world and that the library was a means of universal education so urgently needed to make the world safe for democracy were in full cry. Library was considered the crowning glory of education. 'How much more ignorance would thus he removed" thundered John B. Wright in his defence of the Public Library Act of 1851, "how much vice reformed, how much slumbering talent awakened, how much awakened talent aided and made efficient, how much done to make many in a high degree intelligent, well informed, useful and respectable citizens, and to correct, improve and elevate the general character of the whole community..."[20]. The

18. Shera, op. cit.,
19. O.W. Holmes, cf. Shera, op. cit, p. 140.
20. Ibid.

author of Les Miserables, asked "Light, light in floods, no bat resists the dawn, illuminate the bottom of society"[21]. And the library was the logical development to disseminate knowledge for creating enlightened citizenry. Today we look upon library as a service agency, selling mental food free of cost.

Cosistent to its dynamic and changing role, the library plays a vital role in strengthening democracy. J. Ortega y Gasset has written : "Democratic society is a daughter of books, the triumph of the book written by man over the book revealed by God, over the book of laws dictated by the autocracy"[22]. More concretely, libraries exist, today, for the sake of freedom of thought. Its vital role lies in the creation of thinking people, cultivated men and women gifted with disciplined minds, high intellect and moral calibre, nurtured in a climate of freedom of thought and expression and capable of holding opinions independently arrived at, to shoulder stupendous responsibilities. This remarkable function of training the mind and spirit of man enabling him to work for the social, cultural, moral and material advancement of society is the basic function of library social pursuits. One can conclude with A. Broadfield : "The human being is the most ultimate of ends, his free condition his highest condition, freedom of thought the most fundamental element in his freedom, and the library one of the first essentials in maintaining it"[23].

J.S. Shera sees the library principally as an agency of communication, but in a very special way which depends on the librarian's interpretation. He writes that in this age of specialization and social fragmentation the library can become a great force for cohesion. However, by the word "cohesion" Shera does not mean the achievement of conformism. As he puts it, whereas the mass media—such as newspapers and television are declaratory, "the library is interrogative". In fact, the library, now-a-days serves a society in flux poised between annihilation and utopia, torn asunder by great social movements and tremendous political changes, and confused by a babble of conflicting traditions. Such a society needs, as never before, effective access to the wisdom of past for its very survival and its provision

21. Victor Hugo cf. Ibid.
22. "*The Mission of the librarian*", *Antioch review* (v. 21, 1961).
23. A. Broadfield, *A Philosophy of librarianship* (Lond., Graften, 1949), cf. Thomson, *Library power*, op. cit.

is the library's foremost duty. It enjoins upon the library to collect together all available recorded information and to socialize it and serve freely all such information to each according to his needs at the moment. As Shera concludes : The responsibilities which society often quite unwittingly placed upon libraries are very heavy.

In sum : the foregoing discussion projects three roles of the librarian : Custodian, Mediator, and Organizer. The first of these, traditional but narrow in approach, saw the job as concerned with collecting, preserving and classifying books and other graphic materials which were, of course, available to those members of the public who sought them out. Today this may be giving way to a second, more outward-looking, role in which the librarian, from the profusion of published material, excercises more discrimination in presenting it, identifies those who can make use of the information and encourages by display, study guides etc. to utilize it. Probably the librarian of the future will have an even more dynamic role as an organizer. He will go out into the field, creating relationships, activities or groups which did not occur spontaneously but which will enable the library to benefit all sections of the public disseminating cultural traditions more widely; in fact becoming a positive social force within the community[24]. Shera echoes the same view when he writes : "Gone forever is the librarian as soercerer-priest with his papyrus rolls, as monastic recluse pouring over vellum codices of Biblical texts and commentry, as bibliophile perched high on a ladder in a book-lined vaulted chamber, as maiden aunt presiding, with muted voice and padded footstep, over the whispered silence of the library reading room. Each in his own way was a response to to the social needs of his time, the creation of the cultural milieu in which he pursued his career; and by the same token, and for the same reasons, the modern librarian, in whatever branch of librarianship he selects to serve, must be well-educated, professionally competent, and highly qualified to play an important part in the communication process of today's world".

It will be better to close this chapter in the words of S.R. Ranganathan—the prince among library and information scientists : Libraries produce material happiness, mental joy and spiritual delight : they are social institutions charged with the duty of

24. Bryan Luckham, *Library in society* (Lond., LA., 1971).

providing the means for the perpetual self-education of one and all; and contribute to the circulation of ideas, the harnessing of leisure, the demands of democracy, the spread of literacy, and the success of commercial and industrial organizations.

Great libraries have rightly been called the roots and fruits of great civilization. They show light to enable people to become better citizens. Library, thus, affects society and is an acknowledged agency with which society must be concerned.

3

LIBRARY AS DISSEMINATOR OF INFORMATION

Man with his tremendous capabilities of intellect, wisdom and mind has been mastering his situations since his very creation. With the development of our thinking, growth of our experiences and minuteness of our observation, the knowledge has been growing considerably through the ages. But parallel has also been the course of human recording which grew and developed in relation to man's requirements. In the light of material and demand of the society at a particular juncture of the human history the man had been developing methods of recording his experiences through pictographs, hieroglyphies, clay-tablets, wax tablets, papyrus rolls, and through modern books as well as electronic publishing.

Recorded information, however, in itself is of no use unless it is stored in such a way that it can be retrieved easily and made readily accessible for use. It is the basic function of the library to store communication to this end—accumulating, processing, and preserving information for dissemination. In libraries, one can find facts on every subject, from ancient literature to the development of the wheel. Without such storage of information and knowledge, progress would be impossible, for each new discovery in the realm of sciences and ideas is based on the work done in the past. Over the centuries man has gathered immense mass of information. As the sum of his knowledge grows, he must continually seek more efficient and effective methods of storing and retrieving information pin-pointedly, exhaustively and expeditiously on demand.

Information embodied in documents is a great national and international resource Scientific and technological knowledge has been expanding at a terrific speed and there is every likelihood that the growth rate will continue to mount, consequent upon the ever expanding activities in the fields of scientific research, technological development and Industrial production. The headings in professional journals "Information Explosion"; "The Flood of Literature"; "The Rising Information Tide"; and "How to Cope with Literature" are some of the phrases that partly identify this problem.

Information Explosion

In order to appreciate the role of the library in the dissemination of information[1], it is better first to know what we term as information explosion.

The nascent information is usually communicated through the medium of the periodicals and the research reports. Several attempts have been made to estimate the number of periodicals being published in science and technology. C.P. Bourne puts the figure at 15,000 significant journals. C.M. Gotts-Chalk and Desmond put the number at 35,000 with a fallacy of 10%. Martin and Jett's estimate is of 60,000 Derek J. De Solla Price in his article "A Calculus of Science" has stated that by 1800 A.D., there were 100 different scientific periodicals. By 1830, there were more than 500, far too many for any one man to assimilate or even to read. By 1850, this number had grown to 1000; by 1900 to about 10,000; and in 1950 to about 100,000. By the year 2,000, that number will increase manifold, though not exponentially. Little wonder the term "information explosion" is used. S R. Ranganathan puts the number at 50,000 carrying about 10,00,000 learned articles. The swelling sea of recorded knowledge has generated a high-powered flood of literature even in specialized areas of subject fields. To take a concrete example, Bio-Medical Sciences alone have now about 10,000 periodicals and these carry about 2,20,000 titles.

The problem does not end here, rather it is becoming more formidable, because scientific and technological knowledge doubles itself within 7 to 10 years. A million or more scientific papers are poured like rain over the scientific world a year. Fields like atomic energy and television are piling up enormous new masses of materials. Similarity in the pattern of growth has been observed in different systems. For example, exponential and logistic patterns have been recogniz d in the increase of knowledge about animal species, the number of publications on

1. **Information is the input to knowledge. The longest lived, most porsistent sort of information is called knowledge.**

specific subjects such as on Drosophila, Laser, Computer Technology, and Particle accelerators.

The impact of this explosion of micro-documents has been estimated. A scientist can read technical literature at the rate of 200 to 300 words per minute of, let us say, 15 minutes per paper. If all the publications were to stop and a man were to try to catch up with a single year's cutput alone, reading 24 hours a day, 7 days a week, it would take him 50 years. Clearly the problem is out of hand and has been for a long time; as far the scientist is concerned, the end of century could not bring a worse situation[2].

In this regard one is tempted to recall what Charles Bernier, Associate Editor of *Chemical Abstracts* said long back :

> Today's scientific literature is so large that, one person can no longer read the output in one great branch of it, such as Chemistry. If a chemist, fluent in 30 languages, started on January 1st to read all papers in his particular field, 40 hours a week, at a rate of 4 articles an hour, then by December, 31st, he would have read not more than one-tenth of the material published during that year, for which the benefit would he nil, as he would have no time left to do anything with knowledge thereby gained.

The picture projected by Allen Kent (1963) was no better. He wrote :

> "For every 60-second period during the day and night—Saturday and Sundays included, it is estimated that, 2000 pages of books, newspapers or reports will have been published somewhere in the world. If you attempted to keep fully, informed of everything going on in the world—through reading—you would fall behind an estimated 1,051, 200,000 pages every solid year you would devote to reading". This problem though worsened now faces industrialists, military planners, scientists, techonologists and lawyers in keeping abreast of what is published in their own specialized fields.

Commenting on the growth-rate, R. Isenon has written that the rate of growth of knowledge can be expressed as an equation embodying a number of limiting factors. Lenz has pointed out

2. Lewis H. Sarett "The Scientist and scientific data" *Amer. Doc* (v. 19, 1968).

that the exponential growth curve is similar to the growth of biological population under constraint. This accounts for the S—shaped logistic growth noted in the increase of knowledge in different fields. Hartman projects scientists and technologists encircled by the swelling sea of information, and considers the information, as the life-blood for the creation of new ideas. He maintains that occasionally a bit of information collides with a scientist or engineer, sometimes triggering a new idea and sometimes not. Because it is impossible to predict what piece of information will collide with which scientist or engineer and whether a particular collision will be 'elastic' or 'inelastic', the process is only satistically definable.

In sum : Innumerable ideas are being generated every minute. Some of them get documented. But a study of the history of development of ideas in different subject fields would show that the degree of impact of a new idea on the universe of knowledge is not of the same order in all cases. There is the seminal contribution, probably grasped intuitively which makes a powerful, deep and extensive impact and even turns the course of development of several subjects. It may contribute to a considerable disturbance in the pattern of schedules for these subjects. Then there is a large number of near-seminal contributions, which probably constitute the flesh and blood of the document retrieval system. In a study of the mode of development of the Universe of Knowledge it is helpful to evaluate the frequency of incidence of the seminal contributions and of the near-seminal and perhaps even of the pedestrian contributions, during the two or three centuries.

De Sola Price in his study *Calculus of Science* suggests that a theory similar to statistical thermo-dynamics may be helpful in considering the ratio of the total number of papers to the number of good papers, and the number of scientists to the number of good scientists. The basic theory is that all the indices in this respect show regular exponential growth with a doubling in about 10 to 15 years. Such a growth has been happening in the field of the Natural Sciences during the past three centuries. Therefore, the number of documents in the Natural Sciences has increased by a factor of 10 with every doubling of the world population. To understand the statistical mechanics of exponential and logistic growth of the contributions to science, Price considers the productivity distribution of science. He concludes that the number of people writing in papers in a life-time is proportional to $1/n^2$.

At DRTC (Banglore) in a study carried out by Pramodi Bavadekar et al it was experienced that : (1) the frequency of disturbance of the rate of development of the Universe of Subjects is much greater after 1900 than say in mid 19th century. In fact, the Universe of Knowledge has now become turbulently dynamic; (2) the disturbance is highly frequent in the natural sciences; and (3) the disturbance is becoming appreciable and frequent in the social sciences also.

The crux of the problem, however, is that information, even vitally needed information, takes months or years to reach most in need of it. The research is staggered by the findings and conclusions of thousands of other workers—conclusions which he cannot find time to grasp, much to remember as they appear. It may be easier for a researcher to discover a fact by experiment or to build up a theory, than to ascertain from the literature, whether these have been discovered or deduced before.

It is followed by the Seepage Problem of Micro documents; it implies the Bradford's 'Law of Scattering'. It means that the articles are published not only in the periodicals of specific subject fields or of bordering areas but also are scattered among periodicals in subject fields of different and un-anticipated removes from umbral subject-fields. Pertinent information has to be located, collected and shifted from different types of sources.

The problem of information has become formidable one with the proliferation of subjects generating inter-disciplinary approach. Herbert Menzel summarizes this situation as under :

> There has been a vast increase in the demand for information by scientists : There are more scientists to demand information, they demand it at a faster rate, they demand wider geographical coverage, and they demand wider cross-speciality coverage. At the same time, and largely for the same reasons, there has also been a vast increase in the supply of information—and we are, strange as it may seem, dealing with a field where an increase in supply does not alleviate the demand problem but aggravates it. At any rate, the increasing number of researchers

who have made increasing demands for information have also thrown increasing bits of information into hopper. This fact, plus new forms of specialization, is reflected in the increasing number of scientific periodicals in existence. Added to this is the increasing importance of new types of documents appearing on the shadowy frontier of that which is published and that which is not. Such documents place their own peculiar burdens on the science information system, both as to physical handling and dissmination, and as to coverage in the secondary media[3].

In addition to this is the problem that information is not an entity by itself. It is embedded in the various types of documents—Books, periodical-articles, preprints, notes, monographs, personal letters, diaries, punched cards, computer print-outs, magnetic tapes, data (tables), diagrams or charts, photographs, abstracts, indexes, conservations, lectures, conference papers, technical reports, reviews, advances, dissertations, microforms, and the like.

What we witness in the 1980s is a virtual deluge of 'information explosion'. Licklider, however, objects to the use of the word "explosion". He argues that only in hyperbole does a thing 'explode' that takes 10 or 15 years to double its volume. He suggests instead the analogy of flood, in which the rise is gradual, hitting first one area and then another—not all simultaneously, and in which the overflow may be sudden and dramatic. For most of us the flood of information is a major factor in our lives[4].

The torrents and rivers of current literature pour themselves into libraries adding, without cease, to what is already there. As a result, the size and cost of every research library are growing, not at a constant rate, but at an ever increasing rate. The problem is based on the fact that on one hand, every scientist's reading time is limited, whilst on the other hand, there must exist, somewhere among the millions of items of literature available, the particular ones which contain the ideas most appropriate to his needs. The scientist's need, time, and power of attention are highly precious and must he scarcely saved; and to achieve this objective, information be collected and disseminated more promptly, be better processed, and be better summarized and indexed.

3. Herbert Menzel, "The Information Needs of Current Scientific Research : *LQ* (v. 34, 1964).
4. J.C.R. Licklider, *American Psychologist* (v. 21, 1966).

Library as a Disseminator

The flood of information—created by the development of the Universe of Ideas which tend to become turbulently dynamic—raises very serious problems in storage, retrieval, and dissemination. Moreover, most of the members of research team are not self-helpers. They are in need of the stimulus created by knowing the work done by others. This stimulus has to depend on information techniques like documentation work, documentation service, reproduction service, translation service, and indexing and abstracting services. Transmission of scientific information is a precision job, demanding special care and clear perception as to not only how the information is to be dealt with but also what that information is, who is it intended for, and to what degree does the process of transformation of information help in the advancement and use of science. Today, the research potential of each nation and the world at large should be conserved with the least dissipation. Society is now finding it helpful to assign the function of document search, retrieval, and service to library profession rather than detracting for this purpose, the research, production and managerial personnel from their legitimate sphere of work. The library profession is also sharpening its tools and techniques to retrieve and disseminate graphic knowledge to individual members and groups in society.

By studying the attributes of the information explosion, it is easily realized :

1. That a scheme for classification and the methodology for its development that were adequate to meet the state universe of ideas, say, a 100 years ago is inadequate to meet the requirements of the classification of the universe of ideas in it present state;
2. Today, a methodology for the development of schemes for classification is likely to become inadequate and obsolete at a much faster rate than it might have been done a century, even half a century ago; and
3. Methods should be developed to overcome such a quick obsolescence of the design methodology[5].

5. A. Neelameghan and M.A. Gopinath "Research in library classification", Lib.Sc., with a slant to documentation (v. 4, 1967).

The explosion of information has also led to its storage and retrieval through international agencies like UNISIST, ICSU, IFLA, and international information systems and services like INIS, AGRIS, DEVSIS, INSPEC, MEDLARS and SPINES; and through national agencies like INSDOC, SENDOC, DESIDOC, NISSAT, SSDC (India); BLAISE, INFOLINE, EURONET (U.K); LOCKHEED, SDC, OCLC (USA), and VINITI (USSR).

Similarly, indexing and abstracting services like MARC, INDEX MEDICUS, etc. have flourished. Every agency or research institution is equipped with a library serving as an information bureau.

To cope with the very serious problems of information storage, retrieval and dissemination, machines particularly computers are being pressed into service.

The library, thus, helps in the contemporary development of knowledge and conserves the precious research time of humanity by separation of literature search from positive research. The library and its staff act as a catelyst to transmit the ideas, facts and feelings from the mind and soul of the author to the reader who, in turn, generate new ideas. They keep a researcher or a scientist or an academic of today abreast of the torrential down-pour of micro-documents published in any form, and in any part of the world by studying the needs of their clientele as intimately as possible. The librarian and his professional staff have thus become a partner in research work taking up search of literature side. This is the high water-mark of library service reached today.

The social role of the library is highly complex and the responsibilities which society has placed upon it are stupendous. Certainly there is no one library form that can achieve them all : there must be many types of libraries to to assume this responsibility. In modern society there are different communities of clientele with different interests : public, academics, students, researchers, businessmen, workers, agriculturalists, specialists, etc. To meet the varied demands one may recognise the following types of libraries :

1. **Public Libraries.**
2. **Academic Libraries.**
3. **Special Libraries.**
4. **National Libraries.**

No one plan can describe all libraries, because the purpose, form, collection, and programme of each library are determined by the specific needs of its users. But the activities which are common to all libraries have to do with :

1. organising and administering the libraries,
2. building the collection;
3. making it (collections) available for use pin-pointedly and promptly; and
4. serving the users

The number and variety of these activities and ways of performing will vary according to the size, purpose, and user of the library, influenced, of course, by the availability of finance, facilities, equipment, and the availability of competent and highly qualified staff. But some objectives or functions are peculiar to a particular type of library; and the libraries having the general types of objectives and functions have come to be identified as a group or as a kind of library service. An attempt is made in the chapters 4-9 to discuss the purposes and functions of each type of library.

REFERENCES

S.R. Ranganathan, "Documentation and Kumar-Avatara", Lib.Sc. with a slant to doc. (v. 7, 1970).

—*Prolegomena to Library clasification* (Asia, 3rd ed).

A. Neelameghan, "Research on the structure and development of the universe of subjects", Lib.Sc. with a slant to doc. (v. 4,4, 1967).

Herman M. Weisman, *Information system, services, and centres* (Becker-Hayes, 1972).

4

THE PUBLIC LIBRARY AS AN EDUCATOR

The province and purpose of the public library is to provide for every person the education obtainable through reading. This does not mean education in any narrow or formalized sense but, rather, the culture of mind and spirit that books can diffuse in life. As Helen E. Haines puts it : "Education in its ideal fulfilment is not simply fact finding nor the assiduous pursuit of information. It implies the use of books for spiritual and intellectual as well as for material and vocational profit, books for mental resource, reading for individual and personal joy—all elements in the diffusion, perhaps not of specific knowledge, but of culture in Mathew Arnold's sense—"in becoming something rather than in having something, in an inward condition of the mind and spirit, not in an outward set of circumstances". This is the ideal that has inspired and directed the development of library service...."[1].

Three dimensions emerge for discussion : What is Education ? What is a Public Library ? How Public Library Educates ?

Education is defined by Louis R. Wilson as the process by means of which the individual is brought through training to an understanding of himself, of the life about him, and of the infinitely numerous relations which connect him with it. It is the process through which he passes in gaining for himself a proper knowledge of the various circumstances of life; from which he acquires the ability to adjust himself properly to them; and by which he learns to know the standards of the true, the good, and the beautiful with which to measure them. It is the highway over which the individual passes in reaching an ultimate point from which he can view with greater clearness than he otherwise could, life and the issues of life, in their true perspective. To pass this

1. Helen E. Haines, *Living with books: the art of book selection*, 2nd ed. (Columbia Univ. Press, 1961).

way, is to become educated; to help another on this course, is to be an educator; and to be an educator in this sense, is to be Godlike[2].

Admitting that education is the source of individual's enlightenment, happiness and self-fulfilment, the modern welfare states have established the school, the museum and the institutions of higher learning for importing education to help man to know himself and his role in society. The role of public library lies in helping the students to learn when they are away from their teachers by providing learning environment.

Definition and Characteristics

Unesco Manifesto[3] defines a Public Library as a library :

1. which is established under "the clear mandate of law";
2. which is "maintained wholly from public fund";
3. which levies no "direct charge" (fees) from its users for any of its services; and
4. which is open "for free and equal use by all members of the community" regardless of race, colour, caste, creed, religion, age, sex, nationality, language, status or level of educational attainments.

Characteristics

The above definition of a Public Library is pregnant with vital characteristics; it is better to analyse them :

First, a public library should be provided by a local authority and financed for the most part out of its funds. It should be governed and managed by the local authority or a committee wholly or largely appointed by itself. The public library should be a product of local government at least for four reasons :

(i) people should take pride in their possessions;

(ii) people can achieve variety, richness, and excellence in their model and resist any pattern being imposed from above;

(iii) closer the library, better it serves the public; and

(iv) it provides a common platform for the local community for exchanging their views leading to cross-fertilization of ideas,

2. ...., *Education and libraries* (Crossby, 1966).
3. Unesco Manifesto, 1972.

to develop the quality of appreciating others' point of view, to learn sympathy, tolerance, friendliness, understanding and mutual cooperation.

Nonetheless, the local unit must be economically viable. Moreover, the local unit cannot function in isolation. These local units must be assisted and encouraged by state, regional and national agencies—not to control the local libraries or to dictate their actions, but to provide centralised bibliographical and informational services; regulate book supply; provide professional courses for training personnel and above all to make grants from national, regional or state exchequres both to stimulate development and to overcome local inequalities and poverty of funds.

Second, the public library should be "free" in the sense that the users should not be required to make payment for the services they use. If a man has the right of using the mine of knowledge or information, he must not be deprived of it because of his financial disabilities, keeping in view that many of the library users who would most benefit are just those most hesitant to pay. Moreover, no librarian can do his duty of disseminating knowledge with dedication if he is at the mercy of subscribers. The only one admissable and satisfactory method of financing public libraries is, that they must be reared at the expence of whole community.

Third, a public library is a dynamic, living force and the intellectual nucleus of the community it serves. It is an institution of the public and for the public. Therefore, they must be open to all, without any let or hindrance. They must be quickly and highly accessible. This principle implies that there must be appropriate public library service points available to everyone in the community. It requires the provision of urban as well as rural libraries. That the public library keeps its doors open for free and equal use by all members living in area of its operation distinguishes it from an academic or a special library.

Finally, a public library must provide to its users the world's best thought giving reliable information, in an unbiased and balanced way, on as wide a variety of subjects as will satisfy individual's personal, professional, or political aspirations. It means that our libraries must be unfettered, impartial and serving no ulterior purposes. It is useless expecting a man to think for his intellectual development if he is given censored, limited, and pre-digested material to conform with someone's idea of what he should know and believe. When this is the case, library servicцs will not only be ineffective but also constitute a gross denial of a vital human right. They will fail to safeguard democracy and prevent people from falling a prey to anti-social, anti-national, and anti-cultural forces. Thus public libraries are vital for individual's liberty, and freedom of thought—the bed-rock of modern democracy

In brief, a public library will be accepted as such when it is open to all and has a stock of books and other graphic materials adequate for the educational, recreational, informational, and research needs of its public. It must never be the instrument of political propaganda, or of proselytism, religious or anti-religious.

Objectives

In his work "Library Manual", S.R. Ranganathan hails the library as a "Social Institution" and lays down for it the following objectives :

1. it should help the life-long self-education of one and all;
2. it should furnish up-to-date facts and information on all subjects to one and all;
3. it should distribute, in an unbiased and balanced way, all shades of recorded views and thought to one and all, as a help in discharge of their political functions in respect of local, national, and inter-national affairs;
4. it should contribute to productivity-drive by informing top-managements of the latest trends in diverse enterprises, by ploughing back into the minds of researchers, designers, and technologists every piece of relevant new thought, promptly and pin-pointedly;
5. it should provide to one and all a harmless and elevating use of leisure;
6. it should preserve the literary remains of humanity for posterity, as vehicles of culture and as source materials for antiquarian research; and in general
7. it should work for continued social well-being, as the agency in charge of all socialized recorded thought.

Thus a library has educational, informational, political, economic, industrial, cultural, and antiquarian objectives.

Functions

1. Providing Materials

Functions follow the objectives. Being a social institution, the public library has to perform multi-faceted functions : But one function remains constant; to provide and service materials for enlarging the mind and dispelling prejudice and ignorance. It implies the necessity of making access to the truth easy and rapid for anyone who seeks it. For the overwhelming majority, the quickest and easiest access to the world's best thought is through the public library. It means very recent facts and ideas as well as the wisdom of the ages; the library must be current as well as retrospective[5]. Its materials are provided :

—to facilitate informal self-education of all people in community;

—to enrich and further develop the subjects on which individuals are undertaking formal education;

—to meet the informational needs of all;

—to support the educational, civic, and cultural activities of groups and organizations;

—to encourage wholesome recreation and constructive use of leisure time[6].

Provision of materials means more than occasional availability It means a supply sufficient to make the library a dependable source for most people most of the time. In addition to books, the public library selects and provides pamphlets, documents, and other non-book sources in printed form, and films, tapes, discs and other non-print stores of knowledge and opinion. All activities of the library are designed to facilitate use of resources—to remove barriers, to invite use, to guide reading towards the goals of each invidividual.

5. Gerald Johnson, "Role of the Public Library", cf. J.L. Wheeler and H. Goldhor, Practical administration of public libraries (Harper, 1962), p. 3.

6. *Minimum Standards for Pnblic Library System*, ALA. cf. W.J. Murison, *Public library*, 2nd ed. (Lond., George H. Harrap, 1955).

2. Servicing the Materials

Providing materials is only the first step. The second basic function that which differentiates a library from a mere collection of books and other materials, is service. The services performed by a modern library include :

1. the organization of material to make it easily accessible through shelf-arrangement, classification, and cataloguing;
2. lending of material so that it may be used at the time and place most suited to the public;
3. guidance to assist the user to find what he wishes, either in the materials immediately at hand or in whatever library may possess it;
4. a programme of public information to make its resources not only available but eagerly sought by its community[7]. It includes stimulation of use and interpretation of materials through publicity, display, reading lists, story hours, book-talks, book and film discussion, and other appropriate means either in the library or in community organizations. The materials, services, personnel, and physical facilities of the public library cover the interests of all ages and groups in population. The public library, thus, has to serve not only the earnest seekers for knowledge, but also those who are merely gratifying an elementary curiosity, and those who are seeking relaxation and recreation.

In essence, the public library provides materials and services to promote the general diffusion of knowledge and information; to stimulate freedom of expression and a constructive critical attitude towards the solution of social problems; to educate man to participate in a creative manner in community life and to promote a better understanding between individuals, groups and nations; and to extend the activities of the centres of learning, offering new educational possibilities to the people. The basic principle underlying the library service is that it exists for the training of the good citizen. It must aim at providing all that printed literature can provide to develop his intellectual, moral, and spiritual capabilities.

3. Prime Educational Functions

Convinced of the fact that books and reading have a powerful influence on society, the public library under dynamic leadership

7 Ibid.

can become an active, and effective education centre. Of course, L. Stanley Jast[8] warned : "The librarian should carefully avoid tresspassing the ground of the educationalist", but he was contradicted by Carl Thomsen[9] who said : "Public libraries cannot fulfil their responsibilities in isolation from educational work". To J. H. Shera, the library is "handmaiden of universal education", with the aim of bringing enlightenment, improvement and happiness to one and all. In the words of Ranganathan, "libraries are social institutions charged with the duty of providing the means for the perpetual self-education of one and all", leading to material happiness, mental joy, spiritual delight and the spread of mass literacy. Books remain the sole comprehensive and proven method of self-teaching; and public library being the repository of our cultural heritage provides opportunity and encouragement for children, young people, men and women to educate themselves continuously.

It is the duty of the public library to co operate with the school in its endeovour to awaken in the children an inspiration to make the most of his powers, to give him the alphabet of learning and activity, to train his power of thought and expression, and to supply him with the implements with which he may attain culture. Apart from its connection with the schools, its chief function is to serve as the lifelong university for the individual, in which he may find freely, without money and without price, an opportunity for the continuous development of all his powers. This point needs further discussion.

4 Adult Education

The idea of adult education lay embedded in the realization that education is a life-long process, and that universal education is the very life-blood of modern society.

> The Adult Education Committee of Great Britain defined it to mean "all the delibrate efforts by which men and women attempt to satisfy their responsibilities as citizens and members of society or to find opportunities for self-expression"[10].

8. Library and the community (Lond., Nelson, 1939).
9. Carl Thomsen et al. *Adult education activities for public libraries* (Paris, Uneseo, 1950).
10. Great Britain, Reconstruction (Ministry of-). Adult Education Committee, 1919, *Final Report* (HMSO), p. 34.

The American Association for Adult Education[11] states that the aim of adult education is "to ins pire grown-ups to be something more than they are now, and to do their work better than they do it now. Its beginning is wherever one finds onself; it ends only when ambition ceases to function. At its best, it leads to constantly increasing richness of life, better appreciation of what life offers, greater satisfaction in the use of mind and body, and better understanding of the rights and duties of one's fellowmen".

The above definitions reflect that adult education is an effort put forth by a mature person to improve himself by acquiring new skills, information, understandings, attitudes, or appreciations or the effort of an agency to present the opportunity and the encouragement to mature persons for improving themselves or their community (Houle). It further aims at combating ignorance and prejudice, fanaticism and bigotery which divide them. It must guide the energy of the people into heathy, creative channel and stimulate their intellectual, educational, social and spiritual interests so that they may not only elevate the individual but may enrich the life of the community as well.

In India, the concept of adult education has been broadened. Maulana A.K. Azad, once the Union Education Minister of India, gave a new orientation, a new life, and later on a new name to this concept by enlarging its base and giving it the apt title of Social Education—an education for the complete man. "The real aim of Social Education", says Humayun Kabir, "is to create an educated mind among the adult literate," for helping them to evolve a philosophy of life and to develop interests which will enrich their leisure. It is an attempt to salvage a generation by giving it the minimum of education needed to improve its way of life, its health, its productivity and its social, economic and political organization.

From the aim of adult education or social education as given above, it is clear that many social agencies will have to work in unison to provide adults the means for educating themselves continuously. But as adult education is varied, informal and practical, library is the most appropriate agency of adult education in so far as it provides both the requisite reading

11. J.E. Russel "Help to Self-Realiztion, Survey", Libraries and adult education (Macmillan, 1926).

material and environment for informal reading. Probably, it inspired Alvin Johnson to hail the public l brary as a People's University and assigned it a vital role in fighting illiteracy and helping people in their intellectual, cultural and material advancement. He commented that as education is needed from cradle to the very end of life, "library is so obiviously its proper cent e that not even the purest of the pure librarian can be against it"[12].

As an egency of adult education, the public library has used various iustruments of mass-communication, with increasing use of audio-visual materials for disseminating knowledge.

An integral part of the library's educational function is to supply motives for reading. Lectures, study circles, dramatic clubs, book review groups and exhibitions have been purposively organized and programmes of work planned to serve the interest of special groups, like women's club, association of parents and teachers, and Church groups. The libraries themselves have helped in the formation of many other groups, viz., among young adults, old adults, rural folks and labour groups. Group discussions have judiciously been deviced and forums encouraged and run with the premises of the library to enhance intellectual interests and afford valuable educational experiences. Today, many groups flourish under the library's leadership. Opportunities to discuss critical issues of the day, community problems, burning problems, great books of the past and thought provoking books of the present draw people together in community-wide meetings and small neighbourhood groups. It may, however, be added that the library is not the sole agency engaged in adult education, nevertheless, it forms a permanent nucleus around which such activities can easily grow. And Dan Lacy is more objective when she says "Perhaps the g eatest opportunity for expanding library usefulness lies in closer identification with all the manifold wealth of group discussions and informational activities which we loosely call adult education"[13]. It is maintained that the public library is not so much a place where adults get education, as where educated adults get books It is not Robert D. Leigh states "the people's university but a library of people's university"[14]. As the library of the People's University

12. Alvin Johnson, The Public library—A People's, University (N. Y., Amer. Asso. for Adult, 1939).
13. Dan Lacy "The Adult in Ca hanging Society..." LQ, V.27,1957. p. 292.
14. op. cit.,

one of the functions of the public library is to follow-up mass education programmes by providing books of all types (viz., books for the neo-literates, semi-literates and the literates) so that what has been learnt in adult education classes is not immediately forgotton again through lack of reading materials.

In the communities where there is no flow of appropriate reading material and no stimulus to write, literacy itself may have little significance. The wisdom and patient service of school teachers must be supplemented when the students have left their schools by liberal provision of means such as public libraries provide for self-education of those whose ambitions and interests, having been stimulated, are active forces in the development of the individual and of society.

Curiously enough, the Govt. of India has not appreciated the role of Public Libraries in adult education. The National Adult Education Programme launched by the Central Government through Ministry of Education and Social Welfare on 2nd Oct., 1978, could have worked mueh effectively through the efficient public library services. Their due recognition in NAEP would have given an opportunity to public libraries to educate people to learn to be useful citizens by developing their abilities, individual judgement and sense of moral and social responsibility.

5. Community's Information Centre

In 1924, a thesis was put forward that the chief business of a "community library" is to produce a general "diffusion of knowledge" among "small, ill-defined, and constantly, shifting groups, where each need is peculiar to the individual himself, and must be dealt with separately". Thus a view was held that the public library "is an indispensable basis for a community intelligence service". It was prophesised that "a free community book exchange is destined to be transformed into an active intelligence centre,-- a genuine community university, bringing intelligence, systematically and persuasively to bear on all adult affairs"[15]. The author of this statement, William S. Learned, persuasively enunciated the concept of the public library as the community's intellectual power-house, a centre for reliable, useful and up-to-information

15. William S. Learned, The American public library and the diffusion o knowledge (N Y., Hartcourt, 1924), p. 27-28.

A.H. Bill, too, argues that the library is not a collection of books but a collection of information in various forms, which has to be gathered, organized and fully exploited to be more fully and promptly available to each user according to his needs. The public library also provides facilities for the study of arts, trades and professions which contribute to the occupation of the inhabitants.

6. Recreation

The term 'Recreation' in library discussions denote "such use of leisure time as will promote personal happiness and social well-being". In persuance of its recreational function, the chief role of the public library is to provide material for relaxation, entertainment, adventure and escape. This has led to the division of library materials into two categories : fiction and non-fiction.

The new generation of library users are strongly oriented toward audio-visual materials. It, therefore, follows that libraries must not be concerned only with books; they should contain all the principal media of communication.

The logic of this "cultural" interpretation of recreation is also underpinned by extension activities undertaken by the public libraries : exhibitions, lectures, book-weeks, talks, films, gramophone recitals. Library also organizes cultural activities for the entertainment of the public. The Public Library and Museums Act of 1964 (U K.) allowed "the holding of meetings and exhibitions, showing of films and slides, the giving of musical performances, and holding of other events of an educational or cultural nature"[16]. Recreational uses of library services shade imperceptibly into those of an educational nature and from increased leisure matched by greater educational opportunity comes a readership that requires access to information and to recorded knowledge on a greater scale than before.

7. Stre gthening Democracy

The public library is a product of modern democracy and a practical demonstration of democracy's faith in universal education

16 cf. G. Jefferson, *Libraries and society* (Camb. James Clarke, 1969). Also Ronald C. Benge, *Libraries and cultural change*, (Lond. Clive Bingley, 1970).

as a life-long process. By throwing open the mine of recorded knowledge for effective use, critical evaluation and exploration, library encourages individuality, variety and dissent within a climate of tolerance—the anti-thesis of authoritarianism.

Through the diffusion of education, the library strives to enhance equality and social justice, to promote intellectual freedom and advacnement of knowledge, to generate in the young generation a sense of purposefulness and maximum dedication, confidence in themselves and faith in democracy's future.

The strongest threats to democracy come from ignorant classes who vote wrongly because of their "untutored choice" or by the influence of unscruplous politicians. In democracies where every thought and deed affect the socio-economic mechanism of the whole, it becomes the duty of whole to educate its parts to have an informed body of voters for the success of democracy. And we shall not have a democracy until we have a well-educated people : the library can play a vital role in the spread of education, thus, paving the way for the success of democracy. The public libraries disseminate works of all kinds calculated to promote the life-long education of one and all; to serve books where no good library exists. Doubtlessly, books written by zealots and propagandists, and newspapers which tend to be sensational, can be potent weapons of subversion. But a good library service providing materials in open, balanced, many sided collections on policies, mass movements, economics, citizenship, and government can help to make democracy safe, informed, stable and real.

One may conclude with Ranganathan that public libraries generate 'material happiness, mental joy and spiritual delight'; they are social institutions charged with the duty of providing the means for the perpetual self-education of one and all; and then contribute to the circulation of ideas, the harnessing of leisure, the demands of democracy, the spread of literery, and the success of commercial and industrial organization.

Speaking in the same veins, the Public Library Research Group (U.K.) stated that the whole aim is : "To contribute to sustaining the quality of life in all its aspects—educational, economic, industrial, scientific and cultural and promote the concept of a democratic society in which equal opportunity exists for all to develop into true citizens, with whole and balanced personalities leading to an increase in the sum total of man's happiness and aware of himself, his fellow men and his environment".

5

UNIVERSITY LIBRARY :
The Sun Around Which Teaching and Research Revolve

The concept of the library as the "heart" of a university, the sun around which teaching and research revolve is widely hailed.

There is, however, difference of opinion as to the precise nature of the functions of the university library. In their work "The University Library", the Association of University Teachers made a bold statement : "The prime function of the university library is to provide facilities for study and research for the members of its own institution. At the same time there is considerable support for the view that it should serve a wider circle of users and not to adopt too restrictive an attitude which would be contrary to academic traditions". The statement implies three functions of the university library : teaching, research and extension services.

Elucidating the functions of university library, Arthur T. Hamlin concludes that conservation of knowledge is an important function of the university as a whole, and that it is through the university library that it carries this function to its conclusion. Hamlin mentions two other subsidiary purposes. These are : the extension of knowledge, carried out mainly through library cooperation; and the transmission of knowledge, which he feels can best be achieved by the encouragement of programmes of independent study by students who are thus obliged to use the library. In other words, according to Hamlin, there are three functions of the university library : conservation of knowledge, extension of knowledge (research) and transmission of knowledge (teaching)[2].

1. cf. Donald Davinson, *Academic* and legal deposit libraries (Lond., Clive Bingle, 1965).
2. 'The libraries of the universities of Italy', Libri, 15(2), p. 138-158.

In their oft quoted work, "The University Library", Wilson and Tauber assign six functions to the univesity library :

1. Conservation of knowledge and ideas
2. Teaching
3. Research
4. 'Publication
5. Extension and service
6. Interpretation.

It may he noted that in practice one can identify the "conservation of knowledge and ideas" function with the teaching function. Moreover, the 'interpretation' function can be associated with the second, third, and fourth functions. Finally, the function of 'publication' is not of significant potency, particular in the Indian university libraries which almost do nothing in this context.

That is why one may say that teaching, research and extension services are the three major functions of the university library.

How does the university library perform teaching, research and extension services functions. For answer one may look toward S.R. Ranganathan, Wilson and Tauber, Rogers and Weber among others.

S.R. Ranganathan's Views On Teaching and Research Functions of University Library

Ranganathan writes that the university library helps the academic community in five stages. Three of these are correlated to work in the class-room and in the laboratories.

In the first stage, which Ranganathan calls *preparatory study*, reading materials should be gathered, organised, and attractively presented to the students—on all the subjects of study and in all levels—for preparatory study before the class lectures. This is to rouse *curiosity*.

The second stage is called *parallel study*. The librarian should provide another set of reading materials for parallel study immediately after class lecture. This is to maintain curiosity.

At the third stage, a still another set of reading materials should be served for *follow-up study*. This is to harness curiosit and to take the students to a higher level of curiosity and work. This spirit should be further enriched at the fourth and fifth stages.

The fourth stage in library service is concerned with the use of leisure. The library should feed students with entertaining and elevating books for use during leisure time.

The fifth stage of library service, according to Ranganathan, arises only in the case of the more advanced students, the research fellows and the teachers themselves. At this stage, the university library is concerned with the conservation of the research-potential of the academics. To conserve the research potential, it should pick-up and organize the nascent thought in every field of knowledge and plough it back into the minds of the research-workers. The librarian has thus become a partner in research-work by taking over the literature-search. This is the high-water mark of library service reached to-day. To emphasize this new role of library, the term DOCUMENTATION came into use. It consists of the following work :

Scanning the contents of the current periodicals and picking out all new thought relevent to the research work in progress in the several departments of the university; Ranganathan calls it "Nascent Micro Thought";

Classifying each article minutely and cataloguing it with all the necessary cross-references or subject analyticals and alphabetical indexes;

Making a systematic or classified list of the entries of all the relevant nascent micro documents with helpful feature headings to guide the research-worker, so that he can arrive at his spot in the list without any waste of time; this Ranganathan calls "Documentation Service"; and

Voluntarily bringing to the notice of each research-worker any new published thought likely to be relavant to his work.

Thus, documentation service should be given both on demand and in anticipation. This does not mean spoon-feeding. This does not take away the right of any research-worker to use his leisure in browsing widely among periodical literature.

Library service of this kind is essential to get an adequate return on the capital sunk in the laboratories and the buildings and on the money being spent on the teachers and research-workers. "It is not proper", writes Ranganathan, "to blame the students, the teachers, or the research-workers for poor out-turn, when they are not served the necessary mental food from time to time in the exact measure of their needs". The enrichment of the collection in the library and of the actual services to be rendered should be reviewed from this economic angle[3].

In brief : in order to participate in the teaching and research functions of the university, the library performs duties at two levels :

1. Duty to Teachers and Students

The library staff should keep itself in close touch with the progress of work in the class-room. In collaboration with the professors and lecturers in different subjects, the librarian and his staff should plan for the students to pursue *preparatory*, *parollel* and *follow-up* study in each of the subject, and mobilize the resources of the library to facilitate this pursuit.

2. Duty to Research Staff

Secondly, the librarian and his professional and technical staff should make themselves familiar with the wave-front of knowledge in which research is in progress in the university. They should analyse the current periodicals and feed the research staff with nascent thought embodied in them pin-pointedly, exhaustively and expeditiously[3].

Wilson And Tauber's Views On Teaching And Research Functions of University Library

Administering the library at teaching and research level, according to Wilson and Tauber, is based upon two assumptions :

1. that learning is promoted by means of various methods. including library use as well as the lecture, the discussion group, the laboratory exercise, and the field trip; and
2. that the library may be administered in such a way that it may make a maximum contribution to the learning process.

Provision of effective library service conducive to good teaching, learning, and development of research, continue the learned writers, calls for two major factors : *Orientation*, and the *Stimulation of students' interest in reading* Each factor

3. UGC (India) *University and college libraries*, Report (1965).

needs a brief discussion to drive home the vital role of the university library in the promotion of teaching and research.

1. Orientation

Orientation of Student

The basic purpose of *Orientation* or what Ranganathan terms *Initiation* is to make student feel at home and to acquaint him : how to look up material in the catelogue, how to find it on the shelves, and how to charge it out. To the freshman, the card catelogue seems enormous and hopelessly complicated. The book-stock is so large as to overpowering his sense of determination in selection. Everyone on the library staff seems overbusy and productive. The freshman is hesitant to interrupt; the library looks bewildering—even forbidding place.

During Orientation, the freshmen are given a homely introduction to the library usually through a lecture combined with a tour of the library : the freshmen are taken through the stacks, shown the special materials, past the card catalogue, circulation desk, exposed to the reproprographic facilities, if available, then given a brief talk on the use of the primary, secondary, and tertiary sources of information. Like his colleagues in the class-room, the librarian gives advanced lectures and demonstrations in the compilation of bibliographies, union lists, and on the writings of reports, abstracts, and guide to theses. The usual method of lecture and discussion (if facilities exist) is illustrated by slides, charts and films on the use of books and libraries. Sometimes, this procedure is replaced entirely or augmented by videotape instructions.

A GUIDE to the library is another invaluable device to assist and instruct students about the use of library. Such a guide may vary from single mimeographed sheet to well-printed, well-designed and well-illustrated handbooks. The usual pattern includes the description of resources of the library, with particular emphasis on collections of unusual significance; library services including inter-library loans, reprography facilities, abstracting, indexing, instruction in the use of library, preparation of special reading lists; information concerning rule and regulations, location of rooms (often shown in maps and floor plans), library hours; the scheme of classification used; the type of catalogue in operation and the arrangement of books on the shelves. Such information is supplemented by suggestions about the nature and use of the card catalogue, the guides to periodical indexes, encyclopedias, dictionaries, atlases, ghazetteers, directories, year-books, and other reference works, including titles or directions on such subjects as how to study, how to take notes and how to prepare bibliographies and manuscripts. The availability of reference service or subject specialists should be highlighted. It should contain a list of key telephone numbers, addresses of different libraries within the system, the procedure for becoming a member of the library, and finally make a point of welcoming users' suggestions and requests for information or advice.

The guide or handbook should be written in a simple language and style and particular attention be paid in the production of its cover, arrangement, illustrations, diagrams, and typography. It should he made available to all fresh-men at a nominal cost.

In libraries with highly decentralized system of materials, the use of *Posters* and *Signs* are helpful in orienting the student in regard to the facilities available. Wilson and Tauber maintain that not only do such devices directly aid the student, but they also reduce the number of questions to be answered by the over-worked library staff.

The librarians can also take help from Students' Magazine, Alumni Bulletin or other university publications to project information concerning acquisitions, changes in library policy, the addition of new services, current exhibits, public readings and the addition of new services like the loan of records, and tapes, rare material of local history or special collections, services to the disadvantaged, the short loan collections, the requests for inter-library services, and privileges.

The *Orientation* and direction of the students may also be facilitated by providing *Annotated Book Lists* relating directly to their studies and by the preparation of displays and exhibits. The judicious use of book jackets in a distinctive place in the library preferably in the entrance hall, corridors, display windows, and announcement of latest titles may stimulate the interests of students in the materials which concern their course work.

Exhibitions represent an effective device to arouse the interest of students in the library and its activities. Exhibits are mostly organized to publisize little known or rare materials, stimulate reading, promote interests in a specific field, celebrate anniversaries and special occasions, relate books to specific courses, publicize gifts, encourage hobbies, and emphasize the work of student organizations, or the research work of faculty. Each exhibit, write Wilson and Tauber, should have a specific objective. Skillful use of colour contrasts, backgrounds, lighting and equipment should aid considerably in attracting the interests of students and other users.

Orientation of Faculty-Members

Of course, every faculty member has the competence to teach his subject, but his knowledge of current literature in his subject is likely to fall short because of literature explosion and proliferation of subjects. The subject specialists in each area have a special function here to forge a link between the library and the academic staff—to promote better book-selection; better reading lists for students; better use of materials already in stock, current awareness of new books, periodical articles; reports, conference proceedings, statistics, and theses.

The second important factor involved in administering the library at teaching and research level is the promotion or stimulation of reading habits among the students. And to achieve this purpose, the library scientists of the stature of L.R. Wilson and M.F. Tauber, R.D. Rogers and D.C. Weber[4], G.R. Lyle[5] and S.R. Ranganathan have suggested the following techniques.

2. Promotion/Stimulation of Reading

Created as a facility for shared use by the university community, the library exists to provide reading material and other graphic sources to support the purposes of the institution. As a major depository for reading matter, it is in a unique position to promote reading; as a service organization, it must facilitate reading; as part of a pedagogical institution, it should play an active role in making books a significant part of a university education.

The teacher can be the prime motivator to student learning, yet the librarian is in a most unique position to contribute to such motivation. The central role of the librarian is to help students

4. *University library administration* (H.W. Wilson, 1971).
5. Administration of the college library (H.W. Wilson, 1961).

learn when they are away from their teachers by providing a learning environment. The underlying idea is to establish conditions conducive to developing creative enquiry.

Freedom of Access to Collections

The most significant step the library can take in fostering reading habits among students is to provide freedom of access to collections. By allowing individuals free access to all the ideas and facts, from all ages and all societies, which are contained in libraries, one inevitable result must be the creation in some students the desire and inspiration to innovate. The ease with which one can reach the collections provides stimulus in every aspect of students' activities—intellectual, social, and artistic.

Another significant aid, according to Rogers and Weber, is omission of "red tape" in the use of the collections. How much irritating are some circulation procedures ! What better way to suppress enthusiasm for scholarsh!p than by placing hurdles in the path of a youth who seeks on his own to follow the example of the teacher who has stimulated his inquisitiveness. Classic frustrations include the information void that occurs when a book is recorded in a catalogue but cannot be found, when a desired journal has been in professor's office/home for months, or when a volume has departed to spend months at a bindery. A library staff sensitive to the needs of its clientele must be aware of such failings and do what it can to prevent them. The basic test of the quality of any university library is its ability to get into the hands of the reader the book he wants and at the time when he wants it. It requires that library materials should be highly accessible; and assistance in the location of matericals and in the use of the library for information and research should also be available.

Teaching Techniques

In order to promote love of reading, the teaching technique should move away more and more from notes-dictation, narration of facts, and strict confinement to the letter of the syllabus and the prescribed text-book. The present system of education encourages students to the application of purely mnemonic tests, stuffing their brains with the "abracadabra of geometry and physics, algebra and logic". It aims at the filling of the memory of students once for all with every possible piece of information and knowledge likely to be needed by them in their entire life's journey after leaving education.

The true aim of education and the true purpose of teaching technique should be to equip the student to face the intellectual challanges and the ups and downs of life. For this, he must be trained to keep himself in finding out by himself any information or knowledge needed to satisfy his curiosity and intellectual attainments. The teacher should inspire and fire the imagination by a few lectures and make the students help themselves with the books in the library. Under such a system of teaching "Students demand more relevance, greater freedom, and more opportunity for individual learning. Any educational program that places more responsibility on the student for his own education necessarily involves greater use of books and libraries"[6].

This method of teaching requires that the librarian must serve teacher and student as he has always done, but no longer with mere technical information about the place of books and their titles; this time he must have a first-hand knowledge of their contents and their value, he must in him and by himself be an intelligence agency, be the glowing point of contact between his library and the inquiring mind[7].

Although, the library should facilitate use and encourage general reading, faculty members bear the major responsibility for developing reading habits among the students. Courses must be shaped toward the stimulation of independent reading. The teacher should stimulate curiosity, arouse critical faculties and encourage among the students the innate desire to learn. The teacher should invite the librarian in the class-room to expose the students to the use of reference books and bibliographical aids pertinent to their studies and research. The purpose should be to sharpen their power of discrimination, sensitivity, reflection and of analysis and judgement to have recourse to books that inspire him to to think and feel for himself. In fact, the students should be encouraged to use the library as a workship for learning "how to manage their own education"; how to use it in preparation for discussion in class, seminars, reports and papers. But this kind of teaching requires that there must exist a two-way flow of information between teacher and librarian to propagate that

6. A.M. McAnally; "Status of the university librarian in the academic community" (1971)
7. Jacques Barzun 'The new librarian to the rescue' *Library Jour.* (Nov. 1, 1969).

the library is an extension of the class-room and a generating source of knowledge and ideas. If the intellectual atmosphere in the class-room and the nature of class assignments foster the use of a large number of books, the library effort will be rewarded.

Courses of Instruction

Instruction in the use of libraries through formal courses, write Wilson and Tauber, has long been recognized as an effective means of increasing library use. The university is a tool for instruction, and the librarians should work closely with the faculty to this end.

Such courses of instruction, when provided, have been offered at three levels—undergraduate, graduate, and professional. Such courses are usually offered in three forms : (1) complete courses for freshmen, which may be required; (2) elective courses for freshmen or more advanced students; and (3) abridged courses that are offered as a minor part of a course in some subject field. Whether required or elective, the courses in library instruction have followed a pattern. They include the mastery of information and working on problems which involve the parts of the book, encyclopedias, dictionaries, periodical indexes, indexes to collections, yearbooks, documents, pamphlet materials, reference books in special fields, the card catalogue, classification of books on shelves, facilities of special collections, and methods of constructing a bibliography. Most courses include a detailed tour of the library.

Service to the Undergraduates

The undergraduates require introductory level instruction. Basic use of the library should be coordinated with particular undergraduate needs—e.g., the first library problem, the first bibliographic essay, the first major research paper, and the first independent study project. Audio-visual techniques* can be used effectively concerning topics being studied by the class. Librarians should make every effort to offer these services to professors responsible for key courses. Collaboration with the faculty may also serve to stimulate their use of the library method of teaching. Cordiality and every evidence of a wish to be of professional service are essential while dealing with the undergraduates.

*a few films, filmstrip, or slide programmes, etc. Instructions/are given in class sessions as well.

Instruction Courses for Graduates

Graduates require a for more specialized level of instruction, and their needs are best served not by mass treatment (as with the undergraduates) but by small sessions with seminar classes. The instruction may include information on such topics as bibliographic form, library catalogues, national and trade bibliographies of sources of data about current publications, bibliographies of bibliographies, indexes, abstracting services, union lists, union catalogues, bibliographies of dissertations and research projects (e.g., Dissertation Abstracts, International), resources and special services of the library, directories of library resources, and facilities for inter-library loan and photographic reproduction. Many of the manuals issued for faculty members and graduates are designed to help them in orienting themselves to the resources, services and facilities of particular libraries.

Service at Professional Level

Professional school libraries (viz., of agriculture, business, law, education, medicine, and engineering), too, have introduced bibliographical and reference courses to aid their students. Much of the stimulus for courses of this type has come from the professionally trained librarians.

Open Access System

Another well-tried means for promoting reading habit is for the library to adopt the Open Access system. Walking amidst books, browsing under guidance, and handling books freely form the bed-rock of Open Access. A well guided stack room with books arranged and displayed in a minutely classified way is a perennial exhibition. Open shelves make possible the intelligent exploitation of library and is the basis of Second, Third, and Fourth Laws of Library Science.

Browsing Rooms

Browsing rooms represent another effort to make books easily available to users. Books included in browsing rooms should have contemporary interest, should be non-techical, should not be text-books or reference books, and should be of recreational value to various groups of interests. Judicious selection for current relevance is the key to any browsing collection. Its value in the promotion of reading is based upon the fact that the freshman will appreciate the careful selection of the "best" recent books on a subject that interests him. The encouragement of reading through discriminating selection of the best books has been widely appreciated. Such browsing collections are welcomed by the student who is hard pressed for time yet wishes to broaden his intellectual interests. Such a collection should be placed in an alcove or in an easily accessible room and should be displayed in an attractive manner which enlightens, entertains and attracts students.

Dormitory, Fraternity and Sorority Libraries

Through dormitory and residence-hall collections, university librarians have tried to stimulate the reading habits of students by making materials immediately accessible. The dormitory library is small, comfortable, informal and close at hand (reading facility provided) to the students. These are akin to the browsing rooms because they contribute in generating an atmosphere in which books other than reference and texts are made as much an integral part of the student's life as possible. The most popular titles are fiction. historical novels, periodicals, books of current interests, speculative, and imaginative literature and science.

On many university campuses, fraternity and sorority houses have provided collections not only to serve as recreational reading but in many cases items needed in curriculum also. Practically, all dormitory and fraternity libraries permit the circulation of books in students' rooms. If funds available, such libraries are a mark of quality education.

Book-shop

An attractive book shop-allowing open access-with an assortment of books covering a wide range and with radiant flair will form a good appetiser. A well organized campus book-shop serves as a "cultural institution". It provides a platform where scholars, students, and books of educational, and recreational value and literary merit are brought together, where literary judgement may be developed, and where ownership of personal collection is encouraged. It will be better if it is run in the library building itself. The university should encourage it. The university book-shop makes an effort to provide promptly, accurately, and economically the books needed by the students and faculty.

Reference/Information Services

The methods of promoing reading habits as described above are a bait to attract the students to the library. They are necessary but not sufficient. Something more is required to make the student to visit the library of his own accord. To make him a regular customer, he should be given prompt and exact service in a personal way. He is a human being; and a human personality alone can keep him in good humour. Till an appreciation of the value of books blossoms in him, transforms him into a willing beneficiary of the library, and make him love to come back to the library quite often, he must be attended to by a library host. This humanized, sympathetic, and personal aid given to users engaged in teaching and in research of any sort is called reference service.

S.R. Ranganathan has aptly defined reference service as essentially a human process of establishing contact between the right reader and the right document at the right time in a personal way. According to him, reference service is the most distinctive achievement of modern humanism in library science. The way in which users' information needs are handled can do a lot to promote reading, teaching and research.

The reference function of the university library includes :

—building up reference collections.
—assisting in selecting materials for the general collections;
—maintaining a clipping and pamphlet file;
—exhibiting materials for publicity or for public information;
—compiling special bibliographies, and making annotations and abstracts when necessary;
—preserving university ephemera;
—reviewing books;
—providing a translation service;
—cooperating with bibliographical centres and in the compilation of union catalogues;
—amassing information regarding iibrary resources of the region, nation, and of foreign origin;
—borrowing and lending material on inter-library loan;
—helping the students in locating documents, citations, quotations, proverbs, in identifying an obscure person and providing informational and bibliographical advice;
—compiling list of faculty publications; and

—giving instruction to the users in the most effective methods of using library materials and facilities by conducting classes and by giving instructions to individuals or groups and administration of personal reference assistance from a desk, lectures or group tours, hand-books or guide books and selectively prepared bibliographies.

As a rule, the reference librarians should be instructors in the use of libraries and should ass it with all the general collections of the library, not merely with the "reference collections". Their role lies in interpreting library collections for study and research. They are the hyphen that joins, the buckle that fastens the users and their documents in a personal way. This makes the reference librarian a friend, a guide and a philosopher and reference service the hub of all activities of a library.

In addition to the foregoing basic inducements, librarians have taken number of steps for encouraging the minority of regular readers to read more widely than they might otherwise. These include student book clubs, book collection prizes, bookstore tie-ins, rental collections with extra copies of popular titles, exhibits, display shelves for new acquisitions, publicity via the student paper or radio/TV, series of public lectures, reading circles, distribution of lists of significant new titles or readings related to books or printing. Each activity has its value in promoting reading and should be considered as part of the total library programme. Staff talents, space limitations, exhibit facilities, special fund opportunities, student interests and responses, and other factors may shape the specific programme.

3. Extension Services

Some universities offer extension services by supplying large quantities of printed materials to numerous individuals (alumni, friends of library) and groups. The researches conducted by the faculty of Universities especially those on agriculture and technology are made available to the society for the solution of the socio-economic problems. Moreover, the university crosses its campus walls and through such means as extension courses, correspondence courses, agricultural fairs for the farmers, publications, cooperative bibliographies, reference, information and reprographic services, radio and TV programmes, community recreation, dramatics, music, art, visual education, child welfare, adult education programmes, and research through experiment stations contributes actively to the furtherance of the education of individuals and society in general.

One may conclude the functions of the university library as under :

—The university library is the heart of academic pursuits; directly so, as regards its research work, and, indirectly as regards its teaching work, which derives its life from research work. Scientific research needs library as well as its laboratories, while for humanistic research, the library is both library and laboratory in one[8].

—Methods and fashions change from generation to generation, but each generation uses the library as a means of realizing its aims; hence the library remains a great conservatory of learning. An investment in a library is a permanent investment, guaranteeing returns for centuries to come.

—A quality education is impossible without a quality library.

—You cannot have a quality faculty without a quality library. The university library's ability to make really good collections available acts as a kind of 'bait'[9] to attract really able men to the university.

—A library is "a must" for cultivation of intellectual excellence.

—The library is essential to the maintenance of free access to ideas, and to the functioning of untrammelled mind, though controll will never be successful so long as books are freely and widely available. Here the laboratory can never take the place of the library[10].

The analysis of the functions of a university library given in in the foregoing pages make it amply clear that it is the soul of a university, the sun around which all teaching and research revolve. Hence, maintaining a university library is worthy of consideration by all those who value learning. The words of U.G.C. (U.K., 1921) still echo in our ears :

"The character and effiiciency of a university may be gauged by its treatment of its central organ, the library. We regard the

8. India. University Education Commission, Dec. 1948–Aug. 1949.

9. Parry Report...

10. Paul Buck, *Libraries and universities*, p. 9.

fullest provision for library maintenance as the primary and most vital need in the equipment of the university..."[11]. It is, therefore, not only right and proper but it is indispensable for the right conduct of their ordinary teaching end research work that the universities should provide great libraries on their campuses with great scholars to direct them.

11. cf. UGC (U.K.) Committee on Libraries, *Report* (Lond., H.M.S.O., 1967, p. 9.

6

COLLEGE LIBRARY :
The Pulsing Heart to Quicken Activities

What is the place of the library in modern college? Definitely, it is not a useless accessory. It is the pulsing heart which is to quicken every activity which goes on upon the campus; it is the easily accessible mentor to which every alumnus should look for guidance; and it is a beacon light whose rays should illumine more and more the path of those leaders of men who are entrusted wtth the conservation of equality of opportunity and the solution of problems of civilization that daily assumes a greater and ever increasing degree of complexity[1].

The function of the college library, therefore, is threefold. First, its service to the college community; second, duty towards the alumnus; third, it must become a positive influence in society for the expansion of knowledge and helping men and women in their quest after truth.

Each of these services may be explained in some details. Guy R. Lyle[2] has made significant contributions in this respect, and the following explanation is based on him.

1. Servce to the College Community

The college community uses the library at three levels, viz., the *text-book* level, the *reserve* book level, and the *independent* study level.

At the first level, the college library serves as a central study hall for students reading their own textbooks. It is mainly because the teaching programme consists of lectures, text-book assignments, and frequent tests.

1. L.R. Wilson, *Education and libraries* (Crosby Lockwood, 1966).
2. ...... *Administration of the college library*, 3rd ed. (H.W. Wilson, 1961).

The second level of service is reached, when a required or an elective course goes beyond the text-book At this level the library is called upon to put on reserve a few essential titles or a large number of titles from which students may select a few to read.

The third level of library use is brought about by the kind of teaching which is associated more often with the laboratory than with the library This level of library use has been referred to as "independent library use". It is the product of the kind of teaching which goes on in the laboratory where the biology or chemistry student learns to work out his own problem, observing the processes of growth and reaction from the plants and animals and chemicals used in the experiment. Instead of listening passively to the class-room lecture, the student comes to the library to select, sift, organize, and evaluate such information as he needs for the purpose of class discussion. The purpose here is not merely to give the student experience in securing information that is pertinent to his topic or problem but also to sharpen his power of discrimination and his critical faculty.

Any attempt to foster the habit of "independent library use" among the students is based on two pre-requisites :—Faculty Motivation of the kind of teachihg that will inspire more students to work independently, and secondly, adequate instruction in the use of the library and bibliographical tools. Each of these pre-requisites deserves further explanation.

1. Faculty Motivation

The teachers should actively engage their students in using the library as a kind of laboratory of learning "how to manage their own education." The library must be taken as an extension of the class-room and students be expected to use it intelligently in preparation for discussions in class, seminar reports, and papers. But for this kind of teaching, there must be two-way flow of information between the teacher and the librarian. For his part the teacher should :

—"Know the library's resources and adapt his teaching so that the student has the chance to use them in pursuing the subject matter of the course";

—consult with and give effective direction to the student in the library. Without the availability of the teacher in the library for consultation and guidance by the students for utilization of appropriate materials, the "presence of a magnificent library on the campus is merely ironic";

—make assignments for library investigation which do not require an exceptional degree of ability and insight for the young student to do a creditable piece of work;

—make library problems vital and interesting to the students.

—invite the librarian in an early meeting of the class to discuss general reference books and bibliographies;

—consult the librarian of the availability of special materials;

—urge students to seek the assistance of the reference librarian in learning more about special bibliographical aids pertinent to their studies as they proceed with their research.

The teacher can be the prime motivator to student learning, yet the central role of the librarian is to help students to learn when they are away from their teachers by providing a learning environment. The idea is to establish conditions conducive to learning and to maximize the utilization of materials. To achieve this aim, the librarian should :

—be personally acquainted with his teaching colleagues and know as much as possible about their characteristic methods of teaching;

—make himself familiar with the curriculum and keep informed about current changes to update his materials;

—remind faculty members of the varied opportunities for using library resources in teaching;

—know what tools and materials the instructor is using so that students are not only given assistance in using them properly but encouraged to learn of other tools;

—bring new materials and library services to the attention of the faculty;

—acquaint faculty with unique and unusual materials available in the library's special collections that might profitably be used by the students;

—provide resources necessary for research in the fields of interest of the academic staff;

—keep the faculty members abreast of developments in their fields for teaching;

—bring documents, students and the academics together under environments which stimulate reading for pleasure, sel-realization, personal growth and development, and the cultivation of intellectual excellence;

—seek teachers' help in formulating iibrary rules and regulations;

—plan library orientation programme with teachers and correlate it to instructional situation in their class-rooms;

—make recommendations for improving the collections of primary and secondary sources, for filling up gaps in literature, and also seek teachers' help in weeding out materials in library collections;

—provide patient, studied assistance to individual students in using reference and bibliographical tools.

—provide if possible, a seminar room for advanced classes where it is necessary to use library books and bibliographies in connection with the class discussion[3].

In sum : The programme must be all-embracing, must include the whole of the teaching faculty and the whole of the library staff working together and informed of each other's activities.

In persuance of his teaching role, the librarian converts the library into a live, intellectual, and learning laboratory. This tempts us to probe the educative functions of the college library.

Educative Functions of the College Library

To participate effectively in the college instructional programme, the educative functions of the college library lay in—

—providing materials to the college community adequate for their various needs and purposes;

making material easily accessiable physically through open shelves, orientation, or other efficient means and bibliographically through catalogues, bibliographies, and indexes;

—making them available for library use and home use through reasonable loan period;

—by giving formal and informal instruction in the use of the library;

3. Ibid.

—by encouraging wide reading through easy accessibility of materials, reader's guidance, displays and book discussion;
—by enlisting the cooperation of the faculty in making the library a study centre;
—by providing bibliographical information and special materials for the faculty;
—borrowing needed materials on inter-library loan from other libraries;
—providing adequate and comfortable physical facilities for study including carrels for work on special projects; and
—by extending the hours of service to meet the needs of the users.

The college library also promotes cultural activities for the college community and often serves as a nucleus for community academic and cultural affairs.

2. Service to the Alumni

Another major service rendered by the college library is that to the alumni. The alumnus is given a special status; he should always be welcomed for brief periods of time. The services rendered to the alumni may take the various forms :

—full use of the library;
—distribution of reading lists on a specific subject;
—direct loan service; and facilities for inter-library loan;

3. Service to the Nation

The library, in common with the college as a whole, has the duty of training more adequately the leaders of a state who will actively advance the intellectual life, the morale and material progress of the country. Brilliant men and women who are thoroughly informed, who know the use of books as tools, who have learned to seek after wisdom, and found joy and inspiration in the doing of their tasks, are demanded by any nation to put it on sound footing.

College Libraries in India

College library holds a distinctive position as its services, organisation and administration significantly contribute to the realisation of the objective of college education. Unfortunately, peeping into the working of college libraries in India, one finds, with few exceptions, a gloomy and depressing picture. To quote S.R. Ranganathan : college libraries consisted of closed cupboards. Most of them were concentrated in one or two rooms called general library. A student could at best reach up to the barrier, select all by himself a little from a tattered volume of printed catalogue, and drop an application for it into a tray, one morning each week. By the evening, the available books would all stand piled up on the desk. A lucky student might find his book in the pile, but he will often feel disappointed by the book not suiting his standard or by its being something different from what he thought it to be[4].

Ranganathan's description of college libraries is more or less true today also. The college libraries are insufficiently financed, under-staffed and poorly managed.

The main source of revenue for the college library today is the library fee collected from the students, supplemented by periodical Government or UGC grants. The library fee vary from state to state, within the same state, from college to college, with the result there is wide variation in the financial resources available to the different college libraries[5].

Booksellers often contact the principal and or the heads of the departments and try to tempt in getting such books selected as would decrease the quality and utility of the book stock. During their busy academic arrangemeut they fail to verify the uptodateness of the book-stock. The result is that out-moded and unwanted books often enter into the library.

In many college libraries, card catalogue is still a luxury on the ground of economy. The catalogues used in most of the college libraries cannot be termed a catalogue proper as in most cases they are not made on any sound cataloguing principle.

Most of the college libraries do not have their own buildings, and are located in a class room or a multi-purpose hall. Books are

4. S.R. Ranganathan, "Norms for College Library". cf. Proceedings of the *Seminar on College Libraries in Rajasthan*, (Jaipur, 1965) p. 15.

5. K.A. Isaac, "What Are College Libraries And What Can They Be ? A Blue Print for Action". *New Frontiers in Education* 8 : 3 : 6.

kept on the shelves in more than one row, they are actually dumped. Consequently, retrieving of books becomes awfully difficult. In many colleges books can be borrowed from the library only on a particular day in a week, thus denying the students the privilege of borrowing books during the whole week. Reference is conspicuous by its absence. Students are quite ignorant of the effective use of the book stock and bibliographical tools available in the library. Certain college libraries exist only to serve the teachers The books are purchased to meet the needs of teachers and no heed is paid to meet students requirements. There are teachers who regard the borrowing of advanced book by a student as an infringement on his personal prerogative. Far from getting books, students are not even allowed entry in some libraries. The rules of the library which are inflexible and even oppressive in the case of needy students are usually flouted by the teachers. The number of books a teacher can borrow from the library, the length of time he may retain them in his possession and the scrupulous manner in which he is expected to use them are some of the major problems for which a college librarian has not been able to find suitable solution.

Majority of college libraries suffer from grossly inadequate book stock and annual book grants, unscientific technical organization, inadequate staff provision, poor services, unsatisfactory physical facilities and, above all, a lack of recognition of their important academic role.

The staff position of the college libraries is deplorable. Usually it is only one man show. The authorities still regard the libraries as an administrative accessory and the librarian a storekeeper of books. He is never looked upon as a responsible and trust-worthy person. He has all the responsibilities for keeping the stock in tact but no authority to take independent action and frame policies for opertating library on academic lines. He has no independence of ideas and action, no credit for the work done by him, no opportunity for personal growth and development, or self-esteem and consequently college librarians are simply cog in the academic machine having no independent status.

The probable reasons for this sordid state of affairs is that we still do not seriously consider that the aim of education is to promote intellectual freedom aud advancement of knowledge, to generate in the young generation a sense of purposefulness and maximum dedication and faith in the country's future. In simple words, if the aim of education is to educate the students to stimulate research and build-up the character of their youth, then, it must be admitted that we have miserably failed. Our educational system is bereft of any motivation. The degree is looked upon as a passport to get into a job, to earn bread and butter, and the values of humanism, tolerance, rationalism, the adventure of ideas and the search for truth have been ignored. Moreover, inadequate staff, and insfficient funds for the development of the libraries in an educational institution has accounted for the depressing conditions. Poor conceptions of administrators of educational institutions regarding the role of library in educational settings has also hampered the growth. Library consciousness has not yet been sufficiently aroused in colleges. The library is still regarded more or less as a useless accessory, an adjunct to the principal's office. Consequently, least can be expected that students will realise the importance of library in their textbook oriented education. The librarians have also done precious little to demonstrate the value of library in education either to the students or to the teachers or to the administrators of college. The comments of Rabindra Nath Tagore made in 1926 that most libraries are possessed with the passion for accumulation of books—the facilities offered for their (books) use that should have been its (library's) glory are not deemed necessary for its pride, still hold good today.

The wayout is to emphasise the educational role of the library as being the source of information rather than a depository of books. The more the academics and pupils learn to use its resources and utilise its services, the more effective it should become. Report of the Education Commission (1964-66) succinctly remarked :

(a) We should completly break away from the traditional view that a library is a conventional but more or less a useless accessary.

(b) No new university, college or department should be set up without taking into account its library needs in terms of staff, books, journals, space, etc. The library should be an important centre for attraction on college campus.

(c) The object of the library planning should be to relate book selection. organisation of the books, conditions of access and all library activities to the daily needs and activities of the teaching community.

Madhuri R. Shah has aptly remarked :

Today, the greatest need of education is a system in which the students are able to shed their role of passive bench-sitters and emerge as active, alert and motivated people seeking not only academic excellence but also learning to appreciate the cultural values of their country[6].

6. Madhurai R. Shah, in her forward to R.N. Trikha and Manmohan Singh's *Library* and development oriented education (N.D., Harnam, 1983).

7

THE SCHOOL LIBRARY : *The Hub of Instructional Programme*

The purposes and philosophy of school library are determined by the purposes of education itself. Therefore, to study the problem of school library, we should first clarify our ideas about "Education" itself.

The purposes of education have been changing from age to age.

To Plato (427—347 BC), the Father of Political Philosophy, the purpose of education is : Fitting the individual to community life; to bring out the hidden faculties of mind to light.

To Sir Thomas Moore (1478—1535 A.D.) the purpose is : Giving a grind in Classics.

To Lord Bacon (1561—1526 A.D.), the purpose is : Advancement of science.

To John Dewey (1859—1952) : Transmission of the acquired powers to the new generation in order to secure the continued existence and growth of the community.

To S.R. Ranganathan (1892—1972), the purpose of education is : Releasing and exercising the creative ability of each member of the community in his own field and in his own measure[1].

The Secondary Education Commission appointed by the Ministry of Education (India, 1952-53) remarked that the aim of Secondary Education is to train the youth of the country to be good citizens who will be competent to play their part effectively in the social reconstruction and economic development of their country.

1. S.R. Ranganathan, *New education and school library*, (Vikas, 1973).

From the definitions given above, it is clear that the purpose of education is to produce young men and women of character and ability having disciplined minds, an intellect of high order and moral calibre, and capable of arriving at matured and unbiased decisions.

Since the aim of education is the cultivation of intellectual powers, self-education becomes of great importance. And of all the means of educating the people, library is in a most central place to serve as the agency of self-education.

By disseminating knowledge, the library can play a most constructive role in moulding the character and sharpening the thoughts of children. It is essential, therefore, that our education be more library oriented rather than class-oriented.

School library is, in fact, the cradle of the intellectual conditioning of the child. It awakens and fosters reading habits among children, and enlightens the immature minds. Keeping this in view, the Report of the Secondary Education Commission has gracefully accepted that "no school can function without a good library which will be the hub of the intellectual and literary activities of the school and play the same role as a laboratory or workshop plays in a science or technical institution".

Purposes

To meet the intellectual challanges, the librarian must be ever aware that the growth and development of the boys and girls is of paramount importance and he must design the library to fulfil the specific purposes, which are :

—to participate effectively in the school programme as it strives to meet the needs of pupils, teachers, parents, and other community members;

—to provide boys and girls with the library materials aud services most appropriate and most meaningful in their growth and development as individuals;

—to stimulate and guide pupils in all phases of their reading so that they may find increasing enjoyment and satisfaction and may grow in critical judgement and appreciation;

—to provide an opportunity through library experiences for boys and girls to develop helpful interests, to make satisfactory personal adjustments, and to acquire desirable social attitudes;

— to help children and young people to become skilful and discriminating users of libraries and audio-visual matereials;

—to introduce pupils to community libraries as early as possible and cooperate with these libraries in their efforts to encourage continuing education and cultural growth;

—to work with teachers in the selection and use of all types of library materials which contributes to the teaching programme;

—to participate with teachers and administrators in programmes for eontinuing profession and cultural growth of the school staff; and

—to cooperate with other librarians and community leaders in planning and developing an overall library programme for the community of the area[2].

FUNCTIONS

A Service Agency

It functions to help school in the achievement of the general educational objectives. It has no distinct subject-matter but provides materials for all subjects and all interests of pupils and teachers. Through thc library, books and other materials are distributed to individuals, groups, and classes. From all parts of the school, pupils, teachers, committees, classes and Individuals go to the library to use books, magazines, picture, maps and audio-visual materials; to find facts and illustrative materials, to read.

A Teaching Agency

The school library has a positive, active, teaching function. It suggests the readings. It supplies all types of materials for developing and expanding interests; it stimulates new interests. Through its reference books, indexes, bibliographies, and catalogues, the realms of information and knowledge may be explored. The library cooperates with other agencies of instruction in helping pupils learn how to use libraries and their materials, how to

2. A.L.A., *Schaol libraries for today and tomarrow : functions and standards* (Chicago, A.L.A., 1945). 43 p. p. 9-10.

find information, how to study. By its bulletins and exhibits, by its posters, direction sheets, and guides, by its guidance, the library teaches informally and encourages learning. By its introduction to the public library, it suggests the life-time use of this public service to further any interest or experience. The beauty, order, and quiet of the library, the efficiency of its organization, the appeal of its materials invite reading, make study attractive, carry on and increase the enthusiasm, zeal, or motive started within its own walls or in the class-ropm, assembly, shop, laboratory, or gymnasium.

A Resource Centre

In it the books, films, filmstrips, records, and transcriptions, periodicals, pictures and maps to meet the needs of the pupils and teachers of the school are organized, catalogued, shelved or filed and displayed so as to be easily found and used.

Knowledge Disseminating Centre

The school library is a knowledge disseminating centre. It is a place for enjoying books, for invetigating problems, for study : for using all sorts of materials—atlases, maps, clippings, pamphlets, magazines and books of information, inspiration, recrereation and reference.

The physical feature of the room—particularly the provisions for lighting, for seating, for ventilation, make the reader comfortable and facilitate reading and study.

The school librarian—skilled in matching books and their readers, understanding school needs and prepared to cope with school problems, ready to utilize the results of the school's needs and prepared to cope with school testing programme, quick in discovering reading difficulties and in finding aid for dealing with them; alert to improve the conditions for study and to help individuals improve their study habits, effective in relating books to the happenings of the world and the interests of the world to books—is so subtle a guide, a friend, a leader that the reader is almost unaware of his services. The school librarian makes the library a knowledge disseminating centre, a resource-sharing laboratory, and an intellectual workshop for the entire school.

Promoting the Effective Use of Materials

The school librarian uses various devices for promoting the use of library materials and stimulating the students to use the library as a resource laboratory, a reading workshop, a work centre for the entire school. Mary Peacock Douglas in her book *"The Teacher-Librarian Handbook"* summarizes the various devices used by the school librarians for encouraging the use of materials :

1. *Devices employed by librarians to encourage pupils to use the library* :

—encourage reading by telling pupils of books which may interest them;

—encourage pupils to go to library individually as need for reference materials arises;

—encourage reading by giving pupils lists of suggested readings;

—encourage teachers to take classes to library for periods of reference work;

—encourage reading by means of displays and book jackets on class-room and library bulletin boards;

—teach pupils how to use the library as situations requiring its use arise in connection with class work;

—devote a unit of work in one or more courses to teaching pupils how to use library materials;

—take classes to library to spend periods for pleasure reading;

—have pupils prepare publicity for the library;

—read excerpts from library books to stimulate interests;

—take library materials to class-room to "sell" them to pupils;

—post articles and clippings on class-room bulletin boards and inform pupils where additional materials can be found;

—exhibit interesting materials;

—become acquainted with books in library which pupils may enjoy reading;

—teach pupils how to use reference books related to specified courses;

—recommend magazines to be used by pupils;

—recommend to pupils materials relating to their extra-curricular interests;

—emphasis current problems and encourage pupils keep informed with magazines and newspapers to be found in library;

—have pupils keep record of books read;

—consult with teachers regarding pupils who reveal poor reading habits;

—call attention to services available from the public library;

—use films, filmstrips, and phonograph records in stimulating interest in, and understanding of, problems; and

—use films and filmstrips in interpreting library service and how to use libraries.

2 *Devices Employed by Librarians to Encourage Teachers to Use the Library* :

—notify teachers of new books and materials received;

—have frequent informal talks with teachers;

—send teachers lists of interesting magazine articles;

—attend and talk at departmental meetings;

—place library notes on principal's bulletin board;

—ask teachers to suggest new materials to be ordered;

—attend to teachers requests promptly;

—attend the talk at faculty meetings;

—work with teachers' in developing units of work on library services to be included in course of study and to be taught to all pupils;

—become familiar with course of study and assist in developing new courses of study;

—have a faculty reading table in library;

—invite new teachers to library at opening of school year;

—visit classes;

—send all teachers each week a form asking what library assignments will be made to the pupils;

—mention names of teachers making outstanding use of library in monthly news-letters or school paper;

give to teachers names of little-used materials relating to their courses;

—send teachers' suggestions for book week activities;

—ask teachers for suggestions for book week activities;

—post on bulletin boards reviews and jackets of new books;

—have library exhibits at faculty meetings;

—have faculty meetings held in the library;

—hold open house for teachers between semesters;

—at each faculty meeting use five-minute period to discuss new library materials and features of library service;

—devote at least one entire faculty meeting to discussion of school library and it use; and

—encourage use of audio-visual materials related to class work and give help in selecting and locating suitable ones.

3. *Devices Employed by Librarians to Encourage Recreational Reading.*

—place book and library news in school paper;

—make scrap-book of clippings from book jackets;

—cut book reviews from book jackets, paste on different coloured cards, fill in box where easily accessible;

—prepare and distribute book news bulletin;

—cooperate with public library by advertising available books;

—have informal talks with pupils;

—give book talks to home-room groups, school clubs;

—visit classes and when opportunity arises discuss materials related to the subject being studied;

—notify new materials in which members may be interested;

—display books in library and elsewhere;

—devote one section of library shelves to books concerning hobbies, one to books recently made into movies, etc;

—make study of pupils' reading habits and interests;

—present book plays at assembly programmes; and

—advertise books through library instruction.

4. *The Library Hour for Elementary Schools Pupils*

—each child may select and borrow from the library a book or books which he wishes to read. Opportunity for returning or exchanging books during the week should be provided;

—children should be encouraged to do some reference reading. Primary grade children may find pictures and easy books with the teacher's help that answer some of the questions connected with their activities while intermediate grade children may do real reference reading;

—poetry hour may sometimes be held during a library period. This is a time for enjoyment, when children can search through the poetry books to find their favourite poems to read aloud to the group or to read silently for personal satisfaction. Teachers should take this added opportunity to introduce the children to new poets and new poetry;

—story hour may be held sometimes during library periods in which the teacher tells or reads stories or plays recorded stories for the children;

—children may tell or read good short stories which they have found. Teacher may introduce the children to some of the great stories that have been written for them;

—children should be given some free time in the library to spend browsing to find things in which they are particularly interested;

—teachers should read classic to children by reading aloud to them;

—children should be encourged to read current news during library periods;

—information about authors and illustrators are of interest to children. The library period is an appropriate time to expose them;

—teachers should include instruction in the use of books and libraries as part of the plans for library periods;

The foregoing activities aimed at promoting the effective use of library matarials cannot be carried on during any one library period. Teachers and librarians must use their own judgement and plan use of time so that children are benefitted most from it.

In as much as a prime purpose of the librarian is to foster development of good thinking and learning habits among boys and girls, he must make conscientious efforts to see that young people

—Learn to enjoy reading.

—Develop judgement in selecting worth-while books.

—Acquire ability to use factual books and materials.

—Form the habit of using libraries and library materials.

—Respect the rights and privileges of using public property.

Scene at Home

If library is an organic part of the school, changing, growing, and developing with the whole school programme, then, it must be confessed that the school library in India is the worst and least used technique. The condition of High and Higher Secondary Schools (except Central Schools and some Public Schools) is deplorable. Honestly admitting. there are no libraries worth the name. The libraries are weighted down with dcad and antiquated text-books. The stock is not being renovated and kept up-to-date. The libraries are invested with astray and unwanted books purchased without paying any heed to the tastes and interests of the children. The collections are poorly quartered, unclassified, neither catalogued nor readily accessible for use. The books are arranged either according to accession number or sizewise in closed sequence.

The collection of books range between 500-2000 on an average. Books are kept in locked almirahas and sometimes left to repose in corners or corridors. About 95% of school libraies have no room of their own. Reading tables, chairs, and other items of furniture are conspicuous by their absence. Library rooms generally are unattractive, unhealthy and un-airy giving a shabby outlook.

Books are not issued regularly. The students go to the library only once a week—class-wise. In some of the schools the librarian issues/returns books before or after school hours. There is no provision of regular library period in the time-table. As a result, many of the students gradually loose all their interest in reading books. Moreover, even those who continue to visit library have to face the grunt and scowl of the librarian who happens to be one of their teachers; they are not even given the liberty to choose the book of their satisfaction. Thus instead of inculcating the habits of reading in children, these neo-votaries of the profession, curb it in the budding stage

Mostly, three registers are maintained in school libraries viz., the Accession Register, the Issue Register and the Newspaper Register. The Issue Register narrates the distressing story of circulation of books. The average issuing of books vary between

1-5 in a day and in some of the schools it even comes down to 10-50 in a year.

By and large, the books for school libraries in many states are purchased at the state level by the Director of Public Instructions, who distributes them to the schools. The book-sellers and publishers directly send their books to the D.P.I. for approval. Approved Book Lists are circulated to each school by D.P.I. from time to time. Thus the tastes, needs, demands and interests of the readers are controlled by the selectors who have not met even a single reader. The net result is that collection becomes seedy, ragged and dead.

The school library is no librarian's land. In the government schools and majority of the private-owned schools, there is no post of School Librarian. A clerk or a teacher holds the charge of the library. But the teacher-librarian does not take any interest in library work. as he is already crippled by heavy teaching load. His only award is an honorarium of Rs. 15/- but that too starts when library possess more than three thousand books. For want of any incentive, he looks upon the charge of the library as an additional burden. If any book is lost, its price is deducted from his salary. For fear of losing books, he keeps the library usually closed.

Some Ways Out

School libraries are concerned with generating understanding of the intellectual, moral, spiritual, cultural, social, and democratic values, and with the preservation of these values through the development of informed and responsible citizens. To achieve this end, school libraries deserve more attention than even college or university libraries for the simple reason that schooling age is the most formative period for building the character of the students and inculcating good reading habits among them. Some ideas for injecting new blood in the paralysed school libraries may be considered :

—To coordinate and promote the alround development of libraries, a *Directorate of School Librasies* be instituted. All school libraries would be under its jurisdiction. Its functions would be to regularize grants, exercise control and supervision, administration, preparation of statistics, formulate school library standards, compilation of bibliographies, promotion of professional education, library extension services. production of literature for children, adolescents, or young adults. It would also produce materials for the gifted, special areas, for special purposes, and on topics of current interest to children and young people. It would also produce magazines, pamphlets, periodicals, films, audio- visual aids, and develop standards for school library buildings, and furniture. It must generate reading habits. If the establishment of a Directorate of School Libraries is not feasible at present, a new post of Deputy Director for Libraries be created who may be entrusted with the responsibilities for the promotion and control of library services. A professionally competent per son should hold this post.

—A professionally trained person be appointed in each High School/Higher Secondary School, One gets support from Mudaliar Secondary Education Commission which strongly recommended that there must be a library in every Secondary School under a well-qualified and professionally trained librarian with salary scale and status of a senior teacher. The practice of appointing teacher-librarian should be discontinued.

—A library period be introduced in school time-table for each class to enable the students to use the library fruitfully. Books should be distributed among them in the light of their tastes and interests, so that the students may develop the reading habits, power of thinking and imagination, and become library-minded, An annual library award for the best reader of the year may be awarded and some library assessment numbers may be given in annual examinations.

—At least 6 per cent of the school budget may be spent on library development. Regular and handsome non-planned annual grants in lieu of books should be allocated by the D.P.I., to each library school in addition to the planned grants. Anuual appropriation may be counted @ Rs. 25/- per student and Rs. 50/- per teacher in each school. A capital grant should variably be provided at the beginning of the school to build up the basic collections.

—Each and every school library must have its own building. The school library building must be constructed with a capacity of 10,000—20.000 books and 50 reading seats. In case the funds do not permit a separate library building, a well-lit, airy, tastefully decorated big room be provided in the heart of school building. This is as much essential as the room for the Principal/Headmaster.

—A School Library Committee may be appointed charged with the responsibility of recommending books for purchase. The librarian would act as the Vice-Chairman or the Secretary of the Committee and will have power for the acquistion of books or materials. Students may participate in this committee for suggesting books for purchase.

—The collections of school library should be dynamically correlated with changing curriculum.

—Production of attractive, informational, inspirational. recreative and educative literature in all Indian languages be taken up and encouraged by the central and state governments. Unesco can prove to be of great help in developing Indian School Libraries by taking up the supply of latest and modern materials through publications for improving the faculties and international materials. To strengthen the national integration, inter-state periodicals, and other publications should be sent by the National Library or on agency like NCERT to every High/Higher Secondary School of the state to promote nationhood.

—For effective use of the materials, open access system be introduced. Losses up to 5 books per thousand of volumes circulated be written off.

—The State Government should encourage the library training programme for the school librarians. The syllabi of certificate course in library science be shortened. At present, there is not much difference between the contents of courses of B. Library Science and C. Lib. Sc.

Finally, a competent, effective librarian is the key to efficient and effective library services, He must understand the psychology of children and have the ability to manage and direct them. Among essential qualities, he must possess a wide variety of interests, vitality, personality, tact, imagination, enthusiam, energy, and ability to work with children and adults.

He must keep in mind that his function is to assist these Indians of tomorrow to a greater knowledge of the wolrd about them, to a happiear participation in the work in which they will be engaged, and to a more creative use of the leisure which will be theirs. But he cannot perform this function properly unless he receives more adequate support, and unless the importance of the library is better understood by the authorities, and unless he makes it the hub of all instructional programmes.

8

SPECIAL LIBRARIES :
The Power-houses for Generating Information

Special libraries in the form they are known today, began to emerge and develop in the beginning of the twentieth century, in response to the increased tempo of industrial, scientific and technological advances. The term 'special library, means a library which is concerned almost exclusively with the literature of a particular subject, or a group of subjects. Special library serves a special clientele located within a single establishment or group and all engaged in working towards one *common purpose*. Special library exists to serve the personnel of the parent body and caters to to their information needs. So much important is its 'information' function that it is called an *Information Bureau*.

It is quite apparant that a special library serves specialist clientele, located within a single organization or group and is responsible for the collection, organization, storage, retrieval and dissemination of information directly concerned and ancillary to, the work of the specialized institution with which It is attached.

Thus, there are three basic elements in a special library, i.e., special readers, special collections, and special location. If we closely look at these three elements, we can establish that the word 'special' originally applied to the subject area, which is restricted, and this is still the *main* distinction. The material is not *necessarily* different from that in other types of libraries, but it usually includcs a large proportion of items on very specific topics or segments of information. Finally, the readers are usually members of a particular organization having a *common purpose*.

At this stage, it is worth-while to examine some definitions of the term 'special library', though there is no agreed-upon meaning for the term 'special'.

Definitions

To L.M. Harrod[1], "Special Library is a collection of books and other printed, graphic or recorded material dealing with a limited field of knowledge and provided by a learned society, research organization, industrial or commercial undertaking, government department or even an educational institution. It may also be a special branch of a public library serving certain interests or occupational groups such as a technical library or a special subject library, meeting the needs of all enquiries on that given subject such as a music library".

Speaking almost in the same veins, J.E. Wright uses the expression "special library" to mean a library which is concerned almost exclusively with the literature of a particular subject or group of subjects. He further includes in this category those libraries which are collections of particular form of materials. Moreover, under the heading "special", Wright lists libraries of colleges, universities, and schools, of learned and professional societies, of government departments, and the libraries of research, industry and commercial organizations[1a]

To Broadfield on the other hand, a special library is neither academic, commercial, national or public but it intends to serve the needs of a portion of a community requiring detailed information on a limited subject field.

L.H. Morley defines "special library" as that unit in the organization responsible for locating and supplying whatever knowledge and experience that may advance its activities.

D.V. Arnold contends that "a special library is one, that serves a group of readers who have an 'extra-library' existence as a group".

Strauss, Strieby and Brown are of the view that, "any organization, actively concerned with the sciences and related technologies must be cognizant of the great body of published information that comprises the scientific literature...To take full advantage of this important resource, it is imperative that there be a unit in the organizational structure that is charged with

1. L.M. Harrod. *Librarians glossary of terms*...(Lond., Andre Deutsch, 1971).

1a. J.E. Wright, "Special Library and Information Service". In Handbook of special librarianship..., ed. by Ashworth (ASLIB, 1967), p. 12.

the responsibility of locating and making available, whatever knowledge and experience that may advance its activities. This unit is commonly called 'special library', because of its unique functions"[2].

Edward G. Strable veering close to J.E. Wright quoted above, uses the term "special" to "subject branches or departments of public or university library complexes, such as the business branch of a public library or the industrial relations library or a university library system"[3]; and it is used to designate certain types of agencies called "information centres".

However, the renowned library scientist D.J. Foskett defines a special library as one serving a group, having an extra-library existence, whose members direct at least some of their activities towards a common purpose. This excludes academic libraries as their users pursue their individual ends, and are in no sense united by a *common purpose* The group served, according to Foskett, may be a government department, a professional association, an industrial firm, a research association or an institute or any similar organization. Special libraries serve organizations with a clearly defined group policy, and members of the group have indicated their acceptance of this policy by the fact of their joining, which implies their recognition of a common interest[4].

It is clear that if Foskett agrees with Wright and Strable that special libraries have a limited clientele, depend on specialilization in subject interest or both, he excludes from this category departmental academic libraries or public libraries having strong science and technology divisions, and serving the interests of industries or commercial organizations within their areas of service.

It is very difficult to arrive at a completely clear and agreed-upon definition of a "special library"; it is important, however, to have a basic understanding of the differentiating characteristics of the term "special library". A special library deals in a particular

2. L.J. Strauss et al. Scientific and technical libraries : their organisation and administration (N.Y. Wiley Becker, 1972).
3. Edward G. Strable, *Ed., Special libraries : A guide for management* (N.Y., S.L.A., 1966), p. 1.
4. D.J. Foskett, *Information services* in libraries (Lond., Crossby, 1967).

subject, or a group of related subjects, or form of material. Its task is to locate, select. process, and disseminate information in specialized fields of knowledge as soon as it is available in written form. As such a special library is a particularized information service centre designed to meet the research needs of the 'specialists', the 'experts' and 'top management' of the parent body. Probably to remove confusion, S.R. Ranganathan* prefers to call it the 'Specialist Library', to supply detailed information regarding some subject field—scientific, technological or otherwise. The resources are specialized and the users are specialists. Ashworth, too, defines a 'special library' as one which is established "to obtain and exploit specialized information for the private advantage of the organization which provides its financial support"[5]. Thomas Landau also in his "Encyclopedia of Librarianship", defines special library as a "service unit" devoted to the information requirements, both present and future, of a specific organization.

The emphasis, then, is on *information services*, on providing the specialized user with information rather than with material. "Putting knowledge to work" is the watch-word of special librarianship; it is this characteristic that best defines 'special' in in special library.' Such a library is run primarily for its own members, who support it both financially and intellectually. Paul Wasserman endorses this view by defining special library as "an information facility designed to provide access to specialised information and placed within range of and addressed to meet the needs of a special clientele[6]. It is apparant that the most distinctive feature of the special library is not so much its subject-matter as its service. Before everything else, it is an an 'information bureau'; its function is to make the information available to the members of the parent body. This parent body could be a :

Society—Learned or professional;

Government—Administratrative departments and Research departments; and

Business houses—Industrial research and commercial.

*S.R. Ranganathan, "Special library vs. specialist library", Lib. Sc. Doc. 4 (3), 1967, p. 290.

5. Wilfred Ashworth, *Special librarianship* (Lond., Clive Bingley, 1978), p. 6.
6. Paul Wasserman, *Library journal*, v. 89, No. 4, Feb. 1964, p. 79.

In other words, the parent body of a special library could be an agency, organization, institution, bnssiness or industry—private or governmenal, and its sole purpose is providing information and knowledge resources which are vital to the parent organization's specific objective, product, or service.

Difference Between a Special Libraıy, University and Public Library

Special library's emphasis on the dissemination of information differentiates it from a university or a public library. Whereas a university or a public library provides documents, special library provides information for immediate utilitarian application and to bring together the users and the information they require in whatever form it may be available, in the most effective way possible, at the time when and in the place where they need it, if possible. The emphasis, then, is on *information services*, on providing the specialists with information rather than with documents[7].

S.R. Ranganathan maintains that the difference between a general library and a special lay only in the nature of the clientele and the material or the documents served.

Important distinctions between a special library and a general or an academic library are observable :

The first difference lies in the unit of materials which is the basis of the organlzation : In general or an academic library this unit is usually a book, pamphlet, periodical, map, or other physical items; in a special library or an information centre the unit is a particular piece of information irrespective of the form of materials in which it is embedded;

The second major difference is that a general or an academic library usually exists to give what is asked for, but a special library must also draw attention to unrequested relevant information; and

Finally, a special library is intended to serve a section of the community qualified by interest in particular subjects[8].

In short, the distinctions are observable in respect of *Material, Clientele, and Service.*

7. J.K. Gates, *Introduction to librarianship* (N.Y., McGraw-Hill, 1968).
8. L.J. Anthony, *Ed.* Handbook of special librarianship and information work, 5th ed. (ASLIB, 1982).

The nature, purpose, and service patterns of a special librar would become more clear if we distinguish it from an academic or public library in respect of Location : Subject scope : Collection/Stocks : Service : Clientcle : Size and Equipment. The study of these characteristics will amply make clear the difference between a special library and an academic or public, national and other types of libraries.

Characteristics of Special Libraries

1. Location

The first differentiating characteristic lies in respect of location. The parent organization of a 'special library' could be:

—National libraries with special materials, e.g., National Library of Medicine, National Library of Science, INSDOC, DESIDOC, National Lending Library for Science and Technology (now British Library), National Archives, etc.

—Government department libraries. e.g., libraries of Ministries of Labour, Finance, Commerce, Education, Food & Agriculture, Law, Parliament, etc.

—Government Research Laboratories, e.g., CSIR (Council of Science and Industrial Research); NPL (National Physical Laboratory); BARC (Bhaba Atomic Research Centre);

—*Research Associations and Professional Societies*, e.g , Indian Standards Institute (ISI), Indian Institute of Public Administration (IIPA), All Indian Agricultural Research Institute, National Dairy Research Institute (NDRI), Royal Asiatic Society, Lalit Kala Academy, American Chemical Society.

—*Public* Authorities, BOAC, BBC, and the large public corporatlons as of drugs, chemical, petroleum and electronics;

Private Business and Industrial Organizations—banks, insurance companies, advertising agencies, engineering firms;

Special libraries are located in medical schools, divinity schools, hospitals, Churches, religions organizations, militrry instalations, prisons, news-paper agencies, music organizations, etc.

Subject Scope

As the major source of information in the organization it rves, the special library identifies, collects, processes, and maintains informational materials in subject or group of subjects pertinent to the work of organization, for use by or on behalf of its clientele. The collection includes all basic, frequently used, and potentially useful materials to meet both the current and anticipated needs of its users. It goes without saying that even those special libraries which are most highly specialized contain of necessity a certain amount of material on related and bordering subjects. For instance, a library attached to a bank may have collections concerning not only banking but also dealing with Management, Industry, Politics and Sociology. Nevertheless, the choice of books in the allied subjects perforce will be more selective and restricted.

Sometimes, the special libraries are designated by the *forms* of *materials*, viz., Map Library, Film Library, Record Library, etc.

Depending upon the nature of the supporting organization, the special library collection may contain a variety of forms—(1) Reports, preprints; (2) Theses; (3) Periodicals—learned, trade, popular, news-papers, regular conference procedings; (4) Standards; Patent specifications; (5) Drawings, illustrations; (6) Photographs, slides; (7) Plans; (8) Maps; (9) Punched cards, Films, tapes, discs; (10) Pamphlets; (11) Monographs; (12) Treatises; (13) Standard specifications, codes of practice; (14) Official publications; (15) Trade literature; (16) Company reports and accounts; (17) Reviews; (18) Hand-books; manuals; data books; (19) Compendia of statistics; (20) Encylopedias; (21) Year-books; almanacs; (22) Dictionaries, glossaries—monolingual, multi-lingual; (23) Atlases, gazeteers; (24) Biographical reference materials; (25) Concordances; (26) Biographical reference material; (27) Directories, buyers' guides; (28) Bibliographies, guides to the literature; (29) Abstracting and indexing sources and services, translations; (30) Current awareness periodicals and service; (31) Citation indexes; Periodicals lists; (32) Guide to sources; (33) Research and laboratory note-book; (34) Clippings; (35) Blueprints; (36) Index to expertise[8a]; (37) Individuals; (38) Organizations etc.

The size of the collections depends upon the objectives of the supporting organisations and, of course, the availability of funds and materials.

8a. Ruther Finer, "Reference and Enquiry Work", *in Handbook of special librarianship*, op. cit., pp. 319-20.

3. *Reference/Information Services*

Specialized, intense, customized reference service is frequently the prime raison d' etre for establishing the special library. It is the provision of such services that differentiates the special library from the public, university or government libraries. Special library is often called an "Information Bureau". The main function of a public or an academic library is to make books available; the function of the special library is to make information available[9]. In other words, whereas the objectives of the public or special library is to provide reading facilities for recreation, academic attainments and scholarly research, the distinguished characteristic of the special library is to provide the Right information, to the Right Reader, at the Right Time, in the Right Amount and in the Right Form : The laudable function of a special iibrary is to file, retrieve, and disseminate information for immediate and utilitarian purposes. To fulfil its major goal of providing information promptly and even in the anticipation of demand for it, calls for special techniques connected with registering, correlating, interpreting, utilizing, and handling information for the constant use and benefit of its restricted clientele or the organization it serves.

Clientele of Specialists

Special libraries are also differentiated by the nature of clientele they serve. They are not open for "everybody". They serve a "specialized clientele"—having special interests and skills, located within a single establishment or a group and all engaged in working towards a common goal.

The clientele of special libraries particularly those housed in business and commerial enterprises are awfully busy persons. For business organizations, time is money and money is time. They cannot find time to hunt up for information. Their time is all required in the pursuit of their specific business. The library department of a business house owes its genesis to a realization of the need for a division of labour. The provision of information pin-pointedly and promptly is the labour falling to the share of the library department. The special librarian is presented with a problem and is then expected to come up with an answer, no matter how detailed, and how complex. In the process the

9. William A. Katz, *Introduction to reference service* (McGraw-Hill), v. 2, p. 161.

special librarian may carry on an extensive literature search and present his findings in the form of a bibliography, abstracts of articles, translations, or even an interpretation of the materials at hand in relation to the question presented. As an ongoing service; he may scan and refer current information and new materials to the appropriate individuals.

4. *Smallness in Size & Equipment*

Another important characteristic of a special library is its "smallness". By and large, a typical special library is small in size of the staff, often consisting of one professional librarian together with non-professional hands. Nevertheless, some special libraries do have a number of professionals and specialists on the staff, such as a translator, an abstractor, an indexer, or an information systems specialist. The special library is also small in *space* occupied, and small in its *collections.*

The function of 'filing information' to be discharged by libraries requires special equipment for reproduction, translation, reading and storing documents.

In sum : from the study of characteristics of a special library, it is clear that its predominant characteristic which differentiates it from other types of libraries, is, that it files information rather than material and speedily disseminates that information. The unit material, which forms the basis of special library organization, is a particular piece of information, irrespective of the physical form of material in which it is contained—whether a book, a pamphlet, a periodical, an atlas or any other graphic record.

Secondly, a special library is set up with a purpose to supply information on specific subject rather than literature; it draws attention to its (information) existence and evokes the demand for it. The information demand may be related to research in industry for high standard of manufacture and design; research in defence and military installations; research in humanities and social sciences; research in natural and biological sciences; and research in engineering and advanced technology. And it is obligatory on the part of the special librarian to supply information which will be pertinent, factual and accurate. This requires special techniques connected with the filing and dissemination of information, e.g., Current Awareness Service, SDI, and the like. It is the emphasis on the supply of information pin-pointedly, exhaustively and expeditiously that the terms like "Information Bureau" or "Information Centre" have been accrediated to a special library and its librarian is designated as an "Intelligence Officer", or "Information Scientist" charged with the sacred duty of recording, organizing, and disseminating the published information directly concerned with, and ancillary to, the work of the specialized (parent) institution. And the speialized institution which ignores the literature of the research-field concerned, will achieve less in the way of results than the concern which takes advantage of recorded information. This makes special library indispensable for any organization which has to depend heavily on recorded information and research. Special libraries have proved to be the most dynamic and progressive force in library profession, covering a wide area of contemperary activities.

Functions of a Special Library

The functions of a special library are based on the objectives set-forth by the organization with which it is attached. Of course, the main functions of *Acquistion*, *Organisation* and *Dissemination* of *materials* and information remain the same in special libraries as in other libraries. But there is difference in approach, performance and techniques as well as materials collected.

The acquisition function involves identification and acquisition of relevant records, which are potentially capable of catering the needs of the clientele. The special librarian has the responsibility to see that the materials he collects are used. He is, therefore, always on the alert to hunt up every new relevant publication, to know its thought-content and place it before the researcher who needs it most to save his precious time. To quote Foskett in this context, "Save the time of the reader" might well be called the First, rather than the Fouth Law of Special Library Speed and selectivity are the new dimensions, in the context of special library's information needs.[10]

Knowledge must be indexed, filed and made readily accessible to the specialists to enable them to take quick decions. As the special librarian deals with highly specialized collections, with

10. cf. A.K. Mukherjee, *Fundamentals of special librarianship* and documentation (IASLIC, 1969).

technically detailed data and as the area of enquiry has been growing more and more complex, he finds conventional methods of information storage and retrieval only of little help. Efforts have been made to devise an entirely new system of bibliographic control including new schemes of classification, printed check-lists, indexes, computer prlnt-outs, catalogues, and electronic data processing equipments. Computers are being used effectively in printing bibliographies of useful references, predicting what materials may be of use to an individual user and providing the source of such materials. The most effective factor in the organization of collections is the necessity for generating information for each user when he needs it, in a suitable and useable form, and at a time when he needs it.

The special library is a particularized information service centre aiming to provide to its user apposite. factual and correct information. It requires of the staff the duty of preparing authoritative, timely, and specialized reports of the evaluative and analytic, monographic, or state-of-the-art type, in order to render alerting service to its clientele both in groups and individually. It implies that the staff responsible for the location, selection, accumulation, processing, storing, retrieving, and dissemination of information should be fully acquainted with the sources of information, and are aware of the needs and interests of users.

The special library as nucleus of intellectual gravitation of its parent body performs the following functions :

—collects, maintains. stores, and retrieves information and data keeping in view the evolving needs of its parent organization;

—analyses, synthesizes, and evaluates information and data;

—provides critical reviews, monographs, reports, and/or collections;

—provides critical compilations;

—provides states-of-the-art report;

—provides replies to quetries;

—provides reprints, bibliographies and references;

—performs literature searches and translation services;

—provides abstracts, indexes and extracts;

—prepares accession lists, bulletins, news-letters, summaries, hand-books or manuals;

—disseminates current information, and SDI and thus stimulates research;[11]

—uses inter-library loan to provide additional needed materials;

—maintains organization's archives through its staff;

—encourages the use of its materials through displays, lists of latest additions, and liberal loan polices: and developing programmes to retrieve information through the use of computers.

Ordinarily, the special libraries issue the following products for the advancement of their organizatioal activities, research programmes, and keeping their clientele of specialists currently aware of literature being published in their areas of interests :

(1) Hand-books (2) Bibliographies : (3) Current Awareness Bulletin; (4) Periodicals; (5) Abstracts; (6) Indexes; (7) News-letters; (8) Directories; (9) Translations; (10) Thesauri; (11) Accession lists; (12) Library catalogue and union catalogues; (13) Local Documentation Lists; (14) Data banks—information available indexed on cards.

The underlying aim of all the above services is to provide Current Awareness Service or alerting service including SDI. This users-oriented service enables the users or specialists, by scanning only selected items, to have freedom to browse, or carry more serious study or research, in the time they save.

The functions which a special library performs require a man of super qualities and distinct qualifications to operate it. What should, then, be the skills of mind and talents of the special librarians or the information officers or information specialists. The following section is devoted to this discussion.

Special Librarian/Information Officer : Qualities

—The "special" librarian must know the structure and policy of the organization or agency which he serves in order to be able to see the place of the library in the achievement of the organization's goals and objectives.

—He must be well-grounded in the subject speciality of his library and efficient in the techniques of reference and information service.

11. For details, See Ruth Finer, op. cit., Herman M. Weisman, *Information systems, services and centres* (Willey—Becker—Hayes, 1972).

—He must know both the literature he collects and the particular interests and needs of his clientele of specialists and be able to act as shrewed match-maker between the information source and user. He will need to be able to interpret documents in terms of user.

—He must be able to perform such special services as indexing, editing, abstracting, and translating, .or know the sources of their location for procuring.

Special librarian role as an indexer and disseminator of information require in him a flair for the organization of materials, a noose for information, a wide range of intellectual interests, a genuine desire to help the inquirer. He should have an analytical, critical and logical mind in pursuing details.

Special librarian's role as a producer of abstracts, bulletin of of current awareness, reports and other products require of him the qualities of writing precisely, persuasively and relevantly. Moreover,

—he must understand the basic principles of classification in order to adapt or device systems to meet the needs of the diverse materials and forms of materials. Many a "special" librarians creates subject organization systems tailored to his needs, such as classification, subject heading lists, and design filing and retrieval systems for special collections like patents, maps, pictures, etc.;

—he must familiarize himself with outside sources which can be of assistance in locating authoritative information in the developing new areas of knowledge;

—he must have the tenacity to see a problem to its successful conclusion as well as be able to move quickly from one problem to another;

—he must he able to change established procedures for more efficient, and to innovate; and

—he must be able to work under pressure[12],

The nature of services to be rendered by the special librarian are most demanding and requires that he should have among other qualities a good memory and imagination; he should be thorough, orderly, persistent, observant, accurate and a good judge of the needs and interests of his clientele and documents. Above all,

12. Gates, op. cit.

he w.ll be characterized by two outstandihg attributes : the first is intellectual *breadth* and *depth*, and the second is *creativity*. He must be able to meet his patrons at least as an intellectual equal, and he must be able to communicate effectively with them : *Creativity* is the capacity for innovation and intellectual independence. Moreover, he should have a "penchant for scholarship", and be a "potential manager of people and organizer of work.

The towering functions to be performed by the "special" librarian make him to act as the "Merchant of Light".

Generalist or a Subject specialist ?

Should a "special" librarian be a subject-specialist; or specialist in documentation techniques, in communication and information sciences, and in computer technology. The answer depends upon the mission of the services/centre he is called upon to serve. The more evaluative functions a centre performs, the greater is its requirement for *subject specialists*. In view of the rising tide of literature and proliferation of subjects, judgement on which document or data to acquire, to abstract, to index, to evaluate, and to disseminate the right information to the right reader through approaches to current awareness services, depend on the knowledge of a subject specialist. The greater is his subject knowledge, the greater his understanding of the thought-content of documents he handles, and the greater is his ability to recognize what is useful for his research staff. But many subject specialists may not like to become librarians often feeling that it is below their dignity, and full-time information work may become a hurdle in their professional growth and advancement. Moreover, real specialization implies a narrower field than in which most of us work. The term as used in information work has almost become synonymous with an understanding of the intricacies of the automated information retrieval; or with an information officer, who is an expert on all aspects of information—from how it is created to how it is used.

For both these reasons, a special librarian having a broad subject knowledge, professional qualifications, and a mastery of the library techniques may prove a more success than a specialist in one particular subject. As Ashworth puts it : Knowledge of of librarianship techniques certainly assists a person to carry out the duties of acquisitton and organization of information, and teach him about sources of information; so that it is possible to achieve what, to the uninitiated, would seem to be a surprising degree of success in locating information in a quite unfamiliar subject area. On the other hand, subject knowledge gives the edge in understanding; a greater facility in selection, and a better capability in interpretation and presentation of results to suit different types of users. Neither qualification has any obvious overriding superiority. The ideal person to seek would have qualifications in librarianship and/or information science, and also in a subject, appropriate to the library concerned. It should be remembered, however, that the range of topics handled in any special library is never so restricted as the uninitiated might expect, and also that anyone who has specialised narrowly in one field may well be less well informed in the broader aspects of his subject. For both of these reasons, the most successful librarians and information workers have tended to be all-rounders within the broad area of their organization's interests, rather than specialists in one particular part. Thus, a general degree in science and a knowledge of scientific method, would probably prove more useful in practice than a specialist degree in (say) Chemistry or Physics.

In addition, the special librarian should have a skill in the techniques of indexing, abstracting, report-writing and the zest for conducting literature-searches. A working knowledge of the languages in which the material is coming into the library will add to his proficiency. In libraries dealing with science and technology, a knowledge of languages like German, French, Russian, Chinese and Japanese beside English have special significance. In the finale, he should be able to compare, assess and integrate his findings so as to present them in the most appropriate form to his users. It requires that he should have sufficient training in academic investigations and in the most effective bibliographical methods to be adept in literature searching and thus, capable of giving clear, accurate, and adequate information on damand; have proficiency in selecting and evaluating materials; ability to work effectively with subject specialists and research teams; and an understanding of the interrelationship of the subject fields.

Status of the Special Librarian

The tremendous reponsibilities put on the shoulders of the special librarian for disseminating information require that he should be vested with all the powers of the head of a unit in the organisation. He should have responsibility only and exclusively to organize, and to operate the library in the way he thinks best to meet the needs of his clientele; and for this he should be directly responsible to the chief administrator of the parent organization, with whom he should have easy communication, in the matters determining policies. It is only in this way that the librarian can derive the necessary knowledge of the continually changing aims of the organisation, of the potentials for future growth and of the constraints under which the organisation has to operate. This will enable him to access which information can be profitably used; and also that which is unlikely, from lack of proper resources, to be exploitable. The nature of his work subjects him to a constant flow of new information from outside, and this makes him one of the best informed people on the staff about external developments in the organization's fields of interest. As a manager of information, he would be able to use this information more directly in policy-making and not merely be a passer-on of information to others who might distort or fail to use it. The fewer steps there are in the transfer of information the better, as there is always a risk of distortion and inaction. The librarian's task is to use the knowledge he acquires from his position to enable his unit to tap most appropriate sources of information and select that part which has the highest potential for exploitation[13]. It is only in this way that the special librarian can make his library a permanent living force in the life of the research team so that no member of it feels inclined to think either "Why a Library" ? or "Why a Librarian" ?

Sufficient care, of course, will be taken in selecting the librarian-a person who is eminently capable of performing the complex task of transforming the library into a dynamic agency for the dissemination of information, and has the potentialities of keeping the title *Special Librarian,* a dignified one equivalent to that of a Scientist or a Professor in the organization. Besides having a penchant for scholarship, integrity, cultural background, competence as administrator of the library and expert in human relations, he should be strongly familiar with modern techniques of librarianship. It must be emphasized that a Ph.D. degree will enhance his status and creditability in the eyes of his clientele of specialists, experts, engineers, scientists, technologists and academics.

13. Ashworth, op. cit.

9

NATIONAL LIBRARIES

The Reservoirs of Nations' Literary Products

National library occupies the highest position in the national library system of a country, yet we still do not know what a national library really is, nor can we name with certainty the functions it must fulfil in order to be called 'national'[1].

The reasons for failure to formulate a precise and acceptable definition of a national library may be :

—that national library is comparatively a 'modern product', and its idea is still expanding;

—that national libraries are currently passing through a period of ferment; and

—that national libraries are wonderously complicated organisms;

—that national libraries have come to possess separable personalities and bear proud markings of dissemination[2].

We must also remember that national libraries do not have a unified origin : some came into existence to fulfil the objectives they discharge at present; others developed as a result of great donations of books; many have attained their present status through a gradual extension of their privileges and facilities to an ever-enlarging patronage[3].

Definitions

Since national library is a vital phenomenon of librarianship, S.R. Ranganathan ventured to define it as the library having the

1. Pierre Bourgeois, Unesco : national libraries; their problems and prospects, (1958), p. 2.
2. Gonzague de Reynold, Foreward, National libraries; their problems and prospects (New Delhi, Universal, 1974).
3. *Library Trends* (1955).

duty of collecting and preserving for posterity, the literary products of that country. It is the central station for assembling and disseminating thought energy[4].

Inspired, probably by Ranganathan, Unesco's General Conference (1970) gave a more comprehensive definition. which runs as under :

Libraries which irrespective of their title are responsible for acquiring and preserving copies of all significant publications published in a country and functioning as a deposit library, either by law or under other arrangements. They will also normally perform some of the following functions :

—produce a national bibliography;
—hold and keep up-to-date a large and reprentative collection of foreign literature including books about the country;
—act as a national bibliographic information centre;
—compile union catelogue;
—publish the retrospective national bibliography.

The recommendation of the Unesco conference was that the libraries which may be called "National" but whose functions do not correspond to the above definition should not be 'placed' in the 'national library' category.

Functions

Library scientists also differ with regard to the functicns that the national libraries should perform. Such difference of opinions seem to flow from one or more of the below mentioned factors :

—the role of the library in the progress of the country as perceived by the government;
—size of the country in terms of its area and population;
—availability and quality of other comprehensive collections in the country;
—bibliographical and information services rendered by academic, special, public and research libraries of the area;
—the existence of other organizations performing the functions falling in the purview of a national library;

4. S.R. Ranganathan, *Plan* : a thirty year programme for India (Univ. of Delhi, 1950).

—the financial resources that are available.

Notwithstanding these limitations, we can determine the basic functions which a national library should perform in its own interests and in order to retain its due place in international network of cultural relations. Basing our observations on the discussions and proposals of Unesco's seminars, Ranganathan's work, and the working of four great national libraries of the world viz , British library (London; formerly Britirh Museum); Library of Congress (Washington); the Lenin Library (Moscow); and the bibliotheque Nationale (Paris), the following important functions may be noted :

—The primary function of the national library is clear enough. National libraries are set up to preserve the literature produced in a particuiar country, and this function is carried out under the terms of the Copyright Act or the Legal Deposit. This concept is often extended to include documents relatlng to country and its nationals, published anywhere and in any language outside the country. If some of the material is stored elsewhere, the national library should have a record of it.

—It acquires comprehensive, representative current foreign literature. It should try to be as international in range of their collections as financially possible.

—It bears the responsibility of publishing a current national bibliography, and also of retrospective national bibliographies where needed.

—It undertakes the publication of catalogues of materials in its possession, and also compiles Union Catalogues of holdings in the country's libraries. It should also establish a Union Catalogue of Manuscripts held in other libraries and archive repositories.

—It sets up a national reference and bibliographical service throughout the country, based on libraries and other organizations which possess information services. The national centre in the National Library should corrdinate the system and act as a Clearing House for enquiries to and from similar centres overseas.

A new and very important trend among national libraries is that of separating the national libraries' reference function from lendings ones There may be two national libraries in each country, one for conservation and reference, and the other for lending and photo-copying.

—It should provide leadership for the country's library system; initiate or participate in any schemes of a cooperative nature concerned with such matters as shared cataloguing; resource sharing; and coordinated information retrieval system. It is a valuable instrument for furthering nation's material, intellectual, artistic, and spiritual progress. It implies that the national library should be at the head of other libraries as an aid in social engineering. Of course, it does not create a new social order but helps to stabilize on agreed upon social order, and this it accomplishes by identifying itself with the problems and aspirations of its social milieu,

Effective leadership is much more possible in the acquisition of foreign materials for libraries, often essential for technological and economic development. In fact, Unesco sponsored seminar at Manila (1964) suggested a policy of Cooperative Acquisition on national level on the lines of the Farmington Plan, Scandia Plan, and West Germany Research Libraries Plan. In addition to purchasing materials in the areas alloted to it under the cooperative purchasing plan, the national library may acquire secondary and 'fringe' materials as a supplement to the acquisitions made by other libraries in the plan. Some national libraries also take the responsibilty for the national archives, and all national libraries have substantial collections of manuscripts. National libraries should establish a Union Catalogue of manuscripts held in other libraries and archive repositories.

There are certain functions which are desired from a national library :

—that it organizes inter-library loan system for procuring research materials on national and international levels;

—that it does pre-natal cataloguing and classification;

—that it renders reference and information services, and offers reprographic and translation services;

—that it renders book service to the local population; and to the blinds; and maintains *Contact Libraries* abroad;

—that it standardizes classification and cataloguing codes; and renders technical help to other libraries;

—that it should provide dynamic leadership, aiming at the development of 'systems and procedures' which will make available the total library resources of the nation for the benefit of the whole national commuuity;

—that it receives as 'gratis' collections of personal papers, rare books, and other valuable materials; and distributes duplicates;

—that it should conduct research in the fields of library science and bibliography; also organize professional training.

—that it should provide bibliographic, reference, and information services to their country's parliamentarians, ministers and government departments. Such a service may consist of the provision of factual data, the formulation of arguments for or in favour of predetermined action, and assistance in speech writing both within and outside the legislature;

—that it should provide services to the government. Library of Congress is rendering such a service.

Of the numerous functions of national libraries, the most important ones beyond being the repository of nation's literary products are that of collecting or selecting current foreign literature, the setting up of national bibliographical and information services, and a leadership role in the planning of library services generally—a role which may include library training and education. These are merely four of the most important of possible functions, and of these, the colleetion of world literature is of special significance. It increasingly happens that this type of provision is carried out by special libraries in particular fields; these come to be regarded as national libraries, and some of them also benefit by legal deposit. The outstanding example is the National Library of Medicine in America.

Keeping in view the multifarious responsibilities and functions of national libraries, one may go back to Pierre Bourgeois's statement stated in the beginning of this chapter (1) and ask why "We still do not know what a national library really is"? Once one goes beyond the legal deposit definition, the answer surely must be, first, that the pattern must be different in each country, and second, that it is impossible to define these wider functions without reference to a national library system as a whole. This conclusion, implied in the Unesco discussions, if correct, is most important, because plans and policies for national libraries are often worked out in isolation, and a national library is, or should be, merely one part of a national structure. That is why the term 'national librarianship' is meaningless, and why a wider definition of functions for one particular library is not possible (Ronald Benge, op. cit.).

Organizational Set-up

The organizational set-up of national libraries of different countries varies according to the needs and functions to be performed by them. In his *Library* Development Plan, Ranganatthan writes that the organizational set-up of a national library should be similar to that of a big public library. He ascribes the following departments to the national library in addition to usual departments : (1) The Home Section; (2) The National Bureau of Copyright; (3) The National Bureau of International Exchange; (4) The National Library for the blind; (5) Contact Libraries abroad for propagating national culture; (6) The National Library for the seafarers; (7) The National Bureau of Inter-library loan; (8) The National Bureau of Bibliography; (9) The National Bureau of Technical Services; and (10) The National Library Secretariat.[5]

Role of National Librarian

The National Librarian has tremendous responsibities for running the national llbrary and developing its each part. His duties are enumerated by Ranganathan as under :

—to manage the National Central Library;

—to superintend, direct, and deal with all matters relating to the Copyright Act and to the maintenance and service of the material deposited with the national library under the said Act;

—to manage the central libraries of India and libraries for Sea-Farers of India established in India and foreign countries;

—to centralize all technical works like acquisition, and cataloguing and to co-ordinate the services and maintenance of reading materials in the departmental libraries;

—to promote cooperative and centralized classification, cataloguing and bibliography in India;

5. Ibid. pp. 82-83.

—to assist the National Library Authority and submit to it an annual report on the progress and working of the library system of the country;

—to manage the Contact Libraries of the country established abroad;

—to take part in all discussions for the improvement and extension of library services and of library resources generally;

—to speak for the national library in all international meetings, conferences, or councils concerned with library activities of all kinds.[6]

It goes without saying that for this high and pivotal post in the Library System of a country, a person with intellectual exellence at academic level and professional competancy should be appointed. The provision of a National Library is the moral obligation of every modern welfare state towards its people. The State is also responsible for the expenses occured in the maintenance of such an institution of national importance, People of the country should not be taxed separately for this purpose. Ranganathan has suggested to maintain a National Library Fund from which these expenses will be met.[7]

REFERENCES

—K.W. Humphreys, "Role of the National Library" *Libri*, v. 14 : 4, 1964.
—"National Library Functions", Unesco bulletin for libraries, v. 20, 1966.
—U.G.C. (GB) Report of the committee on libraries, (H.M.S.O. 1967).
—S.R. Ranganathan, Library development plan, Op. cit.

Ibid., p. 184-85.
7. Ibid., p. 185.

10

DEVELOPMENT OF LIBRARY SERVICES IN MODERN INDIA :

Plans and Proposals

Education is no exotic in India. She has been the cradle of one of the earliest and brilliant civilizations. The greatest and wisest of her monarchs found in the promotion of learning their noblest and most beneficent achievements and saw in the foundation of the university the most enduring memorials of their thrones. There is, in fact. "no country where the love of learning had so early an origin or has exercised so lasting an influence. From the simple poet of the Vedic age to the Bengali philosopher of the present day, there has been an uninterrupted succession of teachers and scholars.[1]"

The well-equipped libraries with vast, choicest collections of manuscripts and other materials of ancient wisdom attached to the internationally-renowned Indian universities like Takshasila, Nalanda, Vikramsila, Valabhai, Banaras and Kanchi in ancient India were solely organized and functioned with a view to advancing the traditional, philosophical, ecclesiastical and classical education for its own sake. They were the handmaidens of scholarship, and during the centuries when learning was so individualistic, they were almost the sole recourse of philosophers and scholars.

The libraries in the Medival and Mughal India were created of, by, and for the elite; This close association of the library with the elite soon brought to it a prestigious status, and it is not suprising that the patronage or possession of library became a symbol of aristocracy in the Mughal period. Nonetheless, the benefits of

1. F.W. Thomas, *The History and prospects of British education in India* (London : George Bell, 1891), p. 1.

these libraries were confined to royalty and nobility; the poor had no access to knowledge.[2,3]

We may trace the development of library services in modern India in respect of University Libraries, Public Libraries and Special Libraries.

I Development of University Library Services

Pre-Independence Era :

The modern universities in India, began as institutional transplants from the Great Britain, on the pattern of the London University as it then was. Sir Charles Wood's Education Despatch of the 19th July, 1854, recommending the establishment of the three universities each in the presidency town of Calcutta. Bombay and Madras proved to be a cornerstone in the arch of modern university education in india. Because of its historical importance, the Despatch has been hailed as the "Manga Charta of English Education in India.[4]" It enunciated in clear terms the missions of the university education as the diffusion of Arts, Science, Philosophy and literature of Europe.

Yet the praises showered by the admirers of the Despatch are nothing short of exaggeration. The first three Indian universities created in 1857 were not places of accumulation, preservation and dissemination of knowledge, or the cultivation of intellectual excellence. Nor they were corporations of scholars, graduates, postgraduate departments, or physical agglomerations containing museums, libraries, and other real estates normally associated with modern idea of university. These three universities were, in fact, "bureaucratic devices"[5] for testing the value of learning obtained in colleges which did not form an integral part of the universities. Nonetheless, the Despatch set the ball rolling and the capture of citadel was but a question of time.

When two more universities were created, one at Lahore in the Punjab in 1882, and the other at Allahabad in 1887, these universities followed in the footsteps of the three earlier universities

2. For details see, Bimal Kumar Datta, *Libruries and librarianship of ancient and medieval India* (Delhi : Atma Ram, 1970).
3. P.N. Kaula. *Ed., Lil rary movement in India; papers* (Delhi Library Association, 1958).
4. J.A. Richey. *Selctions from educational records* (Delhi: Govt. of India, Manager of Publicatlon, 1965); pt. 2. 1840-59, p. 364.
5. Ruldolph and Rudolph, *op. cit.*, p. 16.

by restricting their activities to affiliation and examination, though, they were authorised by their constitutions to undertake teaching functions. Post-graduate departments and advancement of learning developed only in the 20th century.

In all these universities, at the time of their inception, the libraries were not considered to be of central importance, as they were not seats of teaching, learning and research. The teaching was done in the colleges which did not feel the necessity of having libraries with books other than the meagre stock of text-books. This is well borne out by the comments of the Indian Universities Commission, appointed by Lord Curzon, under the chairmanship of Sir Thomas Releigh, on 27th Jan. 1902[6].

In the absence of the university and college libraries the students had no opportunity of forming the habit of independent reading and they took to cramming—a practice which continues till today. Curzon aptly condemned an educational system which encouraged students to the application of purely mnemonic tests, stuffing their brains with the "abracadabra of geometry and physics, algebra and logic"[7].

It was the *Releigh Commission* which attached great importance to the formation of good "reference libraries"[8] for both uuiversities and colleges. Yet one is distressed to record that the authorities continued to look upon the libraries as useless accessories even long after the enactment of the Indian Universities Act of 1904, based on the Commission's report.

As regards the pathetic conditions of the university libraries, the *Calcutta University Commission* appointed in Jan., 1917 in the time of Lord Chelmsford, under the chairmanship of Dr. Michael Sadler, Vice-Chancellor of the University of Leeds, succinctly remarked : "one of the greatest weeknesses of the existing system is the extra-ordinary unimportant part, which is played by the library in it. The libraries were found to be inadequate not only for the needs of the students but also still more for those of

6. Progrees of education in India, *Eighth Qutinquennial Review*, 2 vols. 1917-22 (V. 1 and 2, 1923), Vol. 2, p. 386-88.
7. Thomas Releigh, *Ed., Lord Curzon in India; speeches 1898-1905* (London : McMillan, 1906) p. 317-18.
8. Progress of education in India, *Loc. cit.*

teachers. Even the best, that of Presidency College, was very defective"[9].

If such was the sordid state of affairs in Calcutta, where besides the college libraries, the university library and the Imperial Library were also available, the fate of libraries in other parts of the country can be well-imagined. The Commission, therefore, recommended that "to maintain a library on the amplest scale and to make it as useful as it may be to all teachers and serious students, must be the most intellectual function of the university"[10].

The publication of the Report gave a great impetus to the advancement of the university education in India resulting in its wake and that of the Act of 1919 in the establishment of 8 new universities[11]—unitary, teaching and residential in character and opposed to affiliation. These universities had some types of libraries as they were upgraded from the colleges, but the service of these libraries was of no consequence in the general structure of the university.

Of course, with the implementation of the Govt. of India Act, 1935, three more universities[12] were created, thus, bringing the total to 18 universities in the pre-independence India, but the library service in these universities was not a shade better.

An Appraisal of Library Services (Before 1947)

Honestly speaking, there were no libraries worth the name in these universities. The libraries were weighted down with dead and antiquated reference and text-books, astray and unwanted documents purchased without paying any heed to the tastes, interests, needs, demands or standards of the readers. Moreover, these small collections of books were poorly quartered in locked almirahas or even in sealed cup-boards, sometimes left to repose in corners or corridors, neither classified nor catalogued properly nor readily accessible for use[13].

9. India. University Commission (East India), *Report of the committee appointed by the Government of India to enquire into the conditions and prospects of the Caldutta Univeristy* (London : H.M.S.O., 1919); 5 Vols V. 1, pt. 1, p. 407.
10. *Ibid.*
11. For details see, Education Commission, 1964-66, *op. cit.*, p. 538.
12. *Ibid.*
13. Information collected during personal discussions with the university librarians.

The librarians were held responsible for any loss of book and in the Calcutta University, the library staff was required to deposit a security of Rs. 1,000/- before appointment. Since the fear of losing books continued to haunt the minds of librarians like a nightmare, suffocating their sleep, many librarians did not loan out books for home study and kept the libraries opened for minimum possible hours. Very few libraries allowed their readers direct access to the collections. Reference service and bibligraphical assistance were practically ineffective; documentation services were unknown. The non-book material was conspicuous by its absence. Photo-reproduction facilities were unheard of, and no systematic effort was ever made to publicize the activities of the libraries.

The buildings of the university libraries—those which were fortunate to have them—were not functional but rather works of art and beauty. The authorities never bothered to seek any expert advice of the librarian. Even where they did take such an unusual step, they rectified it later by making summary changes on their own, with the most undesirable results[14]. The furniture and equipment adorning the libraries were also of "old and antiquated types"[15]. Worse still many libraries were housed in buildings meant for some other purposes. Among the more serious defects of these library buildings were lack of sufficient space for the books, or arangement for seats where readers could consult the books[16].

If the service of the university libraries was deplorable, the status of the university librarian was no better than that of a watchman of books. The small collections which the libraries had were left to the charge of cleaners, care-takers, and some clerical staff to keep them dusted and accesstioned. In fact, the university libraries provided a heavenly abode for university administrators to accomodate good-for nothing persons—a teacher who had miserably failed in his teaching, the official who was physically disabled

14. N.N. Gidwani, Indian university library problems and prospects. *In first seminar of university librarians in India held at the Rajasthan University, Jaipur from 16th to 19th Nov., 1966*, ed. by N.N. Gidwani, 4 Vols. (Jaipur : University of Rajasthan, 1967), (Mimeographed), V. 2, p. 2.
15. S.K. Mukherjee, *Development of libraries and library seience* in India (Calcutta : World Press, 1969), p. 103.
16. India, University Education Commission, Dec. 1948-August 1949, *op. cit* p. 110-11.

or mentally abnormal or a deaf or a dumb or both[16a]. Moreover, every Tom, Dick and Harry was considered fit for the positions in the library.

Hardly did any well-qualified person dream of joining the library service. A wrong tradition had thus come into vogue regarding the library staff which was taken to consist of peons, book-lifters, and at the most a clerk with a literary bent of mind. The new universities which saw the light of the day after the deliberations of the Calcutta University Commission were put into circulation and by virtue of the Acts of 1919 and 1935 were solely guided by the traditions of colleges in respect of their libraries. They, therefore, put an honorary librarian—usually one of the professors—over the library staff. This deprived the librarians of all initiative and infused in them an attitude of inferiorty complex and the habit of pleasing the professor-in-charge, who in most cases did not know even the alphabet of librarianship to win his benedictions. It not only adversely affected the efficiency and the status of librarians but also had its inevitable banal effects on the library image, as "cheap sycophancy" took the place of "true spirit of service"[17].

On the whole, the libraries in the pre-independence era were like a museum and a librarian was a "mouser" in dusty books closely guarding these treasure-troves like a watchman lest their loss be made good out of his salary, and the visitors looked with curious eyes at the ancient manuscripts and out-of-date books. Under the circumstances the word library merely implied a collection of books; it did not matter how or where it was housed, or how the books in the collection were arranged or who administered it; nor was much variety sought in the quality of the book-stock. All that the librarian had to do in its wake was to keep watch over the wares in his custody and grudgingly leave the chair in order to let a stray reader have the book he wanted[18]. Instead of inculcating the habits of independent learning and reading, these neo-votaries of the profession curbed them in the budding stage.

From the above it can be concluded that the concept of library as a useless accessory dominated throughout the pre-independence

16.a S.R. Ranganathan, Vitalising the education of university librarians. *First seminar of the university librarians in India, op. cit* p. 137.

17. S.R. Ranganathan, University library then and now, *Library Herald* (V. 6, nos. 2-3, 63), p. 1966.

18. S, Bashirudin "Twin requisites of modern library" *Journal of Library Science* (V. 6, no. 1, 1963), p. 4.

era. As a result, the libraries even in the well-established universities were not properly organized and the status of the librarian was pathetically low. Little did the university authorities realise that the library's quality is a major contributory factor in determining the quality of education that a university can provide. It is, therefore, not only right and proper but it is indispensable for the right conduct of their ordinary teaching work that the universities should provide great libraries on their campuses with great scholars to direct them.

The Post-Independence Era

August 15, 1947 is a red letter day in the history of India as it marked the dawn of our independence after centuries of subjugation. Once the captains and kings had departed, we launched ourselves on a great adventure of national reconstruction whose principal objective was to raise the standards of living of the people and to create a new social order based on freedom, equality, justice, and dignity of individual. The Sovereign, Socialist, Secular, Democratic Republic which proclaims equality as its ideal requires university education of the type in which learning and social application, ideas and practice, are superbly blended. Unless democracy becomes a part and parcel of the bone and blood of the people in daily life; unless it is buttressed by the presence of democratic methods in all social relationships; and until we practise and infuse it in our educational institutions, it is bound to be destroyed in the larger complex of the state[19]. Great strides were, therefore, made to understand and to grapple with the complex, difficult but significant problems of higher education—specially university education. But to embark upon a programme of university education without assigning due place to the library in the educational set-up sounded like "staging Hamlet without the Prince of Denmark"[20]. Therefore, alongwith the reformation of the university education, the library also started marching from the position of a uselese accessory to be the heart of the university academic life.

The first great milestone on the road was the appointment of the *University Education Commissson,* in Dec., 1948, consisting of reputed educationalists from India, the United States and the United kingdom under the Chairmanship of S. Radhakrishnan.

19. John Dewey, *Democracy and education; an introducttion to the philosophy* (New York : McMillan, 1961), Chapt. 7.

No doubt, the Commission paid a glowing tribute to the library by hailing it as the "heart of all the university's work"[21]. Yet, the modern librarian is constrained to record that the Commission set up as a first step to suggest ways and means of raising up the cultural standards of the country and headed by a man of letters, did not suggest any concrete measure to cleanse the Augean Stable and restore to library and his controller the place they deserve[22-23].

The Radhakrishnan Commission, however, made a recommendation revolutionary in spirit. This concerned the setting up of an autonomous body to foster the development of university education in the country. This unique recommendation blossomed in 1953, when the University Grants Commission was set up. It was, however, in 1956 that it was infused with statutory life.

The *University Grants Commission* (U. G. C.) under the guidance of its Chairman, C. D. Deshmukh injected new blood into the hitherto paralysed limbs of the university libraries. To him : "the students are the body of the university, the administration is, of course, the head, teachers are the soul and the library the heart"[24]. In pursuance of this full-blooded faith in the role of the library, he appointed a library committee headed by S. R. Ranganathan in 1957 to advise the U.G C. on various problems connected with the provision of grants to libraries for the purposes of book purchase, development of reading habits and and help to students in the use of libraries, documentation work and service to research workers, departmental libraries, library personnel and their functions, classification of positions, qualifications, status, salary scale and strength alongwith standards for the design of library buildings, fittings and furniture.

20 G.D. Bhargva, *University libraries and the educational set-up of India, Indian Librarian* (v. 14, No. 3, 1959), p. 117.

21. India, University Education Commission, Dec. 48—Aug. 49, *Loc. cit.*

22. For details see, O P. Sharma, History of the development of university libraries in India; an appraisal, *Indian Librarian* (v. 19, No. 3, Dec. 1964), p. 128-43.

23. Also Anis Khurshid, Growth of librariesi n India, *International Library Review* (v. 4, No. 1, 1972), p. 21-65.

2 . University Grants Commission (India), *University and college libraries; a report* (New Delhi, University Grants Commission, 1965), p. 158.

25. *Ibid*, p. 1.

After accepting most of the recommendations[26] of the Committee, the U G.C. gave liberal grants to the universities for uplifting their librares from their pitiable conditions in which they were before independence. The universities in their turn ear-marked for their libraries a sub-standard share of their resources. This lamentable position was highlighted by the subsequent Education Commission with D. S. Kothari as Chairman.

The *Kothari Commission* touched the heart of librarianship when it stated that with ever-increasing enrolment in universities and colleges, the demand for library service has been mounting. Unlike in the past, the library staff have now to cater to the diverse needs of undergraduates and research scholars. Because of "torrential rain of micro-documents" and with the emergence of researeh in our universities, the Commission rightly felt the need for conservation of research potential through documentation work and service. It, therefore, recommended the appointment of a team of documentalists in university libraries who can speak the language of research workers and undertake the work of documentation-search, indexing and abstracting[27].

Still one is disappointed not to find in the report any recommendation of a revolutionary import with regard to the role of the library. The objective of student-oriented education so much emphasized by the Commisaion itself depends upon establishing conditions for developing creative inquiry which is the very spring-board for mental growth. The library is the only effective agency for making a substantial contribution to the provision of individualized enquiry and learning. But because, of "an aura of mistaken veneration"[28] and misplaced emphasis however, library's potential for providing the learning environment was conveniently overlooked by the Commission.

In fact, to recapitulate, all the Commissions—right from that of Sir Thomas Raleigh's, 1902 to Prof. Kothari's through Sir Michel Sadler's, 1917 and Sarvpalli Radhakrishnan's—have treated library as an adjunct to research; but definitely not a process that permeates the academic life of the university campus. No

26. For details see, *Ibid.*, p. 9-127.

27. India, Education Commission, 1964-66, *op. cit*, p. 519-23.

28. Robert S. Taylor, *The Making of a library : the academic library in transition* (New York : Willy-Becker-Hayes, 1972), p. 1.

heed has been paid to bring the library—both its book resources and its staff—into full participation in the teaching process.

The Sadler's Commission, of course, recommended that the "University Librarian ought to be a functionary of great importance, ranking with university professors and having a place in the supreme academic body of the university"[29]. Such a recommendation was reiterated by the Radhakrishanan Commission after 40 years when it aptly remarked : "The library should have adequate and well-qualified staff. At the top will be a man of the calibre of a university professor—(having) qualifications corresponding to a Doctrate in Library Science"[30]. Unfortunately, such a novel idea was never put into practice.

The credit of yeoman's service rendered to the cause of university libraries and their staff, as already pointed out, goes in its entirety to C.D. Deshmukh who invited S.R. Ranganathan to head the U.G.C. Library ad hoc Gommittee in 1957. Anxious to motivate brilliant and talented university trained young men and women to embrace and hold librarianship proudly as a profession, Ranganathan took a revolutionary and unprecedented step in procuring from the U.G.C. academic status and scales of pay for the librarians, Deputy Librarians and Library Assistants[31]. In no other country were the librarians placed so easily as in India, on the same footing as that of Professors, Readers, Lecturers, and Assistant Lecturers.

Librarian and His Staff : An Appraisal of Their Services

Alongwith procuring the status and scales of pay at par with the academic staff, Ranganathan had recommended that as participators in the university's "teaching and research" programmes, the librarian and his reference and technical staff should get themselves thoroughly "acquainted with the wave-front of knowledge in which research is in progress in the university"[32]. It does not behove to blame the academic commuuity, both teachers and students for the poverty of their thought, when they are not fed with the requisite mental food, pin-pointedly, exhaustively, expeditiously and unerroringly. In fact, the librarians and

29. Calcutta University Commission, *op. cit* , v. 2, p. 279-80.
30. Report of the University Education Commission, 1948-49. *op, cit.*, p. 112.
31. U.G.C. (India) *University and college libraries op. cit* , p. 63-74.
32. Ranganathan, In *Untversity and college libraries; a report*, op. cit., p. 64.

professors should work as partners in a cooperative academic enterprise[33]. This is now becoming the accepted practice in the universities all over the world, India cannot stand outside this stream[34].

Sustained efforts have been made to show that the librarian is primarily an educator and the library is no longer just connected with education, but it is the centre of the intellectual community. But truth compels the admission that the recommendations of Ranganathan to the university librarians "to speak the language of a professor, understand his literature need, make literature-searh, for him..."[35] are more honoured in breach than observance. Even in most of the well-organized libraries, operating the library on "teaching and researeh" levels has come to mean, by and large, making books easily available in the reading halls or at the most providing books to the readers. The bibliographical and documentation services are conspicuous by their absence. It is a sad commentary that even the instruction in library use, which so many academic librarians regard as one of the highest forms of library service, remains ill-defined and poorly organized. In brief, though the university librarians claim their service to be essentially a teaching function, yet in practice they are neglecting the opportunities to contribute directly and dynamically to the educative process. The academic staff often remarks that despite the revision of scales of salary, the functions of the library and the role of the librarians have not proved easily adaptable to the changing modes of education.[36] The librarians "huff and puff for achieving lilliputian ambitions, and pin-head achievement followed by a loud drum beating"[37].

We must look at the other side of the coin. Admitted that the university librarians are responsible for lack of transmission of the

33. *Ibid.*, p. 166. 65, 64,

34. *Ibid.*, p. 65.

35. *Ibid.*,

36. S.R, Ranganathan, Productivity and partnership in university education, *Library Herald* (v. 19. No. 1, 1968), p. 15.

37. H.N. Gidwani, Library documentation service to social science research. *In progress of libraries in free India : being a symposium on library science by some eminent and experienced librarians in India*, ed. by N.B. Sen (New Delhi, New Book Society, 1967), p. 23.

"new profile of academic librarianship"[38] But teaching is a co-operative effort. There must flow opportunities for closer and conscious cooperation and collaboration between librarians and teachers as enterpreneurs in the industry of knowledge. The academic community, however, is notorious for its innate conservatism and stubborness. The library method of teaching is eloquenly upheld by teachers—but more in theory than in practice. The university librarians rightly complain that such of their colleagues have done little to deserve a good library service. If some of the university librarians are more "resource-minded than people-minded"[39], it will not be wrong to say that some educators have a sordid record of using the library as a teaching instrument. It is, thus, the educational philosophy of the the institution. and the way it is translated by the faculty, which decides how the library will function[40].

After weighing both sides of the coin one fact emerges conspicuously that though the service rendered by the university librarians has improved somewhat after increase in their emoluments and enhancement of their status, yet the university library has not become a laboratory for teaching and research.

Two reasons are advanced for this by a veteran university librarian, S. Bashiruddin[41]. First, the new scales of pay were given to the existing library staff on human considerations rather than as token of recognition of merit. But, to the author's mind, it is only partly true. In India, in most of the service organizations, one does not always go to the top or hold the middle or the lowest rank by merit of what one knows but by virtue of whom one knows. And the library profession is no exception. Individuals working in organizations often are surprised to learn that honesty, sincerity, energy, enthusiasm, and above-average ability are not the assets they thought. This can be disillusioning and frustrating.

38. H. E. Holland, Academic librarianship in three educational journals. *College and Research libraries* (v. 27, no. 1, 1967) p. 31.

39. C. Dyer et al., *School libraries : theory and practice* (London : Clive Bingley, 1970), p. 63-64.

40. H. Hauf et al., *New spaces for learning : designing college facilities to utilise instructional aids and media* (New York : Renssolaer Polytechnic Institute, 1961), p. 24.

41. Cf B.S. Saini, *Library organization for higher education* (Delhi : ESS ESS, 1976), p. 60.

Moreover, the immediate deterioration in service could be very well anticipated. The present generation of librarians was not prepared for the stupendous responsibilities which the intellectual challenges as a result of the explosion of literature and proliferation of subjects have placed upon their shoulders. One gets support from S.R. Ranganathan, who in a personal letter no. 2w of 24th July, 1972 addressed to the present author writes :

> "My friends tell me that this degeneracy was partly due to my having succeeded in putting the library profession on a par with the academic profession in respect of status and scale of pay. I knew that this would be the immediate result, because for human reasons, the libraries will have to promote the existing lower intellectuals to the higher grades but the benefit which I had in mind was a long term one. The acceptance of the higher grade by authorities would make men of higher intellect to take library science course and when they enter the profession in sufficient number, the profession itself will get completely transformed in the higher level. This would mean no doubt waiting for about one generation. Knowing this I deliberately got my recommendations accepted.
>
> For it is a case of seed first or tree first. If we wait to change the grade until better librarians come in, you know that it will not happen. If we raise the grade even now, better librarians will come in at least within a generation—
>
> I am not sure whether I was wise or foolish in the philosophy that guided me.—"

However, heart of the problem is touched in the second reason given by S. Bashiruddin : the total failure on the part of the traditionalists in our midst to recognise the fact of change in the pattern of demands on the libraries resulting from rapid changes taking place in the university education itself.[42]

In an age of tremendous technological advancement when images are moved at the speed of light from the moon to earth, most of the university librarians in India spend much of their time on purely custodial and clerical functions. Many librarians are not only suspicious of intellectual achievement, but welcome

42. *Ibid.*

routine and pedestrian tasks. As a result, the average user does not except the librarian to be able to help him with more than routine matters; the scholar suspects that the librarian is relatively ignorant Little thought is given to finding out why many groups do not use the library and demand reference service.

Nevertheless, the university librarian in India, if he is to be sensitive and true to the ideals of our day and age, must serve as a dynamic agent for the social transformation, for development of truly Indian political systems, for the elevation of standard of living, for the survival and advancement of people he serves by disseminating truth. The diffusion of knowledge to each according to his needs may be regarded as the role in which the functions of conservation and education coalesce. And just as he maintains his interest in the source and synthesis of all knowledge he should likewise remain closely identified with and sensitively cognizant of Indian society. How he shapes the energy, motivation and values of the next generation by providing an easy and systematized access to the recorded knowledge will determine the shape and direction of national progress. Unless he is vital, we are all in trouble. The university librarian would only be rewarded by such a distinguished service. This is, therefore, high time for soul-searching.

Instead of appointing another library committee consisting of eminent librarians to diagnose the lapses in the growth of library organism and its service based on empirical study, the University Grants Commisiion after having done a right thing, out of regrets probably, caught the wrong end of the stick and withdrew the academic status and scales of pay. But tragedy becomes too deep for tears when one learns that among those who advised the U.G.C. to set the hands of the clock back were no others but our own professional brethren but who had never lived the profession, who did not believe in the profession, who even went about preaching the powers that be that all the qualities necessary in a librarian are tact and administrative ability, and some knowledge of library techniques may be an additional qualification. But these neo-votaries of the library profession are whole-time courtiers spending their time in the government offices as they do precious little in their libraries. Previously, the university librarian in India was only worried over devising the ways for improving the library service; now he is dismayed over his own degradation as well which may further affect his morale and efficiency, probably.

Hardly did the U.G.C. pay any heed to the sane advice that money is one of the motivators and "that material rewards are ineffective beyond the subsistence level excepting to a very limited proportion of men, that most men neither work harder for material things, nor can be induced thereby to devote more than a fraction of their possible contribution to organised effort"[43]. Industrial psychologists have proved, that far more important motivating factors in the work situation are such inducements as the opportunity for distinction, status, prestige, personal power, desirable working conditions, ideal benedictions, a chance to experience pride of workmanship, sense of adequacy, the feeling of working toward altruistic ideals, pleasant association with others, the opportunity for participation in the course of events, and the feeling of belongingness.

After having a bird's eye-view of the role of the university library and its staff both in theory and practice, we are in a position to determine what actually impedes the development of an efficient library service and a favourable professional image. The following major obstacles seem to stand out prominently : lack of clearly-defined university and library objectives; lack of co-operation and understanding from university authorties and faculty; inadequate financial support; failure to appoint a competent university librarian and to give him authority commensurate with his important responsibilies; and above all shortage of brilliant and highly motivated staff, without which no library can serve scholarship and no administration can be distinguished by wisdom.

It reflects the conviction that the librarian must continually strive to perform two functions. First, as the university library is an organisation which promotes educational and scholarly pursuits, he has to assemble, preserve and make available to readers the recorded knowledge. Secondly, to perform the first function he must build up and sustain an effective and satisfied working team of reliable, honest, informed, enthusiastic and skilful workers who could act as canvassing agents for documents and help the university in disseminating knowledge, and provide them with the organization and working conditions to obtain maximum turn out of work and efficiency.

43. Chester I. Barnard, *The function of the executive* (Camb., Mass., Harvard University, 1938), p. 144.

Unfortunately, peeping into the working of the university libraries of India, one finds that they are infested with the problems of underutilization of abilities, frustration-bred behaviour, unfavourable job attitudes, alienation, and low morale breeding cynicism towards the profession. This leads to the question of tracing the genuine causes of this distressing situation and to suggest effective measures to arrest the process of further decline.

Proposals

Sufficient Finance

Finance is the life-blood of every organization but more so of a spending institution like a library. Unfortunately, majority of the university libraries continue to suffer from lack of proper financial support. The financial position has become more distressing because of stagnant grants and ever-rising cost of documents.

Moreover, the universities give a step-motherly treatment to their libraries so far as the equitable distribution of their funds is concerned. But as is aptly remarked : "Poverty may force a university to have a sub-standard library, but not to give the library a sub-standard share of its resources. Here, then, is a test of the sincerity of university administrators, who so often say that the library is the heart of the campus". Stinting on library costs is a folly

—The universities should ear-mark at least 6.5 to 10 per cent of their total budget or Rs. 40 per capita on the basis of students registered in the university and Rs. 300 per teacher as the annual grant to the libraries. These figures may be revised periodically.

—No new university department should be set up without taking into account its library needs in terms of staff, books, journals, space, etc. Nothing could be more damaging to a growing department than to neglect its library or to give it low priority. On the contrary, the library should be an important centre of attraction on the university campus. The funds provided for the purchase of various types of library would in a very large measure determine the quality of the library resources.

Rich and Balanced Collections

—The object of the library planning is not to build a collection of books unrelated to class work, laboratory research and conference room. The object should rather be to relate book selection, organization of the books, conditions of access and all library activities to the daily needs and activities of the academic community, both professors and students.

A balanced collection of the documents must be built up with the cooperation of the faculty members. The resources should be of the requisite size, scope and quality so as to include text-books (with multiple copies of collateral reading material, reference and bibliographical tools, journals and serials). It should also contain the latest works in different disciplines, to keep the members of the teaching faculty abreast of development in their field and also assist them in their professional growth. There should be a strong and up-to-date reference collection in the major fields of knowledge. A strong collection must be built of bibliographical sources of information. The periodicals and other serial publications, should be carefully selected so as to be well-rounded collection to fulfil the needs of the students and the faculty.

Quality is the hall-mark of the library collections. What is required are "good, live. worth-while, great, important, substantial, basic books of merit and character"[44] meeting the needs of both students' and faculty. Ample foreign exchange should be available to import foreign publications.

Service to Students and Faculty

Libraries have often been referred to as the hearts of universities from where flows the invigorating blood of knowledge to nourish and sustain life in all the teaching departments of the university. Unfortunately, our libraries are the weakest at the service point. Sufficient attention has not been paid to qualitative reference services. The Radhakrishanan Commission (1948-49) recommends that lectures and tutorials must be supplemented by work in the library. The teacher should give the students more guidance as regards supplementary reading. "The reference assistant if he is properly qualified, will be in touch with the teachers and guide the students to the proper volumes and the proper pages in each volume, which would be helpful to them. These reference assistants can be of help not only to the students but also

44. INDAL Newsletter, Oc.t, 1980.

to the teachers in their special subjects of the study[45]". The Koshari Commission, too, emphasized the need of reference service in the university libraries. It recorded that the library should :

—provide resources necessary for research in fields of special interest to the university;

—aid the university teacher in keeping abreast of developments in fields of his interest;

—provide library facilities and services necessary for the success of all formal programmes of instruction;

—open the doors to the wide world of books that lies beyond the borders of one's own fields of speciaiization; and

—to bring books, students and scholars together under conditions which encourage reading for pleasure, self-discovery, personal growth, and the sharpening of intellectual curiosity[46].

The Commission, in fact, recommended a teaching role for the librarians.

Library Staff

True that as an integral part of research, the library is a temple that emits all knowledge, but the revelation will only be achieved through the help of both men and women who operate libraries and who forming the link between the man and the intellectual thought-content of the documents at once create the public image of the library as a nerve-centre of the university and the very nucleus of the idea of education. Without such a staff. the most luxurious building or extensive book collection may have little to recommend. In fact, the very efficiency, service, and the ultimate success of the library as an agency for the diffusion of knowledge depends upon its staff.

Fortunately, the U.G.C. has re-instated the academic status and scales of pay for the librarians and his professional staff after a decade of hard struggle. It is high-time that the librarians should begin to take their teaching reponsibilities rather seriously. By giving lectures, person to person introduction to the library, by providing reference service, besides maintaning readers' profiles, it should be possible for the librarians to perform their teaching

45. Report, op. cit., p. 113.
46. Report. op. cit., p. 288.

functions adequately. It should be possible to design a course about the introduction to the library for research students tutored to their respective requirements.

To give impetus to research activity it is necessary for the libraries to develop a viable system of information retrieval. The librarian and his staff should keep themselves in touch with the research activity of the teaching departments. They should analyse the current periodicals and feed the research staff with information pertaining to their research.

The role of the library staff has acquired geater significance and new dimensions because of the virtual 'information explosion' resulting from astounding and unprecendented proliferation of literature in science and technology, the dissemination of natural and classical literature, and the flowering of literary criticism opening the flood-gates of knowledge and making the scholars, the researchers, the scientists and technologists, dependent upon library services. It is the reference service or information service which is required of the library professional staff. The librarian and his staff must, therefore, bring to the point of maximum utilization the graphic records by interpreting their collections to the readers. The librarian must function as an active participant in the process of teaching and research and thereby become equal partner in the academic pursuits. This will entitle him to academic status and scale of pay in the university hierarchy and not the slogan shouting.

Librarian as Manager

The librarian as a manager of the industry of knowledge must have the ability to energise, direct and sustain the behaviour of his staff at work, He must keep in view three behavioral requirements :

First, brilliant men and women must be motivated not only to join the profession but also to remain in it.

Secondly, persons must perform the task for which they have been recruited.

Finally, working environments must be conducive for creative, spontaneous and innovative work.

In simple words, to make the library organization effective and efficient, the librarian as manager must motivate his staff to participate in the task of operating the library at teaching and research level by applying the techniques of management to their organizations.

2. *Public Library Services*

The genesis of the public library movement in India may well he traced with the advent of British Raj. Although the British came to dominate India, but they also brought with them an ideology and literature embodying the ideals of common man with which the whole of Europe was imbued at that time. They could not rid themselves in India of the ideals in which they were brought up in England. Incidently, they inspired, though they may not have actively encouraged the setting-up of public libraries in this country[1].

The first great land mark in the history of the public libraries in India was visible in 1808 when the government of Bombay Province started a scheme for registering institutions to which copies of books to be published from the "Funds for the Encouragement of Literature" were to be given.

The second milestone in the history of public libraries was enactment of "Press and Registration of Books Act, 1867". It desired the printer of a book to deliver one or more copies to the Provincial Government, if it so desired, for the purpose of preparing a Quarterly Catalogue of such books.

The Calcutta Library, established in 1784 by the Royal Asiatic Society of Bengal was thrown open to the public in 1820. The Calcutta Public Library was established in 1836 to serve people without any distinction. The reading room of this library was opened for the public in 1900. It is now known as the National Library of India.

Connemara Public Library came into existence in Madras in 1860.

By the end of the nineteenth century, all the provincial capitals and even many of the district towns of Bombay, Calcutta and Madras had their public libraries, founded mostly with the active support and initiative of the Europeans in these Presidency towns. Even some of the Princely States like Indore and Travancore-Cochin had the distinction of having established public

1. India, Education (Ministry of—) Advisory Committee, *Report*, 1961.

libraries in their capitals. But it may be kept in mind that the benefits of these libraries were confined to a thin upper layer of the society. Moreover, they were subscription libraries, and not free libraries, which, alone, can have the proud title of public libraries. Nevertheless, these libraries opened the flood-gates, the capture of the citadel was but a matter of time.

The advent of the twentieth century marked the dawn of a new era in our public library history. If in the nineteenlh century the public libraries flourished on the official backing and patronage, the period from 1900—1937 was characterized by the Indian intelligentsia taking up the cause of public libraries.

The most significant achievement of this period was, of course, the library movement in Baroda. Sir Sayaji Roa III, the enlightened ruler of the State had visited U.K. and U.S.A. He was struck by the social good flowing from their nation-wide public library system. As a result he established a grid of public library system in his State. He availed of the services of U.S. born librarian W.A. Borden who was able to establish an elaborate and well-integrated public library system composed of the central library, village libraries, travelling libraries, cinema libraries and manuscript libraries. Vernacular libraries were also established for people not knowing the English language. Separate wings were opened for women and children as well as audio-visual section for the illiterates and semi-literates This was the dawn of public library system in the modern sense and for years to come this pioneering work of Sayaji Roa Gaekward III fired the imagination of Indian librarians and served as a beacon-light to lovers of libraries all over the country[2].

The epoch-making event of this period was the foundation of Indian Library Association (ILA). The ILA gave the librarians, for the first time, a status and a voice, which feeble as it was in the beginning was bound to be heard in due course of time. The ILA assumed an international stature and performed commendable library work under the Presidentship of S.R. Ranganathan.

The passage of the Government of India Act, 1935, and the initiation of the Provincial Autonomy ushered in a new era in the history of the library movement. The Government played a dominant role in setting up libraries for which there was strong

2. Ibid., p. 2.

demand. But the village libraries set up in provinces—Assam, Bihar, Cochin, Orissa, Punjab and some other states through governmantal efforts, were never run on scientific lines. With the fall of the Congress governments in many provinces and the outbreak of the Second World War, the library movement suffered a severe set-back.

The Library Development Committee, Bombay, appointed under the chairmanship of A.A.A. Fyzee in 1939 marks another great milestone. In its report, submitted in 1940, the Committee recommended building up a strong network of public library system in Bombay with State Central Library, Regional Libraries, District Libraries, Block Libraries linked with each other in the form of a chain.

Critical Appreciation

There were no good public libraries before independence with the exception of few cities as Calcutta, Bombay and Madras. Nevertheless, the library movement in India had begun. The contributions of the twentieth century toward the growth of the library movement in India may be noted :

—the first training class in library science was started in 1911 at Baroda. The great experiment of free public library service was started here;

—the first library periodical entitled the *Library Miscellany* was put into circulation in 1912;

—the Punjab Library Primer—a book on library science by A.C. Dickinson was published in 1916 Earlier, John Macfarlane—the first librarian of Imperial Library had written a book under the title *Library Administration* in 1898. It was followed by B.H. Mehta's book entitled *Hints* of *Library Administration*;

—the first All India Library Conference sponsored by the Government of India was held in Lahore in 1918;

—the first All India Public Library Conference (in association with the Indian National Congress) was held in 1926 at Calcutta;

—*the Five Laws of Library Science* was published in 1931;

—the Model Library Act forming Chapter IV of the *Five Laws*, was presented to the All Asia Educational Conference held at Banaras (now called Varanasi) in 1930;

—the golden age in the history of Indian Library Movement in general and library literature in particular dawned in 1930. Colon Cassification was born in 1933. Ranganathan's methodological and scientific study of the different branches of library science led to the various publications which have projected the name of India on the library map of the world.

The first library van in India was inaugurated in Mannargudi. Among universities, Madras was the first to start a course in library science.

Post-Independence Era

The first great milestone on the road was declaring the Imperial Library (Calcutta) as the National Library of India in 1948.

Another significant step was the establishment in 1951 of the Delhi Public Library, a Unesco Pilot Project for Asia.

The Government of India created a history in the Public Library Movement by including the scheme of Improvement of Library Service in the First Five Year Plan of Educational Development. Proposals were formulated to set up a National Central Library at Delhi and an idea was also mooted that each State should have a Central Library of its own with a net-work of circulating libraries in villages served through deposit stations and mobile vans. During this Plan 9 states (Assam, West Bengal, Madha Pradesh, Punjab, P E.P.S U., Rajasthan, Saurashtra, Bhopal and Vindya Pradesh) had decided to set up State Central Libraries, and by the end of this Plan period (1951-56) these states (except Punjab) had either set up or were in the process of setting up District Libraries in 100 of their Districts.

In 1952, the Government of India initiated the Community Development Programme laying stress on the development of rural libraries. A pilot project type of integrated library service was taken in hand in 29 areas—each comprising a 100 villages.

On May 21, 1954, the Government of India enacted the Delivery of Books (Public Libraries) Act, 1954 making it obligatory for the publisher of every book to deliver at his own expense a copy of the book each to the National Library, Calcutta; Connecmara Public Library, Madras; Asiatic Society Library, Bombay. In 1982, Delhi Public Library also got the copyright privilege. In 1956, through an amendment, the Government wisely extended the Act to include newspapers as well. The Act has laid the foundation of the four National Book Depositries in India.

Under the Second Five Year Plan (1956-61)the Government spent about Rs. 12,943,000 on public libraries for setting up a country wide net-work (excluding Assam and U.P.) of libraries in her 320 districts. An additional provision of Rs. 10 lacs was made to set up a Central Institute for Training of Librarians at Delhi affiliated to Delhi University. The first refresher course on "The Public Library and National Development" was inaugu-in March 1959. By and large, the achievement of this plan period was not encouraging.

Advisory Committee For Libraries

The Ministry of Education, on the recommendations of a Seminar on the 'Role of Libraries in Social Education' set up an Advisory Committee for libraries with the following terms of reference :

—to enquite into present reading needs of the people, how they are met;

—to enquire into the reading tastes of various sections of the people;

—to recommend the future library structure in India;

—to recommend the forms of co-operation between the library and social educational set-up;

—to go into the question of training of librarians and the condition of their service;

—to make recommendations on the administrative and financial measures necessary to support the future set-up in India.

The Report recommended that library service should be free to every citizen of India. Secondly, the library pattern in the country should consist of National Library, State Central Libraries, District Libraries, Block Libraries, and Panchayat Libraries. Thirdly, it was deemed desirable to have an independent Directorate of Social Education and Libraries in every State. Fourthly, it strongly recommended the levy of library cess @ 6 paisa per rupee on property and house tax. Finally, it was recommended that the State and Central Governments should supplement the amount collected by levying cess.

During the Third Five Year Plan (1961-66), the Central Government realized that "an adequate system of libraries is an essential part of any well-organized system of education... Steps will be taken to set up or develop all the four national libraries at Delhi, Bombay, Calcutta. and Madras". Provisions were also made for strengthening libraries at State head-quarters and for increasing the number of libraries at the district and taluqua levels.

If in the Second Plan an Institute of Library Science was established for training of librarians at Delhi, during this plan some universities were encouraged for research in library science aan training library personnel.

Working Group on Development of Libraries

During the Third Plan, the Planning Commission (India) appointed the Working Group on Libraries in June, 1964. The Group formulated over-all polices, priorities, and programmes of public library development costing Rs.30.99 crores.

The coustitution of the Working Group comprising of eminent librarians and educationists under the chairmanship of Dr. V.K.R.V. Rao raised new hopes.

Like the Advisory Committee, it surveyed the existing conditions of library services and made recommendations regarding the structure, hierarchy, and administrative set-up of the libraries.

The major recommendations of the Working Group were :

—creation of a separate division/branch in Central Ministry of Education for library affairs;

—setting up of Directorate of Libraries in each State with a qualified Director;

—setting up of an All India Library Advisory Council with Union Minister of Education as Chairman; and

—establishment of at least three Model Libraries in the country on the pattern of Delhi Public Library. The Group also recommended a Model Public Library Bill which was circulated by the Government of India to the states for adoption.

The Group strongly recommended that 1½ percent of education grants should be ear-marked for public libraries. Unfortunately, its recommendations like those of Advisory Committee's were not honoured by the State Governments. Hence, it is futile to indulge in the evaluation of the result of these exercises.

Raja Rammohan Roy Library Foundation

To stimulate and support the Library Movement in India, the Government of India took a highly laudable step by establishing Raja Rammohan Roy Library Foundation in Calcutta in 1972. It is an autonomous body with Union Minister of Education as its President. It aims at vitalizing the State libraries to work more effectively and set-up a nucleus of district libraries so as to disseminate knowledge for the benefit and improvement of the layman. A good and an integrated net-work of public libraries is highly necessary for the development of human resources on which depends our socio-economic and cultural progress.

The rural libraries will be served by means of mobile vans operated from respective districts. The reading needs and requirements of the children and handicapped have especially been emphasized.

The Foundation also proposes to have core collection of books in regional languages. At each district library, it is proposed to have the stock of Hindi and English books.

In addition to having a strong District Library System, a proposal was formulated to establish three Central Libraries at Delhi, Bombay and Madras to offer book preservation and reprographic services.

There is also a provision to strengthen the Science and Technology divisions of National Libraries, Calcutta.

The major objectives of the Foundation are to :

—work for the development of the public library movement in India;

—disseminate the idea of library legislation and to vigorously persude the State Government to adopt it;

—formulate a national library policy;

—advice the Government on all matters related to the library development in India;

—act as a *clearing house* of ideas and information on library development in India, and to publish a review of library development in the country;

—keep in touch with other institutions engaged in similar

activities in India and abroad with a view to achieving the objectives of the Foundation;

—undertake or sponsor compilation of directory of libraries; and

—render financial assistance to libraries, library associations and other organizations engaged in the promotion of library development.

In persuance of its aims the Foundation has given assistance to more than sixteen thousand public libraries. It is, in fact, the first concerted effort to promote an integrated public library service on a national level, and to spell out a national library policy for adoption by the state and central goverments.

The eradication and attaining self-reliance were the two watch-words of the Fifth Five Year Plan. With regard to education including libraries, this plan put emphasis on :

—ensuring equality of educational opportunities as part of the overall plan of ensuring social justice;

—establishing closer links between the patterns of education on the one hand; the needs of development and the employment market on the other;

—improvement of the quality of education imparted; and

—involvement of the academic community, including students, in the tasks of social and economic development.

No separate mention was made of libraries. Similar is the case with Sixth and Seventh Five Year Plans. Nevertheless, Rs. 352 crores have been ear-marked for education for the year 1986-87. One can take clue from the U.G C. (India) which allows 25% of her grants allocated to the universities for the purchase of library books and journals.

Suggestions for Development of Public Libraries

The British did not encourage the development of public libraries under the psychological apprehensions that free public library service might accelerate political urge for freedom. The library movement started gaining momentum with the advancement of education in post-independence era. The need for library development was emphasized by the Advisory Committee for Libraries (popularly known as K.P. Sinha's Committee) in these words:

With such universal acceptance of the important role of libraries in national reconstruction, it would appear strange that their establishment and maintenance should have failed to receive the priority due to them.

The major bottleneck is the lack of finance. A good amount of money is being spent on education and if a fraction of it could be spent on the development of public libraries, at least initial incentive could be provided to the movement. But our governments seem to hold the opinion that libraries can only be effective among a literate population. Without the ability to read and write on the part of majority of the people, the establishment of libraries would be like the lighting of streets in a city of blind. This argument does not contain the whole truth. Literacy is a by-product of a profitable occupation. People are not easily persuaded to take the trouble of learning to read and write until they are convinced that the knowledge will open up avenues of advancement; that they can gain competitive excellence in their professional career by making proper use of reference and information services, and specialized collections; that they have an opportunity of improving their artistic and aesthetic sensibility and making such wholesome use of their leisure as will promote their personal happiness and social well-being[3]. Commenting on the problem, Ranganathan writes :

We are in a vicious circle. The mental resources go unused. The material plant and animal resources go uncultivated. Wealth does not increase. The taxable capacity continues to be poor. Tnerefore, money cannot be spared for the development of library service. The chain becomes re-entrant. A vicious circle is formed. Finance blocks everthing includiug its own growth. The only remedy is to develop fortitude to plough back finance. One per cent of the nation's annual production of wealth should feed the library service. The history of development of other countries has demonstrated the wisdom of so doing[4].

To achieve her aim of providing "one village-one library", India has to have an integrated plan from national level down to the village level, with the super-structure of a National Library, State Libraries, District Libraries down to librachins-whether

3. Ibid., p. 33.
4. S.R. Ranganathan, Library legislation, Handbook to Madras Library Act (M.L.A., 1953), p. 253.

in the form of mobile vans or boats or cycles. But to have this structure and an adequate, uniform, effective, dynamic and a coordinated net-work of libraries all over the country, library legislation becomes of utmost importance.

Legislation alone, however, is not the answer. Alongwith legislation, standards of public library service on National, State and Local levels should be laid down for the creation of an effective, efficient and economic public library system in this country. Moreover, library consciousness should be created among people; library service should be demanded as a matter of right. As a responsibility of library service, documents selected should be choosen for values of interest, information, and enlightenment of all the peoples of the community; no library material should be proscribed or removed from libraries because of partisan or doctrinal disapproval; censorship should be challanged by libraries in the maintenance of their responsibility to provide the public with information and enlightenment.

Librarian should encourage a general realization of library service. They should participate in public and community affairs and so represent the library that it will take its place among educatinnal, social and cultural agencies. The librarian's conduct should be such as to maintain public esteem for the library and profession.

To conclude : the right way to give stability and impetus to library movement in India is to provide legislation; it will maintain the national library system with the least effect of "the caprices of individuals", and party politics, as well as "whims and finances of the person in power". The service, creation of library conciousness and making the materials highly accessible will create the image of the library as nucleus of intellectual gravity of the community it serves, ultimately strengthening the roots of library movement. Public library networks should be spread all over India in such a way that everyone can reach the library within a few minutes walk.

3. Special Libraries In India

The special library movement has no romantic and historical antecedents. As a matter of fact, before the beginning of the 20th century, one is hard pressed to find any record of the existence of special libraries.

In fact, the history of the growth of special libraries in India is directly related to scientific and technological research and industrial development and the urge for social progress and prosperity through trade and commerce. This created social demands for organizations related to the categories of human activities[5], to possess libraries serving interests germane to them. Therefore, in order to trace the development of special iibraries in India, we have to sketch the growth and development of science and technological institutions and associations in India. Each such organization is building up a library suitable for its needs. It implies that special libraries originated because of a specific localized need for organized services. They have grown in a more or less haphazard manner. No real plan has been followed in the establishment of these libraries. But it is encouraging to note that our librarians and Library Associations like IASLIC have realized the importance of these llbraries and trying to do a lot in this direction.

With the development of modern science, several learned societies and associations have grown up in India. Particular mention may be made of the Royal Asiatic Society of Bengal (1784); Indian Association for the cultivation of sciences (1876) which is promoting investigation in physical sciences; Minning, Geological and Metallurgical Institute of India (1901); Bombay Natural History Society (1902); Indian Mathematical Society (1907); Indian Botanical Society (1921); Indian Chemical Society (1924); Institute of Engineers, India (1929); Indian Statistical Institute (1931); Indian Psychological Society (1935); Indian Society for Social Social Sciences; Zoological Society of India (1939); Horticultural Society of India (1922) and Indian Dairy Association (1948).

All these associations have as their objective—the promotion of a particular branch of knowledge in all its aspects. They are obviously building up very good special libraries around them—an essential tool for scientific research and development.

Besides, there are many institutions, associations and societies in India, engaged in applied research such as Indian Council of Medical Research; Central Research Institute, Kausauli; School of Tropical Medicine, Calcutta; Indian Council of Agricultural

5. A.K. Mukherjee, *Fundamentals of special librarianship* and documentation (IASLIC, 1969), p. x.

research; Central Potato Research Institute; Forest Research Institute, Dehradun; Sugarcane Research Institute, Coimbatore and Central Rice Research Institute Cuttack.

Organized scientific research had started even before independence with the establishment of Survey of India (1800). It is doing a very useful work in collecting data under irrigation project and conduct of mineral surveys namely (i) The Geological Survey (1851), (ii) Botanical Survey (1889) and (iii) Zoological Survey are also doing excellent work in the interest of country's economy. The Indian Metrological Department (1857) has well equipped laboratories in Pune, Delhi and other places in India. All these Government organizations charged with the collection of factual data about the natural resources of the country have developed special libraries in their respective organizations for preserving and processing data. The Geological Survey of India Library is the oldest of its kind.

Industrial Research is the most important branch of Applied Research. But it was only in 1934 that the Indian Industrial Research Bureax came into existence. After the Second World War, industrial research was given importance and Council of Scientic & Industrial Research (C.S.I.R.) was started.

C.S.I.R. has now to its credit more than 40 national laboratories spread throughout India providing facilities to scientists for individual research which were not available before the inception of the Council. All these laboratories have good special libraries on their respective subjects.

The C S.I.R. at its headquarters has built up a unique library serving as a clearing house of information on raw materials of India and the industrlal products, attached to its publication Division, formed in the year 1952. In addition to several scientific monographs, this divison has compiled a dictionary of economic products and industrial resources of India called the "Wealth of India"—a very useful and well documented compendium of raw materials and material resources of India. Another series entitled 'Industrial Products of India' 8 vols. has also been published.

The establishment of these national laboratories under C.S.I.R., has opened up a new chapter in the history of the special librarianship and scientific documentation in India. It has within its embrace an agency like INSDOC.

The progress of science in Indian universities has resulted in the genesis of a number of research institutes for post-graduate research of an advanced character. Schools of research have also developed round promising teachers and experts in science. The institutions included in this category are :

The Indian Institute of Science, Banglore. It is one of the first Research Institutes to be established in this country, providing facilities for research and teaching in Bio-Chemistry, Organic and Inorganic Chemistry, Fermentation, Technology, Cytogenetics, Physics, Electrical Technology, Electrical Communication Engineering, High Voltage and Power Engineering, Aeronautical Engnieering, Internal Combustion Engineering, Chemical Engineering, Minning and Metallurgy, and even Economics and Social Sciences. Each one of these sections has built up a special library round it, with the result, we are having a nucleus of special libraries. Probably the central library of IIS in one of the best science libraries in India today.

Next comes in this category Tata Institute of Fundamental Research, Bombay; Raman Research Institute, Calcutta; and the Indian Institutes of Technology at Delhi, Kanpur, Bombay, Madras and Khargpur. These institutes are building up excellent libraries in their specific fields of research.

The demand for the establishment of special libraries in India has become the moment's call and more special libraries are cropping up alongwith various information centres. Attention may be paid to the scientific and technical special libraries of BARC, INSDOC, DESIDOC, SENDOC, NPL, the National Science Library and the National Medical Library. Special libraries have also grown within the information centres like :

—Food Science Technological Information Centre at the Central Food Technological Research Institute, Mysore.

—National Information Centre for Leather Technology at the Central Leather Research Institute, Madras.

—Machine Tool Information Centre at Central Machine Tools Institute, Banglore.

—Drugs and Pharmaceuticals Information Centre at Central Drugs Research Institute, Lucknow.

—Crytallography.

Mention may also be made of the proposed National Agricultural Documentation Centre and Library; the Standards Information Centres and the Library of Indian Standards Institute; and the libraries of the Atomic Energy Commission; the Space Research Commission; and the Electronics Commission.

In the field of Social Sciences Indian Council of Social Science Research, Indian Historical Society, Indian Institute of Management, All India Law Institute and the like are also building up libraries with vast and rich collections. Central Government department like Railways have also a Railway Board Library System.

In brief, the development of special libraries is associated with the growth of science and technology in this country. To keep pace with the scientific and technological development of other countries and to keep the advanced studies in various subjects, better organisation of special libraries is essential. Without better bibliographical control, coordination of research results cannot be obtained. It is suggested that one special library on each important subject may be raised to the status of the National Library on that subject. Indeed, the All India Institute of Medical Sciences, Library; the National Physical Laboratory Library; INSDOC Library and the I.A.R.I. Library are to form a nucleus of the National Library of India,

REFERENCES

—Some poineering articles on this topic are :

—H.N. Rangachar. "India and its Special Libraries", *Indian Librarian* (v. 7, 3, Dec., 1952), p. 71-73.

—......, "Nucleus of Special Libraries in Renascent India...", *Indian Librarian* (v. 10, March, 56), p. 147.

—A.C. Ray, "Special Library in Aid of Research", *Indian Librarian* (v. 17,3. Dec., 1962), p. 15.

—Paul Wasserman, "The Special Library—Past, Present, and Future", *LJ* (v. 89, 4, Feb., 15, 1964), p. 797.

—S. Mukerjee, "Special Libraries, Our problems", *IASLIC Bulletin* (v. 4, 1, Mar., 1959), p. 118.

11

BRITISH PUBLIC LIBRARIES :
A Wonder of Legislation

That the public library is established by state legislation; is financed out of local taxation and voluntary gifts; is managed as a public trust; and every citizen of the city, town, county, region which maintains it has an equal share in its privileges of reference and circulation—, is an "Anglo-Saxon idea". Such an idea germinated and developed in Britain and United States almost simultaneonsly, "and was original in both countries".

Britain is credited with having the most extensive and the finest library system in the world both in its variety of libraries and their coverage, But Britain's available public library system has directly emerged from its library legislation. Therefore, to study the growth and development of public libraries in Britain, one has to trace the history of library legislation simultaneously.

The Public Libraries Act of 1850

This Act was the first great landmark as it gave birth to public libraries throughout England and Wales. It permitted any town of ten thousand population to set up a library service by providing a building, a librarian, light and fuel, etc. The rate to believied was ½ d. in a pound on the rateable value. Admission to library was to be free. But the greatest limitation of this Act was that it contained no provision for the purchase of books. Perhaps it was assumed that the books would be donated by the people. Little wonder that there was no great rush to adopt this Act.

Nevertheless, the Act was valuable mainly as establishing a principle. Subsequent development was directed largely to the removal of its limitations.

Act of 1855

This Act enhanced the finances of the libraries as the rate limit was increased from half pence (1850) to one pence in a pound.

But the population limit was lowered from ten thousand to five thousands which proved a grave blunder. But the provision was made in the Act for the purchase of books, news-papers, maps, and specimen of art and science.

Act of 1866

Every Act was a further step in the improvement of library services. The Act of 1866 removed the population limit altogether. The total removal of the population limit, making it possible for smallest town or parish to establish a public library, must have seemed at the time the crowning triumph but, as W.A. Munford pointed out, it was storing up trouble for the future by encouraging the growth of library authorities without adequate resources. The amount of money available, however, was still limited to the product of a one pence rate and it continued upto 1919.

The progress of public library movement was quite slow. All the Acts were passive in nature. It was not obligatory on the part of authorities to adopt the Acts. That is, the local authorities were free to decide whether or not to provide libraries, and they could spend as little and as much as they decided. Nonetheless, these Acts influenced people to appreciate the role of public library in bringing the happiness and pleasures of reading, and as a means of continuing education, information and recreation.

Act of 1892

The Act of 1892 consolidsted all the then existing Acts from 1850 onwards. This Act emphaized that no charge was to be made for admission to the library, nor for the use of lending library by inhabitants of districts. The non-residents could be granted the use of lending libraries either free or on payment. This Act was not repealed till 1964.

Carneige

The Carneige United Kingdom Trust (f. 1913) commissioned Professor W.G.S. Adams of Oxford in 1915 to prepare a report *Library Provision and Policy*. This report paid generous tribute to the Carneige benefactions, "which have had," it declared, "far-reaching influence on the library movement in the United Kingdom, and have made possible at many centres a development which would not otherwise have come into existence". There was, it was stressed, "still wide scope for development in the system of town libraries". The Trust readily acted upon Adams' chief recommendations that attention should be given to the neglected rural areas and that the County Education Authority would be the most appropriate body to control rural library provision.

By and large, the years fron about 1880 to the break-out of the First World War was a great age of library benefactions. Small-scale gifts and bequests of books or money were common, and there were many more substantial donations to provide for building also. The library service was, however, curtailed during the war.

Library history from the close of the First World War until 1965 was dominated by a single Public Libraries Act, that of 1919 to which we many turn.

The Act of 1919 : County Libraries.

Before the enactment of this Act, there were two demands: first to abolish the rate limitation, and second, to empower county councils to act as authorities.

The Public Libraries Act of 1919 authorized the local authorities to spend on public libraries, as much as they could choose and abolish the penny rate system once for all. This act greatly influenced the course of public library movement in England and Wales. By authorizing Country Councils to become library authorities, the Act made possible the provision of library service throughout the length and breadth of the country. The smaller towns were to be provided with the branch libraries and the more remote districts being served by travelling vans. As a result, millions of inhabitants were brought within the reach of public library service.

Secondly, by removing the crippling penny-rate limitation, the Act enabled public libraries to make the most permanent contribution to Britain's growth. The penny-rate was hardly sufficient to pay for the maintenance of the library building, its heating, lighting, cleaning, repair, the cost of newspaper, journals and wages of staff, inadequate as they were. The funds available for the purchase of books were usually meager and consequently no real service could be provided except in large towns. But the Act of 1919 provided :

—the basic ingredients for an adequate public library service-
no arbitrary limit on expenditure was imposed;

—the provision of the county as well as urban service; and

—a voluntary means of getting rid of impoverished and completely inadequate small town libraries to the county libraries.

The efficiency or otherwise of the public library structure was to be determined :

—by the viability of the local government;

—by the advice and encouragement, if any given by the central government; and

—by a professional organization competent to present the case for public libraries at local and central government levels

What was lacking in this Act was a means of coercing the backward authority to do better or enforcing any approved standards of service.

As a result of this Act, public library coverage was greatly extended by the inauguration of the County Library Movement and by the fact that the amount to be spent upon public library provision rested upon the decision of the local authorities.

It must, however, be recorded that the county libraries could hardly have been born in less auspicious circumstances, for the years immediately following the 1919 Act were years of political instability, economic depression and industrial strife. L.R. McColvin in his war-time report to the Library Association highlighted the haphazard and un-coordinated basis of public library structure and variations in library provision and efficiency. Overall qnality of book-stock was found to be poor and there was need for better opportunities for their training. The Act did not have any coercive power to force the small libraries facing financial difficulties to merge themselves with the bigger ones, though it contained such a provision.

Kenyan Committee

On Oct., 8, 1924, the Board of Education appointed a Committee under the chairmanship of Sir F.C. Kenyan with the following terms of reference :

—to explore the adeqnacy of the Public Libraries Acts and the means for extending them throughout England and Wales;

—to examine the relationship existing between the libraries established under the Acts vis-a-vis those provided for by other agencies; and

—to investigate the general system of education in the country[3].

In persuance of its terms of reference, Kenyan Committee recommended :

—that a balanced system should be built up on vountary basis, financial burden should be shared by the participating libraries and the voluntary cooperation should be encouraged in the adjoining areas;

—that the public libraries should be grouped together on regional basis in which the biggest or the richest urban library in the area would be the central library;

—that not only the public libraries but also special libraries should be knit together in a federation and they should pool together their resources and education;

—that in addition to regional basis there should be central committee for the creation of cooperation among the different libraries;

—that the National Central Library for students be converted into the National Central Library and attached to the British Museum for lending of libraries; and

—that special provision must be made for the recruitment and training of librarians. For attracting brilliant people to join librarianship, attractive grades and professional status be given.

Happily, many recommendations of this Committee were accepted. The National Central Library for students was converted into the National Central Library; coordination of libraries was also done; and courses for the training of library were started. The greatest importance of the Report, perhaps. lies in the fact that it "marks the definite acceptance of Public Libraries as part of the educational equipment of the country", and "the stage is passed when Public Libraries can be scoffed at as doing little but provide second-rate fiction for the use of the idle and the foolish."[4] Indeed, this Report is the turning point towards the obvious significance of the British public library.

3. Britain. Board of Education. Report on public libraries in England and Wales (HMSO, 1927).

4. F.G. Kenyon, Libraries and museums (1930), p. 40, cf. W.J, Murison, *The Public* libraries (George G. Harrp, 1955), p. 86.

In September 1957, the Minister of Education appointed a committee under the chairmanship of Dr. S.C. Roberts (after wards Sir Sydney Roberts) "to consider the structure of the public library service in England and Wales, and to advice what changes, if any, should be made in the administrative arangements, regard being had to the relation of public libraries to other libraries"

After a careful review of the problem the Committee recommended :

—that every library authority should spend at least a sum of 2 shilling per head or 5000 pounds (whichever is higher) for the purpose of purchasing books alone;

—that the Miniter of Education should be made responsible for the efficient operation of public libraries;

—that the scheme of library cooperation on the regional level be maintained;

—that the cost of regional library should be borne by the local library authority;

—that the salary of staff should be fixed keeping in view their status and qualifications; and

—that service of the public library was to be free of the charge.

The Committee desired that an act be enacted to achieve these objectives.

The Report was published in 1959. The Minister of Education appointed two Working Parties of librarians to advise him on future legislation based on Roberts Committee's recommendations. In December 1962, these Working Parties' Reports were issued under the titles : (1) Inter-Library Cooperation in England and Wales; and (2) Standards of Public Library Service in England and Wales. Subsequently the Minister introduced a Bill based on Roberts' Committee Report into the Parliament which resulted in the Public Libraries and Museums Act 1964. This Act came into force on April 1, 1965 and replaced the Acts of 1892, 1893, 1901, and 1919.

The Act placed upon the Secretary of State for Education and Science[5] the duty "to superintend, and promote the improvement of, the public library service", and upon every library authority the duty to provide "a comprehensive and efficient service".

5. The Dept. of Education and Science, headed by a Secretary of State, took the place of the Ministry of Education, 1964.

However, the greatest changes in library organization and service have come about not through library legislation but through local government reforms, thus, demonstrating priorities in the mind of the law-makers. Though the local government legislation has been beneficial to libraries on the whole, they have lost a certain measure of independence in having to be regarded as just one of many departments run by a local authority. Their interests are now linked with those of education or recreation; they have become financial pawn in the battle for local government subsides from the government, and are afflicted by a welter of different management theories.

Despite some limitations, the Act is a great landmark in the steady development of the public library system in Britain. With this Act, as Thomas Kelly says, 'the Central Government for the first time assumed responsibility for the supervision of the library service'. And by the late 1960s about 30% of the population of Britain were registered library users, 'making Great Britain one of the most library conscious nations in the world'[6].

The Local Government Act, 1972, which came in into force on April, 1974 divided the country for the purposes of library services into six metropolitan counties with a population ranging between 1.2 million to 2.8 millions; and thirty non-metropolitan counties with a population of 300,000 to 1.5 millions. As a result of this Act, not only small local authorities lost their library powers but also some very large provincial libraries found themselves transferred to the non-metropolitan counties. Economic viability of the library authority is the major consideration of this local government Act.

The public libraries of Britain organized in a systematic and economically viable units, and administered by efficient and energetic personnel is a model to follow. Britain today is served by a network of public libraries.

6. E.D. Johnson, History of libraries in the Western world, 2nd ed., (1970), p. 2.

12

PUBLIC LIBRARIES IN U.S.A.

It is a historical fact that the 'modern library idea' did indeed achieve its full vigour and stature in American hands. Belief that universal education is essential for the welfare of the American Republic; belief in the power of books as a deterrent from vice and a source of education and culture; all this form the bed-rock of American public libraries. To this has been added a slowly growing conviction that only a free library could meet the needs of modern society; a library which should ignore the distinctions of class; and a library offering equal privileges to all the residents of the community maintaining it.

Experience has taught that this library could not be successfully imposed upon the people by authority. For such an institution to accomplish its whole purpose, it must be in the highest sense popular. That is, it must have directly engaged in its formation and use the whole people. If such work is to be done all are to come to it as having an equal or a common interest in it. This institution can only exist through the enthusiasm of the people, and it can be created by that in a moment[1]. The American public library can have no better characterization than the words graven on the present home of the Public Library of the City of Boston :

> Built by the people and dedicated to the advancement of learning.

Arthur E. Bostwick views the development of the public library in U.S.A. as being not only important in American terms, but in a universal context also. He maintains that the American contribution lies not merely in the great impetus that is given there to 'the idea of a collection of books for the use of an entire community, supported by that community from the proceeds of

1. C. Slymour Thompson. *Evolution of the American public library*, 1653-1876.

the tax', but essentially in the "modern library idea"; that is, characteristics such as "freedom of access to shelves, work with children, cooperation with schools, branch libraries, travelling libraries, and the so-called 'library advertising'—the effort to make the library and its work known in the community and to induce people to use it".

To appreciate the contemporary American Public Library Movement one has to trace its origins in the nineteenth century alongwith the socio-economic and political influence which moulded its development. The nineteenth century was period of industrial revolution, territorial expansion, growth of population, and national prosperity. As J.H. Shera has put it : Historical scholarship and the urge to preservation, the power of national and local pride, the growing belief in the importance of universal education, the increasing concern with vocational problems, and the contribution of religion—these aided by economic ability and encouraged by the example of Europe, were the casual factors in the formation of libraries that would be free to all the people[2]. In brief, the Public Library Movement in U.S.A. sprang forth in response to the American commitment to equal educational opportunity and in her democratic beliefs in the rights of individual in freedom of thought and expression, the strive for intellectual excellence, to participate in the political process, to improve vocational capabilities, and the pursuit of happiness.

In U.S.A., the first free library supported from the public funds and opened without distinction to all classes of the community, was established in Peterborough (New Hampshire) in 1833.

In 1848 the City of Boston was empowered to establish and maintain a tax-supported free public library. It opened its doors to all its inhabitants over the age of sixteen on March 20, 1854. Its founders exhibited a breadth of view which justly entitles them to be called the fathers of public library movement.

At the time, when Boston Public Library law was shaping this library, the State Legislature of New Hampshire passed permissive legislation (1849) enabling towns to levy taxes for the support of libraries. Massachussets passed permissive legistation for the

2. Jesse H. Shera *Foundations of the public libraiy* (Chicago Univ. Press, 1949), p. 243.

entire state in 1851. It was followed by Maine (1854); Vermount (1865); Rhode Island and Connecticut (1867); and New York (1872).

Development of libraries and library laws was greatly accelerated after 1880 by the organization of Library Commissions which were established by the states to assist in establishing libraries and to improve their services. Around 1900 A.D. these Commissions became concerned with extending library service to rural areas and promoted a series of laws to secure acceptance of townships and counties as larger and more efficient units of library service.

In 1895 was created the illustrious New York Public Library. Though started as a reference library, it achieved its circulation function on Jan. 8, 1901.

The Public Library Movement in USA was greatly stimulated by the philanthropy of wealthy men and women. The Prince benefactor of libraries was, of course, Andrew Carneige. His grants were mostly utilized for the construction of library buildings to the tune of 1946 in number all over U.S.A.

1876 is a great landmark year in the history of library science. A.L.A. was founded to promote library interests in U.S.A. Melvil Dewey's Decimal Classification, and C.A. Cutter's Rules for making a Dictionary Catalogue were born. Melvil Dewly also started a library science school at Columbia College in 1887. The American Library Journal was also put into circulation.

At the turn of the nineteenth century, there was an increasing interest in public libraries, in the extension of library services on local, county, state levels and in the training of personnel to operate libraries. The first county library was set in Ohio in 1898, followed by other states like Philadelphia. Twenty states established their library laws.

The dawn of the twentieth century saw the publication of U.D C. Book mobile service was floated in 1905 by the County Library in Van Wert (Ohio). The Washington County Free Library in Maryland initiated book-wagon service in 1907.

The first two decades of the present century were also significant for making advances in the municipal public library's programme. Such activities as children's departments, open shelves, cooperation with the public schools, extended hours of service, subject departmentalization, and the establishment of branch libraries were initiated. The purpose of a branch library is to give as much service to as many citizens in its area as possible.

The First Great World War provided an opportunity to the public library to make a distinguished contribution to the community and the nation, and it responded by serving as an agency of War publicity for the government; aiding in the Americanization of aliens; and providing library facilities for soldiers' hospitals, the handicapped, and the blind. The emphasis on democracy focussed attention upon the essentiality of an informed electorate in a democratic society and gave new importance to the educational role of the public library—a role which assumed greater proportion by the enfranchisement of women in 1920. The public library's efforts to meet these needs grew into a planned programme of adult education; informational or educational services to industrial and commercial organizations and to special groups, such as factory workers, national and racial groups, immigrants, and migratory workers; and library sponsored group programmes on books or films, forums, lectures, story-telling, concerts, etc.

Public library service to the public schools expanded during 1940s. Such service includes not only throwing open library's collections and facilities to students and teachers, but also lending boxes of books, setting up school libraries solely by the public library and the public librarian, instructing students in the use of library materials, giving book-talks and arranging story-telling for children, and assisting teachers in the evaluation and selection of materials to supplement the curriculum.

During the Second World War, the public libraries helped the citizens to become enlightened on the issues involved by disseminating information. It also extended new services to government, commercial and industrial houses; sponsored programmes for both recreational and cultural work; provided services to transient groups of workers; and acted as a clearing house of information pertaining to the war efforts.

The essential services and functions of the public libraries in U.S.A. involve :

- logical organization of documents for making them easily, freely, and equally available to all;

—guidance to individuals in the use of educational, recreational, and informational documents;

—providing informational and referral service; and

—assistance to civic, cultural, and educational organizations in locating and using materials for programme planning projects and education of members; sponsoring cultural programmes in library for chiidren, young people. and adults; collecting special materials of interest to the community; borrowing materials on inter-library-loan; inter pretation of materials through publicity, display, reading lists, story-hours, book talks, book and film discussion; extending library service to all points of the community through branches, deposit stations, and book mobiles; organizing library for specialized service into subject departments and coordinating the iibrary programme with other educational institutions (viz., schools, colleges, Churches, theatres, art galaries, clubs, etc.) in the community.

The public library in U.S.A., in 1970s moved actively to take documents and programmes to the very door of the people who were not habituated to visiting the libraries. In particular, it has found that it can make a particular contribution to enriching the lives of men and women over the age of 65. They are provided with books of special interests and books that supply information they need in order to solve their new problems. These libraries also create entirely new interests for them through clubs or disscussion groups that meet in the library. Service is also given to patients in hospitals, blind readers and other shut-ins in their homes.

The American public library has become actively involved in continuing education. Its role as an agency of public communication is to serve the group of adults whose interest, will, and ability lead them to seek personal enrichment and enlightenment. It also serves as the resource centre for those enrolled in the 'Open University' courses. Public librarv services for adults revolve around four major functions :

—information and bibliographic services;

—guidance and advisory services;

—orientation and instruction in library resources and their use; and

—stimulation of the library's pubiic to intensified use of the library resources and services.

The major objectives of the American public librarv are education, information, aesthetic appreciation, research and recreation. But in essence they are two : to promote enlightened citizenship and to enrich personal life. It includes the stimulation for self-education. In particular, the public library provides the opportunity, the materials and encouragement for upkeeping the cherished ideals of American democratic process of group life, and the sanctity and dignity of the individual freedom. In the light of the tremendous contributions made by the American public library, Lowell Martin hails it as "an organ of social democracy and an instrument of personal self-realization".

Laws providing for the establishment, maintenance, and operation of various types of libraries are found in the federal government; in the constitutions and statutes of the states, and the charters and ordinances of municipalities.

The Federal Laws govern National Archives, the Library of Congress, the Library of Medicine, the National Agricultural Library, the libraries of the districts of Columbia, and those of the various federal departments, bureaus and independent agencies—such as the Supreme Court, the Departments of State, Commerce; the Central Intelligence Agency; the Ferderal Bureau of Investigation, the Bureau of the Budget; military, academic, public, special, and highly specialized and technical and scientific research libraries.

As a public agency, the public library is authorised by state laws, supported from special taxes voted for the purpose; and administered for the benefit of the citizens of the city, town, county, or region which maintains it on the basis of equal access to all. Public library service is not mandatory in any state, but all states have general permissive legal authorization for the establishment and maintenance of public libraries.

Each city or town in turn operates its own library system and and under the powers given to it by state laws, taxes itself for maintenance.

Some other kinds of state laws relating to public libraries may be noted :

—General laws relating to municipalities, which may include sections relating to establishment of libraries.

—Separate acts for eaeh kind of public library—municipal, county, regional or multi-county.

—Special legislation concerning particular cities, which may include sections relating to libraries if a Commission form of government is established.

—Special state legislation concerning a particular library such as that which establisned the Boston Public Library.[3]

The Library Service Act was passed by the Congress in 1956; it was amended in 1964 to become the Library Services and Construction Act. It resulted in the institution of service to many un-reserved rural people, in service to the disadvantaged, in upgrading of services at the state level, and in a great number of new library buildings.

Among other important factors in public library development were the development of Standards for Public Libraries in 1933, 1943, 1956 and 1966 by American Library Association. Each set of standards reflected fresh concepts of service or organization.

The 1966 *Minimum Standards for Public Library Systems* describes the least services, the citizen has a right to except from his public library.

Library standards are sharpened by the library scientists themselves and then accepted at state or local level without official authorization. "On one hand", writes Lowell Martin, "are noble professional pronouncements for public libraries; on the other hand, are local laws and traditions which allow each library to be just as poor or 'un-standard' as it wants to be, or more precisely, as poor as its local constituency is willing to tolerate".

Despite the distinctive eontributions of American Public to their culture and civilization, it is beset with a number of problems. Financial support is not keeping pace with increasing costs; and the libraries are under great pressures to give service in more breadth and depth to a wide range of users who vary in age, education and interests. They are limited in their ability to tap new technological sources of information and they are constrained from up-grading their present manual methods to automatic systems. In many instances, these problems have

3. Carleton Bruns Joeckel. *The Government of the American Public library* (Chicago Univ. Press, 1935).

caused the public library to expand its normal resource sharing activity by affiliating with technical processing cooperatives, depending on larger libraries for back-up, expanding inter-library relationships, and joining public library systems and net-works outside their local jurisdictions.

Notwithstanding the limitations of American Public Libraries, no other country could successfully transplant to its own shores the public library system of tne United States, but every country can learn from their experience and can profit from their failures and successes.

American librarians have an unshakable faith in education and the power of the printed word, and as a class they can almost be said to believe that only books and good reading are going to save the world from thermo-nuclear holocaust. As a conseqence of this faith in the contributions that libraries can make to better life, the Americans have left no stone unturned to excel themselves in their libraries.

In brief, public library in the United States is one of the most important servants of its community. It provides knowledge and information on all subjccts for everyone. The strength of public library is its democracy, its service to all people across age, ethnic, economic and cultural lines. It caters to the needs of children, young adults, and senior citizens; and it is a major educational force in American life. Public libraries including smallest, are the backbone of the library system in America, and are the potential windows on any future nation-wide network. Therefore, a great deal depends upon the strength of their human and material resources and on their ability to undertake new programmes of value to their constituents. Most public libraries are well below the A.L.A.'s standards and are inadequate to meet the information needs of the public.

Still, public library in the United States is one of the most important servants of its community. It provides knowledge and information on all subjects for everyone as far as possible. It serves as a centre for arousing and stimulating intellectual curiosity and the desire to learn, and offering materials and programmes to satisfy their hunger for knowledge. Stated in the broadest terms, thc American Public Library, is at once "Calvinistic, deistic, and egalitarian". In fact, the modern public library system reached its zenith in U.S.A.

13

LIBRARY LEGISLATION

A Critical Appreciation

A public library is a social institution. It is owned and maintained by the public of its area for the socialization of its books and kindered materials. Socialization means that no charge is made on per-book basis for the books used by readers.

A stable, uniform, efficient, pulsating and integrated library service can be secured only through a properly laid-out and well-supported state-wide net-work of library system. Library legislation becomes highly necessary for the establishment and orderly functioning of a net-work of library system.

Legislation is as necessary for the constitution of proper supervisory, advisory and administrative machinery as it is for the provisions of steady and perennial sources of finance, The library authorities are so constituted that they become responsive to the public. The legislation, thus, saves libraries from becoming pawns in the hands of bureaucracy.

Statutory provisions of finance also saves public libraries from the whirlpool of party politics, and ensures the provision of universal, standard and adequate library service which may offer to adults and children the opportunity to keep in touch and up-to-date with the progress in sciences and arts. Therefore, to have an effective, and integrated library service system, the public libraries must be kept immune from political ups and downs and parties' caprice. They should be maintained from funds collected from whole tax-paying community and administered by its representatives.

Speaking broadly, the legislation lays down the structure, ensures its development on an approved pattern, and prevents its haphazard growth following the whims and fancies of politicians and administrators. The legislation sets up the proper government or management of libraries, and ensures that the authorities in-charge of libraries are so constituted that they are responsible for the implementation of the law, and are ultimately accountable to the legislature or representatives of the people. The legislation provides for the financial support on a stable and a progressive basis. These elements—structure, management and finance—, are so important that they should be placed on a firm legal footing. Otherwise, the danger is that they become toys in the hands of administrators[1].

Throughout the world legislation has been the potent source of library development. The principle that the library is an educational concern of the state should be established beyond question. In fact, some states of U.S.A. have incorporated in their constitutions the responsibilily on the state "to promote the establishment and development of free public libraries and, to accept the obligation of their support by the state and its sub-divisions and municipalities in the preambles to their library laws"

The Unesco Regional Seminar of Library Development in South Asia (1960) highlighted the need of library legislation in the following resolution :

> This seminar recommends member States to enact library legislation for the establishment of public library based on local taxation with national and state aid to guarantee a basic minimum of funds for public library.

The Report of the Advisory Committee of Libraries (India, 1959), too, recommended a comprehensive State Library Law because it will bring homogeneous and unified library service to the State and it will ensure statutory recognition of State responsibility for the maintenance of public libraries in the State.

The Working Group of Libraries appointed by the Planning Commission (India) urged the need of library legislation. It was stated that "the Group is unanimous and firm,...that there is no alternative to library legislation".

The library legislation for the establishment and orderly functioning of a network of public library is, in any case, an

1. S. Das Gupta, "Library Development of India". *Library Herald* (v. 3, April, 1960) pp. 7-8.

essential condition for the growth of the public library movement. Through library legislation, the State recognizes its responsibility to establish and maintain the public libraries as its statutory obligation.

Objectives

The library law should provide the free public library service with the following objectives :

—to house materials giving reliable information and wholesome recreation;

—to organize them so as to promote their use; and

—to stimulate non-readers to be readers and readers to be purposive students[2].

Functions

Five functions of library legislation may be noted :

—It should clearly define the government's responsibility in the matter of public libraries.

—Legislation should lay down the constitution and functions of the library authority at national, state and district levels.

—Legislation should provide an assured basis for library finance. There are two ways of providing a firm basis for library finance :

(i) a special librarary cess; and.

(ii) reservation of a certain percentage of the education budget.

—Legislation should lay down in outline the structure of the public library system.

—Legislation should provide for participation of the representatives of the public in the work of the public libraries at all levels.[3]

Factors Governing Good Library Legislation

'The development of public Sibrary Services'—a working paper prepared by the Public Libraries Section of IFLA lists the following factors in a Library Act to ensure proper library development.

2. Regional Seminar on library development in South Asia.
3. Advisory Committee, Report, op. cit.

—Appropriate local authorities must be empowered to expend public funds for public library purposes.

—The amount of expenditure should not be limited.

—The public library puposes for which funds may be expended shall be so defined as not to restrict development.

—Local authorities should be empowered to enter into arrangements with other authorities for joint schemes for providing the whole or any part of the service.

—Each local authority should appoint a library committee directly responsible to the local council. The librarian should have the right to attend all meetings of the library committee....

—Each local authority should have the power to appoint staff who shall be employed in accordance with the conditions and regulations applicable with suitable variations to other local government officers.

—The use of all the services provided must be available to all inhabitants free of any charge whatsoever.

—Though each local authority provides services primarily for the use of its own inhabitants and those who work or study in its area, other persons, living outside that area, should be able to use those services if they wish—.

—As soon as practicable, all appropriate local authorities should be legally obliged to maintain adequate public library services.

—All public libraries should give users 'open access' to adequate stocks of books for reference and for borrowing.

—Library staff must be recruited from persons with a good general education and must be professionally qualified.

—Library staffs must be adequately remunerated—.

—Scales of salaries should provide for the varying degrees of responsibility, specialization, and experience involved in the several positions found on the establishment of library systems of different sizes and types; and adequate opportunities for promotion and personal growth and advancement must exist.

—The number of staff employed by each authority must be sufficient to permit all necessary duties to be carried out completely and satisfactorily.

—Schools of library science must be maintained.

—The existence of a well-organized Library Association is essential.

—Where the above requirements are not met, the service for the public as a whole suffers gravely.

—Probably the most important factor in determining the state of library development is the way in which the functions of public libraries are understood by librarians and authorities and by the public itself. If the accepted conception of the service is that it is a natural, essential element in the life of any civilized progressive community, it will be supported by all men of goodwill[3].

Another library scientist enumerates the following factors which a good library legislation should contain.

—The library legislation must be both simple and general. It should allow for future development, without giving opportunity for misrepresentation.

—It must as for as possible be kept above accidents of political changes.

—The law must make library services possible, encourage development, and ensure that libraries shall be provided.

—It should coordinate library activities and control them in full recognition of the people's right to free access to the means of knowledge and factual information.

—The law should stipulate the duties and privileges of public libraries and above all, the terms of financial assistance that they should receive from public authorities.

—The law must make clear the respective responsibilities of local, state and national administration in respect of public libraries.

—The law may provide either for the state establishment of libraries or state aid when local governments are managing them. The library service may be made compulsory if the financial resources of the district are adequate.

—The law must prescribe that public libraries should be free to one and all. The law should also provide for public library resources to be supplemented by those of academic, specialized and scientific libraries.

—All libraries should lend their books free of charge to all citizens in the country in accordance with an approved scheme for cooperation between libraries.

3. cf *Library Advisory Committee*, Report, op. cit., p. 142-43,

—The books in stock should cover every shade of opinion. Censorship should apply only to the type of books which would incite crime and violence. The law should also include a provision for the establishment of libraries for children, and school, for the sick, and the aged, for the blind, for the defence service and merchant marine. The library Act should allocate different tasks to different types of libraries in order to ensure more economical administration, rationalization of methods, specilization in subject fields and altogether a better service to the community as a whole[4].

The acid test of the efficacy of library legislation will be the extent to which its provisions are practically implemented. Library Act passed by five states of India, contain the essential factors in one or the other form. An attempt is made in the following pages to critically evaluate the Public Libraries Acts passed by the five states, viz., Madras, Andhra Pradesh, Mysore, Maharashtra and West Bengal.

1. MADRAS PUBLIC LIBRARIES ACT, 1948

The Madras Public Libraries Act, 1948 came into force on 1 April, 1950.

The objectives of the Act are contained in its Preamble as 'an Act to provide for the establishment of public libraries in the Province of Madras and the organization of a comprehensive rural and urban library service therein'.

Strangely enough, the terms "Development" after the word "establishment"; and "System" after the word "public libraries" are omitted in the Preamble. "Maintenance" of libraries, established with a view to their systemic development is not only desirable but necessary in order to ensure homogeneous and healthy growth, failing which libraries will remain static and cease to have any appeal for the users. In order to utilize the resources of other classes of libraries (viz., Academic and Special, and even privately owned libraries), the Act should have extended its jurisdiction to cover such libraries. As no library can be fully self-sufficient in collection of materials and be provided with unlimited finances, it is always a distinct advantage for a small library to draw on resources of the big libraries. The Public Libraries and Museums Act, 1964, of Britain stands as a guide-post in this respect.

4. C.O. Houle, *Libraries in adult and fundamental* education (Paris, Unesco, 1956).

Section by section comments may be noted. Section 1 of the Act contains short title, extent and commencement.

Section 2(1-9) deals with the definitions of the terms—'Aided Eibrary', 'Director', 'District', 'Government', 'Notification', 'Prescribed', 'State', 'Public Library' and 'Year'.

Obviously, the Act contains definitions which should not ordinarily form a part of a legislative Act. The Act does not make any distinction between 'State' and 'Government'.

Section 3 of the Act stipulates the purpose and scope as well as the functions of the Provincial Library Committee, advisory in nature and consisting of 17 members. The Act does not provide for the Provincial Library Authority.

Ironically, it is also not clear whether the Provincial Library Committee is to be the State Library Authority or the Government, i.e. the Minister of Education or the Director of Public Libraries of the Province, who is appointed by the government and who is invested with a large range of powers to control the public libraries. It is most desirable that either an independent Ministry of Libraries or Ministry of Education be designated as "State Library Authority". It is better to choose Ministery of Education as the State Library Authority, as it is profitable to link libraries and education at the state level. But the libraries should not be made subordinate to the formal educational programme of the state. A.R. Hewitt has rightly commented that the Minister of State (Education) should be the library authority as a Minister is responsible to his parliament (and through it to the electors) and may be called upon to account for therein. It is desirable, of course, that the Minister has an obligation under the Act to seek expert advice and guidance for discharging his duties; an advisory council would be desirable.

A possible alternative to the ministrial authority is the constitution of a state library board with wide representation and powers to grant, direct, and control finance and policy. It would be satisfactory if the present Provincial Library Committee be made the State Library Authority after enlarging the scope of its authority over all matters pertaining to the public libraries.

Section 4 deals with the appointment of the libraries' Director and his duties. The Director will be appointed by the government and he shall be subject to their control. His duties will be to:

(a) manage the Central Library and its branches; (b) superintend and direct the affairs of the public libraries; (c) declare what public libraries are eligible for government aid; (d) superintend and control the work of all local library authorities under the Act; and (e) submit annually a report on the working of public libraries to the government.

Keeping in view the vast powers vested in him, it is obvious that the success or failure of the public libraries in the state will largely depend upon his professional calibre, merit, personality, sincerity and dedication to the profession. But strargely enough, the Director of Public Institutions (D.P.I.) was made an ex-officio Director of Public Libraries. The D.P.I. is a member of bureaucracy, and investing too much power in him is a dangerous thing.

Creditably, wisdom seems to have descended on the mind of the government and a separate Directorate of Public Libraries has been set up since 1972. For one thing, the myth of D.P.I. as the veritable chimera has to be blown out once for all.

Section 5 deals with the constitution of local library authorities—one Local Library Authority for the City of Madras and one each for the districts of the State. These Authorities are responsible for providing public library service in their respective areas. As the public library system is to be free from personal or political considerations, library authority is likely to prove more successful.

Ironically, the District Education Officer (D.E.O.) has been appointed the Ex-officio Secretary of the Local Library Authority. Doubtlessly, libraries are more akin to education and have to be linked with it at some stage or other. But as Ranganathan[5] has aptly remarked that the D.E.O. has proved a fifth wheel almost in every district. His hands are quite full with the inspection of schools. He cannot be expected to feel the delicate pulse of library service. He cannot evaluate correctly many of the legimate activities of the library. As a matter of fact, in many a district, he looks upon the District Librarian either as a competing step-brother whose wings should be ruthlessly clipped or as a subordinate on whom his own toes should for ever press[5]. The solution of the problem lies in appointing the librarians of the City Central Libraries in case of City Library Authorities and that of District

5. Ranganathan, *Library Herald*, 2 : 3 (Jan., 60.)

Central Libraries in case of Rural Library Authorities as the Secretary of the Local Library Authorities[6].

Section 6 lays down the procedure of Incorporation of Library Authorities and their general powers. This section empowers sufficiently a Local Library Authority for discharging its duties.

Section 7 of the Act pertains to the mode of appointment and powers of the Executive Committees and Sub-Committees of Local Library Authorities.

Section 8 governs the procedure of submission of schemes for instituting libraries and for spreading library service within an area by the Local Library Authority for approval and sanction of the Director (now fortunately Director of Public Libraries), who is empowered to alter, modify or approve the scheme.

Section 9 discusses the Powers of Local Library Authorities in respect of provision of land, buildings, furniture, etc. for the public libraries; collections; staff; gifts; lectures and the like.

Too much attention should not have been paid for the provision of the works and specimen of art and sciences as it is likely to convert the library into a museum and obstruct its basic objectives. *Section 10* deals with the vesting of all property in the Local Library Authority of that area.

Section 11 enumerates the Regulations that a Local Library Authority can make, in order to implement the Act; and without prejudice to the generality of the power such regulations may provide for, among others,

(i) the admission of the public to public libraries in its area on such conditions and on payment of such fees as it may specify;

(ii) requiring from persons desiring to use such libraries any guarantee or security against injury to or misuse, destruction or loss of the property of such libraries.

In a developing country like India where about 35% of the people live below the poverty line, intellectual wants are not as pressing as those of bread and butter. An average Indian often feels that he can do without books and reading. His intellectual wants are quite fleeting and, therefore, the levy of fees for the use of public library service may have a crippling effect on the use of library books. The public libraries should be maintained wholly from public funds, and no direct tax should be made on anyone for its services.

6. For change, *see*, p. 161 infra.

A security or guarantee for any possible damage or loss of books by the users may be found necessary for safe return of books by the users. Bnt such a practice is likely to bring down the number of prospective and potential users of the library. It would be advisable either to amend or delete this clause. Till that time, its use should only be for a person whose bonafide is in doubt. The law of contract could be invoked for the realization of compensation, if necessary.

Sections 12, 13 and 14 deals with the Finance and Accounts of the Local Library Authorities.

Section 12(1-a) empowers a Local Library Authority to levy in its area a library cess in the form of surcharge on the property tax or house tax so levied. Section 12(1-b) empowers the said Authority to enhance the rate specified in (1-a).

Making the property tax as the sole basis for library cess is quite an anachronism in the new tax pattern prevalent in the country. There are now more elastic sources available such as octroi, professional tax, and basic revenue. It is not desirable to make the property tax-payer carry the entire burden of the library cess. Moreover, the rate of 3 pies of a rupee levied as library cess is quite insufficient for the proper development of library services. Although the rate of cess has been enhanced from 3 pies to 5 paise per rupee since 1972 under section 12(2) of the Act, yet it is quite in order to tap other elastic sources of taxation.

Under Section 13(3) the Government's contribution to the Library Fund maintained by every Local Authority, other than the Local Library Authority for the City of Madras is fixed at a sum not less than that collected as library cess.

The complete refusal of state aid to the Local Library Authority of the City of Madras reveals the disparity in the policy of State financial aid. This is bound to create a feeling of dissatisfaction amongst the tax-payers of the City of Madras as having to pay for library purposes without getting anything in return from the state ex-chequer for library is quite irksome. Nevertheless, the diverson of this subsidy to smaller Local Library Authorities will definitely improve the financial stability of the smaller libraries, and thus result in equalization of library services to the entire population. Moreover, as Advisory Committee for Libraries has suggested that the State Government should contribute its share "three times the cess collected". The initial cost of the building and of book stock should be borne by the Union Government.

Section 15 authorizes the Government to reconstitute any Library Authority constituted under the Act. Section 16 requires that Every Local Library Authority or aided library shall submit returns, reports and information to the Director of Public Libraries. Section 17 deals with the inspection of libraries. Section 18 authorises the Government to make rules and regulations in order to carry out the object of the Act.

Section 19 is miscellaneous. It contains **Amendment** of the Press and Registration of books Act, 1867, in its application to to the Province. The amendment requires that instead of one copy, five copies of a book printed by a printer or a press are to be delivered to the government which shall deposit four copies in the Central Library of the State and dispose of the fifth copy as it determines.

This section of the Act overburdens the publishers because the Delivery of Books Act, 1954 (amended in 1956) directs every publisher to deposit 4 copies free of charge. It is doubtful if all the Indian publishers are so honest that they will deposit all their publications of high cost with the deposit library.

Present Position and Critical Appreciation

The over-all picture of the public iibrary system in Tamil Nadu may be briefly projected.

Connemara Public Library is the State Central Library. It is priviledged under Delivery of Books Act, 1954 to get one copy of each book published in India and one copy of each book published in the State as provided under Section 19. Immediately below the State Central Library are the District Libraries, Branch Libraries and Village Libraries.

Each of 16 revenue districts (except the district of Kanyakumari) has got one District Central Library to serve the needs of the district library. It means that there are 15 Local Library Authorities, and one Local Library Authority for the City of Madras.

In addition 1,459 branch libraries render a comprehensive library service to the urban and rural areas of the district. Where an independent library service unit is not economically viable, people of areas are served through librarchines-mobile libraries (as in the districts of Madras, Coimbatore, Madhurai and Tirunelvely). Delivery station can be started in a village with a population of

1,000. It is managed by a school teacher on a part-time service basis. Students are also engaged for disseminating the literary products at the very doors of the citizens. But in villages having a population of at least 5,000, a branch library may be opend with a full-time librarian to manage its operations. The branch libraries may obtain books from district libraries which in turn replenish their resources from the State Central Library.

A separate Directorate of Public Libraries headed by a practising librarian was set-up in 1972. He manages the Central Library and its branches; superintends and directs the affairs of the public libraries; superintends and controls the work of all Local Library Authorities under the Act; declares what libraries are eligible for government aid; submits to the government every year a report on the working of libraries under the Act and the like.

To improve the library services at the district level the government created and appointed 13 practising librarians as full time District Library Officers in 1977. Moreover, the services of the employees of the Local Library Authorities have been provincialized, that is, they are treated as state government employeses since 1982.

The Director of Public Libraries is the administrative head of public library system in the State. He is assisted by an Assitant Director and a supporting staff of 25.

The District Library System is managed by District Library Officers who were practising librarians before their present assignments. The District Central Libraries are manned by Librarians Grade 1. Each district has one professionally qualified Inspector of Libraries in the cadre of Librarian Grade 1. He is responsible for the inspection, guidance and rectification of branch libraries under the control of the District Library Officer. Each district has got Stock Verification Officer, Grade II, responsible for stock verification in branch libraries. Branch libraries having a stock of 8,000 volumes and above, with 12,000 volumes of annual lending are manned by librarians Grade II and the rest i.e. libraries having the stock of less than 8000 volumes are manned by Librarians, Grade III.

The library cess has been enhanced from 3 pies to 5 paise per rupee since 1972. The government provides full grants for the maintenance of libraries opened under Five Year Plan Schemes in rural areas. A Model Plan of buildings was approved by the Government in 1978. In order to encourage building programme in Municipal town, the Government sanctioned grants to brancn libraries in 1975. In Madras, three circle libraries and five branch libraries have been built.

Notwithstanding its limitations, this Act is a great landmark in the history of library legislation in India. It has generated library consciousness amongst the people of India and has inspired other states to follow suit. The Act has justified the wisdom of those who brought it on the Statute-Book. The organization of library service appears to be more effective in Tamil Nadu than in any other part of India, mainly on account of the Library Act. Slowly but steadily the Act has laid the foundation of a well laid-out and well-supported state wide net-work of public library system in Tamil Nadu.

The Act should extend its jurisdiction to cover academic, special and research libraries. People's representation in Local Library Authorities should be so modifide as to create earnest enthusiasm in the mind of masses. Provision for education and training of library personnel be provided in the Act. The Act should also provide sources of revenue for library buildings, equipment, initial stock of books, and other capital expenditure. Nonetheless, as M.A. Gopinath puts it : "This Model Act is the seed out of which Library Legisiation grew in India".

2. ANDHRA PRADESH PUBLIC LIBRARIES ACT, 1960

The Andhra Pradesh State was formed on Nov. 1, 1956. The Andhra Pradesh Public Libraries Act came into force on April 1, 1960. Prior to its enactment, Madras Public Libraries Act, 1948, and Hydrabad Public Libraries Act, 1955 were applicable to the areas of Andhra Pradesh.

The A.P. Act both resembles and differs from the Madras Public Libraries, Act. The similarities can be observed in respect of the formation of : (a) A State Library Committee; (2) the constitution of Local Library Authorities; (3) the levy of library cess; (4) the maching of State grants to the library cess fund; and a separate Directorate of Public Libraries.

The dissimilarities lie in the improvements. The advances are that :

—the Librarian of the State Library is the member of Library Committee;

—the decentralization of library administration by empowering Zila Granthalaya Samastha (District Library Committee) to provide library service;

—the rate of *library cess* levied has both a minimum and a maximum limit, viz., 4 paise and 8 paise per rupee respectively; but in the case of Madras Act, it was raised to 5 paise only in 1972, but no maximum limit has been specified; and

—permission for the continuation of the functioning of private/subscription libraries aided by the Government.

Section 2 lists definitions of "Committee" 2(2); "Library cess[5]" 2(6); "State Central Library" 2(11) which are not included in the Madras Act'. In the A.P. Act, certain definitions are too obvious to be included, viz , Section 2(6) and and 2(7) relating to the meanings of 'Library Cess' and 'Notification'. Happily, this Act makes a particular mention of the word "Maintenance" in its Preamble, thus, making an improvement upon the Madras Act.

Section 3 deals with the Constitution and Composition of the State Library Committee and its functions. Like the Madras Act, this Act also makes provision for a State Library Committee consisting of 27 members, as against 17 in Madras Library Act. Obviously, this committee of 27 is quite unwieldy and difficult to manage The Amending Act of 1969 changed its composition giving more representation to the professionally qualified persons and also took away the right of co-option of four members by the State Library Committee.

Curiously enough, under Madras Act, the State Central Librarian is not the member of the State Library Committee. The present Act removes this lacuna. This Act provides for a State Central Library. In case of Madras Act, the Connemara Public Library functions as a State Central Library. Moreover, under this Act the Deputy Director of Public Libraries is to work as Secretary of the Committee.

Section 3(3) of A.P. Act states that the "Committee shall advise the Government on all matters arising under this Act and shall exercise and perfom such other powers and duties as may be prescribed". But the Madras Act under its Sec. 3(1) clearly states that the "......Committee shall be constituted by the Government for the purpose of advising them on such matters as they may refer to it". Obviously, the A.P. Act makes it obligatory for the

Government to refer all matters pertaining to libraries to the State Libary Committee; whereas the Madras Act has made it optional. The term of office (Sec. 4) of the members of the State Library Committee was raised from three to five years under the Amending Act of 1969.

Section 8 deals with the Constitution of Public Libraries and appointment of the Director thereof and his duties. Surprisingly, the duties of the Director includes, among others, the publication of the State Bibliography*; arranging of centralized catalouguing and classification; inter-library laws; co-ordinating book-selection and maintaining the copyright registry.

The responsibily for the publication of a ual bibliography and centralized cataloguing and classification should better he entrusted to the State Librarian as the State Library occupies a key position in the library system of the State. These services require professional skill of high order which can be available only at the State Central Library. These services do not feature in Madras Act.

The Amending Act of 1969 makes it obligatory on the part of the Government to submit to the State Legislature the Annual Report on the working of the libraries under the Act in the preceding year. It also requires the Government to create, in accordance with the rules made under this Act, the posts required, in the office of a Zilla Granthalya Samastha and in the public libraries established or maintained by this body. Section 9(3) makes it the legal duty of the Zilla Granthalya Samastha to provide library service in the area of its jurisdiction.

Section 10 enumerates provisions with regard to the constitution of Local Library Authorities in the State. This Act reduces the number of nominated members to almost half of the Madras Act. It has, thus, made Local Library Authorities quite popular, representative, responsive, and responsible to the people.

The Amending Act, 1969, designates the Librarian of the City Central Library, Hydrabad, and the Librarian, District Central Library, as Secretaries of their respective Local Library Authorities, thus, doing away with District Education Officer who was termed as the ex-officio Secretary under Madras Act[7].

Another important Section is 27. It deals with the Amendment to the Press and Registration of Books Act, 1867. It requires

*Books published in the State.

7. Replaced in 1972, p. 161.

the publishers to deposit three copies as against five copies demanded under the Madras Act, Sec. 19.

The State of Ahdhra has a systematic structure of Public Libraries which broadly conforms to the pattern suggested by the Advisory Committee for Libraries. It consists of State Central Library in the City of Hydrabad as an 'apex-library'; 6 Regional Libraries; 23 District Libraries; 794 Branch Libraries manned by part-time workers; 1540 Panchayat Libraries; and 601 Book Delivery Stations.

A Review Committee was appointed by the State Government in 1974 under the Chairmanship of Justice Gopal Rao Ekbote to evaluate the working of the Act and suggests necessary amendments. The most laudable recommendation of the Committee was that the Minister Incharge of the Libraries should be the State Library Authority charged with the duty of implementing the Act. The Director of Public Libraries shall look after the administration of public libraries in the State. The State Central Library should be developed only as a reference and research library. Most of its recommendations were accepted.

The Government of Andhra Pradesh also took note of the private but aided libraries providing library services both in the urban and rural areas in the State where Zilla Granthalya Samasthas could not establish their libraries. A Committee was appointed in July 1978 under the Chairmanship of V. Gopalakrishnayya to review the role played by these aided libraries and suggest measures for obtaining better services from them and also evolve a system of grant-in-aid to Private Libraries. The Committee submitted its report in November 1978 wherein it has recommended norms for identification, grant-in-aid, inspection and recommended norms for reactivating aided library service in the State. The State Government accepted most of its recommendations in 1982.

It cannot, however, be denied that the government aided private libraries result in a parallel library system, particulary when there is no provision to merge them in the regular public library system. This is likely to result in varying standards of library service in the State.

Critical Appreciation

The Andhra Pradesh Public Libraries Act, 1960 is the first of its kind to create a separate Department for Public Libraries in 1961. The State deserves all the praises for appointing a Minister for Libraries. Its enactment has, in fact, engineered an orderly growth and spread of public library services throughout the length and breadth of the State. A net-work of public libraries is offering effective library services to urban and rural people. The library cess collected under the Act and matching grants provided by the government has enabled Zilla Granthalaya Samasthas to establish a well organized public library system under their jurisdiction. But an adequate library service requires adequate funds. The sole basis of library cess in the form of surcharge on property tax at such rate as 5 paise per rupee is quite inadequate in the present time of ever-rising prices of books and other kindered materials. More elastic sources of library cess as on octroi, professional tax, basic revenue. buildings, vehicles, trade, should be tapped.

Notwithstanding, their limited finances, public libraries in the State are becoming the centres of cultural, recreational and informational activities of the community they serve. Some of the public libraries have their own film projectors and audio-equipment Literacy programmes, lectures, conferences, group discussions and exhibitions are also arranged. With the co-operation of the National Library, the State has brought out a bibliography of Telugu books. Union Catalogue of Telugu books and District Catalogues of books are also published. The Director of Public Libraries has also been designated as the ex-officio Registrar of Publications for implementing the provisions of the Registration of Books Act of 1867. Refresher courses for librarians of Regional Libraries and District Libraries are also arranged off and on. District Central Libraries supply books to school students to generate reading habits among the academic budding flowers. Text-books sections are also maintained by the State Central Library, Regional Libraries and even some branch libraries for college students. Almost all the Districts also maintain children libraries. Many libraries maintain children sections as well. Moreover, there are about 22 branch libraries exclusively for ladies and about 50 libraries have ear-marked areas for them. The State Central Library maintains a braille section.

It is obvious that despite its limited finances, the State has build up a reasonably good public library eystem. This Act marked the dawn of a new era in the history of library legislation in India.

3. MYSORE PUBLIC LIBRARIES ACT, 1965

The Mysore Public Libraries Act, came into force on April 22, 1965. It contains 52 sections. Its purpose is to provide for the establishment and maintenance of public libraries and th organization of a comprehensive rural and urban library service in the State of Mysore.

The enactment of this Act has marked the dawn of a brilliant era in the history of library legislation. It has made significant contributions for developing a net-work of public library system in the State. The important highlights of the Act may be noted.

—Its definitions are wide in range and more comprehensive and precise than those found in Madras and Andhra Acts—Sec. 2.

—The Act creates State Library Authority (Sec. 3), though, a corporate one. The principle of Unity of Command requires that the supreme commanding power should be wielded by one person only and exclusively. And this person in case of libraries should be the Education Minister who is responsible to the legislature and ultimately to the people and has a limited term.

In providing the State Library Authority, this Act is ahead of Madras and Andhra Acts as they do not provide for such a library authority; they make provision only for a State Library Committee, having an advisory function. That too is limited because they can advice only on such matters as are referred to them. This creates a serious lacuna because the bureaucracy is in an advantageous position to ignore the Committee by not referring the matter to it. This is dcterimental to progress in a democratic way of life. In comparison, the Mysore Act is an improvement, in so far as it has created an authority in the form of a corporate body. But this does not leave the library development to the caprice of any single government official. In democratic environment, polices regarding educational and library development are likely to emerge from interaction between legislature, executive, pressure groups, and public, with one influencing all others but none determining the out come so that frequently the public approval is given only after the policy has been enacted or has been in operation for some time. Moreover, ironically enough, the State Librarian is not a member of this governing body, though, the Act makes a room for a representative of the State Library Association for membership in this body. Instead of the Minister of Education of Mysore Legislature, as provided in the Andhra Act, an obviously unwieldy Committee has been designated as the State Library Authority.

—The Mysore Act soars high over its predecessors under Section 23(a) which provides a clause which disqualifies a person for being chosen and for being a member of the State Library Authority :

(i) if he has been sentenced by a criminal court for an offence involving moral turpitude and punishable for a term exceeding three months;

(ii) if he is an undischarged insolvent; and

(iii) if he is of unsound mind and stands so declared by a competent court.

The person in office should have an unblemished character and sound mind : This is one of the commendable features of the Act.

—Section 12 is a highly laudable step. It constitutes a Department of Public Libraries with a State Librarian, having the prescribed academic and professional qualifications, as its head. This provision fulfils the long cherished demand, because professionally trained person is better to understand the needs of the people and appreciate their aspirations to satisfy their intellectual needs and banish ignorance to become enlightened citizens. This provision, thus, removes one of the great obstacles in the smooth development of public library system, in as much as it will not get step-motherly treatment of the Department of Public Instructions. The State Librarian who will be leader of the profession, not by virtue of position alone, but because of his professional competency will be able to direct the path of library movement in a more accurate manner.

—Like Andhra Pradesh Act, Section 15 of Mysore Public Library Act contemplates a State-level separate Cadre of Librarians called 'Mysore State Library Service'. All the librarians working throughout the State are considered as State Government servants and enjoy the same privileges.

It bestows a distinct status on the profession and at the same time achieves economy and administrative efficiency. It brings the manpower of the State in one pool and thus avoids the waste of time and money involved in filling up the posts, that would have otherwise been involved if every Local Library Authority were to appoint the staff independently. It further avoids the influence of the members of the Local Library Authority in a day to day management of libraries. The Act, thus, ensures proper administration and economy through State Library Service. The State Library Service is likely to attract brilliant men and women to embrace library profession.

—Under Section 30 (1) a Library Cess in the form of a surcharge on : (i) tax on lands and buildings; (ii) tax on entry of goods into the local area for consumption, use or sale therein; (iii) tax on vehicles; and (iv) tax on professions, trades, callings and employments, is levied in the area within the jurisdiction of every City Library Authority.

Widening of tax base for levy of library cess in case of City Library Authority areas is likely to yield enhanced amount of library finance. But in case of District Library Authority areas, the source of library cess is only from tax on lands and buildings. This may be used as an excuse for providing sub-standard and inadequade library service in the rural areas.

Moreover, the rate of 3 paise per rupee as the surcharge on on the tax is quite small and the maximum limit of 6 paise for every rupee to which it can be enhanced is also contrary to modern international trends. (Sec. 30—2).

—Under Section 31, the State Government shall make annually a grant to every District Library Authority of an amount equal to 3% of the land revenue collected in the district. But curiously, the Act contains no provision for a State contribution to City Library Authorities. Moreover, the State contribution to District Library Authorities should have been at least on the basis of equal grants to City and Distrtct Funds as being provided in Madras and Andhra Acts. Even the working of these two Acts have exposed the inadequacy of the goverment' share in the shape of matching grants. Libraries being spending institutions working in an era of ever-increasing prices require increasing grants if we sincerely want to provide an adequate and standard library service to all the areas.

Notwithstanding the limited finances, it is pleasing to note that the salaries of the library staff in Mysore State Library Service are paid out of the Consolidated Fund of the State (Sec. 15). This provision releases increased sum of money available for library expenditure.

Another remarkable feature of the Act is the provision of library service to the blind. None of the Public Library Laws enacted so far contains such a provision.

—Sec. 17 needs some comments. It makes the element of nomination by the Government conspicuously predominant in the composition of City Libray Authorities. Out of a total number of 11 members, only two are to be elected. This kind of nomination is quite contrary to democratic spirit.

Although, the provision under Sec. 17(2) for designating the Chief Librarian of the City Library Authority as its ex-officio Secretary is welcome; yet with no stretch of imagination one can justify the r mination of the Mayor of the Municipal Corporation or the President of the Municipal Council as the Chairman of the Authority under Sec. 17 1-a. Likewise, the District Library Authority consists of majority of nominated members (Sec. 18). It is likely to dampen the popular enthusiasm and interest in the development of libraries.

—The Act provides sufficient powers to the Library Authority and Local Library Authorities, which will ensure smooth working of the Act. Adequate guiding principles are also provided by the Act through Sections 41-42 to the State Government and the Library Authorities in order to enable them to frame rules and laws. It may be recalled that it is only at the rules making stage that most of the damage has been done in the operation of Madras Act and to some extent of the Aadhra Act.

At the operational level, the Act has established : 1 State Central Library, 10 City Central Libraries, 19 District Libraries, 320 branch libraries, 204 grant-in-aid libraries, 2101 village and other types of libraries. Mobile libraries are also in operation.

The State Central Library situated in Banglore is at apex of the Public Library System. It directly supervises and controls City

Central Libraries. The District Central Libraries are also under the direct supervision and control of the State Central Library. Branch libraries function under the control of City Central Libraries and District Central Libraries.

There are 3 library authorities. First, the State Library Authority (Sec. 3). It looks after the State Central Library and advice the State Government on all matters relating to the administration of this Act and development of public libraries in the State (Sec. 4). The Minister of Education is the ex-officio President of the Authority (Sec. 3-2-a) and the State Librarian is the ex-officio Secretary of the authority. He functions as the Librarian of the State Central Library (Sec. 14-2), and as Head of Department of Public Libraries.

Second, the City Library Authorities—10 for 10 cities (Sec. 16-1-a), having a population of more than one lakh. The Mayor of the municipal corporation is the ex-officio Chairman of the Authority and the Librarian of the City Library is the ex-officio Secretary of the Authority (Sec. 17). The Authority runs the City Central Library and its branches (Sec. 26).

Third, District Library Authorities are responsible for running, controlling and administrating District Central Libraries and their branches. The Deputy Commissioners of their respective districts function as the Chairmen and the Librarians of the District Central Libraries as the ex-officio Secretaries of the Authority.

The Mysore Public Libraries Act, 1965 is a great milestone in the history of library legislation. An independent State Library Service, widening of the tax base for levy of library cess, the creation of the Department of Public Libraries with State Librarian as its Head, and library staff salaries to be met by the State Exchequer are some of the progressive steps. This Act, in fact, is one of the major achievements of Ranganathan's life-efforts as it contains most of the provisions suggested by him in in his "Model Public Libraries Bill", and smothens the way for similar library acts in India.

4. MAHARASHATRA PUBLIC LIBRARIES ACT, 1967

The Maharashtra Public Libraries Act, 1967 came into force w.e.f. May 1, 1968 to provide for the establishment, maintenance, organization and development of public libraries in the State of Maharashtra.

Sec. 2 (xi) defines public library to mean :

(a) a library established and maintained by the State Government for the use of the public;

(b) a library recognised by the Director for the purposes of grant-in-aid from the Library Fund; and

(c) any other library which the State Government by notification in the Official Gazette declares to be a public library for the purposes of this Act.

Obviously, the definition does not specify that the service rendered by the public libraries shall be free of charge, and that libraries are of the people, by the people and for the people.

Section 3 of the Act creates a State Library Council having advisory functions, with the Minister of Education of the State as an ex-officio President of the Council, and the Director of Libraries, as Member Secretary of the body. No State Library Authority has been named in the Act. By implication, one can say that the State Government is the State Library Authority. The Council will consist of sixteen nominated/ex-officio members and only three elected members. It sounds highly undemocratic. No representation has even been given to public iibraries defined under Sec. 2 (xi) above.

Sec. 8 creates a Department of Libraries with a Director of Libraries as its Head with the qualifications prescribed by the State Government. Such a provision enables a government to make appointment of a person without having professional qualifications and competence for operating libraries. The powers and functions of the Director are comprehensive except that the Act does not create a State agency for centralized cataloguing and classification.

Sec. 10 of the Act establishes a Maharashtra State Library Service. The entire staff of the public libraries are Government servants and draw their salaries from the Consolidated Fund of the State.

Sec. 11 (1) maintains that the State Government may establish a State Central Library for the whole of the State, and a Divisional Library for every Division. But the use of the word "may" makes it clear that it is not obligatory for the government to establish these vital organs of peoples' education. Sec. 11 (2) empowers the Director of Public Libraries to establish and maintain public libraries in local areas where any Society registered under the Societies Registration Act, 1860 or any Trust registered under the Bombay Public Trusts Act. 1950 fails to provide a satisfactory standard of library service to the people. All libraries established under this Section shall be maintained, organized and developed by the State Government through the Department of Libraries.

Sec. 18 makes it obligatory on the part of the State Government to make annually a sum not less than 25 lacs of rupees for the development of public libraries. It does not include administrative and establishment expenditure. Libraries upto Divisional level are fully financed by the Government. Libraries below Divisional level are run by voluntary organizations. They are aided by the Government on the undertaking that they shall provide free library service to all. Grants for buildings and for running mobile libraries are also made available.

Obviously, there is no provision in the Act for raising library finance through the levy of library cess, as is the case with Madras, Andhra Pradesh, and Mysore Public Libraries Acts. The lack of such a provision is most likely to hamper the formation, growth and development of library services to the people of a satisfactory standard, because a library system based on modern concept of service and approved standards needs ever increasing recurring grants. This can be met only if permanent sources of revenue are tapped to provide adequate funds for ensuring a public library system that allows a balanced and even development of library services over large areas, irrespective of local differences in wealth. This provision, therefore, needs amendment, so as make the library expenditure as cess based, which has become a world-wide norm for library finances.

At the operation level, the Asiatic Society Library—a legal deposit library under the Copyright Act, 1955—functions as a State Central Library. There are 5 Divisional Libraries, 34 District Libraries, 275 Taluka Libraries, and 2454 other types of libraries—rural, mobile and circulating.

A Department of Libraries has been constituted with a Director of Libraries as its head. The Director is responsible for the planning, maintenance, organization and development of public libraries (except the State Central Library) and public library system. He publishes annually a bibliography of all the books published in the State; collects and preserves old and rare books, periodicals, manuscripts and other documents of educative value in public libraries; and organizes programme for training candidates in library science, etc. There is one Assistant Director in each of the 5 divisions to assist the Director.

5. WEST BENGAL PUBLIC LIBRARIES ACT, 1979

The Act was enacted to provide for the establishment of public libraries in the State of West Bengal and to regulate, guide, control, supervise and to grant recognition to the existing libraries in the State as also to provide for a comprehensive rural and urban library service in the State of West Bengal. The distinctive features of the Act may be noted.

—Like Maharashtra Public Libraries Act, this Act, too, does not provide any provision for levying library cess.

—The Act provides a Directorate of Libraries (Sec. 7) headed by a Director having professional qualifications. Among his important functions (Sec. 6) are : to manage the Central Library together with its branches; superintend and direct all matters relating to the work of all local library authorities under this Act; guide, control, and supervise the functioning of libraries in the State.

—The Act provides for constituting State Library Council (Sec. 3) with Minister-in-Charge of Library Service as Chairman (Sec. 4-a) and Director of Libraries as Secretary. The council will act as an Advisory Committee on Public Libraries and will render advise to the Government on all matters relating to library system, development and organization (Sec. 3). The Council is a heavily nominated body (Sec. 4).

—The Act provides for the constitution of Local Library Authority in each revenue district with the District Magistrate as Chairman and District Library Officer (having professional qualifications) as Secretary (Sec. 8). In fact, this body, too, is heavily officialized.

—The Act makes provision for appointing District Library Officer in each district (Sec. 16-1);

—The Act modifies the Press and Registration Act of 1867 with a view to ensure the deposit of one free copy to the State Central Library to the publishers. It gives great relief to the publishers who are supposed to deposit 4 copies of each publication under Delivery of Books Act, 1954. (Andhra and Mysore Public Libraries Acts required 3 copies and Madras Act 5 copies).

—The Act provides well-framed library rules.

By merit of this Act, the West Bengal Government has taken the responsibility of rendering library services through its Education Department. It is better to choose Ministry of Education as the State Library Authority, as it is profitable to link libraries and education at the state level. But libraries should not be made subordinate to the formal educational programme of the state. A Minister of State (Education, as provided in British Museum and Libraries Act, 1964, here on state level) should be the library authority as Minister is responsible to his legislature and may be called upon to account for therein. But it is all the more better to have State Library Authority with Minister for Libraries as its Head. It will be responsible for providing state library system. It is common experience that whenever, the State Government is to impose a financial cut the axe falls on education and libraries. Moreover, an Independent Advisory Body with Director of Public Libraries as its Secretary should be provided.

The Local Library Authorities are not empowered to levy library cess. The Government Libraries are fully financed and managed by the State Government. Sponsored and aided libraries get grants. The State spends about Rs. 4 crores on public libraries annually.

There are two sources of financing public libraries. First, through appropriation from public funds; second, from special library cess. The developed countries have adoped one of these two methods for financing their libraries. In U S.A., some federal states follow the former method. But in a developing country like India, it may not be feasible to finace libraries which are growing, and spending institutions, and require ever-increasing funds, particularly when, our state revenues are already meagre. It is common experience that, though, education is a State Subject in our constitution, yet most of the Indian States have failed even to provide compulsory primary education despite their loud proclamations. Whenever, there is, financial stringency, the axe usually falls on education, and if library depends on the mercy of the state government, its fate can be well imagined. The

Local Library Authorities may become financial pawns in the hands of local government for subsides.*

As a result, the recourse to the second method, seems appropriate and necessary in India. That is why, the history of Public Libraries in India, is, in fact, an account of the striving of group of persons to persuade governments to enact legislation to provide library service to cities, towns, and villages. True, that library cess alone cannot meet the entire bill of the public library system, but a simultaneous provision from general revenues could be linked with it to ensure an adequate annual budget. Moreover, for levy of library cess, we must use up-to-date financial tools provided by modern theories of public finance which would permit a strong and flexible financial base for development of public libraries.

A Recapitulation Alongwith Suggestions

The public Library is a non-revenue producing and non-profit making institution. Therefore, its income should have a sound basis in law. Sources of revenue should be ensured, with reasonable limits, and final authority for determining the annual library income should be vested in the legislative body ofthe State in which it is located.

Library legislation is an essential condition for the establishment and orderly functioning of a net-work of public libraries. As Ranganathan aptly remarked : Experience shows that the edifice of free ecucation for the adults, is like a mud house without roof. Moreover, the advent of people's government in many countries make the governments realize the explosive nature of democracy without provision for the continuous self-education of the voters. The library associations, too, make the people book conscious. All these factors lead to realizing that a permanent, continuous free book service for all can be ensured only by legislation. Unfortunately, despite the relentless efforts and thought given to this subject, there are still 18 States (Mizoram included) and 8 Union Territories in India which do not have library law for the development of public libraries. The *Will* to do is there, the sympathy is there, but the problem hinges on taxation. The state governments are hesitant to pass mandatory

*For further comments, see, p. 141.

legislation that will increase the tax burden on the masses. The rural and urban areas have adequate revenue to provide library services; and the states coffers do not receive sufficient amount of revenue to disburse. Ultimately, the problem could be solved by the grants from the Central Government to make up the deficiency in the states' budgets. In present times of inflation, 10 per cent of the amount spent on education should be earmarked as expenditure on libraries.

The longer the Central Government feels hesitant to insist on mandatory State Legislation, the more difficult it will be to provide this basic service through establishing at least one library in every village in India. In this context John Makin has suggested the following practical steps that the Indian Library Association and Indian Librarians should take to bring homogeneous and unified library service in the State :

—an appreciation should be made of the efficiency limit of any service under existing Indian conditions, as the attempt to do too much with insufficient resources will result in an even greater loss of reputation;

—a set of basic standards for public libraries should be drawn up and published, standards beneath whose minima it is known that no library can operate satisfactorily;

—the Association (ILA) should take a firm stand on the amount of extension work that should be done; and

—priorities should be awarded to groups of readers than to an area[1].

The comments made by Makin convincingly show that not only legislation but standards of public library service on national, state and local levels should be prepared for the creation of an effective, efficient and economical public library system in India. Such a system can play a vital role in the eradication of illiteracy, removal of social imbalances and making India safe for democracy.

1. cf. John Makin, Background problem of library provision in India (Lond., LA., 1953), pp. 61-62.

14

FIVE LAWS

Implications and Impact on Universe of Subjects

S.R. Ranganathan conceived of the Five Laws of Library Science in 1924 in embryo form. The statements embodying the Five Laws were formulated in the final form in 1928 and published in 1931 under the same title THE FIVE LAWS OF LIBRARY SCIENCE. The essence of this Classic is that books are for use, and user is the KING whose time must be saved.

The Five Laws of Library Science are :

—BOOKS ARE FOR USE

—EVERY READER HIS BOOK

—EVERY BOOK ITS READER

—SAVE THE TIME OF THE READER

—LIBRARY IS A GROWING ORGANISM.

What follows in the following pages is the summary and interpretation of this epoch-making work.

First Law

The first law of Library Science is : BOOKS ARE FOR USE. No one will question the correctness of this law. But in actual practice, the story is different. The law has been deplorably neglected by the authorities in its implementation.

S.R. Ranganathan reveals that during the fifteenth and sixteenth century, it was not uncommon to find books actually chained to the shelves. The books were fitted with brass frames and rings. Such chained books could not migrate from the shelves beyond the length of the chain. In fact, libraries were then regarded, not as organizations for furthering the use of books, but as institutions for preserving them. The slogan "BOOKS ARE FOR PRESERVATION" had usurped the place of "BOOKS ARE FOR USE".

The old order has changed yielding place to new. The modern library is a service agency charged with the function of disseminating knowledge. A modern librarian is overjoyed when the readers make his shelves constantly empty. He is worried and depressed on seeing those volumes which stay at home. What steps should he take to make the library as the centre of intellectual attainments by spreading the use of books. Ranganathan suggests the following methods for maximizing the use of books.

1. Library Location

If the resources of the library are to be fully exploited; if the library is to play its vital role of community's intellectual centre, it must be located in the midst of its users. If it is a public library, it would be wise to locate it in the heart of the city—at a place near the town-hall, river-crossing, the market place or a religious centre—, to which most of the citizens will be going daily on some business or some other purposes. If it is an academic library, it should be planted in the centre of academic institution or at a distance of few minutes walk from the teaching departments or hostels. A centrally located library will immensely help in increasing the use of the books and becoming the hub of the institution's intellectual attainments.

2. Library Hours

The influence of the law 'BOOKS ARE FOR USE' has been no less profound on Library Hours. Before the advent of this law, the library was more often closed than kept open. Probably, it was more frequently opened for the book worms to be chased out and the books to be dusted than for the readers to enter or for the books to be issued for use.

Happily, in countries where the magic of the Mantra 'BOOKS ARE FOR USE' has taken roots in the public mind, the libraries are kept open for 18 hours a day. The credit goes to the University College, London, where the library remains open round the clock as there is no hour of night or day at which a scholar may not feel the necessity of persuing some book which is not in his possession; the ideal arrangement would be that libraries should always be opened to the public.

3. Library Furniture, Internal Equipment and Buildings

The effect of the law 'BOOKS ARE FOR USE' on library furniture and internal equipment is really commendable. To begin with, in the days when the dictum "BOOKS ARE FOR PRESERVATION" reigned supreme, the library racks were built with a view to accomodate maximum number of books in the least space and at the least cost. To use the least space, the height of the book-racks was as much as the height of the ceiling. Not even an inch of vertical space was wasted. The Rule of the Least Cost was that not an inch of horizontal space should be wasted. As a result, the gangway between book-racks was kept as narrow as 1½ or 2 feet just enough for a janitor to pass through. The racks were fitted with doors, locks and keys. To satisfy the Rule of the Least Cost, the furniture of the reading room was made as simple and cheap as practicable. The reader could not expect any comfortable place in the library where he could sit and study.

The First Law has overhauled the rules of the least space and the least cost. Now-a-days, no rack is built higher than what can be comfortably reached by a person of an average height while standing on the bare floor. Its standard height is 6½′ or 7′. The gangway between the racks is kept broad enough (from 4½′-6′) to permit two persons to pass each other or sit back to back while reading their books. Any reader can go to any shelf to locate his book. It is usually an open shelf system, i.e., the book-racks have no doors, no locks and keys.

The rooms are made vermin-proof, theft-proof and air-proof. To provide best reading facilities, the chairs are made cosy, and comfortable with ample table-space fitted with tube lights, fans, etc. The floor is sound proof and the reading hall is decently decorated with beautiful paintings hanging on walls, flowers, pictures to rest the tired eyes.

The internal equipment now consists of book-shelves, book display cases, the catalogue cabinets, the circulation counters, the loan desks, the working tables, verticle files, pamphlet boxes, cupboard for posters, exhibits, pictures, films, etc.

The modern libraries are now planned especially for the kind of work to be done and the community to be served. The exterior of the building is inviting and the interior attractive. It is not unusual to find airconditioned rooms, browsing rooms, space for lectures, seminars, reading circles, in the libraries. The first law has thus exercised tremendous influence on library furniture, equipment and design of buildings.

4. Book Selection

The First Law had a marvellous effect on book-selection. It entrusts the librarians with the sacred responsibility of selecting books which should meet the needs of the present and potential users.

In order to maximize the use of books, the public librarian should select, in a suitable proportion, informative, elevating, recreative, and inspiring books. The children are attracted by libraries that have pictorial literature, which is instinctive, entertaining and fascinating. Book selection in fiction for neo-literates should prefer short-stories to long novels. In fact, the first law permits only those books on the shelves that are continuously read, enjoyed, understood and acted upon by readers. Worn-out and out-of-date books should be weeded out vigorously. Confirmation to these ideals will increase the use of books.

5. Library Staff

The very efficiency, service, and the ultimate success of the modern library as an agency for diffusion of knowledge depends upon its staff. So long as the motto that "BOOKS ARE FOR PRESERVATION" prevailed, all that the authorities wanted by way of staff was a competent care-taker who could read the spine of books and fight against the four enemies of books—fire, water, vermins and men. In fact, the posts in the libraries were held by persons found unfit for other jobs, or the fellow who was physically disabled, or mentally abnormal, or, a deaf, or a dumb, or both. The terms like 'caretaker', watch-man, or even 'watch-dog' of books were used for librarians in the pre-First Law days.

The march of the First Law has brought to light the central role which the library staff plays in carrying knowledge to the doors of those that lack it and to educate all to perceive the right. The First Law, therefore, requires that to disseminate knowledge and to put the books to maximum use, the libraries must have on their staffs highly qualified and professionally trained persons. To increase the maximum use of books, it is advisable to spend less on books and more on educated staff. It is not the books that lack in libraries; it is rather the key to their effective use. And the key is men and women who operate libraries and who forming the link between the readers and their documents create the public image of the library as the community's intellectual centre.

6. Academic Status & Scales of Pay

The most laudable step of the First Law was to strive for the academic status and scales of pay for the library staff.

Academic status may enhance the efficiency and boost the morale of the library personnel. Money is also important as it rules the world. It determines the status of men as well as the value of the services rendered by them. If the academic status and scales of pay are not given, the library staff may not work up to the enthusiasm necessary for the successful carrying out the missions of the First Law. Exen if they did, the enthusiasm, the zeal, and the solitude of a poorly paid staff would not produce the desired results. The voice of the poor, however, beneficial, is seldom heard. A famished staff will render the efforts of the First Law as futile as the paucity of books or paucity of staff. "Therefore, pay the library staff well", says the First Law.

7. Library Staff and their Responsibilities

Academic status and scales of pay also carry certain definite obligations. The staff should never forget that in libraries the documents are accumulated for use, processed for use, and served for use. The librarian and his staff must bring to the point of maximum efficiency the socialization of the graphic records by interpreting their collections to their readers, by offering them unlimited personal assistanee in search of knowledge or information. It is service, not suggestion, that is at a premium. Besides, the staff should develop certain attitudes and interests which are equally indispensable for promoting the use of books.

8. Library Staff and Readers

First comes the attitude towards the users of the library. The First Law desires that a librarian must be a good human being. He must be approchable, willing and anxious to help. His ultimate destiny, the final goal or salvation is reader. But the readers have extreme tempraments and moods. If one is unable to formulate his question; the other is too arrogant to ask. The librarian must keep cheerfulness and perseverance. He has to put up even with the incivility that may emanate, occasionally, from inconsiderate, ill-natured. proudy, unpleasant, talkative, critical, fussy, bumptuous or self-assertive readers. So, every person on the staff of library should be a good judge of human behaviours; have the ability to understand human psychology and handle difficutl readers. He must find comforts amidst the discourgements of ill-appreciated work. In a word, the librarian should be a friend, philosopher and guide to everyone who visits the library to use it. Only then, the First Law will be translated into practice.

The pleasure of understanding human nature and managing difficult cases should, however, be taken only as means to an end; the end being the service rendered to the readers. Hence, the very soul of librarianship lies in the aggressive personal service given to the people pleasanly and persuasively.

9. Library Staff And Personal Service

Books must be used to the largest possible extent and with the least trouble; they must be used as tools for exploring and extending the horizons of knowledge rather than guarded as treasure-troves. If the books are for use; if every reader is to get his book for reading, research or information; if every book is to be energised for whatever purpose it is designed to serve; if the time of the library user in persuit of of knowledge is to be saved; and if the exponential rate of growth of knowledge is to be reckoned with, it becomes the solemn duty of the library staff to lay bare the hidden treasure in the books, that is thought expressed in the books for the use of readers. It is the reference service which establishes the contact between the reader and his/her book. Nothing else can take the place of a fine reference service. Rather the real future of the library as an agency for the transmission and dissemination of information and essential knowledge lies in the direct provision of "comprehensive and accurate" reference service to readers. This is the kind of personal service that the First Law expects from the library staff, if they mean its full implementation.

In brief, the implications of the First Law have been profound, rich, and revolutionizing. Once the outlook was revolutionized, other things followed in course of time.

Second Law

The First Law revolutionized our thinking about the use of books, the Second Law carries this revolution a step further. As Ranganathan puts it : If the First Law replaced the concept 'BOOKS ARE FOR PRESERVATION', the Second Law widens the concept 'BOOKS FOR THE CHOOSEN FEW'. If the revolutionary cry of the First Law was 'BOOKS ARE FOR USE', the revolutionary cry of the Second Law is 'BOOKS ARE FOR ALL'. If the approach of the First Law was from the side of books, the approach of the Second Law is from the side of users of books. If the First Law vitalised the library, the Second Law magnifies the library into a nation-wide problem. If the First Law threw open the existing libraries, the Second Law plants new libraries and brings about the culture of new species of libraries. If there was hesitation to act up to the First Law, there is, in the initial stages, positive opposition to the Second Law. Thus the revolution brought about by the Second Law, writes Ranganathan, is of a more advanced nature.

Every Reader His/Her Book means Books for All. Books for All symbolises 'Education For All'. In the past education was not for all; it was only for the chosen few. Aristotle deprived nine-tenth of the slave population of Athens and Sparata from their right to education. During the Middle Ages, the common man had no access to books. We are even told that vassal father was punished if his son attended the school. Even the nineteenth century upheld the concept that people belonging to lower strata of society had no right to education; hence no right to books. Even as late as 1918, the Education Bill of H.A.L Fisher was opposed on the ground that, if a shephard, a plowman, or anyother workman was given elaborate course of education, "How are horses to be kept at work, the cows to be milked, the sheep to be tended and the folds to be pitched ? How is education going to help a man who has to spread manure on a field"-

Ewart Bill—the first Public Library Bill of England was opposed on the plea : That too much knowledge was a dangerous thing and that libraries might become centres of political education. Also, in Moscow, at the inauguration of the library school in 1913, it was asked in the National Duma, "How the government tolerate library courses, which would pave the way for revolution ?" The Second Law, thus, had to face not merely an inherited habit of preserving books but it had also to face a strong opposition based on political and economic instincts.

Fortunately, the evolution of the concept of democracy, recognition of the rights of man, the emergence of middle class as a strong force in politics, developments in socio-political thought;

development in industrialization, creation and production of books in abudance, tremendous progress in the field of science and technology led to the spread of universal education which in turn demanded libraries with rich collections. Today countries like U.S.A., England, Denmark, U.S.S.R., Japan, etc. fully endorse the ideals of the Second Law : Every Reader His/Her Book or Free Book Service for All. No distinction in respect of the age, the sex, the vocation, the capacity for self-help and the willingness to read, is made

1. *Education for Women*

In the old days, education to women was considered a bad omen. This concept prevailed even in Europe during the eighteenth and the nineteenth centuries. J.J. Rousseau, the harbinger of French Revolution, regarded woman as "Imperfect man". Women were aimed at breeding, deportment, and the accomplishment, not at learning. But the modern scientific experiments of the psychology of women have revealed that an educated woman can not only make her home an ideal one, but also can be a far better and surer guarantee of the education of posterity than a literate man. Thus, Every Woman Her Book is the guiding motto of the libraries today. The modern libraries provide equal service to persons of either sex.

2. *The City-Folk and the Country-Folk*

Thanks to the Second Law the ruralites cannot be denied their right to education through the use of books. Efforts are afoot even to cover the distant hamlets in the far interior of the countryside through mobile vans and delivery stations. In a country like India where 75% of her population still live in villages, village education assumes great importance. As in the past, the city-folk now cannot deny their rural brethren their consitutional and birth right to educate themselves and reap the pleasures of books. This attitude is the gift of the all-embracing Second Law which urges the authorities to supply the inhabitants of the scattered countryside with the books they want.

2.1 *Rural Library Service*

To have a progressive Rural Library Service, Ranganathan maintains that it should be started, first on a District basis as there were ample resources available and the work of serving books in villages can be operated easily. But the first pre-requisite of a successful district library scheme is the appointment of a well-trained, resourceful and enthusiastic librarian.

2.2 *First Know the People*

The first thing that the librarian should do is to get first-hand knowledge of the people he has to serve. The knowledge of the requirements and tastes of the people would facilitate his work in selecting books for the villagers.

2 3 *Libra'y Publicity*

The next step is to advertise the idea of library intensively throughout the area. The vernacular news-papers of the district should be asked to announce the facilities offered by the District Library as prominently and as frequently as possible. Attractive hand-bills should be widely distributed. First-class posters, with charming colours and catching legends, should be distributed profusely. Local festivals and fairs should be visited and an intensive campaign of propaganda should be launched on such occasions with the co-operation of zealous honorary workers.

2.4. *Choice of Books*

A variety of well-built, well-written, well-illustrated books should be promptly and regularly served. Books on local needs, books on their festivals, books on agriculture and its tools, cottage industries, fruit packing, would be quite useful in converting the ideas of the inhabitants and making them lovers of books.

2.5 *Choice of Extension Materials*

Extension materials selected should concern with education of the people. The district library can send gramophone records and picture collections and circulate slides periodically. Educational work can also be carried through travelling cinematograph shows, which may awaken interest in other countries, in market methods, and in civic hygiene. It will be good to enlist sympathy by first showing films based on the Ramayana, Mahabharta, Shakuntla and the like and alternate them with more utilitarian and informational films. Exhibitions, dramas, musical concerts would uplift the people from their druggery and hellish conditions. Education would open to the villagers new avenues of progress and prosperity.

3. Books for Children

The word 'Every' includes children as well. They too are entitled for books. Their books should cover the entire universe of knowledge in a special key, in a distinctive style of exposition, with a high proportion of illustrations, bold faces of printing and an attractive physical get-up.

4. Books far Artisans

The word 'Every' also includes artisans. To convert them library users, it is necessary to produce craft-centred sets of books. The entire universe of knowledge should be covered by the books, in a set, with one book on each class or area of knowledge, written from the angle of the craft in question.

5. Service to Neo-Literates

'Every' includes neo-literates. The new-literate does not read books as he has not been trained to read books. There is need for a set of graded books for their use. Simple elementary books containing alphabets, simple words and phrases should be provided to these readers.

6. Books for the Last Decile

'Every' includes also the persons of lowest intellect—the ten per cent in the intellectual scale. They need speaking books, well-illustrated books in a simple style, sound records. A sound book will appeal to the reader in a triple way-through the ear, through the eyes, and through the phonetic symbols.

7. Service to Workmen in Factories

'Every' includes also the foremen and workmen at the bench in the factories. They are of the lowest quartile on the intellectual scale. But the rate of production and elimination or avoidance of waste depend upon them. Therefore, the librarians must arouse interest of this group of readers with the aid of latest know-how. This has to be supplemented by an aggressive referenee service to enable them to pick-up the exact details from books especially produced taking into consideration their standard, both in style and in proportion and nature of illustrations.

8. Book Service to the Handicapped

The word 'Every' also includes the handicapped. In this catagory may be included (i) Mentally sick, (ii) Patients, (iii)

Prisoners, (iv) Permanently disabled, (v) Housebound, (vi) Seafarers. (vii) Alumni.

The handicapped, too, have the right to continuously educate themselves. The Second Law desires the librarian to provide them the desired books for their reformation, cure and to fruitfully enjoy leisure.

8.1 Service to the Mentally Sick

Libraries can significantiy contribute towards the treatment of mentally ills. A library can be a place where a mentally sick does not have to be evaluated first. It is a place where he can pick-up what he wants, not just what his doctor has decided is right for him. Their book-stock should consist of fiction of all types. Light fiction will be in heavy demand, so the books on travel, biographies, autobiographies, sports and simple art books. Magazines are quite popular with all types of patients. In brief, the Second Law expects as normal a service to the mentally ills as possible.

8 2 Book-Service to Patients

The Hospital Library plays a curative role, the aim is to make patients to forget their immediate brooding environments and make attempts to better their future. Science has given the patients the ceiling books. He reads the projection of the page on the ceiling above.

For the partially-sighted people, well-illustrated books should be provided.

Illiterates and slow readers need picture-books and talking books.

8.3 Books for Prisoners

The importance of books to prisoners can hardly be overemphasized. The study of books may make the criminals to ponder (reflect) over their follies and generate the feelings of repentence and determination to be good citizens. The library service offers prisoners the chance of human contact, of seeing a different face, and introduces an element of choice into the strict regiment of prison life. Many prisoners may read for educational or vocational ends to become responsible members of society. iction and 'escapist' materials, venture stories will be heavily demanded. Interest may also be shown in certain types of non-fiction, for example, books on war, art and sport. Some prisoners may also be interested in works of philosophy, theology, religion and social sciences. Large print books will be popular with poor readers, as well as those whose eyesight is week. Finally talk-books, audio-cassettes and records can all offer an extra-dimension to the service. Thus library can play a significant role in over-all programmes of reform, training and rehabilitation that are current in many persons today.

8.4 Ranganathan suggests a separate wing for the blinds attached to the national library. Attention is also paid to provide books to the deaf or dumb or both.

8.5 Meticulous care is taken to select books for the delinquents. Books are processed, displayed and publicized among the juvenile readers. Story hours are fixed for the illiterates. Even the needs of MEN AT SEA are not over looked by the Second Law.

8.6 Service to the House-bound

Library service with the house bound concern the elderly or at any rate those over school age. Such services also includes those persons confined to welfare houses or day centres and have no time to visit even the nearest library service point. A survey of the reading interests of superannuates carried out by the Boston Public Library in 1967 revealed that mysteries, romantic novels and biographies are in great demand, followed by recent fiction, nature and animal stories and travel advertures. In Indian conditions, books on Religion, Ethics, Karma, Life after Death and on moral values may also be demanded. Non-book materials like gramophone records, photographic slides, talking books have also proved to be popular and effective. The services of volunteer aides reading aloud to old people have also been used. Materials are also served by mail to service house-bound and other handicapped. In U.S.A. and Canada, it is not uncommon to find out old people being taken by bus to visit the library. In brief, the Second Law aims at providing books to all types of handicapped readers.

8.7 The Second Law enjoins upon the university libraries to provide service to their alumini to retain their interests in reading and loyalty to the institution.

Libraries supported by state funds should make their collections freely available for reference purposes to the people of the state. Most of the university libraries make their materials available to visiting faculty members and scholars. Material is also lent through inter-library loan to the readers of other libraries. The underlying idea is that every reader must get his/her document, whatever its location and the place of publication.

The Second Law desires Free Book Service For All. This involves large financial resources to be provided by the State through the library legislation.

Obligation of the State

There is no denying the fact that library legislation is "a must" for the establishment and maintenance of homogeneous and unified library service. To facilitate the development and orderly functioning of a net-work of public libraries for the diffusion of knowledge, the Second Law provides :

—State Library Act

—State Library Authority

—Local Library Authority

—Local Library Committee and Village Library Committee

—State Central Library

—Finance, Accounts and Audit

For the establishment and maintenance of a National Central Library as well as for the promotion and coordination of a comprehensive library service, the Second Law makes a provision for :

—Union Library Act

—National Library Authority

—National Central Library

—Finance.

To provide Every Reader His book, the Second Law desires an integrated library grid of Public Library System, and Special Library System. A well laid-out, well-co-ordinated and financially well-supported state wide net-work of library system would lead to the strengthening of their resources through co-operative acquisitions, co-operative storage, centralized and co-operative cataloguing and classification, co-operation in dissemination of information, inter-library loans, etc. This would in turn lead to a balanced, economical and uniform development of library service based on approved standards. The integration of all the three systems into an organic whole for the development of a planned programme of library service to 'All' can only come from the government of the State.

Obligation of the Library Authority

A well-thought legislative and co-ordinated measures on the part of state ensuring a perennial source of finance is essential but not sufficient. The reputation of the library depends upon its collections but more so on its staff who interprets the collections. It is here that the Library Authority comes into focus to choose books and provide staff.

Choice of the Books

To provide Every Reader His Book, the Second Law requires the librarians to know the (i) Subject-scatter, (ii) Standard-scatter, and (iii) Language-scatter of the books used.

The Second Law indicates that a library should select books on all the major occupations of its actual and potential readers. The people are also likely to demand biographies and travel books. The Public libraries should also provide books in Fine Arts, Literature, Religion, and Philosophy.

The Second Law also desires that book selection should be closely correlated with equal thoroughness, to the language and style of exposition suited to all the intellectuals. The lib.arians should select and furnish books which satisfy the demands of the neo-literates as well as of the seasoned scholars.

The Second Law further urges the librarians to purchase a large number of encyclopedias and other reference books. With a reasonable good collections of such books, the problem of Every Reader His Book will be solved to a great extent.

Obligation of the Staff

Next to the choice of books, the choice of staff can make or mar the fitness of a library to give Every Reader His Book. If the First Law stresses the need for a well-qualified, trained and properly paid staff, the Second Law urges the Library Authority to provide for an adequate, and devoted staff to show every reader how to use books as tools and libraries as workshops and to make even the limited collections of the library yield to Every Reader His Material. To act as the canvassing agent for the books, the staff must know the readers, must know the books, and actively help every reader to find his or her book. This phase of the work is known as Reference Service.

The hidden contents of the books should be brought out by cross-reference entries, that is Subject Analytical Entries. The readers, too, should request for pin-pointed and exhaustive service without any hesitation. That is the desire of the Second Law.

Obligation of the Reader

There is hardly any library which can afford to get duplicate copies of books to any extent. Hence a reader can get his book only if each reader realises that he is not the only one using the library. It is the obligation of every reader to get only the number of books he is entitled for and return them on due dates. Another rule which the Second Law desires the reader to follow is that books of ready reference, rare books that cannot be replaced, books that are full of plates, books which are by nature frail and easily destructible, should be consulted only within the premises of the library. Similarly, the current issues of the periodicals should be consulted within the library. These volumes contain a vast mine of information that will be frequently used. If a reader appreciates the anxiety of the Second Law to give Every Reader His Chance to use them, it would be an academic crime on his part to confine them at his home, where they may remain idle. The librarian should also see that books and periodicals are not to let or lie for an indefinite period amidst the heap of unused books. It is the library staff who serves as a nucleus for converting the library into an intellectual centre for the community. Nonetheless, the reader should behave in the library in a manner, he expects others to behave.

Adoption of above principles in the organization of libraries will extend the scope of use of books to each and all. If every reader has the privilege of using the books in the library, the responsibility of the library for providing an adequate stock of books of all types simultaneously increases. In order to discharge this responsibility satisfactorily, library authorities require secured and stable finances safeguarded through library legislation. The tastes, interests and demands of the reading community would determine the book-selection policy of a library. Ultimately, it is the library staff which makes the library the centre of community's intellectual attainments.

THIRD LAW

The Third Law stands for the maximum use of books by their readers. While it resembles the First Law in making its approach from the side of the books, it is in a sense a complement to the Second Law. While the Second Law concerded itself with the task of finding for every reader his appropriate book, the Third Law would urge that an appropriate reader should be found for every book. In fact, the Third Law is : "EVERY BOOK ITS READER". The most prominent of the means used by the libraries to satisfy the Third Law is the *Open Access System.* The other devices relate to Shelf-arrangement, Catalogue entries, Reference service, Publicity, Extension service and Book-selection.

1. Open Access System

By Open Access is meant the opportunity to see and examine the book collection with as much freedom as in one's own library. In an open access library, the reader is permitted to wander among the books and lay his hands on any of them at at his will and pleasure.

Open access increases the use of books. Few readers know their book needs. Their interests take precise shape after seeing and handling a well-arranged collection of books. While making a search for books, the readers discover such books which they did not know that their library had. Under such a system there is no need of having book lifters to take out and bring the books needed by readers. They can themselves take any book to the reading hall for consultation or the circulation counter to get it issued for use at home. In almost everyway, this system has been a gain. Doubtlessly, Open Access involves a certain risk of loss of books because of theft. But this loss has to be borne to increase the chances for securing Every BOOK ITS READER.

Moreover, the chances of theft can be put down by the very design of the library buildings. Theft of books can further be minimized by placing rare and costly books, pamphlets and under-sized books, books with too many plates and other books with weak physique in Closed Access. Even text-books vigorously demanded by students may have to be removed from Open Access particularly during examination days, as a temporary measure.

Notwithstanding its limitations, libraries should practice Open Access System without any hesitation as it increases the use of books manifold.

2. *Shelf-arrangement*

It plays a vital role in making the books finding their appropriate readers. The Third Law emphasizes the need for the arrangement of books in classified sequence based on their thought content. If the books on Botany are kept together, and also the books on Pathology of Flowering Plants are placed in close proximity, there can be every possibility for each of them to be picked-up by the readers. In any case no librarian would seriously consider classifying his library without providing an author's approach to the books in the catalogue. This immensely enhances the possibility of books attracting the attention of their readers by either of the two approaches. By means of well-devised guides and labels, aided by the catalogues and indexes to the classification, a reader for more ordinary purposes can find what he seeks without personal assistance.

3. *Recent Additions Shelf*

Another technique for attracting the readers' attention is to have a shelf-marked as 'RECENT ADDITIONS SHELF' placed very near the entrance. Recency is an important device for attracting reader Librarians may also use an attractive show-case with books placed near the reading room using catchy labels such as "Books On Current Events"; "Books In the Reviews"; "Books Worth Looking To"; "Books of the Hour" Old but unused books may also be put on display using labels like "Interesting Books Recently Unearthed"; "Long Forgotton But Useful Books"; or "Do Not Read These Books". 'Novelty' in shelf-arrangement is another device frequently employed to invite the attention of the visitors towards books looking for their readers. An occasional redistribution of the contents of the shelves may establish fresh contact between the readers and books.

4. *Easy Accessibility*

Another important factor helping every book to get its reader is that the books may be placed within the easy reach of the readers. It is observed that the books within the comfortable reach of the readers are more frequently used. Experience has shown that books lying on the intermediate shelves are better used than on the others. Shelves with a height greater than 6½′ defy the very spirit of the Third Law. Finally, we must not have more than one row of books on a shelf. Therefore, the shelf should not be broader than what is necessary to hold one row of books.

5. *Catalogue*

Of course, a well planned classified shelf-arrangement is highly desirable, but it is not self-sufficient in itself to attract for Every Book, Its Reader, It has to be supported by a catalogue. Both are twin processes; one cannot be divorced from the other. The series-entries and the subject cross-reference entries sometime prove of great help to the readers to know the thought-content of the book. The Third Law also expects the technical staff to prepare analytical entries to analyse thread-bare the contents of each document for the benefit of the readers.

6. *Reference Service*

The books are mute; they are inert. They cannot reach the hands of readers till their thought content is interpreted by the reference staff. The Third Law requires the provision of human beings as canvassing agents for books. The reference staff must know the qualities of books thoroughly well and have to act as the match-makers between books and the readers. In fact, in the hands of experienced reference staff, the Library becomes like a Kaleidoscope. They should keep turning its facets in order to win over suitable readers to each of its facets. This is the kind of service that the Third Law expects from the reference staff.

7. *Publicity*

Publicity is a powerful weapon to allure the readers to the library and thereby to increase the chances for Every Book To Find Its Reader.

Continuous publicity is carried through annual reports, library bulletins, and magazines, printed catalogues, subject book-lists, lists of latest additions, special service folders, book week programmes, window displays, press notices, radio/TV talks and public lectures. Libraries with their books, music, gramophone records and tapes, archives, maps, prints, drawings have a great potentiality for visual appeal, and this can be expressed through exhibitions, displays, concerts, lectures, film shows, etc. The library shou d adopt all the recognized methods of attracting the public to the library, so that every potential reader may become an actual reader, and thus enhance the chances for the fulfilment of the Third Law.

8. Extension Services

The laudable purpose of extension services is to convert the library into a social centre to encourage reading; to turn non-readers into regular readers.

Extension services aim at the creation and stimulation of desire for good reading and matching the book and its readers. Those librarians desirous of fulfilling the aims of the Third Law take to extension service with great zeal and enthusiasm. It also recognizes the fact that occasionally man feels the necessity and the urge to read in groups, and to have group discussions so as to enrich, deepen and extend his knowledge; to listen off and on to orientation talks and inspiring lectures by subject specialists to get stimulated. The modern library if it is to continue to develop must provide amenities for satisfying all such needs and urges of its readers.

In persuance of the dictates of the Third Law and as an integral part of the librarian's educational role to provide learning environment, lectures, study circles, dramatic clubs, book review groups and exhibitions have been purposively organized and programmes of work planned to serve the interests of special groups. Libraries should engage social workers to read books of inspiration, information, recreation, or religious value to the illiterates to enrich their lives, and to make them admirers of books and libraries.

To cultivate reading habits among children, libraries also arrange for story hours, display of picture and story books, dramatisations and other attractive form of extension service. The idea is to expose the children to the wonders of the books and make them their lovers.

To satisfy, the demand of the Third Law, the librarians celebrate local festivals, and certain national days dedicated to national leaders or ideas and participate in local festivals. In India where such celebrations attract huge crowds of people, this form of extension service is pregnant with great potentialitles to satisfy the dictates of the Third Law.

9. Book-Selection

The Third Law has an important bearing on Book Selection. One of the means of fulfilling the demands of the Third Law is to give full weight to the tastes and requirements of the clientele to the library. Some of the factors from which the tastes and requirements of the clientele could be inferred are :

—the suggestions received directly from the readers;

—the suggestions recorded by the assistants at the Ready Reference Work;

—the notes made from day to day observations by the Reference Staff on floor duty;

—the main vocations of the local people;

—the prospective events of national or local importance; and

—the impressions gained in interviews with the leading members of the local community.

The difficulties of the Third Law would be minimized to a large extent by a well-balanced book-selection policy.

FOURTH LAW

The main concern of the first three Laws of Library Science is to get the books of the library used as fully and by as many persons as possible. The interest of the Fourth Law almost completely centres round the readers.

The Fourth Law "SAVE THE TIME OF THE READER" expects the library reference staff to follow a reader from the moment he enters the library to the moment he leaves it, critically examining each process he undergoes, with a keeness to save his time. This law puts forward the following tenets for saving the time of the readers.

1. The Close Access System

The Fourth Law strongly opposes the process of the Closed Access System as time has no consideration in it. In a library following Closed Access System the choice of the books has to be made through the help of the catalogue. A good deal of time is wasted in searching out the required title from a labyrinth of entries. Having traced the desired entries, the reader has to write it with great accuracy on separate slips and hand over the slip to the janitor. After wasting time in searching entries and waiting at the counter, the slip may be returned to the reader with the remark 'Entry incorrect' or 'Book 'On loan' or 'Engaged'. It means the reader has to undergo the old process of selection and waiting once again. The process itself is too annoying and cumbersome. Time is money and money is time. Open Access System is the technique for saving the time of the reader.

2. Classified Arrangemenl

The best shelf-arrangement pre-supposes that reader takes little time to take out the desired book from the shelf. To achieve this objective, the Fourth Law demands the Classified Arrangement of books on the shelves.

3. Relative Position of Classes

The Fourth Law also recommends the the closest possible affinity of relative classes accomodated on the shelves. A reader that is primarily interested in philosophy is sure to have some interest in religion and psychology. Hence, to SAVE THE TIME OF THAT CLASS OF READERS, it would be advisable to put religion on one side of philosophy and psychology on its other side. In a similar manner, the Fourth Law must be borne in mind in fixing the relative position of the other classes as well.

4. Absolute Position of Classes

Apart from relative position, the absolute position of the classes also will have to be determined in confirmity to the Fourth Law. The class of books that is in most demand should be put up on the nearest shelves of the stack-room and the class that is least popular should, ordinarily, be put at the farthest end. This broken order of books will save the time of readers.

5. Stack-Room Guides

TO SAVE THE TIME OF THE READER, the library should provide an efficient system of guides in the stack-room. It may be quite useful to keep at the entrance of the stack-room, the whole plan of that room indicating the disposition of the book racks and classes of books contained in them. Moreover, every row of book-rack should have a 'SIGNAL' guide, and every shelf-plank should have necessary number of SHELF-LABELS to SAVE THE OF THE READER. To make reader more convenient and SAVE HIS TIME, books should be property tagged; say one inch from the bottom of the book.

In brief, the STACK-ROOM GUIDES alongwith the proper placing of TAG will enable the readers to promptly find their books.

6. *Catalogue Entry*

The Fourth Law is aware of the composite nature of the books. The various facets of a composite book can be highlighted only by cross-references. Sometimes such entries prove immensely helpful in tracing an excellent account of a book catalogued under some different topic.

The Fourth Law requires the librarian to meet the diverse approaches of readers to books. Therefore, TO SAVE THE TIME OF THE READER, the catalogue is generally bifurcated as ALPHABETICAL part and CLASSIFIED part. Some libraries also have an AUTHOR-TITLE catalogue and a SUBJECT catalogue, generally known as divided catalogue.

Although the library catalogue enables a reader to locate the desired book without any loss of time, yet the position becomes different in case of nascent micro-documents. It is not the knowledge of the name of the author that brings the reader to his material contained in micro-documents; it is rather the name of the subject that does it. The time of the reader in locating his material can be saved if the catalogue is unsparing in making Subject Analytical Entries. But it will lead to the enormous growth of the catalogue. Therefore, TO SAVE THE TIME OF READERS, the library must purchase published bibliographies of individual authors, Subject Bibliographies, Cumulative Indexes to periodicals, Bibliographies of Bibliographies, etc.

7. *Reference Service*

Despite the availability of a good classified arrangement, an elaborate well-prepared catalogue with a profusion of subject analyticals and bibliographical sources, it may not be possible for an average reader to locate his information from the plethora of time-saving devices. This necessitates the provision of trained staff to initiate, to establish the contact between the reader and his books, to derive the best advantages of the bibliographical aids. Even after the initiation, the most readers require the bibliographical service of the reference staff who know the hide and seek character of all kinds of catalogues and indexes, and can handle them with greater ease and speed. The reference staff is the match-maker; they bring together the bride (book) and the bride-groom (reader) by rendering both Ready Reference and Long Range Reference Servicees.

8. Issue Methods

TO SAVE THE TIME OF THE READER, the Fourth Law has completely revolutionized the slow, complex and cumbersome charging and discharging systems, viz., Day Book and Ledger System, Dummy System, Temporary Slip System and One Card System. After number of experiments, it has brought about the most economical time saving charging systems like the Browne Charging System; Newark Charging System; Ranganathan's Reader's Ticket, Book Ticket Method; Detriot Self-Charging System. To find a fool-proof and time-saving methods, help was taken from the machine, and the machine methods like the Dickman Book Charging System, Gaylord Charging System, I.B.M., Circulation Control, etc. were brought into use. The big libraries in the western countries are even using the Photographic, Audio-Charging and Computer Charging Systems to fulfil the message of the Fourth Law.

TO SAVE THE TIME OF THE READER, time of the library staff spent on pedestrian tasks should be minimized to enable them to render reference/documentation/informntion services to readers in their search for knowledge. It invariably includes the various library activities, especially aimed at making information as promptly available as possible; selecting and organizing materials in this context assumes great importance. The invention of the card system dealing with Book-Selection Work, Order Work, Accession-Register, Withdrawl Work, has made work accurate, quite easy and speedy.

9. Centralized/Pre-Natal Cataloguing

Another direction in which an attempt is being made to SAVE THE TIME OF THE STAFF is that of Central/Co-operative cataloguing. Libraries spend lot of money, energy and time on processing same titles and organizing catalogues, which generally fail to satisfy the needs and demands of their users. Entries, call numbers and descriptions are usually incorrect. Precious time of the staff could be saved and released for reference service; duplication avoided and catalogues improved with greater uniformity, and consistency; if bibliographical entries were made by a central agency which, then, send copies to all.

TO SAVE TIME OF THE STAFF, Ranganathan has advocated Pre-natal centralized cataloguing, that is—

—Books should be catalogued by the National Central Library or State Central Library

—Catalogue cards should be printed for supplying to libraries.

—Printed catalogue cards should be given alongwith the book to every library buying it.

Such a centralization of cataloguing, according to Ranganathan's estimate, will release one member of library staff for every 2,000 books added to the library for diversion to reference service. Centralized and printed cards also help in the compilation of the Union Catalogue; helps libraries to improve their catglogues; makes it easier to guide their readers in their readings; helps them to find all the books a library has of any aspect of any subject, and ensure that libraries follow standard methods of processing and classifying books. Ranganathan also recommends pre-natal classification. The Fourth Law also urges the library world to evolve a uniform cataloguing code to make way for international cooperative cataloguing.

10. *International & National Documentation Centers*

TO SAVE man-power and money, it has been found necessary to centralize documentation work even at the international level. But in practice, the production of documentation lists like Chemical Abstracts and Biological Abstracts leads to the time lag of 6 months to one year. This is a serious violation of the Fourth Law. Therefore, Unesco recommended the setting up of national documentation centres. The periodicals scanned are restricted to those in which work in being done within the country. The advance procurment of contents pages of periodicals by Air (e.g. Insdoc List, now ceased) make it possible for national documentation list to reach service libraries almost simulaneously with the arrival of the periodicals concerned. The national documentation centre should also do pre-natal documentation of each of the articles originating within its territory and releasing the documentation list with abstracts. This suggestion of the Fourth Law can save money as such a list may prove sufficient in the case of the specialist concerned.

MECHANISATION of libraries can also save the time of the staff. A combination of facet analysis and machinery for search beginning from Punch-cards and going to Magnetic-tape will SAVE THE TIME OF THE READERS.

THE FOURTH LAW keeps in mind the time taken by the reader to reach the library. It should be so located as to SAVE THE TIME OF THE RFADER The academic library should be centrally located to provide easy accessibility to the students of all the departments.

However, it may be difficult to locate a library in the heart of the city, or at a place which is equally accessible from all parts of the city. Therefore, the Fourth Law desires the setting up of branch libraries in big cities, so that every citizen may find his/her library located within ten minutes walk from his/her residence.

The rural areas should be served by a fleet of LIBRARIES to SAVE THE TIME OF THE READERS.

FIFTH LAW

The Fifth Law is : A LIBRARY IS A GROWING ORGANISM. It is an accepted biological fact that a growing organism alone will survive. An organism which ceases to grow will petrify and perish. The Fifth Law maintains that the library as an institution, has all the attributes of a growing organism. A growing organism takes in new matter, casts off old matter, changes in size and takes new shapes and forms.

S.R. Ranganathan recognizes two kinds of growth : CHILD GROWTH and ADULT GROWTH. Whereas child growth is characterized by an overall increase in size and weight; adult growth, on the other hand, is characterized by the absence of an overgrowth. He examines both types of growth in libraries.

Growrh in Size

According to Ranganathan, a storage library. i.e., the National Central Library and each State Central Library continues to have CHILD GROWTH in respect of reading material and of staff. They may possibly attain the stage of adult-growth only in respect of readers. Practically, every other *Local Service Library* will attain ADULT GROWTH. Such a Library consists only of a new generation of readers replacing the old continuously; of a set of books replacing old continuously, and of new staff replacing the old continuously. But in India at present, hardly any Local Service Library has reached the stage of adult-level Nontheless, we should organize them with a full knowledge of the limit to their size.

The growth in the size of reading materials, the readers and the staff will have its repercussions of different aspects of library organization which Ranganathan examines as under :

1. Reading Materials

Every Local Service Library worth the name must have a live, well-choosen, selective and growing collection. In order to maintain recency, novelty and vitality in its collections, a library must purchase new books and journals, audio-visual materials and other informational documents to operate the library on teaching, research, and informational level. A distinguished collection of materials, therefore, becomes a sine qua non of a library.

The growth of reading materials has its own repercussions as under :

1.1 Library Building

The immediate impact of the growth or stock will be on the stack-room. Its size, its relative position, the book rack, forming unit of which the stack is built, the parts of the book-rack the shelf-planks, label-holders and all such things relating to housing of the books will to be examined in the light of the inevitable growth in stock.

As regards size of the building, the librarian must provide adequately not only for meeting present needs but also for future needs so far as they could be foreseen.

The Fifth Law has been slowly eliminating the old alcove and galary forms of construction for the storage of books. The stack-room is steadily gaining ground and a further development in stack architecture is the *stack-tower*. Another solution to meet the increase in stock is the building of repositories of the warehouse type to accomodate infrequently used books.

The unit-racks of which the stack-room is built should all be equal in every way, so that the additions can be made by any number of units at a time. In particular, the shelf-planks should all be of identical dimensions, so that they can be interchanged in any manner. They should be adjustable to accomodate books of varying sizes to avoid waste of space. Mobility of Shelf-Label also becomes essential,

There is an exponential growth in periodicals publication. But to satisfy the first fours laws in general, and the Third and Fourth Laws in particular, periodicals have to be displayed, But in the light of the Fifth Law, table space must be economized. As a result, at least six rows of periodicals, one behind the other, in ascending order should be accomodated on each side of the table.

New principles of architecture, such as modular design and dry construction are being fully exploited to face the onslaught of the Fifth Law. Modular design keeps the building as open as possible; while dry construction retains its flexibility.

1.2 Catalogue Room

The Fifth Law has influenced the size of the catalogue room in which the catalogue cabinets are kept. A standard unit cabinet, which occupies a floor area of 23"×28", can hold 48,000 cards. Each book on an average has six cards to satisfy the Second, Third and Fourth Laws. Thus, a unit cabinet is required for every 8,000 volumes. It is clear that the number of catalogue cabinets will increase in a dynamic library. This impact of Fifth Law must be borne in mind while designing the catalogue room.

1.3 Pysical Form of Catalogue

The effect of the Fifth Law on the physical form of the catalogue is also obvious. If A LIBRARY IS A GROWING Organism, it follows that the library catalogue will also be a growing one. Hence, the Fifth Law has to fight against the Printed Catalogue as it dces not reflect the actualities of the stock chiefly because of losses and withdrawl of books in the library. Moreover, it becomes out of date the day it is printed. As library grows dynamically, librarians find it difficult to administer this catalogue because of its serious limitations : regidity, inflexibility, obsoleteness, and increasing costs.

Another physical form of the catalogue is the Sheaf Catalogue. Here, too, the insertion of more than one entry in a leaf leads to a break in the sequence, which becomes increasingly inconvenient as the library grows more and more. However, if one entry is made on one page, there is much wastage. As a result of the growing nature of the library stock, the Card Catalogue was invented.

CARD CATALOGUE is an epoch-making contribution of the library profession. It has introduced great convenience, freedom, neatness and up-to-dateness in the maintenance of all kinds of records. Its fine quality is that it is a single, self-contained, flexible unit and is easy to operate Card catalogue is equally good in all kinds of catalogues : Author, Dictionary or Classified. It is also very valuable for preparing bibliographies, indexes and union catalogues for its inherent qualities of up-to-dateness, endless expansion and ease of withdrawl of entries. As at present, the card catalogue can cope with the growth of materials despite its serious limitation that it consumes much of library valuable space.

1.4 *Classification Scheme*

Another important matter that needs to be examined in the light of the Fifth Law, is the classification of books. In the first place, as A LIBRARY IS A GROWING ORGANISM and as the Universe of Subjects is also accelrating at a terrific speed, it is necessary that the classification scheme must be comprehensive, embracing all past and allowing places for any possible additions to knowledge. It means that the classification scheme must be elastic, expansible, and hospitable in the highest degree so that it could accomodate the emerging subjects without dislocating the sequence.

The Fifth Law will soon outgrow any Enumerated Scheme of Classification. The increase in the extension, depth and proliferation of subjects need a freely-faceted analytico-synthetic scheme of classification to accomodate the emerging subjects and thus keep pace with the Fifth Law.

2. *Growth in Readers*

The growth of libraries measured in terms of continuity, eternity and perpetuity depends upon the growth in readers. The growth in readers will invariably have its effect on the following factors :

2.1 The size of the reading room;

2.2 The issue method; and

2.3 Certain safeguards.

A brief explanation of each of the factor is worth-while.

2.1 Reading Room

The growth in readers require that the reading room must be flexible to meet the growth of documents, furniture, and accomodation for readers, A well planned and attractive reading area having comfortable seats with even and uniform lights is a source of inspiration for the reader for painstaking studies.

That the Fifth Law does not outwit the librarian, he should make sitting arrangement for at least 25% of the enrolment. The numbers of the research cubicles may be to the tune of 20% of the number of teachers, research fellows and advanced students.

Keeping in view the Fifth Law, the estimate of floor area required for library materials is one sq. foot. per 15 volumes. And the estimate for seating space is 25 sq. ft. for each graduate, 75 sq. ft. for each faculty member, for staff 100 sq. ft. per person, and 7 sq. meters for each research cubicle.

2.2 Issue Counter

Increase of readers leads to increase of issues. The location, size and shape of the issue counter must, therefore, be taken into consideration to meet the future growth. The issue system will also affect the size of the counter. While we must make provision for sufficient shelving space inside the counter for returned books, space around the counter should be spacious enough to make the readers easy while getting their books charged and discharged. Provision should also be made for a property counter where the readers can deposit their belongings.

2.3 Open Access

Open Access System is the only method of meeting the message of the Fifth Law. Closed Access System is unable to meet the growing demands of the readers because of delay and complex procedures involved in it. It also requires number of attendants for locating the books and to dole them across the counter making this system uneconomical. In Open Access, the readers themselves pick out the books of their choice.

2.4 Issue system

The Ledger System of issue simply breaks down with the growth of issue work as it involves a number of operations in the issue of a volume. Browne Charging System has achieved a spectacular success in coping with the growing issue work.

Ranganathan highlights the advantages of his own issue method known as 'Reader's Ticket, Book Card Charging System. According to him, this method is most economical. The daily issues of statistics are obtained with the least loss of time and labour. The method solves the problem of identifying the borrowers. It makes the readers responsible for their tickets and the reader can draw only the number of books for which he is entitled.

2.5 Single Level Floor

Increase in issue work implies increase in the number of volumes to be replaced. Moreover, hundreds of books will be used in different parts of the library building. These have to be taken back to their respective places in the stack room. Finally the newly received books also have to be transferred from the acquisition section to the technical section for processing, and from there to the stack-room or text book section or for display. It implies that the rooms of library should not have raised thresholds so as to admit loaded book trolley to any part of the floor. Simply, the issue aspect of the Fifth Law requires *even* floors. Different floors of an active library should be connected by electric lifts large enough to carry the book trolley.

2.6. Safeguards

As the number of readers increases, the problem of theft of books from the library becomes acute in open access libraries. It necessitates some safeguards.

Entrance to the library must be by one and only one gate and exist also must be by one and only one gate. The gates should be normally in locked position. They should open only if the counter-assistant releases the catch. The moment the reader leaves it, it should automatically lock itself. The gateway should be big enough to allow one and only one reader to pass through it at a time. All other door-ways and windows should be fitted with Jali-work shutters or weld-mesh shutters, whose meshes are too small for a book to be passed through. Further, no reader should be allowed to replace the books on the shelves. The greatest disservice to the open access is its introduction without proper safeguards.

3. Staff

The growth in staff has also to be recognised. Even those who realise the truth of the Fifth Law in regard to the books and readers, fail to recognise the need for the growth in the Third factor. Little do they realize that the Library's quality is a major contributing factor in determining the quality of education that a university can provide. Fifth Law could urge the library authorities to remember that it is only an adequate and well-qualified staff who can convert the library into an academic workshop.

Admitting that the library top-management provides the needed staff, the growth of the staff brings in its trail, certain new problems of organization. To achieve their aim of recording, organizing, and dissemination of knowledge, the librarians must keep in view three behavioral requirements. First, brilliant university trained persons must be inspired not only to join the library profession but also to remain in it. Secondly, persons must perform the tasks for which they have been recruited. It means that every staff member has to be put in charge of work for which he is best fitted physically, educationally and temperamentally. Finally, working environments must be conducive for creative, spontaneous and innovative work.

3.1. Staff Council

To help the librarians to obtain maximum turn out of work and efficiency, Ranganathan suggests the formation of a staff council. It may consist of the librarian, the heads of sections and one representative of each section. The function of such a staff council will be to advice the librarian :

—in solving problems involving intersectional relationships;
—in the systematization of the work of each section with due regard to efficiency and economy of material, energy and time;
—in developing the library resources in a harmonious manner;
—in developing methods for improving the service to the public; and
—in organizing extension work of all kinds.

The librarians should encourage the members to take effective part in the meetings by providing free and frank environment in which they can apply their intelligences. Such meetings, if democratically conducted, can provide a forum for the interchange, stimulation, and sharpening of ideas often leading to short-cuts and more efficient methods. Such meetings usually lead to high productivity; job satisfaction; improved quality of work; team work; acceptance of change; creativity; commitment to goals and generate a feeling of competence, self-esteem and a sense of belongingness.

Spirit of the Hive

As a library has to work on all days and for long hours, the organisation of the reference section and the counter section requires the greatest skill and care. There should be absolute continuity in the work and the change in the shift should be effected smoothly and quickly with the least dislocation of the work. Indeed, the readers should not be able to perceive that a change in staff has come. In other words, the members of staff should inculcate within themselves the spirit of the hives. It means that the members of staff should have most cordial relations among themselves. There should not be the least trace of jealousy or envy. The tendency to claim credit exclusively to oneself should be completely got over. Self should vanish. Every achievement should be anonymous and common to all.

The spirit of the hive should prevail among the library staff if the inconveniences due to the Fifth Law are to be avoided.[1]

Impact On The Universe of Subjects

Law 1

Books Are for Use is Law 1 of Library Science. Here the term "Book" is a generic name to denote all kinds of documents—book, periodical publication, technical report, patent, specification and non-conventional and meta-documents. The document is a trinity of :

1. Soul—embodied knowledge.
2. Subtle body—language and expression of the knowledge.
3. Gross body—physical body of the document.

The use of a ducument meant by the First Law is the use of its thought-content, that is, the expressed thought embodied in the document; the subtle body is indispensable for the acquisition of knowledge and as a vehicle for its communication; and the physical body of the document is a convenient means of transport of the embodied knowledge across space and through time. A document retrieval system is, therefore, essentially concerned with the classification, search, retrieval, and service of "subjects".

To meet the requirements of the Law 1, the arrangement of documents and the main entries for them should be primarily based on the characteristics of Subjects, embodied in documents. Therefore, one must know the characteristics for the efficient classification, search, and reterieval of subjects and service to readers.

1. **For details of Five Laws, *see* The Five laws of library science Ed. 2 (Asia Pub. House, 1957).**

Law 2

The implications of this Law on the Universe of Subjects is that the classification and arrangement of the documents and/or the main entries for them should bring together at every point of approach, just those documents relavant to the interest of the reader at the moment, and also arrange them on either side in the decreasing degree of affinity. An 'Apupa Pattern' of arrangement—(A—P—U—P—A = Alien – Penumbral—Umbral—Penumbral—Alien)—of the documents and of the main entries is desirable. An 'Every where—Apupa—Pattern will be ideal to meet the requirements of all readers at all times.

Law 3

Its implication is that at the time of retrieval no document relevant to the interest of the reader at the moment should be missed irrespective of his approach. It implies that no single tool of Library Science can fully satisfy this Law. Several of its tools and methods have to be used concurrently or in succession according to the need to meet the interest of the majority as well as of minority.

Law 4

Its implications are that the

—intellectual and mental potentialities of the readers should be conserved; and

—the retrieval of documentss and service should be done in the most economical manner.

The satisfaction of this further requires

—analysis of the Universe of Subjects to recognize each of its constituents and their relevant characteristics; and

—formulation of a methodology for the design and development of a document retrieval system which can implement the findings of the study.

Law 5

Library is a growing organism implies that the Universe of Subjects is ever-growing, the interests of readers is ever-growing and, therefore, Library Science is ever-growing, The comparison of the Universe of Subjects to an organism is helpful in the study of the qualities of the former. The Universe of Subjests is being cultivated incessantly at many points. This leads to change and growth, and consequently to new structures. There may be an overall increase in size, there may be internal changes including division and fusion of parts and utilization and assimilation of elements from the environment.

The Five Laws are the Five Commandments, embodying the rationale for unifying the theory of library science. With their formulation, Ranganathan infused a new life into librarianship and changed it into a science—library science; in fact, a craft into a full-fledged profession and discipline in its on right, with its own fundamental laws and a sound methodology of research, which we study in the following chapter.

15

SCIENTIFIC METHOD IN LIBRARY SCIENCE

Is there a library science? In reality, the answer to this question turns on the answer to another question : "What is a Science ?', Ranganathan discusses this question in his epoch-making work *Five Laws of Library Science*. He shows that the scepticism about library science being a science arises because of the restricted definition of the term science. Two such restrictions are common : and they can be shown to be false. These are :

1. Subject of Study, and
2. Method of Study.

1. Subject of Study

The course of studies and the nomenclature in vogue in universities at first restricted science to cover only the study of the physical world and its phenomena. In course of time, it has been extended to cover also the study of the world of living bodies and its phenomena. Some definitions supporting this view may be examined.

Sir William Dampier defines science as "Ordered knowledge of natural phenomena and the rational study of the relations between the concepts in which those phenomena are expressed",

Bertrand Russel gives a wider definition : "Science, as its name implies, is primarily knowledge; by convention it is knowledge of a certain kind, namely which seeks general laws connecting a number of particular facts. Gradually, however, the aspect of science as knowledge is being thrust into the background by the aspect of science as the power to mainpulate nature".

Of these two definitions, Russel's is comparatively more satisfactory. Dampier's definition relates only to scientific knowledge, and does not take into account either the application of such knowledge, or the power to apply it, towards control and change of man's environment. But though wider than Dampier's definition, Russel's definition too suffers from limitations. It presents science as static whereas it is intensely dynamic. The most vital attribute of science is not knowledge, but its capacity for acquisition of knowledge. Knowledge which science obtains is limited, frequently fragmentary and inaccurate, always liable to revison. The capacity of science to acquire knowledge is infinite.

Notwithstanding their limitations, two things become clear from the definitions given above. First, science is an organized knowledge; second science can be a process or method leading to knowledge. The first approach emphasizes the conservation of knowledge, the resusts, and the second emphasizes the process rather than results. However, both of these approaches are interlinked because progress is possible only through conservation, transmission and accumulation, and conservation is possible only through a process of analysis and verification. Scientists put more emphasis on methods rather than on conservation of knowledge or results.

J.G. Crowther's definition "science as a system of behaviour by which man acquires mastery of his environment" presents a different conception of science. It does emphasize the dynamic aspect of science, but it is open to objection as it is at once far too wide and far too narrow. A definition which appears approximating truth is : Science is a form of human activity through pursuit of which mankind acquires an increasingly fuller and more accurate knowledge and understanding of nature—past, present and future and an increasing capacity to adapt itself to change its environment and to modify its own characteristics.

Gradually, however, there is a growing support to another view of science In this view the subject of study is not relevant in determining the claim of a domain in the Universe of Knowledge to be deemed a science. Karl Pearson succinctly observed : "The field of science is unlimited; material is endless, every group of natural phenomena, every phase of social life, every stage of past and present development is material for science". The two follow- dictionary definitions of the term, 'Science' reflect this generalized view of its subject of study : (1) A system based or purporting to be based upon scientific principles : a method of arrangement. functioning, etc., reconciling practical or utilitarian end with scientific laws : e.g., Domestic Science; Animal Husbandry. (2) Accumulated and accepted knowledge which has been systematized and formulated with reference to the general truths and made available in work, life or the search of truth. The following dictionary definition also does so : A Science is "A branch of study which is concerned either with a connected body of demonstrated truths or with observed facts systematically classified and more or less collected by being brought under general laws and which includes trustworthy methods for the discovery of new truth, within its own domain". These definitions necessitate the study of steps involved in scientific methodology to which we shall soon return

2. Method of Study

At the beginning of the nineteenth century, Birckbeck introduced experimental demonstration in teaching the pure sciences. Since then, in due course, the nomenclature in vogue in universities tended to restrict science to cover only a domain of knowledge admitting experimental study. But this restriction, would exclude, an ancient science like Astronomy, from the right to be called a science; for it uses observation only and not experimentation needing a laboratory. This prompted Jeans to make a different approach : "A science teaches us to know and an art to do; and all the more perfect sciences lead to the creation of corresponding useful arts. Astronomy is the foundation of navigation". Rhetoric, here called an art, is sometimes defined as a science. Both designations are true. Science is systematized knowledge; if the laws and principles of discourse are exhibited in an ordered and interrelated system, they appear in a character of science (Genung). On this analogy, there can be an Art of Librarianship as well as a Library Science.

After showing that none of the above definitions leads to a precise definition of a 'Science', Ranganathan brings in the 'Spiral of Scientific Method'. He defines science as the name given to any domain in the Universe of Knowledge, whose development is characterized by a method called 'Scientific Method'.

In order to understand Ranganathan's concept of 'Spiral of Scientific Method', it is better first to know : What is Research ? What are the levels of Research ? What stages are involved in Scientific Method/Enquiry.

Meaning of Research

Research has been defined as a "careful or critical inquiry or examination in seeking facts or principles; a diligent investigation to ascertain something"[1]. This definition makes clear that research is not merely a search for truth, but a prolong, intensive, and purposeful search. As P.M. Cook aptly remarks : "Research is an honest, exhaustive, intelligent searching for facts and their meanings or implications with reference to a given problem. The product, or findings, of a given piece of research should be authentic, verifiable contribution to knowledge in the field studied". Cook emphasizes that research is laborious, careful inquiry or search with the object of discovering facts by scientific study of a subject.

A comprehensive definition of research flows from the pen of J.H. Shera who defines it "an intellectual process whereby a problem is perceived, divided into its constituent elements, and analysed in the light of certain basic assumptions : valid and relevant data are collected: hypotheses (if any), are through objective testing, rejected, amended, or proved. The generalizable results of this process qualify as principles, laws, or truths that contribute to man's understanding of himself, his works, or his environment". Shera wants to convey us that research is the systematic attempt to discover new facts, or sets of facts, or new relationships among facts through the formulation of a preliminary exploration or hypothesis which is subjected to an appropriate testing for appro-..., amending or disapproving (the hypothesis).

Simply stated : research is a systematic and a refined method of reflective thinking employing specialized tools, instruments, and procedures in order to obtain a more adequate solution of a problem than would be possible under ordinary means. It starts with a problem, collects data or facts, analyse them critically and draws conclusions based on the actual evidence. It involves original work instead of mere exercise of personal opinion. It evolves from a genuine desire to know not only what but how much, and measurement is therefore, a central feature of it. One gets support from Ranganathan who writes that "Research is critical and exhaustive investigation to discover new facts, to interpret them in the light of known ideas—laws and theories—, to revise the current laws and theories in the light of newly discovered

Webster's New international dictionary.

facts, and to apply the conclusions to some practical purpose". The findings of research enrich the universe of ideas.

Research is often equated with invention. But that category of invention is called research which attempts to collect data from various sources and variety of ways and subjects that data to a severe and intensive scruitny. The prefix 'Re' in the word 'Research' means "frequentative" and 'intensive'. Therefore, research means "a systematic, frequentative and intensive study of the collected data" with a view to extend the horizons of knowledge.

Levels/Types Of Research

From academic view-point, S.R. Ranganathan has categorized research as under :

1. Observational/Expermertal Research

Researcher is primarily a discoverer and his main source of information is his own experience derived from observation and experiments. Science begins with observation and must ulmimately return to observation. Observation implies the use of close contacts on personal level to seek the desired information data. It is the accurate watching and noting of phenomena as they occur in nature with regard to cause and effect relations. Observation, to Ranganathan, is the act of taking note of facts and depositing them in the memory either directly or after being correlated with already known facts. The accumulated knowledge of biologists, physicists, astronomers, and other natural scientists is built upon centuries of systematic observation of phenomena in their natural surroundings rather than in the laboratory. In the social sciences the term is often used in a much wider sense. The participant observer, for example, shares in the life and activities of the community, observing—in the strickest sense—what is going on around him, supplementing it by conversation, interviews and studies of records. The distinguished feature of observation in the extended sense is that data required are obtained directly rather than through the reports of others. Observation often involves the measurement of some quality or quantity.

Ranganathan defines experimental research as the act of observation coupled with the manipulation of the context and the conditions of observation. It is often done in order to discover some unknown principle or relation among facts, or to test and illustrate an already known principle. The distinctive mental process involved in observation and experiment is perception. The primary senses may be unaided or be aided by instruments. Experiment, observation, survey, and other similar acts are denoted by Ranganathan by the term 'Observational Research'. This forms one level of research.

2. Empircal Research

Research can take over the results of observation, sort them out, and induct from them (with the help of statistical methods including equations and correlation) certain generalized relation between facts. These are called by Ranganathan 'Empirical Laws'. The distinctive mental process involved in arriving at Empirical Laws is induction. It is essentially the intellect that is brought into play in induction. Ranganathan denotes it by the term "Empirical Research". It is really a matter-of-fact research. Both Observational Research and Empirical Research are denoted by Ranganathan by a generic term 'Pragmatic Research'. This forms another level of research.

3. Fundamental Laws

Unlike the Empirical Laws, which are the products of the intellect, it is also possible to have fundamental laws apprehended by intuition without the mediation of intellect or perception. A man having abundance of intuition is called 'Seer'. Sometimes, it is called "divine or trancendental apprehension". Ranganathan writes that transcendental apprehension of fundamental laws through intuition should not be taken to be research; it is beyond research. It is the ultimate starting point for deep *a priori* research.

4. A Priori Research

The distinctive process involved in a *Priori* Research is deduction. Intellect plays the vital role in deduction. It moves from assumed cause to its effect. It has two levels—Pure Research and Applied Research.

5. Pure Research

A *priori* research—and occasionally even pragmatic research—may be pursued unbiased by any possible use of its results. It may not be directed towards the solution of any practical problems of any known, immediate or ultimate utility. Ranganathan denotes it by the term 'Pure Research'. We can have pure research in any subject. Pure Mathematics is the field *par excellence* for pure research. For, as Bertrand Russell aptly remarked : "Mathematical research is pursued without even caring to know whether it has or does not have any correlate in the phenomenal world. A pure mathematician pursues his research without even caring to know whether his results are meaningful". Pure research usually establishes a variety of tools and models. And when factual experience grows, society may find some of those models to be meaningful to some utilitarian purposes. The utility of pure research may be found only years later—sometimes even centuries later. Nevertheless, pure research occasionally gives us remarkable, highly significant as well as unexpected discoveries.

Under the term pure research, F.L. Whitney includes two types of research : Free Fundamental Research and Oriented Fundamental Research. The former type of research is done by an individual. He has freedom of his invention. He tries out his own ideas as appeal him. The aim of pure research is not found directly in the realm of specific human need. Under the latter type, the research worker is concerned with knowledge and understanding of nature. But this field is limited. It is usually a team work. Such research is useful for both the theoretical discoveries as well as practical application.

6. Applied Research

Applied research is pursued for some specific purpose outside its own domain, either for an immediate distinct utility concerned with a specific human need or as an aid to the development of some other subject. Applied Mathematics, Applied Mechanism, Applied Chemistry, Applied Psychology and Applied Sociology are examples.

6.1 Developmental Research

Some people also add the term – Development Research. It is the final stage where a new process discovered in applied research is put to use for social and economic benefit. The need for this type of research is now recognized in almost all industries. Many industrial houses are now having wings for developmental research.

In the modern world, Applied Research dominates, particularly in developing countries to find better, quicker and cheaper ways of doing things for the betterment of people. Nevertheless, a proper balance between Pure Research and Applied Research is necessary for social progress. Pure research is a search for broad principles and synthesis without any utilitarian objective, e g., Franklin's discovery of electricity. This is more an intellectual exploration arising from insatiable intellectual curiosity. On the other hand, Edison's work, e.g. electric lights, phonograph, is an example of applied research associated with particular projects and problems. Such research being of practical value, may relate to current activity or immediate practical situations. Now-a-days, practical orientation dominates most fields of study.

Pure and Applied type of research, however, are not distinct and separate activities. One always involves the other. As Joseph Needham succinctly writes : "There is no sharp distinction between "pure" and "applied" science. There is really only one science with long term promise of application. The knowledge emerges from both kinds of science. "Basic research resembles the sowing, whilst the judging of practical problems can be compared with the harvest".

7. *Deductive and Inductive Research*

Deductive research is the proc ss by which theory is tested when from posulates or from known scientific principles, scientists draw conclusions or generate new theories relating to specific cases using deductive reasoning. But the accuracy of a conclusion reached at depends on the accuracy of the postulates or principles.

Inductive logic, on the other hand, is the process by which theory is developed; whereby observing many individual examples, the scientist draws general conclusion or general theory. David J. Buckley writes that if the researcher does not have an answer to a question and hence embarks on a fact finding mission, he is engaged in inductive research. If he has what he believes to be an answer to a research question, but wishes to confirm or apply it through further testing he is engaged in deductive research. In other words, deductive research is guided by a priori hypothesis (i.e., existing in mind prior to and independent of experience) which are either proved or disapproved during the course of investigation. Inductive method is employed to generalize from the known and verified facts of a given class to the known and as yet unverified facts of same class.

8. Seminal Research

In every discipline, over a period of a century or so, a few men of genius make landmark contributions. Their work exposes the fundamentals and lay the foundation of the subject. It will be charged with a high degree of intuition. It is likely to make a great impact on the course of development of the subject; generate several lines of applied and development research and attract upon itself a large number of works from its own as well as other related fields. Research of this kind cannot be done to order nor can it be directed. Any such attempt will harm rather than help. But the society can play a vital role by spotting out such men of genius; ensuring that the solo research done by them is not interfered with or pressurized, but that each is allowed to dream un-disturbed, scientillate, and radiate at his own time and space; and finally to reduce to a minimum the environmental handicaps (e g., difficulty of access to documents); and the expenditure of intellectual, mental, and physical energy on the necessary routines associated with the work.

9. Team-Relay Research

In its early stages of growth, a discipline may have to depend largely on the work of a few genius. When society discovers the value of the work, the kinds and number of demands on the discipline increases, and thereby the number of practitioners of the profession increases. The need for a wide application and full exploitation of the findings of fundamental research for utilitarian ends will call for some of the following lines of work : First, working out specific procedures for application to particular pieces of work; second, analysis, testing, and evaluation; third, devising suitable methods for productive utilization of the findings of fundamental research; fourth, developing techniques for progressively reducing the dependence on mere flair; and finally, thereby making the work more and more objective.

It will be wasteful to depend upon and engage for this purpose the few men of genius. Team-relay research among intellectuals would be more productive form of organization in such a context. It will also help in bringing to bear on a problem specialized knowledge in different branches of the subject and even from other disciplines. However, team-research would call for proper division of labour, co-ordination of the work, and avoidance of wastage of effort.

10. *Role of Intuition in Research*

While research is essentially intellectual, it is occasionally lighted up by a flash of intuition in some researcher or other. The intuition coming into play is so slight and so fleeting that it does not reveal any fundamental laws. Intuition may also reveal the value of something seen or done, which escapes apprehension by intellect alone. Here too the intuition coming into play is so slight and so fleeting that it does not reveal fundamental laws. Perhaps its role in research may be described as analogous to the water flowing in a river being occasionally added to by a feeble underground spring. A large dose of intuition alone can flood-light the phenomenal world down to the near-seminal level and reveal fundamental laws. It was intuition which helped Ranganathan to formulate the Five Laws of Library Science in 1928. It took nearly two years for the intellect to make inferences from the Five Laws. Even today—45 years later—the intellect has to work on the Five Laws and get more inferences to suit the present-day social concepts influencing library services. It was intuition that helped Newton to "see" the fundamental laws of gravitation and of motion, but it was the intellect in him that led him to deduce from them the theorems on Planetary Orbits. This was pure research.

Though intellectually separable, the different kinds of research are not separated in actual practice. On the contrary, they are blended at various stages and in different combinations. This is a matter of judgement in each situation. Researeh in physical sciences is concerned with the behaviour of matter and energy; in the biological sciences with the behaviour of life that has emerged out of matter and energy; in medical sciences with man who has grown new dimensions of consciousness like "mind"; in the social sciences with the behaviour that human being aggregates like family, community, society, nation, etc., and in humanities with the inner world of human inspirations and realization involving the movements of the mind and the infinitude of the spirit.

Through the following schematic diagram, Ranganathan represents the relation of the various kinds of research to one another and to the fundamental laws which are beyond research.

	Fundamental Laws	Through Intiuition
	↓	
A *Priori* Research	Pure Research	Through Intellect
	↓	
	Applied Research	Through Intellect
	↓	
	Developmental Research	Through Intellect & Perception
	↑	
Pragmatic Research	Empirical Research	Through Intellect
	↑	
	Observational Research	Through Perception

SCIENTIFIC METHOD

Francis Bacon (1561-1626) planted the seeds of the scientific method when he attacked the *deductive method* of reaching conclusions on the basis of observed facts. By deductive method we always arrive at a conslusion from general to specific. Man devised *inductive* reasoning to complement *deductive reasoning* as a means of searching knowledge. In inductive reasoning, an investigator collects evidence that wil enable him to establish a generalisation as being probably, true. He initiates his inquiry by observing particular instances or concrete facts, and from his examination establishes general conclusion about the whole class in which these particular instances belong. Each method has its merits and snags.

To construct a more practical method of attaining reliable knowledge, men such as Newton, Galileo, and their successors eventually combined the *inductive* and *deductive* thought process. This synthesis of *reason* and *observation* produced the modern scientific method of research.

The purpose of research is to discover answers to questions through the application of scientific procedures. These procedures have been developed in order to increase the liklihood that the information gathered will be relevant to the questions asked and will be reliable and unbiased. Scientific Method involves certain stages which invariably lead to systematic, controlled, empirical, and critical investigation of hypothetical propositions about the presumed relations among natural phenomna. However, two points need to be emphasized. First, when we say that scientific research is systamatic and controlled, we mean in effect that scientific investigators can have critical confidence in research outcome. This means that research situation is tightly disciplined. Secondly, scientific investigation is empirical. If the scientist believes something to be so, he must somehow or other put his belief to a test outside himself. Subjective belief, in other words, must be checked against objective reality. As such scientific research means a "systematic, frequentative and intensive study of collected data".

Stages Involved in Scientific Method/Inquiry

I. A Felt Difficulty

Man encounters some obstacle or problem that puzzles him, may be, that (a) he lacks the means to get to the end desired; or (b) he has difficulty in identifying the character of an object; or (c) he cannot explain an unexpected. Problems : India is a rich country inhabited by poor. Why the First war of Indian independence (1857) failed ? Why an apple falls down and does not float in the air ?

II. Gathering Data

Data may be gathered on the problem or within a selected field by applying *observation* method. Observation can fairly be called the classic method of scientific inquiry, a scientific procedure for comprehending things, events, quantities, qualities and relationships

Three modes of observation may be distinguished.

1. Visual Observations

Data are recorded through sense experiences but sense experience is subjective. Science results in unrelinquishable search for objectivity: science reaches the objectivity in 3 ways :

(a) The observation of different persons similarly studied must lead to the same result.

(b) It must be repeatable by the same persons or others.

(c) The quality observed of data by one should agree with that observed by another.

2. Aid of Scientific Research Instrument

Observations by human sense must be assisted with suitable instruments like telescope, and photographic plate because these instruments help in recording facts which would be otherwise unobservable.

3. Experiment

In nature the conditions under which we have to observe a phenomenon may occur in its own time. But in experiment we can arrange the conditions under which an observation is to be made. Thus experimental method makes possible a more reliable analysis that the observer may repeat the experiment over and over again at will and thus greatly lessen the probable error of his determinants. Few merits of the experimental method are worth mentioning. First, results are more reliable. Second, the whole experiment can be divided into suitable parts or stages to make it a detailed observation. Third, it can be studied or observed under a variety of conditions. Finally, it can be observed by several people at several places.

One can say that observation must be accurate, must be extensive, and must be done under a variety of conditions. Observations must be recorded in definite terms and measurments and in specific statements.

Be it noted that observation is only one of the methods for gathering data. The other important methods are : 1. Interview Method. 2. Scheduled Method. 3. Questionnaire Method. 4. Case/life History Method. 5. Experimental Method, etc.

III Analysis of Data

At this stage the collected data are classified and arranged on the basis of the similarities, variations, activities, processes, causes, results, etc. Distinction is also made between essential and superficial characteristics.

IV Formation of Hypothesis

Next step is the formation of hypothesis. A hypothesis is the generalization in the form of a proposition derived on the basis of induction, i e. reasoning. Inductive inference helps to arrive at general principles or statements or theory from particular instances. But this method of inductive inference suffets from two drawbacks :

1. A single instance can destroy the generalization. For example, if after inductive inference, the fact is taken for granted that all swans are white. 2. Induction is based on observation

and so in many cases any principle or generalisation can be a creation of mind only not based on observation as Mendel's hereditary theory of genes. Genes were never observed by him and none has been able to isolate them till now.

Thus a hypothesis may be a free creation of scientific imagination—a leap of imagination. Researchers use constructive imagination, discernment, known principlcs to formulate reasonable generalizations that solve the problem or explain known facts in the selected field. Many researchers accept a mass of classified data and verified generalizations and then proceed to solve some problems by formulating hypothesis thereon and verifying them without including general gathering of data and classification work.

Hypothesis is in a sense a type of supposition or assumption or imagination on the basis of which a researcher makes a proposition which may or may not be proved. Even a negative result, under certain circumstances, can be the crown of research. But formulating a hypothesis scientists cannot know what things to observe and what not. In this step we get theories and principles in tentative form or hypothesis. Nevertheless the hypothesis must explain or describe known facts; it should not be inconsistent with principles in the field; it must be experimentally verifiable; and it must be simple.

5. Testing of Hypothesis

Testing of a hypothesis or verification of generalisation is done by applying the method of deductive inference. Deductive inference is reasoning from general premises to specific derived instance thereof. The procedure involved may be summarised in a simple hypothesis. If proposition (p) is true, then, proposition (q) is likewise true. If it rains, the streets will be wet (if p then q). This method of deductive inference proceeds in the following fashion.

—the general principle is stated;

—a special case is deducted as an instance of general principle; and

—inference, conclusion, proof or demonstration results therefrom.

By this method a hypothesis is tested and accepted in two ways :

1. a hypothesis must tally with the already existing theories;
2. the consequences derived from it must tally with experience and observation.

Consequences from this hypothesis are derived by means of deductive inferences. This basis must he said to be the logical basis of testing a hypothesis. Thus when we say that a hypothesis is verified, it means that the hypothesis explains the concepts or facts which it set out to explain. In science, it may mean that hypothesis gives the cause of the phenomena explained.

Hypothesis are verified in science by controlled experiments, by tested predictions of results. by repetition of experiments and the gathering of additional data.

The Scientific Method, thus, consists of three processes: observation, formation of hypothesis and testing of hypothesis. It is one of the most important and the most recognised method for developing knowledge. When a hypothesis is tested and proved it becomes the theory.

6. *Reporting*

The research in full and subjecting results to criticism and verification by other competent collaborators.

7. *Announcing* the results of the research to the general public for practical use.

Commenting on the stages involved in Scientific Method, Ranganathan writes that in any subject or discipline, progressive step of abstraction is itself an intellectual process and Scientific Method makes intellectual process in any discipline perpetually round and round in a never ending succession of cycles. He explains the process in 4 steps :

1. *Empirical Phase* : This phase starts with facts or individual experience and ends in the distillation of few *empirical laws.* All this work is through intellect.

2. *Hypothesing Phase* For this one must be endowed with a considerable intuition.

3. *Deductive Phase* All the known empirical laws can be derived out of hypothesis by deductive reasoning and work in this phase is solely intellectual.

4. *Verification Phase* : The new deducted laws point to facts and experiments left unnoticed till then. The work in this phase

consists of verifying them by observation in the phenomenal universe. It is done through the senses and intellect.

Spiral of Scientific Method

Ranganathan has characterized the working of the *Scientific Method* by a never-ending spiral movement. It is schematically represented in the diagram on the next page. The cycle implied in the spiral will be followed in the clock-wise direction. For convenience of reference, the four cardinal points of the cycle are denoted by Ranganathan by the terms *Nadir*, *Ascendent*, *Zenith*, and *Descendent*.

The *Nadir* marks the accumulation of facts, obtained by observation, experimentation, and other forms of experience.

The *Ascendent* marks the accumulation of inducted or empirical laws got out of the facts accumulated at the nadir, by inductive logic including normal equations and other aids from statistical calculus.

The *Zenith* marks the fundamental laws formulasted with the aid of intuition of some degree or other so as to comprehend all the inducted or imperical laws accumulated at the ascendent as compelling implications.

The *Descendent* marks the accumulation of the deduced laws got from fundamental laws at the zenith, with the aid of deductive logic including general semantics and all kinds of mathematical calculuses.

The four cardinal points give rise to four quadrants in the cycle implied in the spiral. For convenience of reference, the quadrants have been numbered 1 to 4 respectively, by Ranganathan, as follows :

Quardrant 1 is the one between *descendent* and *nadir*

Quadrant 2 is the one between *nadir* and *ascendent*

Quadrant 3 is the one between *ascendent* and *zenith*; and

Qudarant 4 is the one between *zenith* and *descendent*.

Ranganathan gives the description of the quadrants as under :

Quadrants 1 corresponds to the stage in the development of a domain of the universe of knowledge, confirming to scientific method, in which :

—primary senses are used either in their native state or with the aid of instruments of various degrees of powerfulness;

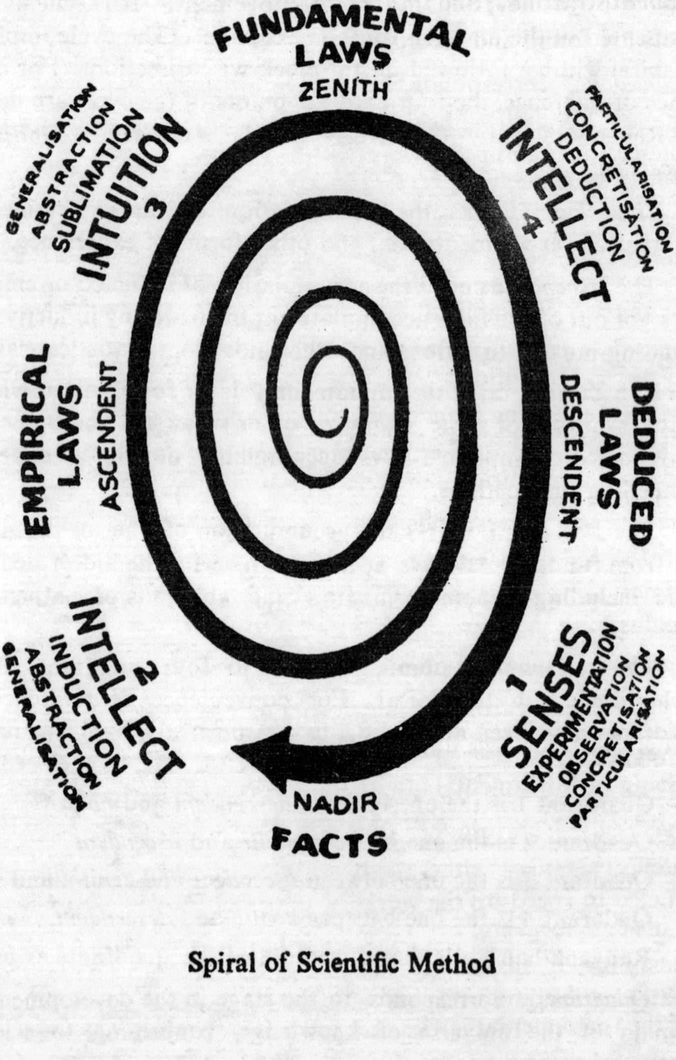

Spiral of Scientific Method

—observations are made of knowees, either with or without experimental interference and conditioning;

—there is progression towards particularisation, and regression from generalization;

—there is progression towards concreteness and, regression from abstractness; and

—facts are found and recorded.

Quadrant 2 corresponds to the stage in which :

—intellect is used either by itself or aided by machinery constructed to speed up the work of the intellect and to give relief to it in some degree;

—reasoning is made with the aid of inductive logic including normal equations, statistical and other calculuses to boil down the numerous facts accumulated at the nadir to a small number of inducted or empirical laws.

—there is regression from particularization, and progression towards generalition;

—there is regression from concreteness, and progression towards abtractness: and

—inducted or empirical laws are formulated and recorded.

Quadrants 3 corresponds to the stage in which :

—intuition of some intensity or other is used unmediated by the primary senses or the intellect;

—the inducted or empirical laws stand boiled down to a very small number of fundamental laws—e.g., Newton's law of motion;

—progression towards ultimate generalisation;

—progression towards ultimate abstractness; and

—seizing of fundamental laws and their recording.

Quadrants 4 corresponds to the stage in which :

—intellect is used either by itself or aided by machinery constructed to speed up the work of the intellect and give relief to it in some measure;

—reasoning is made with the aid of deductive logic including mathematical and other calculuses to workout the implications of the fundamental laws;

—progression towards particularization;

—progression towards concreteness;

—derivation of deduced laws and their recording;

—derived deduced laws include one and all of the inducted empirical laws; and
—the number of deduced laws exceeds that of the empirical laws, if the fundamental laws had been seized with intuition of adequate intensity.

One finds that the process of *observation* corresponds to quadrants 1 and 2; the process of formulation of *hypothesis* to quadrant 3 and *testing* of hypothesis to quadrant 4 in the cycle.

Re-entering into Spiral

The spiral of scientific method begins the next cycle, by re-entering quadrant 1. Two things happen at the this stage of development :

1. observations and experiments are made to verify empirically validity of the new deduced laws; and
2. further observations and experiments are made continuously and this leads to accumulation of new empirical facts.

So long as the deduced laws are empirically verified to be true and the new empirical facts are found to be in confirmity to the implications of the fundamental laws, there is no further movement in the spiral. As and when new empirical facts appear to contradict the new fundamental laws, scientific method is applied and new cycle gets into full swing and carries the spiral of scientific method further. Work in quadrant 2 leads to a new set of empirical laws. Work in quadrant 3 leads to the seizing of a new set of fundamental laws. Work in quadrant 4 leads to a new set of deduced laws. Work in quadrant 1 is again started as before. This cycle is liable to be repeated without end in many a domain of the universe of knowledge. This method is easily applicable to natural sciences because :

—observation can be impersonal and nearly objective;
—experiments can be made without let or hindrance; and
—there has been continuous sharpening of mathematical calculuses over centuries, necessary and sufficient to make induction and deduction.

SCIENTIFIC METHOD IN LIBRARY SCIENCE

Ranganathan writes that the development of library science is fully characterized by the spiral of scientific method. He writes that the development of library science had already completed a full cycle in the Spiral of Scientific Method. The Five Laws of Library Science discussed in the previous chapter demonstrate it. He states that the library practices current before 1931 correspond to quadrant 1 (of the spiral). They state facts of experience corresponding to the nadir. They also mention in a few places some empirical laws derived from the facts by induction, This corresponds to quadrant 2. The five fundamental laws seized in quadrant 3 (by intuition) from the normative principles corresponding to the zenith. Quadrant 4 is well provided for by showing the then library practices as compelling implications of these normative principles. This quadrant receives also new deduced laws not found among the Empirical laws. New library techniques and practices get generated in this way from the normative principles. The formulation of the Five Laws has set the spiral of scientific method into action. These are the normative principles of Library Science.

With the formulation of the Five Laws, a unifying theory for large divisions of library science such as Book Selection, Classification, Cataloguing, Reference Service, Physical Bibliography, Management, Library Buildings, Fittings and Furniture, and Documentation became available. Postulates, canons and principles, based on Five Laws, for guiding the development, study, and teaching of each of the branches of library work could be derived. Five Laws also guide Librarians to make helpful decisions on such minute aspects as "The appropriate width and treatment of the window-sill of the stack-room", "the sequence of the elements in the host section of a bibliographical reference", and "the size of lettering in the shelf guides, gangway guides, and bay guides".

Changes in library practices could be predicted in the context of the changes in the needs and demands of the society; and the effectiveness of each library practice could be tested against the implications of the Five Laws. The discipline of "Library economy" completed a full cycle in the Spiral of Scientific Method and attained the statusof a science[2]. In Ranganathan's own words, the Five Laws of Library Science "Contains, in little, practically everything which is found more elaobrately elucidated in all the succeeding books of the family".

2. **Pauline A. Atherton, Putting knowledge to work, An American view of Five Laws (Vikas, 1973).**

Pauline A. Atherton writes : "If Dr. Ranganathan had done nothing more than publish the Five Laws of Library Science, he would have to be seriously considered for a Library Hall of Fame." The impact of these five succinct statements, first published in 1931, is still being felt around the world. The explication and amplification of these statements by teachers in library science classes who know the importance of these laws stir students to think of and believe in library service above library work as their life goal[3].

In the words of Berwick Sayers "The Five Laws of Library Science, 1931, is a work of great simplicity which conceals depths and yet reveals what may be called the spiritual but intensively practical springs of his activity".[4] F.H. Grave wrote in a review of the Five Laws, "The laws themselves have as much validity now as they ever did. They have been formulated in fewer than 25 words... Every thoughtful librarian will want to spend time and mental energy on a systematic consideration of the implications of these laws."

Five Laws, Re-instated

The word "book" has been replaced by the "document." One finds the re-interpretation of the Five Laws of Library Science in Ranganathan's definition of the term *documentation* by which he means the :

—Promotion and practice of bringing into use of nascent micro-thought by the specialists (First Law)

—Pin-pointed (Second Law)

—Exhaustive (Third Law)

—Expedicious service of nascent micro-thought to the specialists (Fourth Law);

—In spite of the continuous ever- increasing cascade (Fifth Law) of nascent micro-thought on an ever-multiplying number of specialized subjects, communicated through several thousands of periodicals.

G. Bhattacharyya has re-instated the Five Laws into Five Normative Principles of Information :

1. Information is for use;

3. Ibid.,
4. cf. Ibid.,

2. Every Information-user His Information;
3. Every Piece of Information Its user;
4. Save the time of the Information-user;
5. The Universe of Information is Ever growing.

Re-instated, thus, the Five Normative Principles cover the entire problem of the dissemination of information.

In brief, the Five Laws of Library Science have lifted the art of Librarianship to that of a science—Library Science. The Five Laws are, in fact, a "succinct statement of the reasons for our profession". They set the stage for the beginning of research in library science. The use of the Spiral of Scientific Method has also been found helpful in the studies on the mode of development of subjects. The Spiral of Scientific Method being a never-ending one, the development of a subject is never complete, but ever continuing.

A. Neelameghan has emphasized the helpfulness of the Spiral of Scientific Mothod as under :—

—it characterizes a discipline on the basis of its method of development rather than on the basis of its subject of study or the method used in study in studying it.

The difficulties arising in the traditional method of characterizing a discipline as a science on the basis of the subject of study or the method of study is by-passed,

—any discipline may adopt the scientific method in its development.

—certain specific attributes of the different subjects become clear. This is of help to the librarian in learning about certain affinity among large regions of knowledge [such as those comprehended by each Basic Subject; Comprehensive Subjects, etc. This, in turn, helps in placing these subjects in a helpful position in the Universe of Subjects;

—different models of the development of subjects may be formulated to help the prediction of likely developments in each of the subjects or groups of them; and

—the facility for the prediction of the trend of development in a subject is valuable to the classificationist and classifier in particular and the librarian in general.

16

COOPERATION AND RESOURCE-SHARING

Meaning

Library cooperation signifies a symbol of good will, an intent to share resources, knowledge, bibliographical data, facilities and other fruits of technology, man's ingenuity, and the results of accumulated wealth of knowledge[1].

One of the basic objectives of the library cooperation is to reduce wasteful duplica ion of intellectual effort and the expense incurred in providing duplicate coverage of the same material.

Secondly, it provides an opportunity for the collaborating libraries to increase their resources to provide better services and more facilities to the users without corresponding proportionate increase in expenditures. All libraries cooperating in such a scheme are merged as it were into a single unit with vast pool of resources. It is the transmigration of the individualistic philosophy of library service into a cooperative service.

Finally, greater cooperation and coordination of services could reduce the number of sources that a user must check in a given field and would assist in deciding whether services are appropriate or feasible.

Factors Necessitating Cooperation

Library cooperation as a means of extending the services and resources of libraries has its roots in the socio-economic and technological changes being witnessed in the rapidly changing world.

First, the drastic developments in the art of printing and in the field of paper technology has resulted in an inertimable increase in the supply of books, the greater diffusion of knowledge, the dissemination of natural and classical literature, and the flowering of literary criticism.

1. Joe Kraus, *Library Trends*, Oct. 1975.

Secondly, the bewildering discoveries in the fields of science, and technology leading to moon walking, and the analysis of the dust of this planet or the projected Mars walking has, opened the flood-gates of knowledge for common man.

Thirdly, the book, these days, is no longer the primary vehicle for the communication of nascent ideas, and the transmission of the current information. The nascent micro thought is now usually embedded within the bosoms of periodicals. abstracting and indexing journals, preprints, document bibliographies, research correspondence (published and unpublished), patents, specifications, standards, and research reports. No library, however, big is in a position to claim self-sufficiency in this multitude and mass sources of knowledge. Yet any reader, anywhere, might need any book. How can he get it? The answer is "By cooperation" among libraries.

Fourthly, explosion of knowledge and proliferation of subjects has changed the very nature of the demands put forth by the readers With the result, there are more scientists today, to demand information; they demand it at a faster rate, they demand wider cross-discipline and cross speciality coverage. This hue and cry—the hue of ever growing multi-faceted demands for information and the cry of ever swelling ocean of recorded knowledge has made it quite impracticable for any library to meet individually the demands of all it readers. Co-operation seems to be the only panacea for mitigating the disability of limited resources, and to bring standardization of services offered to the reading community.

Finally, the professionalization of library science has been the most important influence on cooperation. The changing role of the librarian from a "keeper" or "lifter" of books to a disseminator of knowledge has enhanced the value of cooperation. Higher standards of education and professional qualifications lead to better libraries, better advice to readers and more specialization, the sum total of which stimulates the demands made upon, and extends, the system of cooperation[2].

Ways and Means of Library Cooperation

The major ways and means of library cooperation include: (1) inter-library loan service; (2) cooperative acquisition;

2. G. Jefferson, *Library Cooperation* (Lond., Andre, 1966), p. 9.

(3) centralized and cooperative cataloguing; (4) union catalogue and bibliographical centres; (5) documentation centres. (6) union lists of serials and bibliographies; (7) cooperative reference and information services; (8) cooperative storage centres; (9) cooperative photographic services; and (10) international cooperation.

Each of the above area of cooperation needs brief discussion.

1. INTER-LIBRARY LOAN (ILL)

The major purpose of ILL is to place every book, manuscript, archive or other graphic record within the reach of persons who need them. Advocated by S.S. Green and E.C. Richardson, the idea of borrowing and leading material within the university, among university and other libraries in a country and on an international level for the use of patron has now become the cornerstone of inter-library cooperation.

The Five Laws of Library Science are the very soul of the theory of ILL. If the books/documents are for use; if every reader is to get his document for reading, research and information; if every document is to be energised for whatever purpose it is designed to serve; if the time of the reader in pursuit of research or information is to be saved; and if the exponential growth of modern knowledge is to be reckoned with, the librarian has to be more than an administrator, technician or a scholar. He has to operate his library under the theory that, given time and a reasonable complete citation, it can hope to provide every item which has ever been printed in any part of the world.

ILL has, thus, two complementary purposes : the first is to aid the researcher in acquiring specialized material of whatever origin and of whatever location; the second is to assist the general reader to borrow material he might not have access to because of lack of proper libraryfac ilities. The idea is to enthuse the patron of a library with the feeling that when he enters the portals of his library, he is, as it were, entering the portals of all libraries not only of his own country but also of the world at large.

By and large the libraries have come to recognize their obligation for providing ILL services. The devices like Teletype,

Facsimile transmission, Ultrafax and Closed Circuit transmission have accelerated the speed of document transmission.

2. COOPERATIVE ACQUISITION

The rising tides of literature, expansion in different form of publications from books and periodicals to 'unpublished reports' and theses as sources of information, the increasing complexity of the relationship between subjects, and the limited financial possibility for the acquisition of all relevant material even for the richest library have obliged the librarians to participate in co-operative acquisition scheme.

The advantages flowing from co-operative acquisition may be counted : It avoids unnecessary duplication of books; may encourage better book selection; takes adventage flowing from bulk purchase, and ensures a faster flow of materials. Centralized procurement of documents on a national or regional levels is quite helpful in overcoming some of the difficulties encountered by librarians in acquiring foreign published materials. For university libraries, a co-operative acquisition plan might be devised along the lines of the Farmington Plan, taking into consideration their subject specialization.

2.1 What is Farmington Plan

The organization of the Farmington Plan took place in 1948. It was a voluntary agreement between sixty research libraries of U.S.A. Its objective was to ensure that at least one copy of the each new foreign book and pamphlet that might be of any interest to a researcher in the United States was purchased under the Plan, promptly listed in the Union Catalogue at the Library of Congress, and made available for use through ILL photographic reproduction. The Plan ceased functioning partly because of the success of two Plans : Public Law 480 (PL 480), and the National Programme for Acquisitions and Cataloguing (NPAC).

2.2 Scandia Plan

Acquisition on a specialized basis has been attempted in the Scandinavian Countries—Denmark, Finland, Norway and Sweden—illusion of self-sufficiency has been abondoned. The Plan was established in 1959. It is based on voluntary co-operation and is managed at the expense of co-operating libraries. The accepted basis of division of responsibity was subject, geographic or logistic. Under this system each library decides independently its own aquisition and exchange policy except that the allocation of special subject-field is made on the basis of a comparative evaluation of existing collections and fields of interest in the different libraries. Each co-operating library has given a commitment to make its materials available to scholars throughout Scandinavia, and has further committed itself to function as a bibliographic centre in their areas of specialization.

Few neighbouring libraries can also co-operate for the acquisition of translations, manuscripts, historical documents, scientific reports, reference and bibliographical publications, newspapers and collections in micro-forms. Such a scheme of co-operative acquisition may better be operated through the national libraries, documentation centres, special libraries association and other professional bodies. Government should take a lead to encourage the idea of co-operation. It must be admitted that attempts at co-operative acquisition have not been quite successful. Though the idea sounds well, it is becoming increasingly evident that forming a network for co-operative acquisition is not being taken seriously as a practical preposition.

3. CENTRALISED AND CO-OPERATIVE CATALOGUING

The centralized and co-operative cataloguing of documents is another important area where co-operation between libraries is possible for saving time and reducing expenses.

The centralized cataloguing is that which is done by a single library or other centralized agency for use of a number of libraries; whereas co-operative cataloguing is done in two or more libraries for the benefit of each participating library and may be made available to others. The objective of each type of cataloguing activity is to economise the processing of materials, to increase the number of titles catalogued, to promote uniformity of cataloguing and catalogues and to raise the over-all levels of the quality of cataloguing by exploiting the services of subject and linguistic specialists. Ranganathan has estimated that if centralized cataloguing is done, national saving would be to the tune of 79% of all publications. The MARC and the Shared Cataloguing Projects of the Library of Congress have shown the way how processing of library material could be effectively and economically undertaken.

Centralization and co-operation in cataloguing should take place within the university as far as practicable, and the university should take full advantage, and participate in such services to keep their records up to date and in making their catalogues more useful to the clientele.

4. UNION CATALOGUES (UC) BIBLIOGRAPHICAL CENTRES

A UC is an inventory common to several libraries and containing all or some of their publications listed in one or more orders of arrangement. Its basic function is to locate publications in order to facilitate access to books. It is a tool for the rationalization of ILL. It also helps in the prevention of unnecessary duplication of little used materials, and to provide information gaps in the collection of the region covered. Special services include supplying cataloguing and classification data. UC also helps in the exchange programmes of libraries[3].

Under university library system, a UC representing all the holdings of the various library units should be maintained. It facilitates library units to consult the UC directly for the location of requisite materials. The main library can also assist its unit libraries by checking bibliographical entries, identifying obscure items and in other ways. The Central library can also help the researcher to know what publications exist or nave been published in his field of specialization.

5. DOCUMENTATION CENTRES

Research is one of the most important functions of a university. But the success of research depends prompt documentation services provided by its library.

The university libraries cannot, however, afford their own documentation centres. As an alternative they should co-operate fully with their national documentation centres and exploit their services. Through their affiliations with similar agencies and research libraries throughout the world, and their indexing, abstracting, and translation services, the documentation centres are capable of becoming strong allies of university libraries in supporting university research.

3. L.R. Wilson and M.F. Tauber, *University library* (N.Y., Columbia, 1956) pp. 464-65.

6. UNION LISTS OF SERIALS AND BIBLIOGRAPHIES

The union list of serials may consist of serials or periodicals of all subjects, or it can be limited to special subjects. Among the libraries units of a single university it may be possible through joint efforts to produce a union list of periodical holdings and to distribute it among faculty members and students. A large group of participating university libraries could produce a consolidated union list. Such a union list of serials can be useful for ILL by providing users with information about the resources of the cooperating libraries. It can also guide librarians to plan more complete coverage of serials and to help avoid unnecessary acquisitions of low-use items already owned by libraries. It can further help the librarians to identify the strengths and weakness in the members' collections. In this regard it may even be possible to combine the partial holdings of several members for the serial in order to get a complete run of that serial.

Similarly, lists of special holidays of manuscripts, newspapers and rare books may be compiled on local or national levels. Many university libraries have assumed responsibility for issuing guides to theses and dissertations prepared of various institutions.

In brief, bibliographies, union lists of serials, checklists, and survey of resourees of cooperating libraries are of immeasurable value to researchers who are concerned about the holdings of specific institutions. But in order to be of assistance to the users, bibliographic access would ideally have accompanied by physical access to materials, such as could be made available through ILL.

7. COOPERATIVE REFERENCE/INFORMATION SERVICES

Cooperative reference/information services can also be rendered among the library units of a university. If the central university library has a strong collection of referenee works and information sources, it automatically becomes the centre of intellectual gravity of teaching and research. It should encourage the librarians of its associated libraries to turn to it for assistance. Likewise, the university central library should stimulate the specialists in its neighbouring libraries for information. The same hold good for inrer-university and nation-wide information services. Interaction among the libraries of a country should permit a free flow of inquiries in all fields of knowledge. The university library may directly refer a user to another library or other information source. In this case, the home library should act as a professional referral agency. John P. Immroth has described this service as an "inter-library loan of ideas and answers".[4]

8. COOPERATIVES STORAGE CENTRES

The basic motivation and logic behind the development of storage libraries appear to be based on two assumptions : First, libraries run out of space, and relief must be obtained. Secondly, a more important presumption is that all large libraries contain a great deal of material that is not being used very much.

It appears advantageous and logical to store little used and rare materials in a common facility built at low cost, located on cheap land, and less costly to maintain than storage facilities operated separately for each library. It may also reduce duplication of materials and free space in existing libraries' buildings, which will then not have to be expanded until much later.

There are, of course, in-built limitations for setting up storage libraries :

First, there has always been, and still is, a reluctance on the part of libraries, especially when faculty members are involved, to have some of their books located at some distance. The inconvenience of having a delay—time taken for delivery and the handicap of having to do one's work at some distance are considered serious.

Secondly, there is concern over the high cost of selecting material for storage and the cost of record change.

Thirdly, how to determine which part of a large collection is not likely to be used.

Fourthly, one cannot overlook the element of local pride in the size of the collection. Many librarians are quite hesitant to see their own libraries shrinking in size.

In spite of the criticisms directed at a coperative storage idea there is truth in G. Jefferson's statement that it is a logical extension of cooperative acquisition and follows from the thesis that coordination of accessions makes more books available than would be the case if individual libraries worked a lone, and enable

4, John P. Immroth, "Library Resource-Sharing" In *Resource-sharing libraries*, ed Allen Kent (N.Y., Dekkar. 1974).

proper economy in book purchase to be made. Also by exchanging stocks among specializing libraries which operate in acquisition schemes, lack of storage space is relieved to the extent that duplicate little used material can be eliminated and a more economic use made of storage space within the whole group.

9. COOPERATIVE PHOTOGRAPHIC SERVICES

Cooperative activity in photographic projects is primarily concerned with micro-reproductions and is a direct extension of traditional library service. Such a service, employing modern copying methods, has become essential.

The university library, if it has photographic reproduction equipment, can well serve not only its units but also its neighbouring libraries. The possibilities of cooperative relationships with well-equipped documentation centres and the national library may be fully exploited. Such services may be international as well as national or local in scope.

10. INTERNATIONAL COOPERATION

Librarians are engaged in problems of international cooperation. At international level, processing of information for sharing it among nations is on the increase. There is mounting emphasis on offering scope for SDI services, improvements in the standards of national bibliographies, abstracting, indexing, training of personnel, etc. Global information systems such as INIS., AGRIS, DEVSIS, and SPINES are examples of sharing the burden of documents processing in a decentralized manner.

International bodies such as UNISIST, FID, IFLA and ISO are providing the much needed guidelines and also assistance in evolving international standards for ensuring greater compatibility between systems, thus fostering measure of success in international exchange of information. The International Serials Data System (ISDS) is another example of cooperative endeavour to disseminate information about current serial publication of the world by setting up ISDS files.

Still another pattern of international cooperation relates to the role of international non-governmental bodies such as ICSU, IFLA, FID, IFIP, ISO, CODATA, etc. Mention may be made of IFLA's two significant achievements. Universal Bibliographical Control (UBC) and Universal Availability of Publications (UAP) with the sole purpose of creating a world-wide scheme for exchange of bibliographic information for all publications, and for making documents available to users speedily and efficiently is another serious attempt in this direction.

Library of Congress MARC projects and MEDLARS, CAS, BIOSIS, ISI, etc. are some of data bases—national in character but international in scope and coverage—that have played a very important role in promoting easy accessibility to literature, thereby contributing to resouce sharing.

The university libraries may participate in a wide variety of international cooperative activities and services including gifts and exchange of library materials, translation services, copying services compilation of national bibliographies, professional training programmes, international conferences, documentation centres and inter-library lending.

Cooperation In India

Library cooperation has not taken roots in India. The philosophy of individualism reigns supreme in India among university librarians; probably they think that by introducing cooperation they will loose their freedom of action. Majority of them may also like to see their libraries great both qualitatively and quantitatively; others are poor in resources.

Nonetheless, we have made some progress. Almost every university library has accepted the idea of ILL and lends documents to other libraries. The provision of study facilities for students, teachers, research scholars of one university in another university library on reciprocal basis is really a laudable achievement. But it should be supplemented by exchange of teachers, and subject specialists between the libraries and the departments of library science. It will be a thrilling experiment invigorating and refreshing to the staff, who in turn will feel better equipped for library service after wider and diverse experience in other libraries and departments than their own.

COOPERATIVE ACQUISTION has never stimulated the Indian librarians to cooperate. But the compelling factors like expanding volume of scientific and technical information; emergence of new disciplines and new links between existing ones; rising cost of materials; inelastic budget and devaluation of the purchasing power of the rupee will force librarians to an efficient and effective cooperative acquisition policy. If cooperation is not possible in all the major fields, a library certainly need not buy the rare, the relatively little used and the most specialised research materials if its clientele has ready access to them at another library.

Mention may be made of the cooperative storage centres in India. The Inter-library Research Centre of the ICSSR was the maiden attempt. S R. Ranganathan as the Chairman of the U.G.C. Library Committee has recommended that there should be a dormitory library in each constituent state. The dormitory libraries should collect and preserve one or two of the best preserved copies of the weeded out books.

Centralized and cooperative cataloguing are practically non-existent. Ranganathan strongly favoured the idea of centralized cataloguing under the concept of Pre-natal cataloguing.

Although the university libraries have taken no significant steps for the compilation of UC and bibliographies, yet INSDOC has compiled 18 Regional Union Catalogues Documentation Centre of ICSSR has compiled UC of Social Science periodicals. ILA, too, brought out the Union Catalogue of learned periodicals Pnblications in South Asia, V. I *Physical and Biological Sciences.*

Some of the university libraries bring out lists of latest additions, theses, dissertations and periodicals. University of Rajasthan is publishing INDEX INDIA—a quarterly documentation list. Indexing, abstracting and bibliographical work is not altogether absent.

Regional centre concept is now gaining ground. The NISSAT Scheme of the Department of Science and Technology may be regarded as a landmark in our endeavour to establish a well-knit and well coordinated system for science and technology. The UGC has also taken up a project to set up regional centres for academic libraries. The ICSSR has also set up data centres.

It goes without saying that we have not been able to make appreciable headway in implementing much talked about scheme of cooperation. The probable reason being that there is no strong National Library System. The recommendations of the Advisory Committee for Public Libraries on cooperation was more honoured inbreach than observance. The university libraries in India are in a leading position to exert pressure on state and central governments to establish a well-organized and highly effective National Library System For university libraries a cooperative acquisition plan might be deviced taking into consideration their subject specialisation. We may start on regional basis. UGC should encourage such centres by financing them. We must establish, on the model of Great Britain, National Lending Library for Science and Technology (now British library) as well as for Social Sciences and Humanities.

One important element in any library network is the unrestricted flow of information in the communication process. This information flow ranges from the purely technical to the highly philosophical. The TWX has become the main instrument for the rapid transmission of ILL requests and technical messages. On-line bibliographic searching is a reality and marks a new level in library and net communication. Probably the most sophisticated of network activities in India would be resource development, shared acquisitions, and cooperative purchasing.

In sum : the modern university libraries are becoming less able to meet legitimate needs of their communities for the reason of information explosion, inflation, more students and continued fragmentation of the traditional disciplines coupled with hard financial times. To overcome these limitations librarians throughout the world, have evolved a system known as inter-library cooperation.

Cooperation is based on a willingness to work together to achieve benefits. The slogan of self-sufficiency makes cooperation un-necessary. Cooperative programmes are based on mutual trust and respect. They succeed only as long as each participant perceives the arrangement as beneficial to his institution. In fact, from earliest times, two principles have controlled the growth of libraries—the principle of local self-sufficiency and the principle of sharing the resources. Neither has ever won exclusive control and the likelihood is that neither ever will.

Before reacting in any way to cooperative system, it must be kept in mind that by the combination of talents and resources, the system provides the means to :

(i) Create a greater depth and range of resources.

(ii) Open avenues for the use of the resources.

(iii) Equalize library services.
(iv) Raise the level of personnel expertise.
(v) Offer the newer types of communication media.
(vi) Take advantage of the new technology.
(vii) Experiment and innovate[5].

Cooperation should not be thought of as a means of saving money. Like most good things, it costs a lot of hard cash. Its raison d' etre is to extend the usefulness of total library resources to readers[6].

5. R.W. Gregory and L.L. Stoffel, Public libraries in cooperative system; *administrative patterns for library service* (A.L.A. 1971), p. 3, 250.

REFERENCES

—L.R. MacColvin and J. Reeves *British libraries*, ed. 2 (Longsman, 48).
—G. Jefferson, Library cooperation (Lond., Andre, 1966).
—Wilson and Taubet, op. cit., chapt. 13.
—M.A. Gelfand, *Libraries in developing countries* (Unesco).
—T.S. Rajgopalan and T.N. Rajan, An overview of problems and prospects of resource sharing......ILA Bulletin, XIV (1978), p. 1-4
—Lyle, op. cit., p. 161.

17

PUBLIC RELATIONS FOR THE LIBRARIES

Meaning

Public Relations means the act or process of putting the library into cordial and understanding relationship with all the people of the community. It means average citizen's understanding of library functions, policies and procedures, the extent and warmth of the community's good-will toward the library, and its appreciation for the quality and morale of the library's staff and services.

Aims

The aim of library PR work is not to blow one's own trumpet. The aim is to build up public belief that it is alert, active, forward looking, quickly responsive to public demands, interested in progressive methods and economy, operated by devoted and highly skilled staff and busy in helping more citizens in every category. PR programme has not to describe services and materials; it has to explain library objectives, problems, plans, projects, personnel, standards and accomplishments.

Objectives

Broadly speaking, the objectives of the library PR programme are :—

—to create library consciousness among the people of the community;

—to spotlight the existence of libraries, where they are located, what do they contain, and to identify the services they can render to help people in their informal self-education;

—to enrich and further develop the subjects on which individuals are undertaking formal education to help people remain well-informed;

—to make constructive use of their leisure hours;

—to become good citizens;

—to help people remain well-informed;
—to appreciate the values of democracy; and
—to increase their theoretical knowledge of their vocations[1].

The purpose of PR programme thus lies in providing the best and most useful material people are willing to use for their sociological, educational, civic and cultural elevation Yet any PR programme which concentrates its activities only and exclusively upon users is at best only a partial success. But if the libraries are to continue to develop, they must look beyond users, and be projected internationally, nationally, regionlly, locally and sectionally with such related activities as central government, education, local government, vocational training, the social services, the book trade and library staff.[2]

PR On International Level

International bodies like UNESCO, FID, and IFLA have played a vital role in projecting library image on international scene.

Unesco has been playing a vital role in the development of libraries in many parts of the world. Although, Unesco is concerned with all kinds of libraries but it has paid special attention for the development of public libraries in those countries which have not been fortunate enough to have them. The initiation of the pilot public library projects at Delhi, Enugun (Nigeria), Medellin (Columbia), and Latin America demonstrate Unesco's faith in public libraries as institutions where everyone can obtain knowledge in the way one likes best. Unesco has generated an idea that public libraries can bring about an intellectual, social and economic revolution by the dissemination of knowledge and information. As a result of this metamorphosis of human mind, librarians, particularly of the less privileged countries, have gained a better idea of the great potentialities of the public 'library'; while the government authorities and the decision-makers are convinced of the utility of these institutions in life-long education and as effective information centres for the whole community; hence their greater support for these institutions of public mental health.

IFLA has also influenced the march of librarianship but in a different way. It operates section for national and university

1. K.C. Harrison, *Public relations of libraries* (Andre, 1973).
2. Ibid.

libraries, for public libraries, for special libraries, for parliamentary libraries and administrative libraries. There are also subsections working for libraries in hospitals, children, astronomical and geographical libraries. IFLA Committees perform work relating to library education, rare books, periodicals, statistics and library buildings. LIBRIS is its powerful journal.

Similarly, FID has made great contributions to spread the latest developments in documentation, information science and UDC throughout the world.

PR Through National Bodies

The national library associations like ALA, and Library Association (Lond.) have magnified library image at international level. They have promoted participation in international conferences, the establishment of fellowships for librarians of developing countries, making arrangements for visiting librarians, and publications of international value. But for ALA's literary contributions, the library profession would have been poorer[3].

Looking at national level, one finds that the governments own national, parliament, state assemblies and departmental libraries. They also give financial aid directly or indirectly for the maintenance and development of public libraries. They also provide financial aid to academic libraries. It, therefore, becomes obligatory that the members of national, parliament and state assemblies, and the bureaucrats be kept informed on the vital role of the libraries. Financial stringencies must be opposed.

Public Relations On The University Campus

The university governing bodies like vice-chancellors, faculty, committees and also students must be kept informed about library's needs and services.

1. Vice-Chancellor/President

The librarian has to educate Vice-Chancellor about library's progress and problems. If the library is poorly or brilliantly organized, the Vice-Chancellor will come to know about it from the faculty, students or even the alumni. But if the librarian requires new equipment for initiating new services, he must keep the Vice-Chancellor informed.

3. Ibid

The Vice-Chancellor is also kept informed about :

—book funds;

—means employed in integrating the library wih instruction, teaching and extension programmes;

—the library costs involved for starting new courses;

—building's expansion for accomodating new acquisitions, and new equipments;

—new activities like the computer application to libraries which call for modifications or extension of buildings or unusual expenditure of funds;

—the advantages and disadvantages of decentraling collections and services;

—the wisdom of separate undergraduate library;

—the money ear-marked for the purchase of special and rare collections;

—the quality of staff and costs involved to operate a first-rate library; and

—the aspirations of staff for recognition and appropriate faculty status, etc[4].

The librarian should be careful to present all sides of his recommendations and problems to enable the vice-chancellor to give whole-hearted support.

2. Library Committee

Another possible way for the librarian to interpret his services and resources is through the library committees. Such committees should be advisory and consultative. The advisory committee can be inmensely helpful in promoting the cause of library : the advisory function should be taken to mean that the teaching faculty advises the library of its wishes and requirements through its representatives on the committee. Its consultative functions should be interpreted as the university librarian consulting the teaching faculty through the committee.

3. Faculty

In addition to library committees, the librarian must work in close cooperation with the faculty for projecting the library

4. L.R. Wilson and M.F. Tauber, *The University library*, 2nd. ed., (N.Y., Columbia Univ., Press, 1956)

image in the university and among students. Since faculty and students are the primary users of a university library, their needs must be of paramount importance to the library in setting goals. Faculty dependence on recorded knowledge in their teaching and research is the mainstay of university librarianship. This dependence can be translated into appreciation or criticism. A wise and an imaginative librarian would endeavour to turn constructive criticism of collections or services towards greater library support. As a participant in the university educative programme, the librarian operates the library on teaching and research level.

For the faculty, the common denominator of library lies in getting the books they want and getting them as fast as possible. The daily association of library staff with faculty and students is more important than any other type of library interpretation. Courtesy, conscientiousness, understanding, sympathy and adaptability at reference and loan desks are the pre-requisites for selling the library idea.

Public Relations Off the University Campus

The off campus groups towards which the PR programme of the university public library may be directed are (1) alumni; (2) friends of the library; and (3) professional associations and organizations.

1. Alumni

The Alumnus is given a special status; he should always be welcome for brief periods of time. Alumni who live near the university may make use of its library directly; others may seek loans by mail; they may also ask for reference and bibliographical services.

The PR with the alumni assumes greater importance when the librarian is interested to build-up library through their help. The alumni can be of vital help to the library in forming a Friends' Group, in making donations, and in listing the support of persons in a position to be of genuine assistance to the librarian. In order to cultivate friendly relations with the alumni, the librarian may organize exhibits for Alumni Day and try to meet as many alumni as possible and keep them informed about library services and needs, outstanding acquisitions, memorial book gifts, special services, and news likely to be of interest to the alumni.

II Friends of the Library

The alumni groups, to a large extent, represent their college and university libraries; public library groups contain a cross-section of members of the community. The former generally carry on efforts to aid the growth of the library collections by means of gifts or by contributions, the latter are more concerned in—

—stimulating increased awareness and resulting use of the library;
—stimulating increased financial support—public aud private;
—coordinating efforts of all groups and individuals interested in the library;
—promoting greatest possible use of the library;
—sponsoring cultural and related programmes for the community; and
—sponsoring and stimulating voluntry service for the library[5].

Friends look upon the library as an informational and cultural force in the community, as a source of inspiration. and as a tool to promote individual, civil, and national development. Friends organizations are established for prumoting understanding of the library—its limitations, its services, its physical facilities, and its resources. More specifically, they may and frequently do promote and encourage gifts to the library either in kind or cash.

III Participation of Librarians in Professional Associations/ Organizations.

Wilson and Tauber enumerate five groups of organizations, with which the university librarian has at one time or another, worked. These are :

1. **Library association—local, state, rsgional, national, and international;**
2. **Educational associations;**
3. **Government offices and departments;**
4. **Educational foundations; and**
5. **Learned societies.**

The type of activities of these organizations which appeal most to the librarians include the following :

5. A.S. Payne "Friends of small public libraries" cf. Friends of the library ed by S.L. Wallace.

—the development of international cu'tural relations;

—the compilation and publication of major catalogues and union lists;

—the establishment of regional union catalogues and bibliographical centres;

—the description of the holdings of individual libraries and groups of libraries;

—the improvement of college and university book collection;

—the improvement and support of education for librarianship;

—the development of physical facilities for the photographic reproduction of materials;

—the reduction of costs of library technical operations;

—the reclassification and re-cataloguing of library collections;

—the study of specific aid to learning; and

—the accomplishment of other undertakings—all of which are intended to contribute to the promotion of research and the advancement of scholarship and librarianship.

Participation in professional meetings of the state or the national associations or the learned bodies may stimulate and refresh the participants and they may return home with new experience, new vision, new ideas and new methods to try with, which ultimately improve services having their impact on educational role of the library. Confident and enthusiastic staff members, receptive to nascent professional thought and latest techniques of operating libraries and disseminating information, gain the confidenee and respect of their teaching colleagues.

Media Used for PR Work

Usually the librarians usc the following media in their PR work to interpret the services of the library to the above mentioned groups :

1. Annual Reports

The annual report of the library is a written document submitted by the librarian to keep his management fully and effectively informed on all aspects of library's services, achievements or regress alongwith plausible reasons of his short-comings to clarify and reinforce the library's request for support. The following topics are usually included :

(i) The state and growth of the collections;

(ii) Services to the readers;

(iii) Statistics of the preparation units;

(iv) Personnel matters, including activities of staff members;

(v) Information regarding income and expenditure;

(vi) Descriptions of improvements made in the building or of equipment added;

(vii) Special problems of administration and organization;

(viii) Description of efforts to improve the services of the library;

(ix) Notes of special progress;

(x) Work of the separate departments for divisions; and

(vi) Recommendations for the future[6].

It is also worth-while to illustrate in the report children's activities in case of public libraries, services to the handicapped, exhibitions inaugurations, book week activities, close-ups of rare books or manuscripts acquired etc; statistics should be given as an aid to comparison.

The report should not be too archival, complex and verbose. The merits of clarity, short paragraphs under cathy headings must be kept in mind while drafting the report. A well drafted, well-prepared, well-produced report, disseminated intelligently to important individuals is a sure way to enlist their support for library development and encouraging gifts.

2. *Library Surveys*

The basic purpose of library survey is to explore, who uses the library and for what reasons; and who does not use the library service, and why they do not. And if people avail of service, or any part of it, are they satisfied and have they any suggestion to make for its improvement ?

Some important results can be expected from surveys whether carried on the national level, regional level, university level or library level :

6. Wilson and Tauber, op. cit., p. 557.

—a survey highlights the serious problems obstructing library administration and services;

—it educates the management about the role that the library plays in the educative process;

—it helps the codification of the library policy of the parent institution;

—it helps to set forth a programme for action for the library; action usually leads to development;

—survey helps to secure funds for the library; and

—the survey stimulates the library staff by reminding them their teaching and research role in the academic pursuits.

The survey report can form a good PR document in itself. But more than that, it can offer a solid foundation for any future PR policy. Library which has been critically and objectively examined in respect of its services, book collections, staff, faculty attitudes and teaching methods, the aequisition policy, financial and administrative support, building programme, operations in the cataloguing, binding, reference, technical or circulation departments, spécial services, major obstacles to its developments, deserves credit for shaking itself out of lethargy.

To secure full understanding and support, the librarian may use a variety of devices to explain and describe library activities and needs. Some of these may be noted :

3. *Handbook*

Small handbooks are a valuable device to instruct and assist the students to help themselves. Sometimes a separate handbook is prepared for the faculty.

The ***student library handbook*** contains a mine of current facts : diagrammatically representation of the main service floor, the location of principal collections and service points; the location and arrangement of books, the method of charging and discharging books; the rules and regulations of the library; the library collections and its special services; description of library catalogue and detailed instructions to use it by means of sample cards and brief notes, tells what a call slip is and how it should be filled out, directs the students to book-stacks and the particular section indicated by the call number. Similary, directions are given about the use and methods of obtaining periodicals, newspapers and government publications. An effort is made to interpret the reference collections and to link special library aids with the students' class-work. The description of periodical indexes offers the opportunity to associate these tools with the preparation of source themes

The availability of reprographic services and the location of text-book and reference sections are highlighted.

The handbooks should be concise, well-arranged and written in simple and clear style. Cartoons, pictures, line drawings, and card reproduction add to the attractiveness and usefulness of the handbook. A handbook can also help those too shy to ask questions.

A library HANDBOOK FOR THE FACULTY serves to keep the faculty informed of library methods, hours of services, rules, regulations, procedures and special services. It describes the means by which faculty and library staff can work together to improve instruction, and explains the significant way in which the library can aid research. It may also include descriptions of library resources intended to serve general education programme, with special emphasis on collections of unusual significance.

Book selection and acquisition policies and procedures are explained. Reference book procedures and special services to the faculty such as inter-library loan, photo-copying, indexing, abstracting, instruction in the use of the library, preparation of special reading lists, reading facilitie —including lounges, seminar rooms and the audio-visual services of the library—, also come in for detailed explanation. The text is followed by detailed floor plans. A detailed index will greatly facilitate use.

4. *Printed Catalogue*

A printed catalogue is an important means for publicizing library contents. It may incl de total holdings of the central as well as branch libraries or may be restricted to special collections of the library. The catalogue should be accurate, well-indexed, well-designed and well-printed.

Attractively produced printed catalogues are quite useful in the library's PR programme, and they should be produced for their bibliographical values as well as their role in the promotion of library use.

5. Library Bulletin

Library publishes a printed bulletin :

—to arouse interest of the public in the library as an institution;

—to keep the public informed of all the library activities and facilities;

—to relate books to the current tastes and interests of the public;

—to relate fresh topics to those about which borrowers already read;

—to arouse fresh interests; and

—generally to stimulate in an attractive "gentle" way—educational, vocational and cultural objectives.[6]

Through the explanation of the work of various departments and procedures, the library bulletin helps to increase the usefulness of the library. By means of brief book lists, it encourages the use of books for general and recreational reading. Through descriptions of important collections and speciai services, it points to ways in which the library may contribute to the educational programme. And through frequent listings of donors and brief description of important gifts, it provides a means for appropriately acknowledging gifts and encouraging further donations[7].

6. News-Sheets

Those libraries which cannot afford to produce costly library bulletins may resort to the issue of printed or mimeographed or typed handbills and news-sheets. Special bibliographies, notification about changes of methods, descriptive notes about the personal service offered by the Reference staff can also be issued in this manner.

Cathcy caption : "Direct From Publishers"; "Facts and Fiction". "Straight From the Shelves"; "On the Shelves"; "New Books"; "Monthly Record" may find the appropriate readers.

6. L.R. McColvin, Library exteusion work and publicity, p. 179-80.

7. G.R Lyle, Administration of the college library (H.W. Wilson, 1961).

7. Press

Those librarians who cannot even afford to produce news-sheets, may profitably use the local press for disseminating information over to users. Many editors would generally be willing to feature library news on a regular basis in respect of latest 'additions', statistics of readers and issues, changes in the issue methods, changes in the working hours, receipt of free gifts of special collections, improvement in the amenities to the public, arrangement of exhibitions and occurrance of events about which special bibliographies may be prepared

PR bulletin of *local authorities* or even students' bulletin is another good vehicle for informing students or the public about the library and inviting them to share its academic, research, information and recreational persuits. Students should be encouraged to write special stories about various aspects of the library, and to encourage them, prizes could be awarded.

It has to be admitted that the image of library projected through the media of press has not been very happy. Library cartoons in a news-paper or students' magazine concentrate upon the repressive characteristics such as commanding silence notices, or upon the archaic, such as library interests with shelving from floor to ceiling. Librarians are themselves usually portrayed as 'Shabby, decrepit, myopic, absent-minded creatures'. Little or no interest is shown in the progressive, imaginative and valuable services'[8] rendered by the profession to the community. The cultivation of good relations with editors, particularly those in locality, will undoubtedly lead to an encouraging flow of publicity for the library.

8. Posters and Bulletin Boards

Librarians use posters and bulletin boards to stimulate people's interests in special resources and services; to invite attention to selected books on a particular topic; to present short, graphic summaries of important national and local news; and to announce programmes and lectures. Posters not only guide and instruct but have cultural values as well. A stricking poster may have an aesthetic appeal comparable to that of a beautiful piece of sculpture or a nicely printed book. Attractive posters

8. Harrison, op. cit.,

should be used to publicize children's services, adult lending services, reference and information services, music and audio-visual materials, mobile library services, and services to the handicapped.

Posters, pictures, book jackets, maps, slogans, notes on special days, authors, and events, constitute the display material for the bulletin board. An effort should be made to connect national, educational, library, scientific, and local campus events with the use of library materials. To command attention, and to be more effective, displays should be neat, simple and visible.

9. Personal Talk

Direct personal talk is the simplest and the least expensive method of publicity. It can convert non-users into regular users of the library. Oral publicity is in effect PR tool for acquainting the people with the contents and services of their own libraries, and also the informational and bibliographical works undertaken by their staff.

The university and college librarians are expected to talk about libraries to new entrants, students' organizations, to faculty members, and often to outside bodies as well.

10. PR On Air

Librarians in U.S.A. are using the radio/TV for publicising their services. If radio/TV talk is to be given life, librarian must be conscious that each item is brief and effectively phrased, revolves around a specific subject, and sounds news :—a new book on babies, house-keeping, child care, marriage, hobbies, current events, etc., or a change in rules or staff, or a new modified service.

11. National Library Week

The organization of national library weeks is one of the most ambitious means of library PR work. This is a cooperative method of publicity including book-sellers, publishers, authors and librarians. It must have a theme, a symbol, and slogan, and stylized recognizable printed publicity.

12. Children Book Weeks

Children's book weeks have been an important element of library PR work. Harison writes that the children's books must be advertised generously, through the press, through poster to be distributed to schools, book-shops, libraries and also by the printing of a folder-type programme.

The programme must be planned carefully. The children love to meet authors and book illustrators whose names are known to them. The librarian should also arrange talks from known authors in children's world; there should also be relavant film shows, puppet shows alongwith a display on painting, photography, wood-carving, and artistic exression.

13. The organization of lectures, concerts, recitals, film shows, play and poetry readings are other PR aspec[illegible] the armoury of the librarians.

14. Another important form of PR programme is visiting groups to the library—whether comprising of international delegations or of groups from conferences or from other local authorities or of groups of students. The librarian must givè a careful thought for planning such a visit as each individual member of the visiting group takes back with him impressions about the library in every aspect.[9]

To conclude : honesty and sincerity underlie good PR work. Through this technique the library can help build a city's/university's pride in itself. Continuous PR work is necessary; repetition builds reputation. It takes a long time to sell facts and ideas; much publicity fails by quitting too soon. Keep it simple : say it often; be sure it's true.[10]

If the best results are to be otained from any PR programme, it should be thoroughly understood by management and by staff what the term embraces. "Public relations" writes Sarah Wallace, "rightly understood and rightly administered, can become the means by which the community knows, appreciates, and uses to the fullest extent the public library which it has established."[11] It is, therefore, an essential part of the operations of the contemporary public library.

9. Ibid., p. 60 81.

10, Wheller and Goldhor, op. cit.,

11. S.L. Wallace, "The Library's public. In Local public library administration ed. by Roberts Bowler (Chicago, IMA, 1964).

18

EXTENSION SERVICES

Of Public and University Libraries

The purpose of extension work is to establish the contact between the librarian and the reader; it implies putting the library into most cordial and understanding relationship with all the people of the community. Through extension programmes the librarians attempt to convert the library into a social centre. Their aim is :

—to mak users of non-users

—to create and stimulate the desire for good reading;

—to act as a link between mind and idea;

—to take effective part in the implementation of the cultural programme of the community;

—to provide library services to schools not having their own libraries; and

—to participate in adult education programmes.

Among the various techniqucs adopted by the librarians for spreading the news of library service, the display of material is the most important.

1. Display

Display is designed to bring together :

—those subjects necessarily separated by the scheme of classification, but which are normally associated;

—subjects normally separated but which are temporarily linked by reason of topical interest; and

—secondary subjects, ignored by classifiers in favour of primary subjects.

The purpose of display is to reveal the thought-content of the documents on display, hence, it is a tool of stock utilization. Display brings to people's notice the latest additions to the libraries. It also gives prominence to special services rendered by the library with the sole aim of prompting people to make use of that service; to make use of the information services; and to highlight special collections of the library. Much of the materials—engravings. photographs, manuscripts, archives, etc. may well be given an occasional airing.

One notices three types of displays : topical, subject and mobile.

1.1 Topical Display

Every display must have a purpose or a theme, something concrete which the reader can see, appreciate and remember. For this reason topical displays designed around a centenary or an anniversary of a local man of prominence, the publication of a new book by a local prolific writer, a Lok-Sabha or Vidhan Sabha election, Independence or Republic Day, silver/golden/diamond jubilee of the library, national festivals, U.N. day and the like may be well organized.

1.2 Subject display

Subject displays are arranged to display together the books having related and allied interests as on Home and Decoration. K.C. Harrison has advanced the view that we can reap real advantages from subject display if we introduce artefacts and non-library material A display of books on sports can be enlivened by such shop-window dressing as the introduction of a foot-ball, a tennis racquet, a skate or a cricket score board

1.3 Mobile Display

Mobile displays are on the increase. Despite best efforts, a branch library cannot offer a full range of library materials. To replenish its resources, the mobile or travelling display is made. Bringing books to people by book-mobile is the most dramatic and colourful and evidently the most efficient and effective way of circulating books for the benefit of the community.

It has an inherited limitation—the limited period of time for it is available at any one stop. Still it plays a vital role in helping to provide a network of book distributing points.

To command attention, and to be more effective, displays should be neat, simple but eye-catching. Few displays should be arranged simultaneously in one room or area. Long paragraphs of explanation should be avoided. When the subject of display is changed, its form should also be changed, or else colour scheme, or both. Pictures, jackets and captions should emphasize one idea. A few jackets neatly trimmed and well-displayed, are more effective than too many displayed at a time. Letters, and lettering should be neat, simple, well-spaced and well-proportioned to the size of board or poster and dynamically balanced. Some libraries have shop-window type frontages, eminently suitable for displays and illuminated so that passers—by after dark will be attracted to them[1]. Colourful eye-catching displays enhance the neat and o derly appearance of a well organised library.

2. Exhibitions

The exhibitions are in essence display work at a much more ambitious level. Exhibitions are mostly arranged to publicize less-known materials, encourage reading, promote interest in a specific field or group of subject fields, call attention to particular anniversary or the centenary of a religious place, acknowledge outstanding gifts, encourage hobbies, or celebrate "Children's Book Week" to highlight their literature and the many facilities provided for them in the library.

Exhibitions on local history, carriers and courses, art, adult education, photogrophy, printings or subjects of common interests, a representative collection of local maps and plans, a pictorial survey of the district's vanquished architectural treasures, or a picture gallery of local personalities afford an opportunity to enrich the library permanently either by encouraging gifs or loan of library materials or by encouraging the copying of materials from other sources which may be borrowed for display[2].

Each exhibit should have a specific objective. Skillful use of colour contrasts, background lighting and equipment should aid considerably in attracting the interests of the readers.

In spite of the merits of displays and exhibitions for popularizing the resources and facilities of libraries for the cultural elevation of the community, over-indulgence in displays and exhibitions should be avoided as much finance and staff are

1. K.C. Harrison, *Public relations for libraries* (Andre Deutsch, 1973).
2. John L. Hobbs, *Local history and the library* (Andre Deutsch, 1962).

required not only to mount the exhibitions but also to man them. Moreover, when documents are removed for display, a gap is created on the shelves which might make the readers inconvenient. For prompt service of each document to its users the gaps ought not remain for long. But these limitations should not restrict the librarians in their normal display work. Moreover, since selective documents on a subject are actually put on display, subject representation is not disturbed. But as an exhibition involves a lot of money, energy and time, they should be well-thought and well-planned in advance.

3. *Adult Education*

Another important technique of extension service urgently needed in libraries particularly of developing countries to remove poverty and illiteracy is the need for educating the illiterates. The illiterate adults can be made to have the benefits of library service by instituting, the 'reading system'. Arrangements should be made to have books read to them at stated hours. To arouse and maintain the interests of the illiterate workmen in books and in hearing books read, it should be necessary to narrate to them, not only books of a religious, or recreational nature, but also books of useful knowledge pertaining to their daily vocation and leading to their work effectiveness.

4. *Reading Circles*

Organising reading circles within the premises of libraries is another form of extension service. Subject speciatists may be brought together by the librarians to consitute a reading circle. The librarians should provide facilities for such reading circles in respect of bocks, perodicals and meeting forum in its seminar room. Such reading circles are usually effective agencies in thoroughly utilizing the library resources for the study of respective subjects by the experts.

5. *Extension Talks*

Inviting local associations to hold their public lectures in the library's lecture hall (usually fitted with a stage, a cinema apparatus and other related appliances) is an important form of extention service. The librarian can also avail of this opportunity for announcing a select-list of books on the subject matter of the talk that could be consulted in or borrowed from the library.

The librarian also frequently arranges for special talk either by the members of his own staff or by library experts on some current topic or on subject of local interest.

The librarians of public libraries receive requests, to deliver talks about their libraries to clubs, associations, or organizations, literary societies etc. Similarly, academic librarians are supposed to initiate new students, and the faculty members to the facilities available in their libraries. Whenever possible, such tasks be illustrated with slides and motion pictures.

6. Story Hours for Children

Libraries also arrange for story hours, plays, talks and other attractive forms of extension service to allure children to come to the library. The librarians also occasionally arrange for dramatic erformance by amateur troops.

7. Fairs and Festivals

The celebration of local festivals and special days of the year dedicated to illuminaries or participation in local fairs is another significant form of extension service to widely proclaim to the community the services rendered by the library and the promotion of books. In India, where such celebrations attract huge crowds of people, this form of extension service is full of great potentialities.

In addition to public libraries, some university libraries particularly in the West also offer extension services.

8. Extension Services of University Libraries

A significant function of the university library is to help the university in fulfilling its extension service aim. For performing extension service, the library usually possesces a special collection which includes various kinds of materials such as package libraries, plays, pamphlets, motion pictures, maps, photographs, slides, prints, phonographs, records, study outlines, readings, recitations[3].

8.1 Books for Courses

The provision of books for courses conducted off campus either through book-mobiles or the setting up of branch libraries

3. This sub-part is based on Wilson and Tauber, op. cit., pp. 242-247.

at off-campus centres is one of the primary functions of the library. Titles have to be duplicated, if necessary, for meeting the needs of the off-campus students.

8 2 Package Libraries

The package library is one of the most important library extension services. Social, political, and economic affairs, current, and international affairs, literature and art, are popular topics. The collection is made up of clippings, pamphlets, documents, and other ephemeral materials.

8.3 Reading Courses and Lists

The reading course is a short introductry presentation of a specific field with suggestions for further study. Some librarians rely on published courses of reading, while others prepare their own in cooperation with the faculty members.

Provision of Reading Lists which range from complete bibliographies to short lists on current topics is another form of extension service.

8.3 Study Outlines

They suggest aspects of the subject that should be studied in detail and they recommend printed materials to help in the preparation of articles on the various phases of subject.

8.5 Dramas and Related Materials

Some universities also have their own art centres in which exhibitions can be arranged. The art centre will arrange dramatic centres, films, lectures, concerts and displays. Plays, readings, recitations, orations, pageants, operettas, and information concerning staging, costuming, lighting, and make-up are frequently made available to teachers and directors of dramas through library extension service. Some libraries also maintain extensive collections of plays which are loaned for reading or for performance. But the dominant feature is provision for the individual to participate in the skills such as pottery, painting, photography, music, puppetry wood carving, etc.

8.6 Information And Reference Services

Some university libraries as part of their extension activities provide information and reference services to individuals who have limited library service or who are entirely without such service. The extended library reference and information service may involve interpretation of or direction to library records, bibliographies and other reference works, information on citations and analytic bibliographies, and use of any part of the library facilities and collections.

William S. Day[4] has advanced the argument that university and college libraries do violence to the ideals which led to their development if they do not serve as wide a public as the nature of their facilities permit. If facilities are lying ideal in the form of books unused, records unheard or films unseen, then, there is a corresponding decrease in the value of the library to the community or individuals who pay for it, and no gain to those who use the facilities. Since university library accepts the role of leadership in the community, it should frame the policies and activities that help the community in the elevation of its moral and intellectual attainments by the provision of partial or complete library privileges :

—to students attending evening courses that are recognised by the university;

—to students following a bonafide programme of correspondence studies under the authority of the university; and

—to private study candidates who would be willing to pay a fee to guarantee good faith.

Further, the university library could make the provision of ALUMNI privileges such as use of reading rooms, loan privileges through an "extension desk", and access to general shelves. The university library could also provide the same facilities to the public, possibly on a more restrictive basis such as a special reading room. Guided reading programmes for professionals—in cooperation with professional associations, be provided.

Conclusion

The PR and extension programme aim at converting the library into a dynamic part of community life. The librarian reveals the sources, analyses the contents of documents for the uninitiated and lead them to use the documents for themselves. Having done this the librarian enters the fields of PR and extension

4. ——. "The University and college libraries and their responsibilities to the community", First seminar of university libraries (Rajasthan), V. 3.

services to spread the news of his service to make his library a living force in a life-long education and the intelligent use of leisure. Through PR and extension programme the librarian wants to proclaim that the purpose of the library as the community intellectual centre is :

—to provide effective service for the children and young people;

—to provide needed information and reference service;

—to promote and stimulate reading for pleasure and recreation;

—to support and re-inforce programmes of adult education; and

—to support civic and cultural activities of groups and organizations.

It must, however, be added that to achieve its objective of extension services, the public library should link itself with other educational, social and cultural institutions, including schools, adult educational groups, leisure activity groups and with those concerned with promotion of the arts. But, it must, if it is to fulfil its purposes, maintain its separate identity, and remain as an independent identity.

19

NATIONAL LIBRARIES

India, U.K., U.S.A., U.S.S.R.

Great national libraries are now to be found in capitals everywhere in the world. Almost every national library is also enthused with the passion of having "one of everything" that is published in the world—an impossible goal of completeness. Most national libraries, therefore, tend to undertake the twin functions of preserving the literary products of national culture and of providing international research collection of high quality for the benefit of their scholars and researchers. A library is called national one when it is an official depository of printed works; a general access library; an information—bibliographical centre of coodination, planning, and stimulation of the entire library system of the nation.

James Thompson writes in his work "A History of the Principles of Librarianship" that a survey of individual histories of national libraries, particulary in Europe, reveals many recurrent features in their origin.

The majority of national libraries are the result of the yoking together of a number of other libraries, either by gift, bequest, purchase or compulsion. Secondly, Royal libraries, indeed figure very prominently in the history of European national libraries : in France on the outbreak of the Revolution, the Royal Library became the National. National libraries seems to have quite benefitted from revolutions. Thirdly, Monastic libraries also found their way into the national libraries of many countries. As a result of the dispersal of books after the French Revolution, many of the contents of monastic and Church libraries were received into the Bibliotheque Nationale. Fourthly, noticeable in the history of most national libraries is also the contribution made by the libraries of individual great book-collectors. Fifthly, another recurrent theme in the growth of national libraries is the privilege enjoyed by each of them under the law of legal deposit. Finally, a universal characteristic of national libraries is that they are indeed nationalistic in their outlook. In this context, a brief history and present structure of the national libraries of India, U.K. U.S.A., U.S.S.R., be studied.

1. NATIONAL LIBRARY OF INDIA

The National Library of India, situated in Calcutta, is an institution of great national importance. Before the dawn of independence, it was known as the Imperial Library of India, founded by Lord Curzon in 1891. The Imperial Library in its turn was born out of the amalgamation of two separate and different kinds of the libraries—the Calcutta Public Library established in Aug. 1835 and the Imperial Library of the Government's Civil Secretariat. The Imperial Library contained the best of European thought, with an emphasis on English. The Imperial Library was fortunate enough to acquire Fort William collections—a priceless treasure of rare publications which form the bed-rock of the present rare book collections of the National Library.

The objectives of the Imperial Library were forcefully stated by Lord Curzon that the new library was not a "public library" or a "lending library" to provide a "desultory pastime" but a place to which people will resort as they do to the British Museum Library in London, or to the Bodleian Library (Oxford), to pursue their studies and research under agreeable conditions with every assistance that pleasant surroundings and a polite and competent staff can place at their disposal.

Curzon's views were reiterated by M.A.K. Azad, the then Union Minister of Education, who said, while throwing open the doors of the National Library of India to the public on Feb. 1, 1953 :

"We have a Reading Room which can, if we wish, create the atmosphere and conditions of the Reading Room in the British Museum".

The National Library (NL) is located at Belvedere, once the winter abode of the Viceroys of India and a nine storeyed annexe completed in 1967. Commenting on its present location, Pt. Jawahar Lal Nehru observed on 8.5.1961 : "I do not want

Belvedere for the mere purpose of stocking books. We want to convert it into a fine central library where a large number of research students can work and where there will be all the other amenities which a modern library gets". The National Library was intended to be a library of reference, a working place for students, and a repository of materials for the future historians of India, in which so far as possible, every work written about India at any time can be seen and read.

The legend at the entrance of the National library best sums up its objectives in the words of Mahatma Gandhi :

> "I do not want my house to be walled on all sides and my windows to be stuffed. I want cultures of all lands to be blown about my house as freely as possible. But I refuse to be blown off my feet by any."

Collections

The National Library of India is studded with fabulous collections like those of Autosh Mukhopadhyay Collection, covering most subjects in the humanities and sciences; the Ramdas Sen Collection, with its wealth of fugitive Bengali publications; the Barid Baran Mukherjee Collection on Indian history and culture, and Bengali ephemera; the Sir Jadunath Sarkar collection, famous for its source material on medieval Indian history and books on Portuguese and French India; S.N. Sen Collection of Indiana; the Vaiypuri Pillai Collection with its wealth of palm leaf manuscripts and classics particularly in Tamil and Sanskrit; the Buhar Collection of Arabic and Persian Manuscripts and printed books: the Thibantis Sansthan Collections; and the Tej Bahadur Sapru correspendene, reflecting the strive for Indian independence. Thus, National Library of India is decorated with rare, precious and irreplaceable collections.

At its inception, it hardly had 100,000 volumes, which rose to 3,50,000 volumes in 1947. At present the NL has 18,10,401 books. In addition, it is proud of having 19,000 periodicals, 76,574 maps, 4,26,444 Indian official documents beside having archival material. The publications received under the Delivery of Books Act amount to 6, 57, 621. The figures are as on 31-3-85. The documents occupy 32 miles of shelf-space. Its annual budget grants as on 31-3-85 were : non-plan—Rs. 1, 12, 55, 000.00 and plan Rs. 40,00,000. Budget grant for purchase of publications was Rs. 25.82

lacs. The total area of the library compound is 30 acres, though, the total carpet area in the library buildings is 2,26,611 sq. ft. The NL has 506 Reader's seats. It has a staff of 783 employees including 211 trained librarians holding a diploma in library science.

Services

The NL functions as a national cum public library. It provides lending and reference services; cooperates with UNESCO for the publication of Index Translationum Indicarum; prepares adhoc biblilographies for scholars; arranges book exhibitions : printed catalogues and mimeographed catalogues have been issued to support these exhibitions. Several indexes have been prepared and published by the NL individually and in cooperation with different government bodies and cultural organizations of India. This Library possesses a highly sophisticated reprographic equipment for the photocopying and microfilming of the documents

Critical Appreciation

Ironically, our NL does not perform even some of the basic functions, a national library is supposed to form. It is functioning more as public than as a national library. The emphasis and concentration on the lending function alone is negation of the functions of a national library. A national library is a reference and source library alone; lending is not one of its functions. The librarians cannot prevent the normal loss of books if the lending function is permited to continue. And the lost documents may be irreplaceable.

The library's reading rooms are mostly used by day (local) scholars with a couple of out-station readers. Surprisingly, though it is a representative library of about 77 crores persons, it has hostel accomodation of only 8 out-station scholars. While it was expected that our national library should be organized as the repository of our literary products and function as an instrument of our socio-economic progress through research and higher learning, one is constrained to record that it has fallen short of these expectations to a considerable degree.

One is really amused to learn that our National Library has a Children's Section. It speaks either lack of work for the staff or lack of vision about the real functions and duties of a national library. It would be far better if the time and money spent on running the Children's Section were utilized to set up a National Bibliographical and Documentation Service Centre to bring out a Union Catalogue of Periodicals or rare publications, to set up a strong reference section and to promote bibliographical activities and inter-library loans. It was proposed to transfer the administration of the library to a statutory autonomous board under the National Library of India Act, 1976. But the Act is silent on role of the National Public Library System; nor does the Act define the functions of the National Library except that the functions of the board as defined in the Act may be taken as functions of the Library.

The Central Reference Library is entrusted with a laudable function of publishing the Indian National Bibliography. Of course, the launching of this project was a great landmark in the direction of bibliographical control, yet it continues to suffer from delayed publication ever since its beginning.

The Author and Subject Catalogue has been subjected to change at different times leading to a lot of confusion. Moreover, there is no proper vigilance over the number and the relevance of entries for a particular document. Cross references provided are inadequate. The library should maintain a *classified* sequence.

On the complaints of inefficient working of the Library, the Goverment of India appointed a high-powered committee in May 1968, under the chairmanship of Dr. V.S. Jha, to review the working of the library and to suggest measures for its efficient and effective functioning and fututre development. The Jha Review Committee submitted its report in 1969 after eliciting the views of scholars, educationists, librarians and learned institutions in India and abroad on the working of of this Library and its future development. Majority of its recommendations for the development of the Library were accepted. As a result, the following basic functions have been enjoined upon the National Library :

—acquisition and conservation of all significant national literary products to the exclusion of ephemera;

—collection of printed material concerning the country, no matter where this is published, and, as a corollary the acquisition of a photographic record of such material that is not available within the country;

—acquisition and conservation of manuscripts of national importance;

—planned acquisition of foreign material required by the country;

—rendering bibliographical and documentation services of current and retrospective material, both general and specialized;

—Acting as a referral centre purveying full and accurate knowledge of all sources of bibliographical information and participation in international bibliographical activities;

—provision of photocopying and reprographic services; and

—acting as the centre for international book exchange and international loan.

It is to be noted that the Jha Committee did not mention the children's library and the lending functions of the National Library.

The Review Committee also recommended that the new Governing Council of the Library should be appointed from among eminent persons from universities, distinguished educationists, administrators of approved worth and academic bent of mind, and scientists of reputed achievements. It was also decided that the Council should be instituted by a resolution of the Government and that the Director of the library should be its ex-officio chairman. His salary and status should be comparable to that of a Vice-Chancellor of a university.

One of its major recommendation which created a storm of controversy was that the National Library should have a delegated autonomy by resolution and not by statute. On the basis of Jha Committee, Report, a National Library Bill was placed in *Lok Sabha* in 1972 specifiying the administrative structure. Notwithstanding the strong public opinion against the Bill, it became an Act in 1976. But the Janta Government in 1977 decided not to enforce the Act and the idea of autonomy was dropped. It is observed that administration of the library is not a matter of rule or the Act of the Parliament. It is more a question of policy, control or direction. This is also a question of continuity of policy. Such a big organization of national magnitude cannot absorb too many and too quick and drastic changes. It is an irony of fate that this institution has become a battleground for the vested interests. In fact, on the recommendations of the Jha Gommittee, the Govt. of India appointed a one man commission headed by justice G.D. Khosla to go to the roots of the strained staff relations and recommend remedial measurers to stem out the rot.

Suggesions

The following suggestions may go a long way in improving the services of the National Library both qualitatively and quantitatively.

—The re-organization of the documents in stacks in a few essential sequences is necessary. The growing number of sequences defeats its own purpose.

—The DDC has also be replaced by a freely-faceted analytico-synthetic classification scheme.

—The Dictionary Catalogue should be replaced by a Classified one. The reorganization of the card catalogue should be introduced and every effort should be made to see that the catalogue should become an effective tool for locating the documents.

—The latest techniques and equipments should be utilised to provide the most effective service. A work study programme should be initiated, examined and evaluated.

—The national library should have a Book Council as an advisory Committee for the library with top thinkers, planners and specialists, as its members. This Council should advise on the improvement of various collections in the National Library and also make each subject area a representative collection of the past, present, and future.

—There should be a co-ordination committee or board of national libraries or institutions with national character to coordinate the activities in individual libraries which can be done centrally or by coordination. Thus all the libraries will be linked up through the committee for providing an inter-library development not only in National Library of India (Calcutta), but also in other national libraries and centres.

—Delivery of Books Act, 1954 (amended, 1956) should now be amended to include films, microfiche (non-printing media), etc.

—Union Library Bill should be taken up to make the National Library as a link in the national library grid of India.

—The National Library should set up a centre for research in Indological studies to promote and support research in all its field such as ancient Indian history, art, archaeology, linguistics, literature and social sciences.

—The National Library should create and develop divisions : Data Base Management Division; Book Museum Division; Personal Records Division; Library and Information Division; Publication Division; Computer Services Division; and Exhibition Division.

—Proposal for the establishment of National Library at Delhi should be implemented. Regional national libraries should be established at Bombay, Madras and Calcutta.

—The National Library can play a vital role in the resource-sharing programme of India.

—The National Library should take up the responsibility of the centralized cataloguing and classification of books. This will save about 80% of the time of the library staff which can better be used for enhancing library services.

—The time lag in the publication of INB should be reduced and efforts should be made to make it more comprehensive.

—Academic status and scales of pay should be given to the staff on the basis of the U.G.C.'s pattern[1].

There is urgent need to overhaul the services of the National Library. The efficiency in the service can be increased by having an erudite scholar and professionally competent person as a National Librarian.

In addition to National Library of India, there are National Libraries in various subjects also, viz., National Science Library; Indian Agricultural Research Institute, Library; All India Institute of Medical Sciences, Library; Indian Council of Social Science Research, Library; All India Law Institute, Library.

2. THE BRITISH LIBRARY

The British Museum Library and the Library of Congress are quoted as two of the most outstanding examples of modern national libraries.

The British Museum was established by the Act of British Parliament in 1753 by amalgamating Sir Robert Cotton's collection of

1. P.N. Kaula, *National library* of India, a critical study (Somaiya, 1970).
———, "National Library of India", *Herald of Library Science*. V. 20, nos. 3 4, 1981, p. 197-99.

historical manuscripts (transferred to the Crown in 1700), the manuscript collection of Robert and Edward Harleys, earls of Oxford and those of Sir Hans Sloane, physician to George II and president of the Royal Society, to provide a repository. The first such repository was founded in 1755 at Montague House, Bloomsbury (which opened as the British Museum to the public on Jan. 15,1759). The Royal Library of the sovereigns (from Edward IV to George II) was dedicated to the nation by George II in 1757. With it came the copyright deposit privileges (one free copy of all books), which with many donations, ensured a rapid growth in the collections. These collections were further enriched by the acquisition in 1801 the Lansdown collection, the library of Joseph Banks taken over in 1827, and the private library of George III in 1828, the Egerton manuscripts in 1829 and the Arundel manuscripts in 1831. The library benefitted tremendously from the dynamic leadership of Sir Anthony Panizzi who became its Principal Librarian in 1856. In fact, "The British Museum Library as most of us have known it", writes Frank Francis, 'is Pannizzi's creation'. By his Herculean efforts he gave to the nation a truly comprehensive unified library supported by the Government which would allow "a poor student to have the same means of indulging his learned curiosity, of following his rational pursuits, of consulting the same authorities, of fathoming the most intricate inquiry, as the richest man in kingdom".

Panizzi laid the foundations for a century of solid growth, so that at present, the stock of the library stands at over 8,500,000 printed books, 160,000 manuscripts (Western and Oriental) and 100,000 charters and rolls.

Distinguished Collections

Collections include the Thomson Civil War Collections; the Garrick Collection of play; the Cracherode Library of fine printed books; the Bagford Collection of fragments of early printing; the Burney Collection of early newspapers, classical manuscipts and printed books; the Sir Joseph Banks library of botanical, zoological and Icelandic books; the Egerton MSS; the Arundell Collection of English historical and literary MSS; the fine printed book library of Thomas Grenvenville, strong in English literature and early printing; the Rich Collection on the Near and Middle East; the Henry Davis Collection of bindings; the Ashley Library of English Literature; the Paul Hirsh Music Library of 15.000

volumes; the Stein Collection of Chinese material including the Diamond Sutra (868 A.D)—the oldest dated printed document in the world. This priceless treasures also include the codex Sinaiticus (4th century); the Lindisfarne Gospels c. 698); the Egerton Papyrus (2nd century); the Westminister Psalter (12th Century); the unique copy of Beowulf (c. 1000); two of the four extant copies of *Magna Carta*; Azzogendi's first edition of Ovid (Bologna, 1471), a unique complete copy; the Gutunberg Bible; the First Folio of Shakespeare's plays (1623); and the only known autograph MS of Coleridge's Kuble Khan.

There is a very large collection of prints and drawings maintained in a separate department of the museum, as are coins and medals.

British Museum was unique in that it combined a great museum of antiquites with a great comprehensive library. In 1972, however, the British Library Act was passed by merit of which the departments of library were detached from the BM and joined with the other national library institutions in England to form British Library in 1973 following the recommendations of Sir Frederiek Dainton's Committee, Report, (1969).

The British Library has three divisions : the British Museum Library has become the *Reference Division*; the National Central Library (NCL) and the National Lending Library for Science and Technology (NLLST) form the *Lending Division*; and the British National Bibliography forming the Bibliographic Services Divison.

1. The purpose of *Reference Divison* is stated to be : "to collect, by purchase, gift and exchange, not only all British books and such British manuscripts and papers as are appropriate, but as much as possible of the world's important printed material in all subject fields, and manuscripts of foreign origin in certain specialist fields. The *Refernce Division* containing rich collections as described above as a part of BM is one of the finest research library on this planet. It has about 600 seats for readers and on an average 28,000 volumes are consulted daily.

1.1 Science Reference Library

British Library Reference Division, Science Reference Library is the largest public scientific and technological reference library in U.K. It provides literature resources in depth as a service to support current research and development in science and technology. It is also the national library for patents, trade marks and designs. Before 1973, the Science Reference Library was known as the National Reference Library of Science and Invention founded by BM in 1960. The Patent Office Library (f. 1855) was added to it in 1968, now the Halborn Branch Science Library. It contains the literature on the inventive sciences, engineering and industrial techologies, while the Bayswater branch has all the rest of the scientific literature but is particularly strong in the life sciences and technologies, earth sciences and the like, and also in documents on any science in Slavonic and Oriental languages. Halborn branch has more than 1.5 crore patents, 700,000 volumes of books, 18,200 periodicals, trade litrature from 2,500 industrial organizations and important series of reports. Bayswater branch (f. 1966) consists of 250,000 volumes and 16,100 periodicals.

2. *Lending Division* :

The British Library Lending Division was established on July 1, 1973. It contains the stock and services of the National Central Library (f. in 1961) and the National Lending Library for Science and Technology (f. in 1961). Its stock nears about 30 lacs books and periodicals and more than 15 lacs items in micro-films. It is located at a site of 60 acres, though, the building is constructed only on a small proportion of it providing 72 miles of shelving

3. *Bibliographic Service Division :*

It publishes British National Bibliography. It is of a very high standard and appears regularly, recording publications immediately they are issued and received in this division by virtue of the copy-right Act, 1911 as amended by British Library Act, 1972. The scope of its coverage could be widened to include-possibly as supplements—such material as maps and charts, goverment and other official publications, etc.

Suggestions

There is a clear evidence that much foreign literature is not being acquired either by the *Reference Division* or by any British library, and that a greater amount is not available for inter-library lending. There is an urgent need for planning on a scale the fullest possible coverage of foreign literature in humanities and social sciences. The British Library should be responsible for the organization of loans and for the maintenance of all types of union catalogues. The British Library should vigorously assume responsibility for information services in social sciences and humanities.

By the publication of its catalogue of printed books it has made available one of the most important bibliographical tools for scholars. The *Reference Division* (as BM) has also published catalogues of maps, of music, of manuscripts, of many other categories of material. The Division should set up a bibliogaphical research and publications department, to initiate the compilation and publication of catalogues of national holdings of various types of material; to undertake research on bibiographical and library problems; and to act as an advisory centre on library techniqnes. It should take part in the organization of the practical training of academic librarians, in cooperation with universities and other appropriate bodies.

The British Library should be the focal point for all library development in the country. It will initiate or participate in any scheme of a cooperative nature concerned with such matters as shared-cataloguing, coordinated information retrieval scheme. The National Librarian should be a spokesman for British libraries in all international meetings, conferences or councils concerned wtth library activities of all kinds.[2]

3. LIBRARY OF CONGRESS

Believe it or not, but the hard fact remains, that the U.S.A. does not have any institution officially designated as a national library. Nevertheless, the combined facilities of the Library of Congress (LC), the National library of Medicine, and the National Agricultural Library perform the functions and provide services of such an institution. The LC is usually considered to be the world's largest library.

The LC was founded in 1800 with the laudable purpose of serving the Congress. It is supported by congressional appropriations and by the gifts of individuals and foundations. Its

2. Colin Steele, *Major libraries of the world;* a selective guide (Lond., Bowker, 1976).

also

U.G C. (G B), Committee on libraries (Chairman : Thomas Parry), *Report* (HMSO, 1967).

Librarian is appointed by the President of America. Today its services have been extended to other branches of the Government, to the library community and to the public at large. But it still works as the research sword arm for the Congress, simultaneonsly performing the functions of the national library of U.S.A.

In 1800 A.D., the LC voted to spend dollars 5,000 "for the purchase of such books as may be necessary for the use of Congress". The library was originally housed in the capital, Washington, D.C., and was destroyed during Anglo-American war, when the capital was burned by the British. Nucleus of the new book collection was ex-President Thomas Jefferson's personal library of 6,487 volumes purchased by the Congress in 1815.

Another fire which broke out in 1851 destroyed 35,000 volumes and almost all of its map collection. Since then the Library has grown steadily.

In 1865, a new act strengthened the copyright system (in force since 1848) in terms of which the LC started receiving a copy of each publication copyrighted in U.S.A., enriching its stock. In 1866, the Smithsonian Institution's collection of proceedings and publications of learned societies, amounting to 40,000 volumes was acquired by the LC laying the foundation for its now unsurpassed scientific collection. In 1867 was brought the Peter Force's historical library containing 60,000 volumes of Americana. These collections added to both the size and magnificence of the library. In this context, it is worth recording the words of an able Librarian of Congress, Ainsworth R. Spofford, who said in 1876 : "As the library of the American people, supported and constantly enlarged by taxation, it is eminently fitting that this library should not only be freely accessible to the whole people, but that it should furnish the fullest possible stores of information in every department of human knowledge", Under the dynamic leadership of Spofford (1864 to 1897) the LC achieved a spectacular growth. Herbert Putnam, Librarian from 1899 to 1939 strained his every nerve to enhance the holdings of the Library, developed better ways of access to these collections through cataloguing and classification, and provided many new and special services, such as printed catalogue cards and inter-library loan. Commenting on the contributions of these two great librarians of the LC, C.A. Goodrum in his work "The Library of Congress" (1974) observes that of the librarians's three duties—

"acquisition, cataloguing, and reference"—Spofford had an "over preoccupation" with the first, to the neglect of the two others. But by so massively founding the collections of LC, he made it what it is today. It was left to his successor—Herbert Putnam to worry about cataloguing, organization, and service; but with such a foundation, the library was bound to grow to its present splendour.

LC—a national reference library in Washington, D.C., is generally regarded the world's largest library, both in number of documents and in physical size. It contains more than 8 crores items including books and pamphlets. In scope, they are universal As David Mearns aptly remarked : "From every region of the earth, from every age, by every means of transportation they have been brought together; and although statistics may suggest their magnitude, enumeration cannot elucidate their lively resourcefulness. To be understood, they must be experienced, they must be used, they must be tested and tried".

Distinguished Collections

The LC is especially rich in material on Social and Political Science, History particularly American History and Civilization; Science and Technology including probably the world's largest collection of Aeronautical Literature; and Japanese, Chinese and Russian Collections. Special collections include Books for Blind; the Cartographic Collection; the Law Library; the Manuscripts Collection, including personal papers of the Presidents, statesmen, military, scientific and literary leaders of numerous enterprises, institutions and societies. The Music collection (sheet music scores, and phonographic recordings of music, speeches, poetry and reading) is probably the largest collection (about 3.5 million items) of music and music literature in the world. Other collections include the Micro-film Collection, the Motion Picture Film Collection; the Prints and Photographs Collection; the Serials Collection, and the Technical Reports Collection. The Rare Books Collection includes Incunabula; the Miniature Collection of Books (less than 12 cm in height); Collection of Type Design; Collection of American Genealogy; Collection of Early Americana and History of the French Revolution; Adolf Hitler's Library; the Woodraw Wilson Library; the Winter Palace Collection of Russian Military, Administrative and Social History; Collections of Magic, etc [3]

3. Colin, op. cit.

In addition, LC collection includes Federal and state documents; professional journals, periodicals, news-papers and broadsides. Although, the LC does not serve children, but it has a large collection as children's books for the use of teachers and other interested adults.

The LC is guided in its acquisition policy by two principles—exhaustiveness, and selectivity. The principle of exhautiveness is applied not to acquistition of national publications, but to foreign literature (which is almost three times more than national acquisition), in all languages and almost without subject limitations. Americana, reference—bibliographical editions, and legal literature are collected with particular thoroughness. In national acquisitions, the LC is guided by the principle of selectiveness; it does not take text-books for high schools; it stores only certain samples of paperbacks, it has only 300 newspapers, and those are in microfilm only; as well as dissertations. Thus the library carries out its main function—collection and storage of a complete repertoire of the national printed publications—to a limited extent.

The information—bibliographical functions of the LC are broadly developed. It publishes and distributes printed cards; carries out cataloguing in source, and publishes a Union Catalogue of new additions to the collection of American and Canadian libraries and a Union Catalogue of publications from the beginning of book printing upto 1956.

It is also the centre of research in librarianship and bibliography giving special attention to the problems of safety of books, holdings and automation of processing operations (MARC project). LC has deviced a subject classification system particularly suited for the use of larger collections. In 1970s together with the libraries of Yale and Columbia Universities, the LC set up an information base for the use of researches, scholars and other libraries.

Most of its rooms are specialized by subject areas, types of publications and languages. Use of the library is free to any adult. The public is admitted to the various reading rooms. Individuals may not withdraw books or other items directly, but they are available through inter-library loan. The National Library Service for the Blind and the Physically Handicapped provides recordings and embossed books. Numerous exhibits, including rare books, MSS., maps, photographs, and prints are on display. From its collections, the library prepares travelling exhibits.

Keeping in view the vastness of its resources and services, the LC is divided into some of the following major departments having their respective sub-divisions :

—The Administrative Department is responsible for the maintenance and preservation of the collections and the physical plant, etc.

—The Copyright Section registers all claims for copyright protection.

—The Law Library provides legal reference services.

—The Legislative Reference Service caters the information and research needs of the members of the Congress.

—The Processing Department includes the descriptive and subject cataloguing divisions, the Decimal Classification section, and the card section.

—The Reference Department renders service on the Library's general and specialized collections. It also looks after the services to the Blind, Handicapped beside taking care of the Rare Book collection.

LC through the Linked Systems Project (LSP) have developed on line, connection-oriented, computer to computer links with other libraries.

Some of the most important projects of the LC are : (i) the National Union Catalogue; (ii) the Union List of Serials; (iii) the National Union Catalogue of Manuscript Collections; (iv) the Monthly Index of Russian Accessions; (v) editing the Dewey Decimal Classification; (vi) the Centre for the Coordination of Foreign Manuscript Copying; (vii) the National Referral Centre for Science and Technology; (viii) LC Classification; (ix) Extensive Research in Library Technology; (x) Centre for a Nation-wide Cooperative Loans System; and (xi) MARC.

4. LENIN STATE LIBRARY OF THE USSR

Lenin National Library of the USSR is located in Moscow. The Soviets claim it to be the "largest library in Europe and one of the greatest libraries in the world"[4]. The library was founded on July 1, 1862, on the basis of the holdings of Count N.P. Rumaintsev Public Museum in Moscow. Since its very inception, it has

4. M.M. Klevenskii and E.L. Sil' Versan "Lenin State Library of the USSR".

enjoyed the privilege of legal deposit (3 copies of national publications since 1945; one copy until 1922 and 2 copies in between the years). During the Pre-Revolutionary period, its growth was slow and its collections (500,000) were relatively inaccessible to the public. Though short of finances and staff, it played a significant role in the development of Russian culture. Its readers included L.N Tolstoy, F.M. Dostoevsky and V.I. Lenin.

After the Great October Socialist Revolution, 1917, more than 1.5 million volumes from nationalized book collections were transferred to the Library. Since 1918, the library has served Central Party and Governmental organs, as well as scholarly and other institutions and organizations, with books and bibliographical information.

Lenin paid special attention to the urgent needs and comprehensive development of the library's work. The decree on increasing the library's staff, signed by Lenin in May 1919, made it possible to proceed with the organization of a general classified catalogue and other projects of primary importance. In 1921, the library began to receive grants to purchase foreign publications and carry on an extensive international book exchange programme.

On January 24, the Rumaintsev Library was renamed the Lenin Russian Library, and on Feb. 6, 1925, it was rechristianed the Lenin State Library of the USSR (GBL). In 1945, the GBL was awarded the order of Lenin.

Writing in 1975, Colin recorded that there were 27 million items in GBL, including 12 million volumes (of books); 10,658,000 issues (not bound volumes which is usually the practice of counting) of periodicals; 432,000 volumes of news-paper; 344,000 units of MSS; 600,000 reels of microfilm and 3,158,000 sheets of maps, etc.

It is estimated that knowledge in Science and technology doubles itself within five to seven years and in social sciences and humanities within ten to twelve years. On the basis of this estimate one can confidently conclude that collections must have more than doubled at least in respects of books in GBL.

The GBL has the most complete collection of Russian newspapers (in more than 200 languages of the peoples of the world including newspapers in 89 languages of the peoples of the USSR) and periodicals in the world and the largest collection of foreign books and journals in USSR[5]. Its manuscript collections contain manuscripts from the 6th through 20th centuries, including exceptional rich collection of old Russian manuscript books (w.e.f. 1092). The department of rare books has collected 15th to 18th centuries books printed in the old style of type; first editions of the works of Karl Marx, Frederic Engels, and V.I. Lenin as well as ends published during their life times, and Russian and foreign classics of science and literature.

Collin records that the Library's collections include over 40,000 volumes of work of Marx, Engels and Lenin; 40,000 volume library of the Sheremetyevs; the 25,000 volume library of the Baryatinskils; the 18,000 volumes of rare 18th and 19th century editions from the Yusupov estate at Arkhangelskoye; and 30,000 Russian and Slavonic MSS of the 11th-18th centuries. Especially rich MSS collections include those from the Troitsko—Sergievskii monastry; the Moscow Ecclesiastical Academy; the 19th century Society of Russian History and Antiquities; and private papers of writers, scholars, painters, and public figures Treasures include the *Archangel Gospels* of 1092; the MSS of Gorgol's unfinished novel *The Hertman*; and first editions of the works of such notable figures as Rabelais Descartes, Voltaire, Rousseau, Spinoza and Machiavelli.

The main building houses the catalogues, the acquisition, cataloguing and classification departments, together with 22 reading rooms with 2,500 seats, including a room for academicians, professors, and doctors of science; three large reading rooms specialized according to the types of collections; and general and young people's reading room. The information and bibliographical department, the services department answer bibliographical inquiries for readers and institutions, as well as provide consultation in the fields of book history, library work, and other topics. Behind it is the 19 storey book-stack.

The GBL publishes the Information Bulletin on New Foreign Books received by the library and provides information concerning bibliographical projects that are being done at country's largest libraries through information; Index of Bibliographical Lists comp by libraries. The GBL provides information on domestic books

5. Ibid.

and periodicals acquired by it; issues Collections Book Annals; and Annals of Journal Articles.

A broad range of research, methodological projects are carried on by the research department of library science and bibliographical heory, the scientific methodological department, the departments of manuscripts, rare-books, and so forth. The Transactions of the GBL (since 1957) and Notes of the Department of Manuscripts (since 1938) are published annually. The collections of the Libraries of the USSR (since 1952), Library Science and Bibliography Abroad (since 1958) and topical collections on the most urgent problems are published several times a year. Between 1960-68 the collective work by the country's largest libraries—*Library Bibliographic Classification* : Tables for scholarly libraries was published in 30 vols Specialists in cataloguing department take an active part in preparing the *Standardized Rules for the Description of Published Works for Library Catalogues*. A great deal of research is done on the history of domestic and foreign publishing.

The GBL is closely connected with foreign countries through an extensive international book exchange, as well as by the mutual sharing of experiences among specialists. The Library participates in the work of F.I.D.

The Lenin State Library of the USSR is one of the great national libraries of the world, the most fully integrated into the national system of libraries. It provides a bibliographic clearing house, lends from its stock, has drawn up a widely used classification : *Bibliotechno—bibliographicheskaya klassifikatsiya*. It also houses scholarly research institution in library science, bibliography and book history, as well as methodological and consultation centre for all library systems of the USSR (except scientific and technical libraries). It maintains : Alphabetical catalogue of books and journals. Classified catalogue of books and journal articles. Card indexes on the history of Leningrad and the history of the University.

20

PROFESSIONALISATION

Criticisms, Dilemmas and Proposals

Profession means an occupation, especially one requiring extensive education in a branch of science or the liberal arts. The *Oxford English Dictionary* defines a profession as "a vocation in which a professed knowledge of some department of learning or science is used in its application to the affairs of others or in the practice of an art founded upon it". The same sense is conveyed by a *Dictionary of the Social Sciences* which says that "the term professions denotes occupations which demand a highly specialized knowledge and skill acquired at least in part by courses of a more or less theoretical nature and not by practice alone, tested by some form of examination either at a university or some other authorized institution, and conveying to the persons who possess them considerable authority in relation to 'clients'... At present the term usually denotes certain occupations whose members give service rather than engage in the production and distribution of goods...[1] Speaking almost in the same veins; the eminent social scientists write : we recognise a profession as a vocation founded upon a prolonged and specialized intellectual training which enables a particular service to be rendered"[2]. Special competence; acquired as the result of intellectual training, is the chief distinguishing feature of the professions.

Professionalization, according to **Herbert Blumer**, seeks to clothe a given area with standards of exellence, to establish rules of conduct, to develop a sense of responsibility, to set criteria for recruitment and training, to ensure a measure of protection for members, to establish collective control over the area, and to

1. N. Elias, "Professions", A dictionary of the social sciences, ed. J. Gould and W.A. Kolb (N.Y., Free Press, 1964).
2. A.M. Carr-Saunders and P.A. Wilson, "Professions", *Encyclopaedia of the social sciences*, XI-XII (1932) p. 478.

elevate it to a position of dignity and social standing in the society.[3]

Librarianship is, definitely, an occupation which demands specialized knowledge and skills. Its study is based on a systematic theory which delineates and supports the skills that chatacterize the profession, It has its professional organizations which promote excellence in the work of the members, influence public sentiment and support, and try to raise it to a position of dignity and social standing. It has at its centre the carrer concept; and from the very beginning it is service oriented[4]. But there are those who do not believe that librarianship has achieved professional status. They question, for example, the intellectual content of its educational requirements, the extent of its authority, and the strength of its code of ethics[5].

It is not the purpose of this chapter to answer the question : Is librarianship a profession ? but rather to trace its evolution, to critically examine its operation in India, to plead for educational programme to provide the specialized intellectual study and training necessary for providing skilled service, and the psychological need for academic status.

Evolution

M.A. Gopinath in a review article "LIBRARY PROFESSION AND ITS EVOLUTION'; recognizes the following three periods in the growth and development of the Library Profession :

1. *Scholarly Period* (roughly till 1850s).

Before the middle of the 19th century, the libraries were largely owned by the kings, noble men, monasteries, and universities. The primary objective of the first two groups of libraries appear to have been more to function as marks of nobility than to get their books widely used But a monastry was interested in the use of their books by the scholarly monks. It was managed by one of the scholarly monks as a secondary occupation. As the monasteries declined, their libraries passed into possession of the

3. Herbert Blumer, "Preface", Professionalization, ed by H.M. Vollmer and D.L. Mills (N.J., Prentice-Hall, 1966), p. xi.
4. J.K. Gates, op. cit., p. 97.
5. William Goode, "The Librarian : From Occupation to Profession ?" *LQ*, 31(1961) p. 306-18.

newly emerging universities. But the tradition of their being used mostly by scholars alone and one of the scholars functioning as the librarian continued till the end of the First World War. This tradition still lingers on in a few stray universities and colleges in India. Under these circumstances, there was little chance for librarianship to emerge as a vocation.

2. *Vocational Period* (roughly from 1850 to 1950)

About 1850s public libraries were started in U.K., and U.S.A. They were manned largely by non-university men. They took their work to be that of providing a "source of information and enjoyment for all men". According to Palmer, this made "the new librarians... to think about their functions anew". As the number of public libraries increased, their common goal of making the public widely use the information embodied in books led to the emergence of librarianship as a new vocation. The arts of book selection, classification, cataloguing, and reference service, were casually developed by methods of trial and error. With the advance of these arts, the vocation got more and more crystalized. Writing in 1950, Robert D. Leigh described librarianship to be merely as "a skilled occupation". Even today, it lingers on in that stage in some places.

3. *Professional Period* (roughly after 1950)

Has librarianship achieved its goal of becoming a profession? asks Gopinnath. This has been a debatable point. Gopinath quotes two library scientists and then maintains that librarianship has become a learned profession. In 1951, Pierce [5a] Butler compared librarianship to the typical professions, such as medicine, law, and engineering, and maintained that the intellectual content of librarianship was not so "abstruse as to become a special professional scholarship". Further, Butler continued, "Librarians always have operated, and still do, with an empirical rather than a theoretical attitude toward their problems. Their techniques are so matter of fact (simple, routine type) that a layman can quickly learn them on the job". In 1961, William J. Goode[6] opined : "Several key elements are missing to prevent its (librarianship's) knowledge

5a. P. Butter, "Librarianship as a Profession", *LQ*, (V. 21), 1951), p. 221.

6. W.J. Goode, "The Librarian : From Occupation to Profession ?" *LQ* (V. 31, Oct. 1961), pp. 306-18.

base from being sufficient for all full professional status. The central gap is of course the failure to develop a general body of scientific knowledge bearing precisely on this problem in the way that medical profession with its auxiliary scientific field has developed an immense body of knowledge with which to cure human diseases". Further, Gocde feels that "In a very general way, it is possible at least to define the major task or problem of the librarian, but I doubt that it is possible to identify the fund of principles or generalisations—the science—which solves it". Gopinath writes that Goode is right in his assumption that a body of fundamental laws is a condition precedent for the formation of a profession. A set of fundamental laws have been formulated as far back as 1931 by Ranganathan as "Five Laws of Library Science". During the past half a century, these Five Laws have helped not only in the inference of the past and the present techniques needed for library service but also in the anticipation of new techniques needed for library service in changing social condittons. These fundamental laws have in a potential form all the intellectual content demanded by Butler for Librarianship to be deemed a profession. Fortunately, however, the laws of Library Science and the application of Scientific Method to every library technique have already begun to permeate widely. Today, the minds of the younger librarians are fully charged with these laws and their potentialities. Thus, the librarians no longer belong to a mere vocation but to a learned profession on a par with the professions of Lawyers, Medical Men, and Engineers.

To this matured judgement of Gopinath, it may be added that the librarianship as a profession is not preceded by a vocat ional growth process which is hypothesized to be the phenomenon behind socially desired professions like medicine, engineering, teaching, law, etc., in India. Vocational growth "refers to the life-long process of developing work values, crystalizing a vocational identity, learning about opportunities, and trying out plans in part time, recreational, and full-time work situations[7]". Growth and development involves increasingly effective investigational choice, and evaluation of occupational possibilities. It is verified by scientific investigations that an individual is involved in a long term

7. E.L. Tolbert. *Counselling for carrer development* (Boston : Houghton Mifflin, 197), p. 25.

process of ariving at a career decision and has many previous choices under the influence of varions persons, conditions, and personal needs and attributes. In short, vocational development begins very early in life and is a life-long process.

Library Profession in India

Librarianship as a profession does not seem to undergo the developmental process as shown by the author in an All India Survey[8]. Majority of library personnel were motivated to join this profession after their college/university education was over and that too for better job prospects. This unambiguously shows that choice of this profession is not preceded by vocational developmental stages, Vocational growth process amounts to the development of an intrinsic interest in profession. This intrinsic interest may have a high motivational charaction, success and morale of the personnel. Because of the lack of this vocational growth library science as a profession is not highly respected either by the "Academic Community", or by the "Public" or even in the "Family"[9] in India.

Majority of us joined this profcssion just to earn our bread and butter. There is nothing wrong if majority of us decided to join librarianship just to get into service, Each new employee makes his psychological contract within organization hoping that it will have a supportive climate, to help him meet his economic, social and *psychological wants.* The perception he has of that climate produces its image in his mind. But an organization tends to attract and keep people to stick to it and to adjust themselves to its climate, so that its patterns are to some extent perpetuated. As library is a service organization, those who prefer and entertain monetary outlook and habits may not prove to be the best persons for this noble and exalted profession aiming at keeping the flame of knowledge burning.

Another distressing feature is that majotity of us would be unwilling to join library profession if we were to start our career afresh. Such an attitude is reflective of a sense of dissatisfaction with the prevailing conditions in the library profession.

Worst of all, our university librarians who are highly paid persons would neither like their children nor even their kith and kin to embrace librarianship as a career.

8. J.K. Khanna. *Personnel management in libraries* (ESS ESS, 1981).
9. Ibid.

Doubtlessly, most of us seem to be fed up with our respective professions and want a change. Almost every one of us also desires that his children should be better placed. But a leading doctor, or an engineer or even an excellent lawyer very much desires that his son should replace him But in case of the library profession, even the most prominent of the university librarians or the librarians of the institutes of higher learning do not like that their children should take up a course in library science[10]

Admitted that parents/guardians are usually hesitant in desiring that their children should join their profession, still the most distressing feature is that majority of librarians would not even like to recommend their profession to their kith and kin. One of the outstanding university librarian commented that he would not recommend this profession even to his "dead enemy". So strongly has the frustration taken root that another university librarian remarked that if he were to know even after his seventh birth that he was once a librarian, he "would feel ashamed of it". This reveals the height of frustration with the profession of librarianship. Of course, K.S. Hingwy observed that he would like to be a librarian even after his hundredth birth.

It is, thus, evident that the library profession is not preceded by a vocational growth process. Neither majority of the librarians pre-planned during their academic career to join this profession, nor would they like to join librarianship, if they were to start their career all over again, nor they would desire their kith and kin, much less their children, to join the library profession. This reveals the height of frustration with the library profession. Explaining the reasons for such a sordid state of affairs it is commented : "Our basic philosophy is erraneous; our proclamations unfulfilled; our ego maligned. We have to change the total set-up of the professional framework which is like a structure being eaten away by white ants."* This type of professional despair may adversely affect the efficiency of the library personnel and they may not feel satisfied with the nature of their job which is pregnant with intellectnal challanges. Perceiving librarianship

10. One observed "Don't Curse Me".

* M.L. Mohindru, in an interview.

as a "noble" and "exalted" profession vis-a-vis a deep disliking for the profession seem to be a defence mechanism. Professional Charm as defence mechanism seems to help the librarians to maintain their psychological equilibrium in a situation which is anxiety-provoking and frustrating.

Deploring this pathetic condition, Ranganathan narrates an incident when one of the leaders of India asked him about a score of years ago.

> "What is there in librarianship to justify your writing 50 books on it ? I hear of your having organized a course for the Master's degree in Library Science and of your having persuaded a University to institute a decorate degree in your subject. It means that you try to glorify mere common sense as a fit subjecct for such degree".[11]

For a layman in India, a librarian is one who can read the spine of books and maintain their records. It is no surprise, therefore, writes Ranganathan. that the thirty posts in the Madras University Library were "indistinguishable". To be instanced, there was an unskilled cleaner in that library named Abdur Razak. Most of the mail of the library had the address "Abdul Razak, Librarian, Madras University Madras"[12].

Happily, the old order is changing, yielding place to new. So far as the numbers go, the provision for training of librarians is quite impressive in 1986*. But it is a different story when we come to consider the quality of training, Part of the deterioration in quality is traceable by the sudden increase in the quantity. The library schools are generally inadequately financed and staffed, are deficient in administration, and medicore in their faculties. Research is looked down upon with utter disdain. A Ph.D. Degree is held in abhorrence. Furthermore, the faculty recruited in the departments of library science mostly does not have sound academic background to train the librarians with special competence in the

11. S.R. Ranganathan, Training for librarianship, *Annals of Library Science* (v. 5, 1, 1957), p. 55.

12. *Ibid*,

* At present, there are 54 schools imparting training in B. Lib. Sc. course; 26 at M Lib Sc. level; 9 in Ph.D., courses. There are some politechnics and library associations which also have provision to impart library training on a lower level leading to either Diplomas or Certificates.

broad areas of the Universe of Knowledge—natural sciences, social sciences, and the humanities—all of these are essentials of the librarian's professional equipment. Experience of working for his research in the various university libraries has convinced the author that lack of sufficient subject knowledge rather than of ample library techniques is primarily obstructing the Indian librarian to render good library service. There is much relevance under Indian conditions in the argument, though, made in a different context, that to "bring about a reasonable degree of efficiency in library service, adequate provision must be made for specialized training"[13]. While library service has been growing more and more specialized, and doubtlessly will continue to do so, the training afforded by the schools has for the most part remained general and static.

Still everything is not wrong with the library profession in India : every cloud has a silver lining. Thanks to the indefatigable efforts of the pioneers like Ranganathan, the Indian University librarian need not feel like a rudderless boat in an uncharted sea. It was he who infused a new life into librarianship and changed it into a science—in fact, a craft in to a full-fledged profession and discipline in its own right, with its own fundamental laws, deducted laws and a sound methodology for reaserch[14].

Another favourable dimension is that library science over the past decade is attracting well-qualified young men and women who have the intellectual capabilities and potentialities as well as moral and mental fibre to face the intellectual challenges thrown up by the explosion of literature and accept responsibilities. Given proper guidance and leadership, their energies can be channelized in such directions that would lead to "more efficient, more purposeful, more directed, more compressed, more specialized, and more individualized service"[5], thereby making the librarian a true participant in the dissemination of knowledge.

13. Charles C. Williamson, *Training for library service : a report* (New York : Carnegie Corporation, 1923), p. 21.
13. The British librarians openly acknowledge England's debt to India See Benhard I. Palmer and A.J. Wells, *The Fundamentals of library classification* (London : George Allen and Unwin, 1951). Further, the creation of a National Research Professorship or Professor Emeritus in Library Science is an evidence of the high value that the society has placed in library science and library service.
15. Bernard Berelson, *Graduate education in the United States* (New York : McGraw-Hill, 1960), p. 260.

What has been achieved is realy creditable, but it is just a clarion-call to achieve more—particularly when the public image of the librarian is also slowly but steadily changing to that of a capable organizer of libraries on modern lines, a specialist, a scholar, and a research worker in his field. To enlarge and retain the changing image, the librarians should constantly be in labour to highlight that "the basic philosophy of the library is the encouragement of learning and that library is a place where learning occurs as well as a place where materials is used and stored"[16].

To be "a live depository of cultural past that anticipates the future"[17] is no longer enough. The documents must be used to the largest possible extent and with the least trouble: they must be used as tools for the exploration of horizons of knowledge rather than guarded as treasure-troves. If the documents are for use; if every reader is to get his/her document for reading, research or information; if every document is to be energized for whatever purpose it is designed to serve; if the time of the library user in pursuit of knowledge is to be saved; and if exponential growth of knowledge is to be reckoned with, the librarian and his staff must bring to the point of maximum efficiency the socialization of the graphic records by interpreting their collections to the clientele, by offering them unlimited personal assistance in search of knowledge or information. It is service, not suggestion, that is at a premium. Nothing else can take the place of a fine reference service. Rather the real future of the library (whether it be public, academic, special or research) as an agency for the transmission and dissemtnation of information and essential knowledge lies in the direct provision of "comprehensive and accurate" reference service to readers. Instructing the user in the technique of information search, is important, but a secondary goal, and is not necessarily a reference function.[18] It is the maximum reference service, today, rechristianed as Current Awareness Service and SDI (Selective Dissemination of Information) that will fire the imagination and remove prejudices of the academic community, who may start looking upon the librarians as true participants in their teaching. The function of the librarian as participant in the process of teaching

16. H. Hauf et al., *New spaces for learning, op. cit.*, p. 25.
17. Ralph W. Conant, Sociological and institutional changes in American life; their implications for the library, *American Library Association Bulletin* (V. 58, Dec. 1964), p 994.
18. Anita R. Schiller, Reference service; instruction or information, *The Library Quarterly* (V. 35, 1, 1965) p. 110.

and research only entitles him to the academic status, and not slogan-shouting.

Finally, as the librarian deals with ideas and their communication, as recorded in various documents, the emergence of electro-mechanical communication media can tremendously help him in distributing 'thought-commodity' pin-pointedly, exhaustively and expeditiously. As a reliable, competent, accurate and cleaner manipulator of library information, the media can bring to fruition many idealistic concepts about flexible library service. Today's efforts, "reflecting the democratization of education and the incandescence of media culture, bear the seed for major alteration of the library's goals, function and organization",[19] particularly when the new media is proclaimed to contain three pre-dominant functions; "socializing and mobilizing" which stand for "the transmission and dissemination of information and essential knowledge...the transmission of a cultural system and the inculcation of values...and the process of persuasion and the development of loyalties and attachments which are essential for collective problem solving."[20] With the use of more and more of media in the Indian University libraries the traditional role of the librarian will change from that of a care-taker of books into the disseminator of knowledge.

In brief, the rising tide of literature, the proliferation of subjects, the explosion of scholarly and informational material in all the major languages of the world and the bibliographical apparatus of the many fields and sub-fields becoming enormously difficult alongwith the introduction of the system of open universities, establishment of advance centres of study, and the mounting spirit of research work in the Indian universities, devolve upon the librarian to assume the role of a subject specialist, documentalist, or information officer, and the media expert as the occasion requires.

While the above steps are essential for bringing about a revolutionary change in the attitudes of the academicians and of the public toward the library profession, some more suggestions are made to allure the young university trained persons to

19. Taylor, *The Mvking of a library, op. cit.*, p. 39.
20. P.H. Rossi and B.J. Biddle, *Eds. The New media and education : their impact on society* (New Jerssy : Anchor, 1967) p 230.

think of joining the library profession while pursuing studies as the students do in case of medicine, engineering, etc.

One of the fundamental criticisms of the education for the librarians is that it abruptly starts at the post-graduate level. In most cases the respondents even did not know about library science courses before they did their graduation. For the growth and development of the library profession, it is essential that it should become all pervasive; an integral part of the entire educational system. As the Chinese proverb goes:

If you plan for one year, plant grain,
If you plan for ten years, plant trees,
If you plan for hundred years, plant men.

Since our aim is to plan for the growth and development of library profession not only for hundred years but for all ages to come, we must carefully plan and educate our future generations—the children. School period is the most formative age for moulding the character and shaping the thoughts of the would be library personnel about the nobility and exaltedness of this profession.

A library period may be introduced in the school time-table for each class to enable the students to use the library intelligently and diligently. Books should be distributed among them keeping in view their tastes and interests, so that the students may develop the reading habit, power of thinking and imagination and become library-oriented. This will invariably generate in the children the appreciation of books; a psychological tempo will blossom in them and transform them into willing beneficiaries of the library. The school library, therefore, is the cradle of the intellectual conditioning of the child which may imperceptibly awaken and foster among the children a love for the library profession which aims at service before self. But this will not be self-sufficient. The love for this profession will actually flower only in graduation courses.

Library science should be introduced as one of the cognitive (elective) courses as history, political science, economics, philosophy, psychology, physics, chemistry, botany or zoology. The point to be emphasized here is that "the focus of the undergraduate treatment of librarianship should be directed toward comprehension of the library system as an integral part of the communication process, and not upon a diluted survey of library skills."[21]

21. Jesse H. Shera, *The Foundations of education for librarianship, op. cit.*, p. 328.

The four years B.A. in library science must not be the terminal for librarianship. Rather it should provide the foundation for further academic study and future intellectual growth. If properly educated and interested, the student should be prepared and encouraged to enter M.A.[22], in library science as is the case with other subjects. Library science should thus pervade the entire education system.[23] Only by such and other methods we can generate a feeling of love and an appreciation for this profession from the school onward and may get library personnel devoted to the profession and ready to make sacrifices for setting it on the right rails.

Further, it must be remembered that the essence of a profession is that, although people enter it to gain a livelihood, the measure of their success is the service they perform, and not the financial gains they carry.[24] At the most, only those persons should be encouraged to enter the field who are interested at least as much in opportunities to help others as in a suitable salary and satisfactory conditions of work.

For the growth and development of the library profession, it is a 'must' that the practice of appointing the Professor of other disciplines as the incharge of library, should be discontinued as it destroys the initiative and dwarfs the intellectual capabilities and potentialities of the library professional staff and breeds in them the habit of sychophancy at the cost of library service, thus lowering their own status and that of the profession in the bargain.

In the altered circumstances, the university librarian should be vested with all the powers and responsibilities previously held by the library committee. It shou'd be the responsibility of the university librarian to organize, and to operate the university library in the way he thinks best to meet the needs of teaching, research and extension services; and for this he will be directly responsible to the Vice-Chancellor. It is only in this way that the librarian can make his library a permanent living force in the life of the academic community so that no member of it feels inclined to think

22. Two years consecutive course.

23. Shera, *op. cit.*, pp. 328-19.

24. B.M. Headicar, *A Manual of library organization* (London : Allen and Unwin, 1941), p. 254.

either "why a library"? or "why a librarian"?[25] Sufficient care, of course, will be taken in selecting as the university librarian a person who is eminently capable of performing the complex task of transforming the library into a dynamic agency for the dissemination of information, and has the potentialities of keeping the title 'University Librarian, a dignified one equivalent to that of a Professor. Besides having a penchant for scholarship, integrity, cultural background, competence as administrator of the library and expert in human relations, he should be strongly familiar with modern techniques of librarianship. It must be emphasized that the possession of a Ph.D. degree will enhance his status and creditability in the eyes of the academicians.

Further, the librarian and his professional staff should not be burdened with part-time teaching work; it is essential for increasing efficiency in the university libraries. Nevertheless, there can be no two opinions that some specialists working in the acquisition section or reference section may be invited to deliver lectures. The students are bound to be benefited from these lectures as compared to those of the teachers, who have never worked in the libraries, as too much theory leads to the sterility of "empty formalism"[26].

The foregoing discussion implies that the department of Library Science in the Indian universities or anywhere else should have a separate entity of its own and the practice of having Librarians as part-time heads of the department should be discontinued. It is absolutely necessary for improving the standards of library education which will in turn lead to better organization and operation of libraries, better service to readers and more specialization, the sum total of which will stimulate better teaching and qualitative research upon which are based our contemporary civilization, our standard of living, and our democratic society.

Further, because of the vital role of the library education in the regeneration of a nation's life, it is of topmost importance that the departments of library science are headed by teachers of eminence who have distinguished themselves in the fields by virtue of their research. As Ranganathan says, "A professor of Library Science should have as the minimum professional qualification a

25. Philip H. Ennis and Howard W. Winger, *Eds. Seven questions about the profession of librarianship* (University of Chicago, 1962), p. 812.

26. Shera, *op. cit.*, p. 216.

Doctorate in Library Science....... He should have the ability to engage himself in research and guide research"[27] As in any other subject, attunement to research is necessary to make teaching creative instead of merely transmissive. Mere transmissive teaching is unworthy of a university department.

Finally, no person be appointed as a teacher in the department of library science in any university till he has worked in a library; this practical training is 'a must' for one to be a good teacher; without it he is likely to be simply a Philistine.

27. University Grants Commission (India), *University and college libraries op. cit.*, p. 86.

21

ACADEMIC STATUS FOR LIBRARIANS

Psychological and Sociological Foundations

Status and role are two sides of the same coin. A's behaviour as determined by the norms towards others is A's role. Others' behaviour, opinions and attitudes towards A as a consequence of the role which A plays, is A's status. One's duty is one's role; the privileges one gets for playing one's role determine one's status.

Status is basic ingredient of our society. 'It is a place in the sun, position in the scheme of things, niche in the town or community"[1] Status cannot, and must not, be ignored because it exists and is important to most people. Man's esteem or egoistic needs (needs for self-esteem, self-confidence, self-respect, advancement, recognition, achievement, urge for independence and freedom, and knowledge) are closely related to the concept of status.

The university librarian in India feels that he has a second class citizen status in the university hierarchy. He is graded neither as an academician nor as an administrator, though, he performs, the functions of both. In the Indian Society, at least, the librarian is still looked upon as a caretaker of books or a book-lifter, and librarianship as a profession meant only for mediocres, This affects the morale and efficiency of the library personnel.

One of the most important motivators required for boosting morale and increasing efficiency of the library professional staff is the restoration of academic status and scales of pay[2]. As Ranganathan succinctly remarked : "The high academic and professional qualifications, the combination of academic and administrative responsibilities, and the practice in the universities

1. Allen F. Briggs. "Status symbol for the librarians", *Wilson Library Bulletin* (36, 3 1961), p. 31.

2. For further details see, Supra, chapt. 10, pp, 111-16.

all the world over indicate that the status and salary scale of the library staff sould be the same as that of teaching and research staff.[3]

The acceptance of the academic status would make persons of higher intellect to take to the library science course and when they enter the profession in sufficient number the profession itself will get suitably elevated. This would mean no doubt waiting for one generation. But this patience has to be kept to attract and hold the best university trained men and women who possess sound educational and professional background to develop into University Librarians, the Deputy Librarians, the Assistant Librarians, the Library Assistants, etc.

If academic status is not given to the university librarian and his professional staff, it is likely not only to divert the attention of the intellectually exellent persons to other professions but may also generate a feeling of inferiority complex in the existing staff thus affecting their efficiency and lowering their morale. Low morale is a sign of deteriorating human relations resulting in (a) apathy; (b) bickering; (c) jealousies; (d) disjointed efforts; and (e) permissiveness.[4] In its more sinister forms it lurks behind wildcat strikes, slowdowns, absenteeism, and employee turnover.

Academic status will enhance not only the social status of the library personnel, but also increase their efficiency and boost their morale, variously decribed in terms of (a) team spirit, (b) staying quality; (c) zest or enthusiasm; and (d) resistence to frustration.[5]

It may, however, be argued that it is only a perception of library personnel that their parity with the academic staff in respect of status is likely to prove conducive to increased efficiency and morale; but in reality it may not happen as the experience of past decade shows. However, it may be stated that motivation is strongly affected by perception, as we noted when evaluating the

3. S.R. Ranganathan, *In University and college libraries; a report, op. cit.*, p. 66.

The Government of India's Advisory Committee for Libraries; and Unesco Regional Seminar on Library Development in South Asia held at New Delhi from 3 to 14th. Oct. 1960 expressed similar views.

4. Norman R.F. Maier, *Psychology in industry* (New Delhi, Oxford, 1970,) p. 120.

5. Ibid., p. 119.

Expectancy/Valence theory as projected by Vroom. The force of motivation is directly related to the perceived probability that effort and success are related, as well as the linkage between success and rewards. Further, as Rogers, the major proponent of self-concept, writes : "The best vantage point for understanding behaviour is from the internal frame of reference of the individual himself".[6] To Rogers, the individual is the centre of experience. To understand his behaviour, one must understand how another views his experiences and what sort of image he has of himself. And the image of the library personnel is that their status is rated on "Average" by the Academic Community, the Public, and the Family; parity with the academic staff could enhance their social status and prove a stimulator to efficiency and morale.

The monetary gains would help to avoid anxiety.[7] For Herzberg and his associates,[8] money serves to avoid feelings of being unfairly treated or economically deprived. Reinforcement theorists,[9] on the other hand, seem to treat money either as generalized entity, functioning independently of specific deprivations, or as a general incentive that has been coupled with various valued goals during a person's total learning history. To Vroom[10] and Gallerman[11] money is important for the symbolic functions it performs. Money not only satisfies the basic physiological needs but the continued supply of money ensures the satisfaction of the higher order psychological needs. It secures for the individual food and protection, but more importantly, it symbolizes even emotional security. It also satisfies the social needs of the person, especially when social life becomes institutionalised. Further, higher-order

6. **Carl Rogers, A Theory of therapy, personality and interpersonal relationships as developed in the client-centred framework, *In Psychology: a study of a science*, V. 3: *Formulations of the person in the social context*, ed. by S. Koch (New York: McGraw-Hill, 1959), pp. 184-256.**
7. **J,S. Brown, Problems presented by the concept of acquired drives. *In* Current theory and research in motivation; a symposium (Lincoln: University of Nebraska, 1953), pp. 1-21. Also his *The Motivation of behaviour* (New York : McGraw-Hill, 1961), Chapt, 1.**
8. **F. Herzberg, et al. Motivation to work; 2nd ed. (N.Y., Wiley, 1959).**
9. **J.G. Holland and B.F Skinner, *The Analysis of behaviour* (McGraw-Hill, 1961).**
10. **V.H. Vroom, *Work and motivation op. cit.* pp. 30-32, 252-60.**
11. **S.W. Gallerman, *Motivation* and *productivity* New York: American Management Association, 1963), 160-71.**

needs like status also could be satisfied by money because at least in Indian culture, money is often considered as an index of social status. Again, only in an economy of abundance can culture become broad-based. One should agree to Lawler's suggestion that pay is a unique incentive, one that is able to satisfy all levels of needs.[12-14]

Academic status and scales of pay also carry certain definite obligations for the librarian. The foremost is the intellectual activity, including a keen interest in the intellectual life of the campus. It highlights that the selection of a highly qualified librarian and his professional staff is of paramount importance to generate a climate that tends to involve us all in a chain-reacting, creative and intellectual endeavour—the pre-requisities for the advancement of knowledge and the educational objectives of the university. The University Education Commission (1948-49) headed by S. Radhakrishnan had recommended that the University Librarian should be a man of the calibre of a University Professor who has specialized in some aspects of library science, and who has capacities for organisation and management. He must have qualifications corresponding to the degree of a Doctor in Library Science.[15]

As regards the insistence on Ph.D. in Library Science, it is asked why such a degree is not required of the administrators viz., the I.A.S. (Indian Administrative Service) officers or the university Vice-Chancellors or the Registrars or of professionals like the Medicos or the Engineers or of the teachers of Art, Painting, Architecture, etc. Simil rly, it is argued that in the case of library profession as well, professional experience and training in librarianship should be the base rather the "Ph.D. octopus".[16] That is why the Library Committee of the U.G.C. headed by

12. E.E. Lawler, *The Mythology of management compensation* (New Haven : Yale University, 1965).

    Conducting research in the industrial organizations in India, the following writers also reached the same eonclusions :

13. H.C. Ganguli, *Structure and processes of organizations* (Bombay : Asla, 1964).

14. D.M. Pestonjee, Effects of financial incentives on job satisfaction, *Indian Journal of Applied psychology* (V. 8, no. 2, 1971), pp 6-163.

15. University Education Commission, Dec. 1948–Aug., 1949, *op. cit. p.* 112.

16. Wlilliam James, Cf. Shera. *The Foundation of education for librarianship, op. cit.*, p. 112.

Ranganathan made the possession of a Doctrate in Library Science as a desirable qualification, whereas the University Grants Commission (U.G.C.) abolished it altogether.[17]

However, the University Grants Commission on the recommendation of the Sen Committee appointed by it withdrew the academic status and scales of pay of the librarians and their professional staff in 1974. Nonetheless, the Sen Committee has recommended the professor's scale of pay for the university librarians having Ph.D., degree in any subject other than Library Science with a good academic record and 10 years research experience. It implies that the U.G.C. prefers scholar-librarians[18]

The pharse scholar-librarians, unfortunately, seem to have become a bug-bear for most of the university librarians creating wrong impressions in their minds that such a person cannot be a successful and competent librarian. But Chamber was a great scholar; he professed English literature. So was Immannel Kant, the greatest philosopher of Germany. But both of them were librarians as well and so demonstrated. What is sometime overlooked is that the management of university library is a stupendous task requiring much more than mere administiative ability, and it is a scholar himself with sound educational background who can fully appreciate how a library can best be made subservient to the cause of scholarship.

Admitted that the expression scholar-librarian is a misnomer; but neither the word technician, nor cataloguer nor classifier nor an administrator is appopriate. In fact, as J.H. Shera[19] has succinctly remarked that librarian is a composite of two bodies in one soul, an amalgam of an academician and an administrator. The two mingle in his varied functions. Library work is an end product of three basic functions—acquisition, organization, and service. As a part of his administrative skill, the administrator in librarian should know how to order means to an end. The acquisitive function expects of the librarian to know what to acquire and

17. University Grants Commission (India), *University and college libraries : a report*, *op. cit.*, p. 66.

18. Indian Association of Academic Libraries, *Newsletter* (V. 1. no. 3, 1978), p. 8.

19. 61 Jesse H. Shera, Mechanization, librarianship, and the bibliograpic enterprise, *Journal of documentation*, (V. 30, no. 4, 1974), pp. 154-8.

how to acquire. The organization function lies in his abilities to arrange and analyse the materials and information for ready use, and this is not possible without a sound academic background. The third function of the service can emanate from his academic and professional abilities to provide the right information, at the right time, to the right reader, in the right amount of all generations of all mankind, and in all the forms to its individual member for enriching his intellect and to perfect his potential talents so that his specific contributions to the society will be superior. It is, thus, in the service part that the effectiveness of the acquisition and organization functions get translated into reality and their utility proved. For this act of professionalism, pedantry and condensation on the part of the librarian are intolerable; cordiality and every wish to be of professional service are highly desired.

To perform his functions as detailed in Chapters 4-9 the librarian must be a scholar (not a pedant). He must be characterized by two outstanding attributes : the first is intellectual breadth and depth; and the second is creativity. He must be able to communicate effectively with the academic community of which he is an integral part. Creativity is the capacity for innovation and independence.[20] Short of this the university librarians will not be justifying themselves for parity with the academic staff which they yearn so keenly.

One. however, feels unhappy about the derogatory decision of the Sen Committee taken in regard to its recommendation that the librarian may have "a Ph.D. degree in any subject other than library science" suggesting thereby that library science is not a discipline.

Needless to comment that library science today is recognized as a full-fledged discipline all over the world, and library is a teaching institution and a process that permeats the entire academic life of the university campus. But in can perform its function of accumulation, preservation. and dissemination of knowledge only if it is directed by one who knows the objectives and the potentialities of the library, the techiques, tools and means of achieveing them, and fully knows 'how and where to find out' the

20. Jesse, H. Shera, The Future, too, is Prologue, *Wilson Library Bulletin* (V. 51, no. 3, Nov. 1964), p. 253.

material as well as is thoroughly acquainted with the 'hide and seek' character of most of the micro-documents which baffle even high intellectuals and scholars of repute. No matter, how great a scholar an individual may be in his own field of specialization, he is not qualified to operate a modern university library on "teaching and research" level without having a sound bibliographical training and expert knowledge of indexing and abstracting services and their techniques.

Expediency and a desire to acquire or enhance prestige may suggest the selection of a distinguished scholar. But such a selection must be condemned too strongly when the individual concerned is without familiarity with modern librarianship and is not in a sense a librarian.[21] In no case, should an unwanted or a disgruntled or frustrated scholar in his own field be permitted to enter librarianship. It will not only dwarf the growth of the library profession irreparably but will also demoralize the qualified librarian and his professional staff. Nonetheless, the author is of the view that the librarian should have excelent qualifications—both academic and professional—to have an edge over his counter part—the university teacher.

In brief, status and monetary gains will continue to play a significant role in the overall library management framework. Fortunately, wisdom has descended upon the U.G.C. and the academic status and scales of pay have been restored. It is for the librarians to come upto expectations by helping the university to engage itself earnestly and vigorously in its intellectual pursuit, which is to assemble, preserve, transmit and illuminate knowledge or wisdom of the past.

21. J. Periam Danton, *Education for librarianship : criticisms, dilemmas and proposals* (Columbia University, 1946), p. 4.

22

NATIONAL LIBRARY ASSOCIATIONS

U.S.A., U.K., and India

The Renaissance and the Industrial Revolution were the primary factors that gave rise to the estabhishment of many vocational and professional associations. B.I. Palmer summarizes some of the motivators leading to the formation of sueh associations as under :

—To protect the good name of a profession and prevent fraudulent, unauthorized practices, e.g., Institute of Chartered Accountants;

—to develop effective techniques, so that they could be identified by the society as a separate group of practitioners, e.g., Institute of Surveyors; and

—to act as a defence organism against the exploitation by non-practitioners who are mainly concerned with mercenary interest rather social interest, e.g., Pharmaceutical Society.

The motivators provided by Palmer indicate that the rise of an association is not only to safeguard the interests of a small group of people, but it also aims at building a better society. They inculcate in each of their member lofty ideals of serving the humanity to live a better life. Thus, the rise of associations symbolises a path of progress wherein the person sharing a common practice and common goal are bound together to bring in a better quality of work which ultimately results in a healthy, productive development of the community.

The Library Association

The library association is a professional association. The establishment of a professional association usually occurs as soon as a profession emerges, for a profession can only be said to exist when there are bonds between the practitioners, and these bonds can take but one shape—that of formal association. Library professional organizations promote excellence in the work of the members, influence public sentiments and support, and try to raise it to a position of dignity and social standing. Their emergence is largely due to a desire to enable the public to draw maximum possible benefit from the use of documents. They contribute significantly to democratise knowledge by promoting the establishment of well-stocked, well-staffed, well-organized and well-financed libraries.

Library associations can be established both at a national and a state level. There can be a library association for a big cosmopolitan city, like Delhi Library Association. Associations at international level are also available, viz., IFLA or COMLA.

Objectives

The Library Association at national level should have the following important obectives: I. It should be a representative body of the profession in a country. II. It should include in its membership all the categories of library personnel and even those who are interested in libraries. III. It should include in its member ship all the categories of library personnel and even those who are interested in libraries. IV. It should have a central office with branches all over the country. VI. It should safeguard the interests of the professionals at various places. VII. It should promote the cause of libraries and the profession. VIII. It should have a definite programme of activity. IX. It should have programme and be a force in the educational set-up of the country. X. It should be handled by honest, diligent, dedicated and hard-working members.

Purposes

The basic purpose of the library association is to speak and act for the profession as a whole in the fields of common professional interests such as the question of revision of grades and enhancement of professional status; standardizing curriculum of library science schools; formulating library legislation; preparation of union catalogues; publication of library journal; compiling, maintaining, updating and publishing library directories; formulating library standards; encouraging inter-library cooperation; creating library consciousness and awareness among the people; organizing educational programmes, training courses, conferences, symposiums, and committees on topics of general interests; helping professionals getting service; and to recommend to individual associations and groups of associations, projects of importance in specific fields and to give such projects general professional assistance.

Functions

Advisory Committee for Libraries assigns five functions for the library association:

—a library association tries to build up a sense of brotherhood among librarians, cutting across the boundaries of caste, creed, colour, and country in a self-conuscious community devoted to the cultural elevation of their fellowmen. This raises the morale of independent librarians and braces them up to their tasks;

—library associations, explicitly or implicitly, help to build up and instil into the minds of individual librarians a code, an ethics of conduct vis-a-vis their communities; this code helps to place the librarian on a platform of respectability in his community;

—library associations make an earnest effort to raise the standards of training of librarians to enable them to perform their tasks with greater competence and for the larger benefit of society;

—a library association is a trade union fighting for better conditions of service of librarians; and

—it is the standard-bearer of library extension service in every country where it exists.

Library associations tend to discharge their functions by holding library conferences, seminars and meetings, by publishing library journals, by holding lectures and conducting study circles and by publicity, exhibitions, and propaganda; by organizing deputations and adopting other well-known pressure tactics and by bringing out basic library literature. Where organs of library research and training are weak, library associations have taken on themselves the task of training librarians and bringing out books on varions aspects of librarianship or compiling valuable bibliographies, book lists and catalogues-tasks which had better be left to special agencies. In all this, the objective of library associations is to strengthen and expand the library movement and not to assist any particular library or section of librarians.

In this context, it will be worth while to compare the foundation, growth and achievements of the library associations in U.S.A., U.K., and India and to see how far they are achieving the objectives, purposes and functions laid down above.

1. AMERICAN LIBRARY ASSOCIATION

Foundation and Growth

Charles Coffin Jewett, famous librarian of the Smithsonian Institution, sowed the seed for the formation of the American Library Association on Sept., 15,1853. In that year the first Librarians' Conference was held in New York consisting of 82 men including librarians, scholars, educationists, and clergymen. In his presidential address Jewett pointed out that they were meeting "to provide for the diffusion of a knowlegde of good books, and for enlarging the means of public access tc them. Our wishes are for the pnblic, not for ourselves". The Conference was indeed the maiden effort toward the organization of librarians as a group, though, the measureable results were few but significant. The Conference significance lay in the fact that it was able to bring it to the knowledge of the public that the distinctive function of the library is to accumulate, preserve, process, and promote the use of books and that special techniques are required in performing this function. It highlighted the need of librarians as a group to confer together; and it emphasized that service is the sine qua non of establishing a library. They dispersed to meet again.

Keeping in view the most significant decisions of the 1853 Conference, another Librarians' Conference was called in 1876 in Philadephia, It was attended by large number of librarians from all over U.S.A., Canada and U.K. This august body of 103 members made history of library science by founding on October, 4, 1876 American Library Association better known as A.L.A. The laudable object of this Association as mentioned in its Constitution, is "to promote the Library interests of the country by exchanging, reaching conclusions, and inducting co-operation in all departments of bibliothecal science and economy; by disposing the public mind to the funding and improving of libraries; and by cultivating good-will among its own members"

Achievements

The activities of A.L.A. are directed toward the achievement of its objective of promoting library service and librarianship.

Over 110 years of its life, the A.L.A. has emerged as a professional body that speaks directly for the profession. Library Science in the world has, in fact, grown with A.L.A., and there has been no important development in the field of library science in which A.L.A. has not played an influential role. The first library school in U,S.A.—the first in any country—opened its doors at Columbia University by virtue of a formal, resolution of A.L.A., under the directorship of Melvil Dewly. A.L.A. accredits the graduate library schools of the United States and Canada and establishes standards for their curricula.

A.L.A. has vigorously concerned itself with the qualifications, salaries, working conditions and the general welfare of librarians and equally with the expansion and improvement of library service. In its infancy it created classification and cataloguing schemes and other techniques for making library materials more easily available both to general readers and to students and scholars. Over the years it encouraged public access to books on open shelves; lending books for home use; special services for children and young people; tax support for public libraries; the extension of library service to rural areas and to outlying sections of cities; the establishment of libraries in schools, hospitals and correctional (reformative) institutions; the expansion of library resources for scholarship and research; and the design of buildings suited to the requirements of library services. Later activities of A.L.A. include the support of federal legislation favourable to libraries. It has also concerned itself with raising the standards of library service by establishing standards for all types of libraries, and of professional performance through education for the librarians.

A.L.A. also conducts programmes to educate the American public opinion in the significant contributions which the library makes for elavating their cultural. social and academic values; provides leadership in planning for the extension and improvement of library services and in securing public and financial support on national, state, and local levels; keeps a constant watchful eye over freedom to read; establishes and encourages the adoption of standards to improve the quality of library service and to ensure the professionally qualified personnel; and strives to maintain equal access to materials, facilities, and services.

In addition to its activities for the Americans, the A.L.A. serves its members directly by giving them an opportunity to discuss their ideas and beliefs, to formulate objectives and purposes, and to develop policies and programmes and by providing the media for publicizing and promoting them throughout the profession. It establishes standards of service and education, protects their professional status by accrediting library education programme, provides guides for their professional performance and opportunities for continuing self-education, self-improvement, and, in general, strives to improve the status of librarianship as a profession. It creates, publishes, and encourages the publication of professional literature by other publishers. A.L.A. is receptive to new trends and new knowledge, and encourages the use of latest technology to improve library facilities and library techniques. Through the adoption of the "The Library Bill of Rights", A.L.A. has "Continuously promoted the concept of man's freedom to seek the truth where and how he will." It means that the A.L.A. preserves the right of every citizen to read whatever he wishes to arrive at independent individual judgements.

From time to time, the A.L.A. has adopted standards for public that communities could use as a measuring stick to evalute their own services and in formulating plans for improvement. The greatest success was the passage of the Library Services Act of 1956 as amended in 1964 to become the Library Services and Construction Act. The essence of the Act is that the "public library service should be universally available".

The A.L.A. continues to publish the greater portion of library literature. It has published over 22,00 titles. They include some of the indispensable tools of the profession :—A.L.A. Catalog; American Library Laws; American Library Resources; Anglo-American Cataloging Rules (A.A.C.R.); Guide to Reference Books; Books for College Libraries; Copying Methods Manual; First Freedom; Liberty aud Justice in the World of Books and Reading, etc.

The Official journal of the A.L.A. is American Libraries, published 11 times a year. Among other periodicals mention may be made of *Choice*; *College and Research Libraries*; *Library Resources and Technical Services*; *the Book list* and Subscription Books Bulletin, etc. In 1968, A.L.A. started the publication of a Journal of Information Science and Library Automation.

In brief, A.L.A. endeavours to promote federal legislation for increasing library services. It is constantly trying its best to enhance the image of libraries in the American Society. It is very prompt in its public relations, and is keenly interested in maintaing and improving standards for education. Library profession as a whole owes much to A.L.A. for its growth and development. In terms of sheer size, resources and range of activities, the biggest national association for libraries is the A.L.A., with its headquarters at Chicago (Illinois). It has now a membership of over 35,000, of which over 30,000 are individual and some 5,000 are corporate members. It has a paid staff of over 300, and it is governed by an elected council of about 150 persons. It is an "Umbrella" organization in which virtually all library interests are represented in greater or lesser degree. But for A L.A.'s contributions, the library profession would have been poorer.

2. LIBRARY ASSOCIATION (LONDON)

Foundation and Growth

It was E W B Nicholson, Librarian of London Institution, who suggested the formation of a Library Association in U.K. This suggestion bore fruit on October 5, 1877, when Library Association was founded with its head-quarters in London. Currently, this Association has a membership of nearly 20,000; it has a modern four storey building of its own and its staff is about 100 strong.

The object of the Association was specified as "To unite all persons engaged in or interested in library work, for the purpose of promoting the best possible administration of existing libraries, and the formation of new ones where desirable. It shall also aim at the encouragement of bibliographical research".

Achievements

The achievements of this Association during past 110 years, may be counted as under :—

—the creation and maintenance of *esprit de corps*;

—promotion of better administration of libraries;

—providing for the training of librarians and steadily improving its standard and now having brought it to the status of a University Degree Course;

—securing the universal adoption of Public Libraries Act and periodical revisions of the Act to make it keep pace with the changing social requirements;

—promotion of the establishment of public libraries in the countri :s of the Commonwealth;

—promotion of research in recent years;

—uniting all persons engaged or interested in library work, by holding conferences and meetings for discussion of bibliographical questions and matters affecting libraries or their regulation or management or otherwise;

—watching any legislation affecting Public Libraries, and to assist in the promotion of such further legislation as may be considered necessary for the regulation and management or extension of Public Libraries;

—collecting, collating, and publishing (in the form of Transactions, Journals, or otherwise) information of service or interest to the Fellows and Member of the Association or for the promotion of the objects of the Corporation; and

—doing all such lawful things as are incidental or conducive to the attainment of above objectives.

These objectives of the Association are quite comprehensive and it has been a character of faith for the Association to follow them in word and spirit. Keeping these objectives in view, the Association did its best to remove all restrictions and limitations of library acts and library systems. The Association has been responsible for bringing into existence 6 library schools for training of librarians. Although, the Association has closed its education office after long and distinguished service, yet it is deeply concerned in the developing pattern of education for librarianship and it maintains close links with the library schools. The Association has taken the responsibility for initiating short courses and study conferences which help to up-date members on the latest trends in librarianship.

The Association also maintains the professional register of chartered librarians. It organizes annually a national conference. Through prizes and awards, it encourages the production of better books in the profession. It was also responsible for bringing into existence National Central Library and many regional libraries. In fact, Great Britain became the first country in the world having a net-work of libraries reaching to almost cent per cent of population through the efforts of the Associaiion. It is the most influential and indispensahle professional body.

Among its world fame publications, mention may be made of :—1. Library Association Record (LAR-M). 2. Journal of Librarianship (Q). 3. Library and Information Science Abstracts (Bi-Monthly). 4. British Humanities Index. 5. British Technology Index (M). 6. Library Association Year Book. 7. Walford's Guide to Reference Material. 8. British Text of AACR-I, etc.

3. ASLIB

Foundation and Development

The association known as ASLIB was founded in 1924 under the title: Association of Special Libraries and Information Bureax. It took its present name in 1949 when the British Society for International Bibliography merged into it. Its purpose was "facilitating the coordination and systematic use of sources of knowledge and information in all public affairs and in industry and commerce and in all the arts and sciences." ASL1B, thus. truly represents a powerful alliance between industry, the academic world, and government. It is also dedicated to the development of special libraries and information services of all kinds. It has now move much closer towards the concept of a research association, with the sharpening of new techniques of information retrieval.

Purposes

The purposes of Aslib may be summarized as under:

—to contribute to the more efficient and effective use of specialized knowledge by means of research into factors affecting flow of information, by the development of improved systems of information control, and by the provision of specialist advice on the organization and operation of library services;

—to assist the development of high standards of work among practising information officers, librarians and other specialists engaged in the collection, retrieval and dissemination of specialized information, by the provision of facilities for both formal and informal education and training, by encouraging the establishment of suitable training facilities in appropriate teaching institutions, and by the provision of advice to employers on the qualifications and training most appropriate to their requirements; and

—to represent the views of its members on matters related to their professional work.

Activities

Aslib maintains a translation index to avoid duplication of efforts; panels of translators and indexers are also kept. Another activity is the documentary reproduction services, whereby Aslib provides photo-copies or microfilms of original documents in libraries. Its information department acts as a referral centre for specialized inquiries, and provides bibliographic checking, locating and searching services. There are also three study groups dealing with technical translations, mechanization, and coordinate indexing. Aslib also has 11 groups on such subjects as aeronautics, food and agriculture, electronics, textiles and the like

Achievements

It is, of couase, true that Aslib does not act as an examining or qualifying body, but its Education Department besides offering advice to teaching institutions, students and employers, organizes courses on information work, patents, translations and translitration related to Russian and other Eastern European countries.

The establishment of a research department designed to make a spearhead of advance in research work is a great landmark. Founded in 1959 this department provides consultancy services and undertakes private research under contracts. It also pursues an internationally generated programme of research consisting principally of mechanization, operational studies and survey work. Among its principal areas of activity so far are a design study for a computer aided system for production of *Physics Abstracts* and a study of reaction to Current Papers in Physics; case study of the information gathering habits of scientists and engineers; studies of the coverage of the literature of science and technology and of the Social Sciences by the major abstracting services. It also includes the coverage and efficiency of abstracting services in the field of documentation, development of the techniques of thesaurus constrction, the ranking of British journals as carriers of original scientific work, test of the efficiency of certain citation indexes, and an examination of possible ways of overcoming language barriers. It draws on the resources of the international organizations worknig in its field for disseminating knowledge. Aslib had also worked closely with Library Association and other bodies in the formation of British National Bibliography in 1950, in the work which led to the publiction of the British Union Catalogue of Periodicals in the 1950 s.

The British Library Research and Development Department decided to support Aslib's research team in 1985.

Information for Decision-Making was the theme of 58th Aslib Annual Conference and Exhibition held in April, 1986 at UMIST, Manchester. The meeting assessed current and anticipated trends in intelligence net-working. It reviwed the way information is used in decision-making and the important role played by information officers and managers, in both public and private sectors.

Aslib has to its credit some well-known publications: ASLIB Directory, Journal of Documentation and ASLIB Proceedings. It also publishes monthly Aslib Book List of recommended scientific and technical books in English, and an annual Index to Theses accepted for higher degrees in the Universities of Great Britain and Ireland. The Handbook of Special Librarianship and Information work, 5th ed. is a recognized standard book for the practical aspects of various areas of librarianship. Aslib is also producing a series of bibliographies designed to act as guides to areas of topical interest; not only for library and information personnel, but also for a wide range of industries, business and professions.

4. INDIAN LIBRARY ASSOCIATION

Foundation and Development

The Indian Library Association was founded on 13 Sept., 1933 at Calcutta at the First All India Library Conference attended by a galaxy of intellectuals, educationists, librarians and eminent citizens of Calcutta. The office of the ILA was shifted from Calcutta to Delhi in August 1964 and at present is housed in its own flat.

The idea of ILA was put across by M.O. Thomas of Annamalai University. In his article, he extolled the achievements of Library Association (U.K.) elaborately and preferred a sort of frame-work for the projected ILA which would act as the main spring of the Indian Library Movement, which in turn would give the same advantage to the people of India as were enjoyed by the people of the West. He said "but neither our longing nor our enthusiasm will carry us far if we do not unite ourselves into a strong association and fight our way through by regular propaganda work. For an Indian Library Movement a strong vanguard of an All India Library Association is absolutely necessary." In this article of Thomas, the shadow of the epoch-making event is crystal clear and is felt like the aroma of the impending first rain of summer.[1]

ILA was, thus, formed to stimulate the library movement in India, and to plead for and encourage the upkeep of libraries in accordance with scientific methods.

Objectives

The objectives of ILA may said to be :—

—The promotion of library movement in India;

—promotion of training, education and research in library and information science;

—bibliographical study and research;

—spread of library legislation for the establishment of public library services in State and Union Territories;

—improvement in the status and scales of pay of the library staff;

—publication of library science literature;

—establishment of library and information net-works in the country in different disciplines such as science and technology, social sciences and the humanities;

—to take all possible steps for the promotion of efficient and effective library and information service in India; and

—cooperation with international organizations with similar objectives

ILA made tremendous progress under the dynamic presidentship of S.R. Ranganathan from 1944-1953. During this formative period, he made the Association superbly scientific and brought it in close association with the UNESCO, FID, and IFLA.

Achievnments

Under the stewardship of Ranganathan, ILA took up the compilation of the Union Catalogue of Periodicals in the libraries of South Asia and brought out a pilot fascicule in 1950 and the Science volume in 1952. Two more projects (1) Rendering of Asian names; and (2) Directory of Asian periodicals were

1. M.O, Thomas, *Modern Libraries,* V. 3, no. 2 (Jan. 1933) cf. *50 years of ILA;* 1933—1983 (Delhi, ILA, 1983.)

entrusted by Unesco to ILA. A Library Research Circle was also formed in Delhi in 1948.

ILA started a library periodical under the title *Library* Bulletin in 1942 which continued upto 1946. In 1949, ILA conducted a learned quarterly *Abgila* (Annual, Bulletin and Granthalaya of ILA). *Abgila* appeared regularly in 3 parts and reached the level of a research journal in library science. In 1953, it ceased publication and the journal of ILA was started from 1955 at irregular intervals. The year 1964 saw the birth of ILA Bulletin. ILA Newsletter (Q) was introduced in 1984.

Critical Appreciation

ILA has seen many ups and downs in its existence of more than fifty years. It has not shown spectacular work particularly after the relinquishing of its charge by Ranganathan. To youngesters in India, the ILA appears to be a game of self-centred personalities belonging to different factions. Lot of leg pulling and snobbery with exchange of hot arguments make the show highly uncomfortable. The prolonged and repetitive appearances of the same faces on dias, till recently, made one feel as if they were the permanent superstars. Still, the youngesters feel that there is no room for young and dedicated workers who realy want to work for the profession. Its publication, too, are not regular. The leaders of the profession do not seem to be interested in their approach to technical subjects much less in subjects pertaing to management of human resources. Probably because of its poor performances, its membership has not gone beyond 1600 (Dec. 86).

Suggestions

State Associations be made the branches of I.L.A. In this way, a member who gets himself enrolled in a Branch Association will automatically become a member of the I.L.A. In this way, membership will increase manifold. It is difficult for the Indian librarians with their meagre economic resourses to pay multiple subscriptions at various levels—local, district, regional, state and national. One-third of the subscription obtained by the Branch Association may be sent to the Central Body. Under this federal structure, all the affiliated associations and libraries will have the advantage of cooperative activities in the fields of common interests while preserving the strength and vigor of the branch associations devoted to specific interests.

Secondly, every student at every library school should be enrolled as a member of ILA or state association. He should take a pledge to serve the association with sincerity and dedication. It should be urged upon him that association is a symbol of experience, competency, and trustworthiness in the profession. These qualities must be amplified by the following statements of ethical standards to which every library professional must adher to.

—A MEMBER performs his duties and personal affairs with integrity and high moral purpose.

—A MEMBER will serve his clientele with professional fidelity, and act only for the clientele's best interests and benefits; and it will be his sincere intetion and whole hearted purpose that the client derive substantial benefits as a result of his services.

—A MEMBER will respect all information relating to the research affairs of his clientele as confidential.

—A MEMBER can be depended upon to be truthful and forthright with the clientele in his observations and recommendations.

—A MEMBER'S promotional announcements will be accurate, and made in a professionally dignified and proper manner.

—A MEMBER strives at all times to uphold the honour and to maintain the dignity of the profession. The member endeavours to hold the esteem of others in his profession who subscribe to these standards; and he will condemn unethical or illegal conduct by other professionals which may come to his attention, and expose it for proper investigation and action.

Ethical codes are voluntary on the part of group members. Enforcement is by various sanctions available to the group, such as fines or even the expulsion of deviant members. Ethical codes persist because of common agreement with the group that such behaviour is the "right" behaviour for the individuals in the group. To keep the confidence and respect of his fellow association members, a library professional must act within the limits of the code. If he does not, he risks losing respect, cooperation, or rights of affiliation. By its very nature, an ethical code exercises a strong emotional and mental hold upon individuals who participate in ethic-forming group.

The existence of ethical codes for librarians serves a number of important functions. They usually specify behaviour that is required for the protection and continuity of the group as a whole.

They reflect a group's unity and cohesiveness, and are evidence of its solidarity. Such codes also provide a measure of protection for the library clientele against fraudulent, misleading, or unfair treatment. The codes reflect the movement of trade associations into sphere of greater professionalization, since they emphasize service and performance within standards and deemphasize monetary rewards for their own sake. It is the professional associations, rather than the trade or industry assciations, that have been the most concerned about codes of ethical conduct and they have gone farthest in the adoption of systematized codes.

During 1975-76, an attempt was made at 'decentralization'. The work of ILA was divided into five geographical zones and a vice-president of ILA was put in-charge of each zone. Thirteen sectional committees with their chairmen and conveners were created to handle the work of various types of libraries.

The recommendations of the 24th ILA Conference at Banglore (1978) were of a technical nature arrived at establishing and promoting resource sharing among libraries.

The twenty-eight conference (1982 at Lucknow)held discussions on *Public Libraries in a Developing Society*; *and Planning for a National Information* System for India. It also recommended that the state governments be requested to (i) enact public library legislation, where there is none, (ii) eastablish separate Departments of Libraries, etc.

The Thirtieth Conference (Jaipur, 1985) had discussions on "Building Library Collections and National Policy and Information Service"

The Thirty-first Conference (Baroda, Nov. 1985) discussed the following two themes :

—Public Library Development; and

—Staffing Patterns in Libraries and Information Centres;

The themes selected for discussion at the various All India Library Conferences of ILA described above clearly shows that ILA is seriously considering the current problems being faced by librarians.

Looking ahead, we may remind ourselves of the article and brilliant Presidential Address (1933) of Dr. M.O. Thomas wherein he lauded the achievements of the Library Association (London) and American Library Association. He had in fact wished to raise an Association in India that would do everything that those associations have done and achieved in their respective countries. We should now try our level best to fulfil the cherished dreams of our prodecessors, particularly because of the changing and and more favourable environments in India as a whole. Since the number of professional librarians in India has grown manifold, salary structures and status of library personnel have vastly improved, and authorities at different levels are more appreciative of the usefulness of librar.es and librarians, we should take all possible steps so as to provide further boost to library movement in the country,

Financial resources are the life-blood of any organization. Different sources of revenue which should be tapped may include a vigorous publication programme, membership drive, financial support from the Union Government and showering of grants and gifts in various forms.

Greater coordination and cooperation among the various national level associations (viz., ILA, IASLIC, INDAAL, GILA, etc.) should be strengthened.

We should honestly and sincerely resolve to accomplish what remains unaccomplished; undertake new programmes to give a fillip to library umbrella in the country that would provide better library and information services; and thereby improve the status and image of the library profession in India.[2]

5. IASLIC

Foundation and Development

The Indian Association of Special Libraries and Information Centres was established as the Indian prototype for Aslib (U K.) and Special Library Association—SLA (U.S,A.) on September 3, 1955 on initiative and inspiration of librarians, documentalists, informaiion scientists, scientists and technologists. It provides fertile soil for their energy, activity and their ideas to grow. Keeping in view the importance of inter-communication of facts and ideas among scientists, technologists and research workers,

2. Ibid.

and of the collection of specialized information among them, Iaslic formulated the following *objectives* :

Objectives

—To encourage and promote the systematic acquisition, organization, and dissemination of knowledge.

—To improve the quality of library and information services and documentation work.

—To co-ordinate the activities of and coperation and assistance among special libraries, scientific, technological and research institutions, and learned societies, commercial organizations, industrial research establishments, as well as other information and documentation centres to the fullest extent.

—To serve as a field of active contact for libraries, information bureaus, documentation centres, specialists, and others having common interests.

—To improve the technical efficiency of the workers in special libraries, information and documentation centres, and to look after their professional welfare.

—To act as a centre of information in scientific, technical and other fields;

—To take such action as may be incidental or conducive to the attainment of the objects of the association, or any of them.

—To act as a nucleus of research in special librarianship and documentation techniques; and to provide forum for libraries in India.

In persuance of its objectives, Iaslic

—provides information on demand;

—provides documentary reproduction service and technical translation service. Such a service includes the provision of micro-films and photo-copies as well as English translation of documents from all European and non-European languages to individual research institution, academic bodies, commercial ane industrial organizations, etc.

—advises on request on problems connected with libraries and information services;

—promotes inter-library cooperation and inter-library loan. An ILL code has already been drafted to this effect;

—holds conferences/seminars, symposia regularly;

—provides incentives to writer of the best articles in Iaslic bulletin;

—maintains a library containing literature on library science.

To render its services effectively, the activities of this association have been devided into six divisions. (1) Documention; (2) education; (3) documentary reproduction and translation; (4) publication and publicity; (5) library and information services; and; (6) inter-library cooperation and coordination.

Assessment

Iaslic—a non-profit organization is doing her best to up-date the scientists and technologists, academicians and scholars. Keeping in vicw her limited resources, Iaslic is probably the most vibrant library association in India. It maintains close liaison with Insdoc, Aslib and SLA. It is also affiliated to F.I.D. and IFLA. It has been fortunate in having the cooperation and guidance of a distinguished scientist or an eminent technologist or an administrator as its President. Prominent librarians are also honored by the Association by being elected honorary members. Of course, it has functioned effectively and efficiently during past three decades of its existence, still the government has not realized her obligation to finance this Association. Assessed from various angles, Iaslic has made significant achievements to improve the efficiency of scientists and technologists and also by acting as a nucleus of research in special librarianship and information services and techniques.

Publications

The publications of Iaslic have been quite impressive, if one bears in mind that it has borne the financial burden of its various activities on its shoulders. Some of the most important publications are : Iaslic Bulletin; Indian Library Science Abstracts; Directory of Special and Research Libraries in India; Development of Societies and Medical Periodicals in India, 1780—1920; Glossary of Cataloguing Terms in Indian Regional Languages; IASLIC special publications containing conference proceedings; Newsletter (M), etc.

23

LIBRARY ACTIVITIES OF UNESCO, FID, IFLA, INSDOC AND SSDOC

Unesco

The Constitution of Unesco (United Nations, Educational, Scientific and Cultural Organization) was drawn up at the London Conference in November 1945. Unesco, however, came into existence on November 4, 1946, when 20 States ratified its Constitution. In 1984, it had 160 members.

Unesco is a specialized agency of the United Nations, but both constitutionally and financially, it is independent of the U.N., though its work is coordinated with the U.N. and other specialized agencies.

Aims : It was designed to promote and encourage international cooperation in Education, Science, Cultural activities among various nations.

Main Objectives

The major objectives of Unesco may be noted :

—To provide a forum for the evaluation of common problems.

—To assist in exchange of information regarding developments in various fields of knowledge between 160 member countries.

—To be a world centre of information for study and travel.

—To collect and disseminate scientific knowledge.

—To promote favorable conditions for intellectual cooperation among artists, musician, curators, philosophers, and men of letters, and to reduce regional racial imbalances.

—To help in translating rare manuscripts in agreed common language; and

—To suggest means for the preservation of national monuments and rare manuscripts.

An analysis of Unesco's efforts to assist its Member States in the development of their libraries indicate three main trends which can be summed up as—Documentation. Libraries and Archives. It is, of course, true that documentation, libraries and archives are not mentioned specifically in Unesco's constitution. Nevertheless, they are implied in it. The Constitution states quite explicitly that—

> The organization will...maintain, increase and diffuse knowledge by encouraging cooperation among the nations in all branches of intellectual activity including the international exchange of publications, objects of artistic and scientific interest and other materials of information; by initiating methods of international cooperation calculated to give the people of all countries access to the printed and published materials produced by any of them."

In this respect UNESCO is quite unique as no other Specialised Agency has such aims and objectives. It is from the very beginning that UNESCO realised the importance of libraries and documentation in the promotion of mutual understanding and in the furthering of socio-economic development.

Documentation and Information Services

UNESCO's major objectives in the field of documentation are closely integrated wtth the organisation of International Conferences. The first two conferences held in 1949 and 1950, though disappointing in certain aspects, are still great landmarks in its history. A brief explanation of the activities of each is a must.

International Conference on Science Abstracting. Paris, June 1949.

This first Conference on science abstracting was attended by 167 participants belonging to 29 countries and various international organisations. The Final Report summarised generally accepted views on the presentation and language of abstracts, their relation to classification, indexing and copyright and the new ideas on mechanical devices for the storage and selection of documents. Some of the recommendations made by the Conference are being put into practice. And yet the conference did not make headway on the important questions of un-necessary duplication, standardisation, sharing the load and the reconciliation of differing national practices.

International Conference on the Improvement of Bibliographical Services, Paris, Nov. 1950.

The fourteen principles accepted by the conference were mainly aimed at the nature and scope of national bibliography and its international coordination. It was agreed upon that every individual country has the responsibility of compiling and regular issue of national bibiography. But subject bibliography is more properly the concern of international organisation. Unesco helps the individual country to set up its own National Bibliographical Centre. To coordinate the work of National Groups and international bodies an International Advisory on Bibliography, Documentation and Terminology was set up.

In 1966, Unesco was re-organised establishing the International Advisory Committee on Documentation, Libraries, and Archives which replaced the former International Advisory Committee on Bibliography, Documentation and Terminology. After an analytical analysis of the current trends in the fields of documentation, libraries and archives, the committee recommended that priority be given to the following programmes :

(1) Improvement in the planning of national, regional and international services. In some way the most systematic and continuous of Unesco's efforts to help member states is the planing and creation of documentation centres within the technical Assistance Programme. Insdoc was estabiished in 1952 with the techinical assistance provided by Unesco.

(2) Training of personnel, using traditional and new methods.

(3) Establishment of common minimum standards for the use of traditional and new methods and for vocational programmes; and

(4) Evaluation and use of new documentary techniques and in particular of data processing.

This important programme is being implemented by the Department of Documentation, Libraries, and Archives. The efforts of the department are directed at achieving a greater degree of standardization in bibliographies and documentation matters, promoting the application of mechanization and automation in library and documentation work. This work is mostly done through contract with professional non-government organisations iike FID, ICSU, ISO, IFIP, IFLA, etc.

In 1967, Libraries Division was improved and the result was the department known as Documentation, Bibliotheques et Archives. This department started operating in 1971 a computerised documentation service with the fundamental purposes of processing, storing and making avilable information on Unesco publications and documents; and also acting as a demonstration project for computer aided methods of information handling.

The greatest contributions of Unesco are the launching of World Science Information System (UNISIST) and the National Information System (NATIS) programmes.

UNISIST is Unesco—ICSU joint venture in the fields of science and technology with the laudable purpose of fostering the improvement of information storage and retrieval systems at international level. Voluntary cooperation is the bedrock of the Unisist system. In the wordings used in the Study Report : "Unisist is a contemporary expression of a long-standing tradition of free interchange of information among the world's scientists".

The functions of the UNISIST as enumerated by General Conference of Unesco held in 1972 are :

—to advance and coordinate the world trends towards information-sharing by creating opportunities for further cooperative agreements among governments, international organizations and operating information services;

—to provide guidance and catalytic action for the necessary developments in the field of scientific and technical information;

—to facilitate the access of published information to scientists and technologists; and

—to help the developing countries in meeting their needs for scientific and technical information.

Unisist further aims at developing national or regional information policies and infrastructures; improving and strengthening the institutional and normative components of information transfer; and development of the specialized human resources essential to the planning and operation of future information net-works.

Among Unisist's objectives mention should be made in particular of the advancement and coordination of world trends towards information sharing, and the taking of necessary measures for the establishment of flexible world net-work of information systems and services on voluntary cooperation.

The UNISIST Advisory Gommittee meeting in May, 1975 and the UNISIST Steering Committee in October 1975 recommended measures to extend the purview of UNISIST programmes in respect of information systems development, systems interconnection, normative action, education, training, future developments, etc.

UNISIST became an integral part of the General Information Programme (PGI) which was formally established by decision of the General Conference of Unesco at its 19th session 1976. At its 20th session, the General Conference decided to create the five themes of the PGI as under :

—theme···5/10.1/01 : Information Policies and Planning at the National, Regional and International Levels;

—theme···1/02 : Promotion of Methods, Norms and Standards for Information Handling;

—theme···1/03 : Contribution to the Development of Specialized Information Systems;

—theme...1/004 : Development of Specialized Information System

—theme ··1/05 : Training and Education of Information Specialists and Users.

The very existence of PGI has greatly helped many Member States :

—to begin the process of formulating a national information policy and plan;

—to establish national structures and institutions for coordinating library and information development;

—to invest funds for such development; and

—to organize the education and training of local manpower and to enter into regional colaborative efforts.

PGI provides a platform for the exchange of views between Unesco's Member States, the UN agencies with sectorial information systems and services and the various professional non-governmental organizations. The basis of PGI was made clear by the Director-General of Unesco at the opening of the UNISIST II

(Intergovernmental Conference on Scientific and Technological Information Development, 1979), when he said that "UNISIST is now directed towards the social and economic value of scientific and technological information for development". One of its objective is to contribute to the United Nations Conference on Science and Technology for Development (UNCTD, 1979). The UNISIST II role is already clear through its recommendations which emphasize :

—the application of information in the service of development;

—the importance of developing user-oriented information systems; and

—the need for national information policies and planning as well as the importance of education and training.

The fifth session of the Intergovernmental Council for the General Information Programme (PGI) was held at Unesco, Paris, in Nov. 1984. The Director-General pointed out that the PGI is now laying more emphasis on national infrastructures and regional networks and the application of new information technologies in the developing countries. The Council was unanimous in recommending that in the selection of programme actions, particular attention be given to the standardization activities; the promotion of national information systems and application of new information technologies in developing countries; inclusion of policy and management elements in the formulation and implementation of integrated projects and regional networks; access to publications and other sources of information; conservation of documents; development of archives and coordination with other information activites with Unesco.

Network for the Exchange of Information in Science and Technology in Asia and the Pacific (ASTINFO) : An ASTINFO Regional Secretariat has been established in the Unesco Regional Office for Science and Technology for South-East Asia in Jakarata, Indonesia, At the Second Consultative Meeting on ASTINFO held in Jakarta from 5 to 7 Nov., 1984, it was recommended that "High priority be given to ASTINFO projects relating to the development of telecommunications and public data networks within and among ASTINFO countries and to those relating to enhancement of national capability for development and use of data bases".

Hopefully, one can say that the UNISIT'S aim of the establishment of electronically inter-connected world-wide bibliographic exchange programme in a not-too-distant future is not merely a dream.

The concept of NATIS (National Information System) was advocated by UNESCO following the Inter-governmental Conference on the Planning for National Documentation, Libraries and Archives Infrastructure held in September,1974. The concept implies that the government—national, state, iocal—should maximize the availability of relavant information through documentation, libraries and archives services, just as in principle it takes responsibility for the basic education, at primary and secondary levels of its citizens. The task of NATIS is to ensure that all engaged in political, economic, scientific, educational, social or cultural activities receive the necessary information to render fullest contribution for the benefit of the whole community. NATIS includes all agencies, resources, process and activities meant to provide information for all sectors of the community and for all the categories of users. It, therefore, requires organizational arrangements for coordination and supervision of policy and programme. The concept of NATIS was reaffirmed in 1979 by UNISIST II. The aim of a national information policy was stated to be "to identify the information requirements of the country and to ensure that they are satisfied as fully, promptly, cheaply and conveniently as scarce resources allow".

As regards the storage and retrieval of information by means of computers, Unesco has stimulated the study of their rational application to the management of information. One may mention here the studies carried out within the frame-work of the UNISIST project especially those concerning the compilation of Thesauri,

Unesco Regional work-shop on Thesaurus Construction and use was organized by Insdoc (New Delhi) in November, 1985. A manual on Thesaurus construction and use specially prepared (by F.W. Lancaster) for this workshop was used.

Unesco workshop on Information Processing Tools was held in Graz, Austria, in December 1984. The objectives of the workshop were to instruct the participants in the use of IV+V Systems and to provide them with general knowledge on the capabilities of computerised information systems which would be useful in selecting hardware and software for information work as well as in the planning and development of computer applications in this area. The modules on machine aspects on bibliographic records, on hardware and software have already been finalized.

The Third Meeting of the Working Group on Methods, Norms and Standards which took place in Coimbra, Portugal In April 1985 discussed the latest developments with regard to the IV+V System software package; which will be one of the software package available to Unesco for free use in developing countries. Unesco aims at providing the first operational prototype version of the IV+V system software package to a few institutions with sufficient experience in the running of automated information systems.

Teaching packages for use of information handling standards :

In order to increase the use of international standards and standard-like materials, Unesco has concentrated its efforts on the conduct of seminars at the national regional and international levels and on the couduct of seminars at the national, regional and international levels and on the dissemination of information on existing normative documents.

In collaboration with FID, Unesco established International Information System on Research in Documentation (ISORID) to collect, organise, analyse and disseminate information on research activities and efforts in the field of documentation, libraries and archives. ISORID provides information on research projects, research reports and copies of research reports. By means of ISORID's computerized records, Unesco has been able to collect information on institutions, and specialists that have contributed through their research work to the advancement of information, library and archives science. Since the publication of such information would encourage and facilitate cooperation between institutions or specialists active in this field, Undsco has prepared the following two reference works :

—ISORID/International Directory of Institutions Active in the Field of Research in Information, Libraries and Archives.

—ISORID/International Directory of Institutions Active in the Field of Research in Information, Libraries and Archives.

Users of information are an integral part of and the final link in the information transfer chain; they are the raison d' etre of every investment made for bettering the storage, processing and retrieval of information. But it is generally accepted that the majority of existing scientific and technical information services are used effectively by only a small proportion of potential users. Recognising this fact as a basic problem intrinsically related to the storage, processing, disseminating and utilization of information, Unesco has paid special attention to the issue of educating and training information users. These efforts were initiated under the UNISIST programme and are now being continued in the framework of the Unesco General Information Programme (PGI).

Unesco's activism is also reflected in operating several pilot projects and programmes of assistance; the notable ones are (1) the Pilot Project in Documentation and Library Services in Ceylon; (2) Pilot Projects in the Mechanisation of Documentation Services in Latin America; (3) Pilot Project in Archives Development for Africa, Ivosy Coast; (4) Pilot Project for School Library services and training for Central America, Honduras; (5) Promotion of development and training services through experts, regional courses, seminars, and symposia especially for building permanent institutions.

UNESCO and Public Libraries

Unesco, through its assistance programmes, helps member states to establish and improve their library services. Particular attention is paid to the development of public library service to support adult education and literary programmes. Unesco Public Library Manifesto gave a new image and a wider scope to this type of library service. Unesco's faith in public libraries as institutions where people can obtain objective knowledge free from pressure of any kind originates in the organisation's constitution which emphasises that since wars begin in the minds of men, it is in the minds of men that the defences of peace must be constructed. The founding of the pilot public libraries at New Delhi, Enugu (Nigeria), and Medellin (Columbia) demonstrated that faith and was a means whereby Unesco influenced the development of public libraries in many of its Member States. The public libraries projects are rendering a service, free, universal, dynamic and with a broad content going far beyond recreation and 'belles letters'. For the developing areas of the world these pilot projects were just as necessary and urgent as primary and fundamental education.

Unesco and School/Technical Libraries

While supporting public libraries Unesco continued to pay attention to school and technical libraries as essential pre-requisites to the implementation of educational programmes. Unesco emphasises educational documentation services as an ideal means of inculcating the reading habit of bringing reading ability to the point where there was no risk of a relapse into illiteracy. Libraries and educational documentation services of this type have been tried in Nigeria and Honduras with profitable results. The delibrations of the Panama seminar on educational documentation and information (1971) highlighted that new conceptions of learning have substanttally altered teaching techniques and the respective roles of teachers and their pupils in the teaching and learning process. If a pupil is to learn, how to learn, to search for and discover the truth, he must have an unfettered approach to the vast mine of recorded knowledge through efficient library service and an educational documentation service. The principles laid down at the Panama seminars in which teachers, librarians and specialists participated have been implemented in Paraguay through a Unesco/UNDP programme. This contact between librarians and teachers could change the whole concept of libraries and educational documentation services, integrating them completely in the educational process. Only in this way can these services be developed and improved and make a real contribution to making education more efficient and effective.

Unesco and University Libraries

As regards the university and special libraries, Unesco has carried out a continuous series of activities—involving seminars, technical assistance mission, grants, publications, etc. aimed at improving the services of this type of library in the various Member States. The result has been a clearer definition of the libraries' aims and functions, their place in university life; the techniques to be employed in administering the various services and determining the budgets they require. The example is the Regional Seminar on the Development of University Libraries in Latin America, held at Mendoza (Argentina), in 1962, whose recommendations particularly with regard to cost indicators and the identification of indices of participation in university budgets were instrumental in improving this type of library in Latin America.

Unesco and National Libraries.

Unesco has played a vital role in the elevation of National Libraries through seminars/symposiums. One may recall Unesco's symposiums on National Libraries in Europe (Vienna, Austria, September, 1958); Regional Seminar on the Development of National Libraries in Asia and Public Area (Manila, 1964).

Unesco's recommendations to the Member States are :

—that they should establish, as soon as possible, a national library in each state;

—that they should encourage the formation of a library association;

—that they should ratify the provision of the Unesco's Convetion, 1958, relating to the international exchange of official publications and goverment documents ;

—that they should ratify the provisions of the International Copyright Convention; and

—that a National Library Legislation is a *sine qua non* for the development of a coordinated net-work of the public library system.

Conclusion :

On the whole one sees that Unesco has striven hard to help its Member States to improve their documentation, library and archives services at national, regional and international level. Unesco has constantly been in for ideas and principles which might enable librarians to identify their goals more accurately and participate in socio economic development of their countries. The principles set forth in the NATIS and UNISIST for the national, regional and international transformation of information are laudable steps and need immediate application. In the next few years many countries will doubtlessly endeavour to organize and operate national systems of documentation, library and archieves services.

The great challange that lies ahead of Unesco is to stimulate, initiate and integrate fundamental and applied research and distil from the international experience what is universally applicable.

In so doing, it has to introduce new substance into the contents of the courses in library schools. Unesco should also play an increasing role in providing books of use in life-long education especially for persons of low educational level. Unesco/UNDP experiment could change the whole concept of libraries and educational documentation services, integrating them completely in the educational process. Unesco public library manifesto has given a new image and wider scope to this type of organization. Finally, owning to the increasing requirements of scientific and techological research, Unesco has introduced new programmes in the Science sector, for the purpose of stimulating and developing scientific and technological documentation centres. In majority of cases these centres have helped to solve the acute problems raised by the 'information explosion' and the increase in scientific and technological research. NATIS and UNISIST together constitute Unesco's greatest contribution helping to place documentation, library and archives services upon national, regional and international foundations.

UNISIST has actively participated in the establishment of a number of international information systems, viz., DEVIS, POPINS GEMS, MEDI, ASFIS, ARKISYST and WISI.

Among the publications of Unesco, note may be taken of—International Standardization of Library and Documentation; Techniques and Minimum Standards for the Training of Library and Documentation Personnel (both prepared jointly by FID and IFLA); Guide for an Introductory Course on Documentation; Guide for the Training of Documentation users; Abstracting Services in Science, Technology, Medicine, and Agriculture, Social Sciences and Humaities; Manual on the Application of Mechanization and Data Processing to Documentation and Library Work (all four projects undertaken by FID); Handbook on Library Statistics and Manual on Library Legislation (both prepared by IFLA). Mention may also be made of Index Translationum; World Guide to Library Schools and Training Courses in Documentation; Standards for Library Service : an International Survey (F.N. Withers) Unesco Bulletin for Libraries. (now ceased), etc.

Coming events cast their shadows before. The withdrawl of financial support which is being considered by some national governments particularly U.S.A,, may seriously bleak the future working of Unesco, FID and ICA.

F.I.D.

FID is the major international non-governmental organization activily engaged in the field of scientific and technical information and documentation. It was founded in Brussels in 1895 under the name 'Institute Internationale de Bibliographie by two Belgians, Paul Otlet and Henri LaFontaine. Presently, its central office is located in Hague (Netherlands) which is administered by its Secretary General and his staff. Its constituents are majorly 'national member' national documentation centre, or similar organization for documentation on one nation one membership basis. INSDOC represents India.

Paul Otlet and Henri La Fontaine had initiated this organization with the main object of creating a 'Repertoire bibliographique universel' for all types of documents on cards which led to the conception of Universal Decimal Classification. But today, FID performs varied tasks. F.A. Sviridov, the Secretary-General of F.I.D. enlisted the following main functions :—

—Coordination on an international level of the documention activities.

—Elaboration of the basic problems of scientific information.

—Studies in the field of theoretical and operational aspects of machine tecniques and systems.

—Survey and evaluation of linguistics and related studies with real potential application to information processing.

—Classification research and standardization of classification terms

—Coordination of the world-wide revision and expansion programme of the Universal Decimal Classification.

—Studies and evaluation of communication forms used tn providing information to industry.

—Promotion of training of documentalists.

—Assistance in creating national information and documentation services in developing countries, and to

—Facilitate the exchange of information in Member States.

FID carries out its activities through its study and special ommittees; a brief summary is as under :

FID/RI : The study Committee on the theoretical basis of formation. Its major field is the prepation of an International esaurus of scientific information terms.

FID/CR : Classification Research—standardization of classification terms.

FID/CCC : Central Classification Committee is responsible for the operation, supervision, revision and further development of the UDC.

EID/LD : Linguistics in Documentation. Its treats linguistics in the creation, improvement, and generalization of indexing and classification tools.

FID/TM : Theory of Machine Techniques and Systems, Cybernatics and Information networks.

FID/OM : Operational Machine Technique and Systems. It is particularly concerned with standardization of information storage formats for mechanical retrieval on the baseis of UDC; international exchange of information on the practical use of data processing systems.

FID/II : Information for industry.

FID/TD : Training for Documentalists.

FID/ET : Education and Training.

FID/DC : Developing Countries.

FID/IM—Informetics Activities : This committee started functioning from India at INSDOC from January 1985.

In addition, there are now FID/PD : Patent Information and Documentation; and FID/CAO : Commission for Asia and Oceania (1968).

The committees have been responsible for organizing a number of significant conferences and useful publications. On the whole the most successful committee in recent years have been FID/RI, which have provided an active forum for fundamental questions of general classification theory and the nature and scope of information—the only true international contributions in these fields,

FID has close relations with Unesco, ICSU and its Abstracting Board, IFLA, ISO, IFIP, CIB and many other international organizations active in the field of scientifi: and technical informatoin and documentation. Of special interest in this connection is the need for increasing cooperation between the FID and IFLA, especially in such areas as training, assistance to developing countries, mechanization, terminology, classification and reprography. As W.K. Lawry puts it : it is imperative that IFLA and FID must work in concert to avoid dilusion of our total resources in working towards common goals."

In sum : FID has acted as catalyst for cooperation of national and international organizations engaged in documentation activities. The needs of the time require an extention and refinement of these cooperative activities. As noted above, the activities of F.I.D. are mainly directed towards documentation, and information and the allied topics like linguistic problems, reprography, copyright, information services, training in documentation, and development of UDC.

FID published Guide to the World's Training Facilities in Documentation and Information Work. Other publications are : Selected Readings on Information for Industry; National Referral Services for Industry; Worldwide Directory; Computers and the UDC, a decade of progress, 1963-77; FID Publications; and eighty years bibliography, 1895-1973.

International Federation of Library Associations and Institutions (IFLA)

Foundation

Library Associations have been set up not only at national level but also at international level. The major international organization in the field of library science is the International Federation of Library Associations and Institutions famous as IFLA. IFLA, in fact, started as an International Committee, but it was only in 1953 that it was constituted as the IFLA General Council.

At an International Conference of Librarians and Book Lovers (Congres International des Bibliothecaires et des Amis du Livre), held in Prague in July 1926, a proposal for the creation of an executive committee consisted of a delegate from each library association, was put forward by Gabriel. The functions of the committee were suggested to be to (i) convene conferences at regular intervals; (ii) defend library interests in the international field; (iii) prepare international bibliographies; (iv) investigate relations between archivists and librarians; (v) examine various problems of an international nature of interest to all members, submitted to the committee for consideration; and (vi) determine a scale of membership fees for member associations.

These terms of reference formed the blueprints for IFLA's future international activity.

In 1926, A.L.A., too, at its Golden Jubilee celebrations (Philadelphia) proposed the establishment of an International Library Committee. Main activities envisaged were : (i) the provision of information about employment; the exchange of librarians; (ii) travel abroad : comparative study of library practices (viz., library management, library training curricula, library statistics. etc); (iii) proposed indexes and special bibliographies; (iv) the study of improved documentation methods; (v) the publicat on, through international cooperation, of manuals and other bibliographical works; and (vi) the organization of international exchanges, etc.

In 1927, the Section for International Library Cooperation of the Library Association (London) examined Henriot's proposals made in in 1926. Its delibrations led to the establishment of the International Library and Bibliographical Committee in 1928. This Committee further set up six sub-committies for : 1. Classification Schemes; 2. Cataloguing Rules; 3. Bibliogaraphies and an International Code of Bibliographical Abbreviations; 4. International Fellowships and Exchanges of Librarians; 5. Education for Librarianship; and 6. for By-laws. At an other meeting in Florence, in 1929, by which 22 associations had joined the committee, its name was changed to that of International Federations of Library Associations, which has been modified by the addition of the words "and institutions" in 1976. This was done to fulfil three purposes. 1. To make it broad-based to allow institutions to become its members. 2. To focus attention on the valuable contributions to international library work made by individual libraries, library schools, etc. 3. To eliminate the effect and influence of large number of associations from developing countries who could have taken the hold of world organization. Whatever the objectives, there were apprehensions in the minds of those who were in control of the organization.

Structure

IFLA is governed by a Executive Board, and it has many sections and committees to conduct more detailed work of the Federation. There are sections for National and University Libraries, Public Libraries, and Special Libraries, while there are sub-sections for University Libraries; Library Work for Children; Libraries in Hospitals; Social Science Libraries; Observatory Libraries; Parliamentary Libraries; Administrative Libraries; School Libraries, and INTAMEL (International Association of Metropolitan City Libraries). There is very important section—Section of the Libraries of Blind. These organs of IFLA coordinate the work at international level.

Among the various IFLA Committees are those on Bibliography; Cataloguing; Exchange of Publications; Statistics and Standards; Mechanization. Library Theory and Research; Serial Publications and Library Schools. There are also a number of working groups : Developing Countries Research and Development; Development in Documentation and Librarianship. There is one Group for English-speaking countries, and another for French-speaking countries.

The work of Sections and Groups developed out of all proportions in the 1960s partly because of the efforts of IFLA to become a real world federation, and also as a result of the greater professionalization. IFLA's membership stood at 1,182 in August 1985 of which two-thirds are from the Third World countries.

The Council is the permanent body of IFLA. But in addition to the Executive Board, there is now a professional Board, and division by type of library activity. IFLA's General Council meets once a year from place to place. The present headquarters of IFLA's permanent Secretariat is at Hague (Holland).

Historical Perspectives : Development

The first great milestone in the history of IFLA was the holding of International Conference in Rome in 1929. But the critics point out that this Conference was more of a national conference with an international flavour than a full-fledged international conference. Its proceedings, published in 6 volumes, were not translated from Italian. They were related to : an international code for bibliographical abbreviations; a list of institutional bibliographies; the conservation of books and manuscripts; a list of libraries equipped with microphotography and projection apparatus; the exchange of staff; professional library schools; lists of member associations with their officers and publications; the importance of legal deposit; international loans; an agreement for the exchange of publications and theses, establishment of national centres for bibliographical information; and the committees relations with the International Institute for Intellectual Cooperation (Paris, 1925). The work of IFLA has grown out of these resolutions.

A Second International Congress of Libraries was organized in Madrid in 1935, and but for the Second World War, the third would have been held in Germany in 1940 on the occasion of the Guntenberg's celebrations. In 1957, an agreement of mutual relationship between Unesco and IFLA was signed, in which each body acknowledged the other's significance in the field of library work. At the London session (1948) the International Council on Archives was created at Unesco's instigation. In this way a trio of international non-governmental orgnizations (NGOS) was eastablished which has been cooperating with Unesco ever since. In the early 1950s relations between IFLA and FID became closer, partly in an effort to coordinate the non-governmental organizations' activities vis-as-vis the Unesco programme. Unesco offered a grant to FID and IFLA, and to the International Association of Music Libraries, to organize a World Conference in 1955 on "Tasks and Responsibilities of Libraries and Documentation Centres of Modern Life". At present the meetings are held annually. For example, IFLA held its Fiftieth Council and General Conference in Nairobi, Kenya in August, 1984. The main theme of the conference was *Information and Library Services : Foundations of National Development*. It was attend by 1,000 professionals from 70 countries.

Similarly, over 2,00 librarians, library Scientists (educators) and exhibitors representing 84 countries gathered in Chicago (USA) for the fifty-first Council and General Conference of IFLA in August 1985. The theme of the conference was *Universal Availability of Information.*

Objectives

IFLA is an autonomous non-governmental and non-profit making organization. Its fundamental objective is to promote international understanding, cooperation, and research as well as development in all fields of library science. IFLA provides expert material which are not usually acquired by other science libraries advice and assistance in the planning and development of library services. Its urges national governments for the development of libraries in their countries. It also channelizes grants received from Unesco and other agencies into practical projects for the development of libraries and library associations. It gives developing countries a more vital role in its activities.

Achievements

1. IFLA has many outstandiug archievements to its credit. Through its annual General Councils and Conferences, it has provided a much needed international forum for the librarians for exchange of ideas and experiences.

2. Another distinctive achievement is the implementation of the International Loan Scheme, which ensures that books and journals could be lent freely from one country to another. IFLA's Committee on International Lending and Union Catalogue has sponsored and approvved a standard form to be used for International requests. This constituted a major advance.

3. IFLA was one of sponsors of the Intergovernmental Conference on the Planning of National Documentation, Library and Archives Infrastructures convened by Unesco, Paris. 1974. It was here that the concept of *Universal Bibliogruphic Control* (UBC) was launched world-wide. UBC can be seen as one of IFLA's tasks to treat international bibliographical control as a single process extending from the printing of books to their cataloguing in libraries. The guiding principle for UBC should be as follows : the information on a book should be produced as compeletly and correclly as possible at the earliest possible date. In the interest of speed, accuracy and simplicity this should be done in the country of origin by the national bibliographies. The date should be made available in machine-readable form. This method is certainly of great value for an individual country, but cannot be regarded as the best procedure for world-wide exchange of bibliographical data, as it would mean a delay for a third country wishing to obtain the data. Moreover, this method must involve the use of certain criteria for selection. Nevertheless, international standardization in bibliographic records is essential and IFLA must continue its efforts.

4. The IFLA Office for UBC administers the programme of ISBDs. The function of the *International Standard Bibliogrephic Descriptions* (ISBDs) is to provide a standard description for library

materials. Its primary purpose is to aid international communication of bibliographic information by (a) making records from different sources interchangable so that the records produced in one country can be easily accepted in library catalogues or other bibliographic lists in any other country; (b) assisting in the interpretation of records across language barriers so that records produced for users of one language can be interpreted by users of other languages, and assisting in the conversion of bibliographic records to machine-readable form. Each ISBD within IFLA's expanding programme of ISBDs is intended to provide the maximum amount of descriptive information required in various bibliographic activities. More pertinently, in considering headings and forms of names, ISBDs by indicating author following the slash show the basis for the acceptance of choice of headings and give the form of name as it appears on the title-pages.

If ISBDs have been accepted internationally, it does not mean that they have been proved acceptable for all languages and scripts. Because of the diversity and complexity of the languages of Asia, their scripts and publishing conventions, an ISBD has not made any appreciable influence. Punctuation symbols for international application should be applicable without any need for interpretation or variation. A punctuation symbol contained in a bibliograhpic record created in accordance with ISBD (M) should perform the same function and convey the same meaning whether the record is created in the U.K., or U.S.A., or Singapore, or U.A.R.

Encouraged by its wide acceptance (in Australia, Canada, German Democratic Republic, Federal Republic of Germany, South Africa, Malaysia, Singapore and the Philippines, and ISBD application to African National bibliographies), IFLA Section on Cataloguing proceeded with the work on ISBDs for other materials—Serials, Cartographic Materials, non-Book Materials and Printed Music and old Books. The concept of UBC which originated with IFLA has been adopted by Unesco as a major objective which is a significant achievement.

5. *Universal Availability of Publications* is a complement to U.B.C. As noted above, UBC has the laudable aim of ensuring that bibiiographical records in standard form are provided for publications all over the world. As a natural concomitant of UBC, efforts should be made both within the country and among countries to improve access to publications, by increasing the availability and speed of inter-lending services and by developing effective

procedures. The ultimate aim should be to ensure that all individuals throughout the world should be able to obtain for personal use any publication, whenever published, either in original or a copy. Thus U.B.C. must be accompanied by a programme of of Universal Availability of Publications. This is now recognized as an objective of parallel importance to U.B.C., and as such included in IFLA's Medium Term Programme. U.A.P. is a very wide-range programme, a system and a concept affecting legal deposit and other methods of acquisition, the coordination of libraries by such means as Union Catalogues, the organization of library systems to offer ready availability of sources of information, inter-library lending and photo-copying, the exchange of publications, and the role of national libraries or national centres. IFLA should play an active role in fostering the universal availability of publications for the benefit of one and all. In this context, one may refer to the First Regional Seminar on the universal availability of publications held in Nairobi, Kenya, in Aug., 1984, by IFLA with the help of Unesco. The objectives of the seminar were to promote the programme of the universal availability of publications (UAP), and to inform on the methods of improving access to publications.

Among the concrete proposals put forward by the seminar were the following :–

1. Establishment of a master plan for the availability of publications in circumstances where a shortage exists.
2. Advertising examples of significant improvements in the area of UAP.
3. Implementation of promotional activities for the benefit of privileged users.

6. The terms of reference of IFLA's section on mechanization reflect its future tasks as follows : –

1. Study of development, management and operation of modern data handling systems for libraries and information services.
2. Elaboration of inter-national standards for methods and data used in mechanized library systems; and
3. Communication of "state-of-art" reports, organization of information scientists, meetings.

IFLA must encourge the generation of new ideas and systems of mechanization, and help in the world-wide dissemination of professional knowledge and techniques of information storage and retrieval.

7. The section of library schools takes a keen interest in IFLA's research activities. These include : coordination of plans for library research, cooperation with Unesco in registering (library) research projects and recording their outcomes: study of research methodology in comparative librarianship; study of multilingual problems in terminology, etc.

8. IFLA Section of Libraries for the Blind held an expert meeting in Washington, D.C., in Aug., 1985. Two hasic objectives were defined and are fundamental to all deliberations and activities of the group :

1. To encourage the establishment of library service to handicapped populations in countrics where it does not exist and expansion of service where it exists.
2. To remove the major obstacles to the free flow of special format materials.

Studies and seminars have identified target populations (of blinds), recommended national approaches to programme and book production, and urged expansion of inter-library loan activity. Free International surface mailing of reading materials for the blind individuals has also been recommended.

9. A number of IFLA's specific activities include computer networking, providing gradually expanding telecommunication links, the preparation of a common United Nations vocabulary, the encouragement of more easy access either on-line or through other means to the numerous important data bases maintained by organizations of the United Nations system and by an active programme of dissemination of information about modern office information management.

10. Among IFLA's important publications, the following are worth remembering : IFLA Journal; IFLA Annual; IFLA Directory; ABHB—Annual Bibliography on the History of the Printed Books and Libraries; National and International Planning; Corporate Headings : their use in Library Catalogues and National Bibliographies; Standards for Public Libraries ISBD (M)—International Standard Bibliographic Description for Monographic Publications; ISBS (S)—International Standard Bibliographic Description for Serials; World Directory of Administrative Libraries; World Directory of Map Collections; Libri, etc.

Before conclusion, it may be stated that IFLA has enriched the profession by its significant contributions. Its latest work was detailed by President Else Granheim at the concluding session of IFLA (Chicago, 1985) in the following areas :

—Inter-national MARC Programme in maintaining and promoting UNIMARC.

—Funding of the Preservation and Conservation Programme by the council on Library Resources*

—Support of the Universal Availability of Publications (UAP) Programme by Unesco;

—Location of the new Trans-border Data Flow (TDF) Proat the National Library of Canada; and

—Establishment of the Programme on the Advancement of Librarianship in the Third World.

A new doeument *25 Essential Points on the Improvement of IFLA's Regional Programme* provides a means to stimulate action.

INSDOC

The Indian National Scientific Documentation Centre (INSDOC) was established with technical assistance from Unesco for providing a complete range of documentation services in the field of science and technology. The organization of Insdoc was entrusted to the Council of Scientific and Industrial Research. In 1963, the CSIR raised the status of INSDOC to that of an independent institute with its own Executive Council and Director.

The fundamental functions which Insdoc performs are as under :

—To receive and retain all scientific periodicals which may be of use to the country;

—To inform scientist and engineers of articles which may be of value to them by issuing Indian Science Abstracts;

—To answer specific enquiries from information available in the centre;

—To supply photocopies and translations of articles required by individual workers;

—To be a national depository for reports of the scientific work of the nation, both published and unpublished; and

***An Int. seminar in this regard was held in *Vienna* in April, 86. For recommendations, see ILA Bul. Sept., 86.**

—To be a channel through which the scientific work of the nation is made available to the rest of the world.

The activities of Insdoc are organised as follows :

1. *Document Procurement Service*

This service is being fully utilized by research organizations, universities, industries, government departments, and individual scientific workers. It supplies, on request, copies of scientific papers in the form of microfilm or photo-copy. More than 22,000 requests for copies of documents are handled every year.

2. *Bibliography and Information Service*

Insdoc compiles *ad hoc* bibliographies on specific topics on requests. The bibliographies are in the form of bare list of documents and include references to books, journal articles, patents, specifications, report literature etc. About 300 bibliographies are compiled every year to help especially the small scale industries sector.

3. *Translation*

Insdoc has got facilities for translating into English from 21 languages. Over 12,000 pages are translated every year. Insdoc supplies translations on orders placed by any individual or organization of scientific and technical documents.

4. *Reprographic Services*

The photographic section of Insdoc is equipped with microfilming and photocoping equipment. It supplies photo-copies and micro-recordings of documents. The work load of this section is over a lakh of prints and 22,000 microfilm strips (each strip convering 10 pages) in a year.

5. *Printing Section*

In addition to a process camera, this section is equipped with dry-copying equipments, such as Xerox 1385, Coronastat Copier, Savin Copier, and electronic stencil cutter. Approximately 25,000 pages are printed in a year.

6. *Information Retrieval*

Insdoc started work on the application of computers for information handling in 1964. The preparation of monthly author, subject indexes and comulative annual author and subject indexes of the Indian Science Abstracts has been computerized since 1966. A major activity in computerization is the development of suitable programme for the compilation of Union Catalogues.

Insdoc is offering SDI on a regular basis from Chemical Abstracts Condensates (CAC) and INSPEC magnetic tapes.

CAS is a weekly tape service having citations from the fields of chemistry, chemical engineering and chemical technology. It scans more than 15,000 periodicals, patents granted by 26 countries, reports, latest books and conference proceedings. But about 85 per cent of the coverage consists of articles. Out of near 5 lakhs citations covered in CAC nearly 60% are in the English language.

INSPEC Data bases cover physics, electronics, electrical engineering, computer and control technology. References are drown from Physics Abstracts (Section A), Electrical and Electronics Abstracts (Section B), Computer and Control Abstracts (Section C).

7. *INSDOC Union Catalogue Series*

1. Catalogue of Serials in the National Science Library, Delhi, October 1965.
2. Cataloguc of Serials in the Indian Institute of Science Library, Banglore, January 1966.
3. Catalogue of Serials in the Indian Statistical Institute, Calcutta, August, 1966.
4. Catalogue of Serials in the Agricultural Research Institute Library, Delhi, March, 1967.
5. Regional Union Catalogue of Scientific Serials; Banglore June, 1967.
6. Regional Union Catalogue of Scientific Serial : Delhi Medical Libraries, Nov., 1967.
7. Regional Union Catalogue of Scientific Serials : Varanasi June, 1968.
8. Regional Union Catalogue of Scientific Serials : Mysore, September, 1968.
9. Catalogue of Serials in National Institute of Sciences of India,Delhi, Oct. 1968.
10. Regional Union Catalogue of Scientific Serials : Kerala, May, 1969.
11. Union Catalogue of Serials in the Geological Survey of India Libraries, July, 1969.
12. Regional Union Catalogue of Scientific Serials : Dehra Dun—Roorkee, Feb., 1971.

13. Regional Union Catalogue of Scientific Serials : Bombay—Poona, April, 1973.
14. Regional Union Catalogue of Scientific Serials : Madras, Feb., 1975.
15. Regional Union Catalogue of Scientific Serials : Hydrabad, Dec., 1975.
16. Regional Union Catalogue of Scientific Serials : Lucknow, Feb., 1976.
17. Regional Union Catalogue of Scientific Serials : West-Bengal, June, 1978.
18. Union List of Current Scientific Serials in India : Dec , 1981.

The Union List of Current Scientific Serials in India was brought out by Insdoc as a preparatory volume, prior to publishing the National Union Catalogue of Scientific Serials. This volume is supplement to the previous 17 volumes in the Union Catalogue Series, (1965-1978), as it updates the information on new and current scientific serials being received in the libraries of 785 institutions.

The *Union List* records information on 11, 511 foreign scientific serials received from 82 countries, and 1,892 Indian Serials. About 2,000 cross reference entries are provided in the list. Insdoc has used computer facility for storage and retrieval of Union Catalogue of Serials data since 1972. The Regional Union Catalogue of Scientific Serials : Bombay—Poona, 1973 was the first volume processed through computer, and a data base of about 9,000 entries, and holdings data of 64 libraries was created. Since then 5 more volumes were published, and till 1978 the data base contained information of about 24,000 entries and holdings data of about 330 libraries At present Insdoc is preparing input for about 20,000 additional entries and holdings data of another 450 libraries for publication of the National Union Catalogue of Scientific Serials.

8. *National Science Library*

A nucleus of the National Science Library has been functioning in Insdoc since 1964. Its purpose is to have at least one copy of every worth-while scientific publication within the country, no matter where it is kept. The library would specialize in materials which are not usually acquired by other science libraries in order to supplement the national collection. It would maintain a depository of Indian scientific publications In addition to periodical collection, the library would specialize in acquisition of conference proceedings, research and industrial reports, foreign language publications, reference materials, publications of library and information sciences, Indian Universities' theses, etc.

9. Regional Centre Banglore

With technical assistance from Unesco, a Regional Centre of Insdoc was set up in Banglore in 1964. In addition to offering document procurement service, bibliography, information and reprographic services, the centre engaged itself in compilation of Union Catalogue of Scientific Serials available in southern region.

10. Russian Science Information Centre

This centre was initiated by Insdoc in 1971. The object of the centre is to acquire current published literature in the field of science and technology published in USSR and to make them available to scientists, specialists and institutions of higher education and research in India. In order to disseminate Russian science information, the Insdoc brought out two lists, viz.. Russian Scientific and Technical Publications—An Accession List; and Contents List of Soviet Scientific Periodicals. Under this agreement about 3,000 publications of 350 current titles of Soviet Scientific periodicals have been received every year.

11. National Science Foundation—US

In 1967, Insdoc concluded an agreement with U.S. National Science Foundation for undertaking cover-to-cover translation of foreign language scientific documents assigned by them. The project runs on a self-supporting basis out of funds provided by the NSF.

12. Insdoc has been entrusted with the responsibility of the centralized processing and acquiring periodicals of foreign origin on behalf of 31 CSIR establishments.

13. Training in Documentation and reprography

This course was started in 1964 with the objective of training personnel for documentation and special library work. At present this course is called 'Associateship in Information Science'.

In addition to the regular course, Insdoc has been offering in-service training to individual librarians, documentalists and information scientists on request by their organizations. Insdoc also started in 1965 an advanced course and a priliminary language course in Russian.

14. Collaborations

Insdoc is a national member of F.I.D. FID/IM—Informetrics Activities' Committee started functioning from India at INSDOC, New Delhi from January, 1985.

Insdoc also maintains close cooperation with Unesco. It is actively participating in the Unisist. It is also participating in world programmes such as ISDS and CODATA. Insdoc is also closely collaborating with VINITI.

At home, Insdoc closely collaborates with ISI in drawing up standards in the field of documentation and reprography. Insdoc helps BARC (Trombay) in the INIS project by supplying nuclear science information from journals.

Insdoc has concluded bilateral arrangements with a number of foreign institutions for receiving microfilms of scientific papers and for exchanging scientific publications.

15. Insdoc has sponsored several conferences and seminars on library and documentation problems and has organized monumental book exhibitions. Second Regional Conference of FID/CR was held at New Delhi on 15 Nov., 1985. The conference was sponsored by ILA and Sarada Ranganathan Endowment for Library Science. The theme was "Classification and Communication".

16. Indian Centre for ISDS at INSDOC

The government of India has designated the Insdoc as the Indian National Centre for International Serials Data System (ISDS) which is an inter-governmental organization responsible for creating a network of the International Centre and 44 national regional centres. The national centres are responsible for registration and assignment of ISSN (International Standard Serial Number) to serials published in their respective regions. and transmission of the serials data to the International Centres and in turn, the national centres have access to the records created in

ISDS database, and can utilize ISDS tapes and microfiches for various purposes.

The Indian National Centre for ISDS undertake systematic registration and assignment of ISSN to serials published in India.

17. Publications

Insdoc list of current scientific literature, 1954-64; bibliography of Scientific Publications of South and South-East Asia; Annals of Library Science and Doeumentation (Q); Directory of Indian Scientific Periodicals (1964); Directory of Scientific Research Institutions (1969); Directory of Current Research Projects in CSIR Laboratories (1972); Directory of Scientific Research in Indian Universities (1974); Directory of Ongoing Research Projects in India; Directory of Testing Facilities in India; Contents List of Soviet Scientific Periodicals (M); Russian Scientific and Technical Publications—a bi-montbly Accession List, etc.

In brief, Insdoc is a vital link in our nation's system of disseminating information services. It has added a new dimension to our scientific and technical research. Its task of compiling bibliographics and meeting technical enquiries on requests from scientists, engineers, medicos, commercial organizations is really praise-worthy.

National Social Science Documentation Centre

The National Social Science Documentation Centre was set up in 1970 by Indian Council of Social Science Research. Like any special set up, NASSDOC has had to adapt to the organization it serves and ICSSR's unique position made NASSDOC task a peculiar challange which it has tried to meet with the help of the following programmes and activities.

Activities

(i) Building up a collection of reference materials; collecting (a) unpublished doctoral theses approved by Indian Universities/and foreign theses on India, (b) research reports of the projects undertaken by ICSSR, (c) working papers presented at ICSSR funded seminars and conferences and (d) Periodicals of research standard in social sciences.

(ii) Providing duplicating and reprographic services.

(iii) Striving for bibliographic control over social science materials by bringing out various documents under Research Information Series. 31 titles have so for been brought out.

(iv) Providing select bibliographies on request.

(v) Providing document supply services to scholars from outside Delhi.

(vi) Providing bibliographical information about Indian publications in social science disciplines to international documentation agencies like International Committee for Social Science Information and Documentation.

(vii) Awarding study grants to scholars for working at libraries of their interest.

(viii) Providing consultancy to social science institutions in setting up documentation and information centres.

(ix) Providing facilities for staff participation in seminars and conferences through contributing papers as well as taking active part in their deliberations. They are also deputed to attend short duration refresher courses.

(x) Organising B.Lib. & Inf. Sc. classes for Andhra Pradesh Open University students in the capacity of Northern Regional Coordinating Centre.

(xi) Processing project proposals for consideration of ICSSR Committee on documentation Services and Researoh Information for financial assistance in the field of documentation.

(xii) Entering into exchange arrangement with national and international organisations for their publications.

(xiii) Supplying ICSSR publications on payment/free and participating in book exhibitions.

Present Position

Collection : SSDC has total collection of 20,500 documents which include Ph.D. theses, research project reports and working papers. Further analysis of the collection is as under :

(i) *Periodical Literature* : The Centre has a collection of back fiies of about 90.000 volumes of social science periodicals. Current issues of most of the Indian social science periodicals are regularly received. The two document

"ILRC Holdings List" and "Periodicals in SSDC : A Current List "provide complete information about the periodicals holdings in SSDC.

(ii) Reference Sources : The library has a good collection of reference materials in social sciences including subject dictionaries, encyclopaedias, bibliographies, indexes, abstracts, etc. Specialised collection includes books on research methodology in social sciences, social indicators, and on status of women. The three NASSDOC compilations, brought out under its Research Information Series, namely. 'Bibliographies in SSDC', 'Reference Sources in SSDC' and Social Science Research Methodology : A Bibliography' can be consulted for locating desired reference tools.

(iii) ICSSR Publications : The Library keeps all ICSSR priced/non-priced publications (books and periodicals, and also those for which the Council has provided publication grants). Besides ICSSR publications list, a 'Guide to Books and Journals Aided/Published by ICSSR' compiled in SSDC, provides an overall picture of ICSSR activities in the publication field.

(iv) Theses and Research Reports : Of special significance to Ph.D. students and other researchers in social sciences is the Library's collection of unpublished Ph.D. theses and research project reports in social sciences. Efforts are made to obtain a copy of unpublished doctoral thesis in Social Sciences accepted by Indian Universities and also foreign unpublished theses on India. So far about 2,000 Ph.D. theses and research project reports have been collected. To furnish access to these, two bibliographical lists entitted 'Theses in SSDC : An Annotated Bibliography', kept updated from time to time have been compiled.

(v) Documents in Microform : The following publications including journals are available on microfilm/microfiche in the library : (i) Annals of Indian Administration; (ii) Anthropological Society of Bombay Journal; (iii) Bombay Geographical Society Journal; (iv) Economic Working Papers (UK); (v) Gujarat Research Society Journal; (vi) Indian Linguistics; (vii) Psychological Abstracts; (viii)

Social Action; (ix) Sharma, (R.A.)—A Bibliography of Mughal India, 1526—1707; (x) Thurston, (E) and Ramachari (K)—Castes and Tribes of Southern India, 7 vols. (xi) A selective number of Ph.D. theses and research reports.

Inter-Library Resources Centre : ILRC was set up in collaboration with Jawaharlal Nehru University in 1975, inviting local libraries to deposit their non-current, infrequently used but important for research serials (i.e. Govt. reports, journals, newspapers, etc.) with this centre. 38 libraries in Delhi have so far deposited their periodicals/serials at the Centre. Sometimes back, due to lack of space, about 55.000 volumes had been shifted to the space acquired at Jawaharlal Nehru University Library, New Delhi.

Documentation Programmes

A modest beginning was made with two broad categories of programmes (i) Programmes undertaken by the Council directly or in collaboration with selected institutions and (ii) Programmes assited by the Council under its Grant-in-Aid Scheme. A brief description of programmes in both the categories is given below.

ICSSR Programmes
NASDOC Research Information Series

Union List of Social Science Periodicals : Four volumes of the Union Lists relating to periodicals currently available in Andhra Pradesh, Bombay, Delhi and Karnataka libraries were broughtout in 1971-72. The Delhi list had been published in 1978, 1982 and 1985. The latest one records the availability of 2,909 periodical titles in 30 libraries in Delhi during 1985. The list will now continuously compiled through microprocessor, and kept updated on floppies.

Union Catalogue of Social Science Serials : The compilation of Union Catalogue was the first major project undertaken on April, 1, 1970 and formally completed on March, 31, 1976. 22 volumes giving location of about 31,125 serials in 550 libraries in the 17 States and two Union Territories with separate volumes on National Library, Calcutta have been published. The union catalogue helps to locate a recognised volume of social science periodical/serial if it is available in one or the other participating library. It also helps these libraries to share their serial resources with one another for the benefit of their clientele.. The union catalogue by its very nature requires revision from time to time to provide information about the current status of serials in our libraries. In some cases, part of these may have been wasted out by certain libraries. Libraries in general will have large holdings in the years to come than what they have now. Unique holdings of some titles may also be discovered at presently lesser known libraries. The revision of the union catalogue is not only necessary but imperative if the time of social scientists is to be saved. It is, therefore, being considered to take up this work on a regular basis and make it a core activity and continuing programme of the SSDC.

Union Catalogue of Newspapers in Delhi Libraries : To update data regarding availability of backfiles of newspapers in Delhi Libraries, earlier part of Union Catalogue of Social Science Periodicals—Delhi Libraries, a separate fascicule with the above mentioned title was brought out in memeo form in 1978, and subsequently revised in 1983. The latest catalogue covers 252 newspaper titles available in 36 libraries and newspaper offices.

Directory of Social Science Research Institutions and Directory of Professional Organizations in India : SSDC has updated the two directories originally published in 1971 and the information is available on cards for reference.

Mahatma Gandhi Bibliography : The first volume in the series 'Mohandas Karamchand Gandhi : A Bibliography' devoted to monographs in English was released on Otober 27, 1974. This has been followed by volumes covering monographs in Hindi, Sanskrit and Urdu. The manuscript of Bengali fascicule is ready.

Retrospective Cumulative Index of Indian Social Science Periodicals : With the Union Catalogue Project behind it, the SSDC planned to prepare a retrospective cumulative index of Indian Social Science periodicals right from their respective first volume. The Retrospective Index Project was started from April 1, 1976. SSDC identified 240 Periodicals for the project, and decided 1970 as the cut-off year. So far, work relating to indexing of journals in Education, Psychology, Anthropology and Sociology has been completed. When the project is completed, it will offer bibliographical control of periodical literature utility to social scientists. The Index is planned to be maintained initially on cards which can be consulted by scholars even while the work is in progress.

It may be printed serially or computerized later on. On completion, the Retrospective Cumulative Index will have the following advantages :

1. The Index will provide reasonable bibliographical control of periodical literature published in this country during approximately the last 130 years.
2. The Union Catalogue volumes will provide location in the country of needed volumes of any periodical for quick and easy access.
3. Inter-Library Resources Centre will try to provide access to three volumes of required articles.

Area Studies Bibliographies : Started during 1979, the project of Area Studies Bibliographies aimed at bringing together all Social Science material of research value pertaining to the different States and Union Territories of India. Under this project, it is envisaged to bring out series of bibliographies which will cover material in social sciences available in any form and language exclusively related to the area concerned.

Under the supervision of a Project Director in each State/ Region, the compilation work has been completed in Andaman & Nicobar Islands, Goa, Daman & Dieu, Madhya Pradesh, Punjab, Haryana & Himachal Pradesh. Rajasthan, Tamil Nadu, U.P. (Eastern Region) and is in progress in the remaining States and Union Territories. About 10,000 titles in English and Indian regional languages have been collected under the Area Study Project.

Language Bibliographies : The project is wider in space and seeks to cover research materials in all disciplines in social sciences in Indian regional languages. The compilation work of bibliographies in Gujarati, Hindi, Kannda and Oriya is in progress. The bibliographical data of about 6,003 references in Hindi, 2,000 in Gujarati and 300 each in Oriya and Kannada languages is in hand.

ICSSR Assisted Projects : The second category of programmes assisted by the ICSSR with a grant-in-aid relates to compilation of indexes and bibliographies.

Publication Assistance : Publication of good reference works has also been promoted by bulk purchase of copies, (1) Civil

Disobedience and Indian Tradition, (2) A Guide to Reference Material on India, (3) Hindi Sandharbh, (4) Index India, (5) Index to Calcutta Review, (6) Indian Behavioural Science Abstracts, (7) Indian Education Index, (1948—1948), (8) Indian Political Movement, (1919—1971), (9) Kesari Centenary Index, and (10) Theses on the Indian Subcontinent (1877—1971) are some examples in the category.

Financial Assistance to Libraries/Documentation Centres

Grant-in-aid has also been provided to the Indian Council of World Affairs, New Delhi, towards the maintenance of the library including subsription of journals since 1980-81 and to the Indian Renaissance Institute, Dehra Dun for the upkeep of M.N. Roy Archives.

Fresh Initiatives

(i) *Automation of Services* : Beginning has been made with the acquisition of micro-processor. The end objective is to have computerised database of research material (books, periodicals, research reports, theses, working papers) in social science disciplines available in Delhi Libraries.

(ii) *Research Projects Data Base* : Setting up a data base of research projects in social sciences, completed and in progress, to avoid duplication and judicious utilisation of resources.

(iii) *Programmes Activation* : Taking vigorously again the ICSSR approved programmes present under by inanimation or suspension like Retrospective Indexing Programme, Union Catalogue Programme, Inter-Library Resources Centre, Sale of Govt. Documents, etc.

SDI Service : Initiating compilation of interest profiles of scholars so as to provide Selective Dissemination of Information Services.

(v) *Resource Sharing* : Initiating a meeting of subject experts and professionals in the field of Economics (to begin with) to find out ways for maximum utilisation of resources available and minimising duplication of services and material like documentation services and purchase of costly foreign books and journals.

(vi) *Micro-filming of Research material* : Micro-filming of theses, project reports and journals is contemplated to cope with space shortage and preservation problems.

(vii) Research Facilities to Scholars : Providing quick document delivery services through adding one more photo-copier and one micro-film reader-cum-printer.

Future Programme :

1. Establishment of a micro-filming unit.
2. Updating of Union Catalogue of Social Science Serials/ Periodicals.
3. A national information grid has also been on the planning board for sometime. The system is expected to link centres of excellence (in social sciences) of the country and make expeditious service to the reader of information a *sine qua non* of coordinated cooperation among the constituents[1].

1. Data povided by S.P. Agrawal, Director, NASSDOC.

24

CENSORSHIP AND COPYRIGHT

CENSORSHIP

The term censorship is of Latin derivation, censere, "to assess". In modern thought, censorship is an attempt made by a government, private organization, group, or an individual to influence human thoughts by preventing, or limiting people from reading, seeing, or hearing what may be considered as dangerous to government or harmful to public morality.

Censorship is as old as humans and will probably exist as long as humans do. Censorship has had been exercised on political views, religious or moral grounds. In the old times, the main emphasis was on the crimes of religious heresy or political sedition, and the modern preoccupation with obscenity and pornography mainly flows from the extension of literacy and the development of the mass media of communication.

In a restricted sense censorship refers to the work of a person or an agency with the authority to come between the producer to publish, and the consumer to acquire knowledge of the censored materials. In a looser interpretation the term is used to describe the enactment and enforcement of laws that restrict the freedom to publish unless these laws deal with the protection of the rights of others, as in cases of slander, libel, or copyright infringement.

In library science, the first two laws : "Books Are For Use"; and "Every Reader His Book" projects the problem of Censorship. For example, the First Law may amplify the term "Use" into the term "Socially Beneficient Use". If this be allowed, it would amount to Book Selection being influenced by considerations of censorship. But against this, the Second Law may argue, "If a reader wants a book, it is the duty of the library to provide it. Consideration of censorship should not weigh with Book Selection. The faith of the Librarian today should be that censorship is not his function. The Government alone can have the duty and power of censorship. Once a book has been allowed to be published and released for use or to be imported, the demand of the reader to have it is "paramount". The First Law may argue, "No doubt the Librarian should not take up the responsibility for censorship. At the same time, the librarian should remember that the public library in his charge is a social institution for the betterment of the society. Government censor may supress only books of immediate social danger or political disruption. But Books with sinister anti-social suggestions set in a minor key and capable only of long term effect, may escape the censors". Therefore, Ranganathan succinctly observes : "The librarian, though not a super-censor, has the duty to abstain from selecting books of such subtle anti-social nature".

Veering close to Rangahathan, James Thompson in his book *Library Power* writes : "It is not part of the librarian's role, educationally or otherwise, to act as a pruner, as a seeker out of dross or as a detergent. A librarian cannot be a censor. He must protect freedom of thought and expression, and the fact that a number of books may be to him personally unplatable can be neither here nor there to him professionally. This principle must be common to every true philosophy of librarianship, and it does not allow for compromise of any sort whatsoever, no matter how well-meaning."

The libraries must ever remain, writes Martha Boaz in his article "Censorship : Contemporary and Controversial", the homes of free inquiring minds. To them, our citizens—of all ages and political persuasions—must ever be able to turn with clear confidence that there they can freely seek the whole truth, unwarped by fashion and uncompromised by expediency. For in such whole and healthy knowledge alone are found and understood those majestic truths of man's nature and destiny that prove, to each succeeding generation; the validity of freedom.

The basic cause of attempts at censorship of library collections derives from the very nature of modern democracies. The democratic societies today are characterized by constant tension between the freedom of the individual and the demands of ganized living. It is clear that in a free society, no matter how much liberty to differ men may have, there must be some areas of general agreement or community life could not continue. Individual freedom without restraints degenerates into licence and lawlessness which ultimately weakens the society. Unrestricted individualism is, therefore, the law of the beast of the jungle: we have to learn to strike the mean between individual freedom and social restraints. Freedom can be gained only through the bonds of discipline, through the sacrifice of personal inclinations, the ultimate freedom is the freedom of self-restraint.

Nevertheless, any restriction in the area of intellectual life is detestable. The concept of thought control is abhorrent to a scholar. Libraries represent the embodiment of human thought. The burning of a book strikes the lover of freedom with something like the same horror as the burning of its author. Attacks on library collections for their inclusion of one book or another, or of one film or another, seem attacks on the human intellect itself. And certainly, as a general principle, librarians ought to stand strongly "for the freedom of communication, for the freedom of intellectual activity, for the freedom of thought which their institutions represent. They ought to resist all attempts to limit the search for wisdom, knowledge, peace of mind, or entertainment[1]".

However, there is a difference between freedom of thought and freedom of expression. The law restrains us from uttering libels and slanders, from false reports of crimes and fires; it limits and restricts the products of our fertile imagination from finding unlimited propagation.[2]

Graphic records are thoughts put into concreate form. Society has laid restricttions on the freedom of those records to communicate, just as it has restricted the individual's freedom to communicate. But the question arises : at what point does a communication in graphic record become dangerous to society and thus subject of suppression[3] ?

This question implies that there is someone who can decide when that point has been reached and that there are measures which can be applied; that there is a calculus of sedition, a yardstick of moral decay. But attitude toward what is evil is not uniform.

1. Mary D. Carter, W.J. Bonk and Rose Mary Magrill. *Building library collections*, 4th ed. (N.J., Scarecrow, 1974), p. 177.
2. Ibid., p. 178.
3. Ibid.

The line marking off the socially permissable from the socially dangerous is not fixed; it shifts from time to time and from place to place within the same period. The basic weaknesses of all demands for Censorship can be put simply : the censor is sure that he can recognize evil—but that the people cannot. The desire for censorship arises from a simple lack of faith in the powers of judgement and discrimination of others. Other people must be protected from evil, we say, but what we are really saying is that they are not bright enough, not good enough, not trust-worthy enough to protect themselves. They cannot see what we see so clearly; so we must not allow them to look upon the book whose evil is so obvious to us.[3a] Such an attitude would be characterized as the most blatant arrogance. The reader must make normal choices for himself, and while we believe that in the long run he will be a responsible and stable citizen, we can not deny to him his basic human right to err, to slip, to stumble and to recover from regression. Broadening one's horizons is not only a matter of going always onward and upward—it includes also the experience of sinking downward and backward. The very basis of man as a being is a contradiction; man is neither an angel nor a beast. And the great play of human life lies in the struggle of man against evil in him. Human character is not fine flower of a beautiful sentiment but the hard won fruit of a painful and prolonged conquest. The making of individual character is spread over years, and that of nations over centuries. Furthermore, it is a mistaken notion that the intellectual conviction of what is good will necessarily lead to good action. There is a gulf between the two : the logic of the passions has to be taken into account by a realist who is anxious to improve man and reform society Therefore, suppression of thought is never more dangerous than in such a time of social tension. Every silencing of a heresy, every enforcement of an orthodoxy, diminishes the toughness and resilience of a democratic society and leaves it the less able to deal with strain and stress, and fret and fear of the world.

Books are among our greatest instruments of feeedom. They are the the natural medium for the new idea and the untried voice from which come the original contributions to social growth. They are essential to the extended discussion which serious thought

3a. Ibid., p. 183.

requires, and to the accumul·tion of knowledge and ideas into organized collections.

Communication without any let or hindrance is the *sin-qua-non* of a free society and a creative culture. The freedom to read is guaranteed under any democratic constitution. The following propositions may be the guiding principles for the preservation of free society and free flow of thought :

—It is in the public interest for publishers and librarians to make available the widest diversity of views and expressions, including those which are unorthodox or unpopular with the majority.

—Publishers and librarians do not need to endorse every idea or presentation contained in the books they make available. It would conflict with the public interest for them to establish their own political, moral or aesthetic views as the sole standard for determining what books should be published or circulated.

—It is contrary to the public interest for publishers or librarians to determine the acceptability of a book solely on the basis of the personal history or political affiliations of the author.

—The present laws dealing with obscenity (in a country) should be vigorously enforced. Beyond that, no extra-legal efforts be made to coerce the taste of others, to confine adults to reading matter deemed suitable for adolescents, or to inhibit the efforts of writers to achieve artistic expression.

—It is not in the public interest to force a reader to accept any book with the prejudgement of a lablel characterizing the book or author as subversive or dangerous.

—It is the responsibility of publishers and librarians, as guardians of the peoples freedom to read, to contest encroachments upon that freedom by individuals or groups seeking to impose their own standards or tastes upon the community at large.

—It is the responsibility of publishers and librarians to give full meanining to the freedom to read by providing books that enrich the quality of thought and expression. By the exercise of this affirmative responsibility bookmen can demonstrate that the answer to the bad book is a good one, the answer to a bad idea is a good one'[4]

Censorship is a negative factor, whereas the basic freedoms are positive and are a mandatory in a democratic society. President Dwight D. Eisenhower was criticising the censorship of free thought when he commented in 1953 : "As it is an ancient truth that freedom cannot be censored into existence. And any who act as if freedom's defences are to be found in suppression and suspicion and fear confess a doctrine that is alien to America". Speaking for liberation and against repression, with specific application to books, President Whitney Griswold of Yale said. "Books won't stay banned. They won't burn. Ideas won't go the jail. In the long run of history, the censor and the inquistor have always lost. The only sure weapon against bad ideas is better ideas". The *freedom to read* prompted the *New York Times* to comment : "The people of this country (U.S.A.) have too long endured the creeping threat of censorship over what they should be allowed to say or print or read or, by inference think. Under the excuse of fighting authoritarian systems we have been urged to adopt one of the chief devices of authoritarianism, with the argument that if we do not accept these inquisitions we will fall into some kind of tyranny. Little men with narrow minds and with great lust for power have tried to dictate to us. To many of us, and obviously to those who drew up the Library Association's documents and those who voted to endorse them these censors are in contempt of the most sacred traditions of American freedom—".

The causal concept of obscenity, most difficult to assess, is still the centre of a controversy that moves from the extremes of absolute freedom to greater restrictiveness. Protagonists of absolute freedom view restrictions as a possible danger to literary freedom, as a stimulant to the sale of pornographic literature because it is surreptitious and further argue that is a form of literature with sublimating effects, which in itself, appeals only to a specialized and limited public with an established taste.

Antagonists, on the other hand, assert that harmful consequences can follow for the individual, and for the society as a whole, from an unchecked flow of literature usually epitomized as

4. *"Freedom to Read"* : A statement prep. by A.L.A. (Westchester conf.) of ALA and the Amer. Book Publishers Council, May 2 and 3, 1953.

"sordid". "squalid" and "perverted". Keeping in mind that pornography can convert and pervert, their belief that literature has the power to deprave and corrupt, requires that some control should be exercised.

Every age has its particular standards of what is and what is not acceptable in terms of sexual morality, and in every age the librarian comes under pressure to reflect these standards in terms of book selection and freedom of access. In selecting the pornographic literature, the librarian runs several risks : his local council might accuse him of providing pornography at the ratepayers' expense; they might appoint some kind of vigilant committee if they think he is putting into the library books which will deprave and corrupt; they might even retaliate by cutting his book fund.

The librarian feels himself in a fix. The concept of items which 'tend to deprave or corrupt' is difficult if not impossible to interpret. Moreover, he cannot use current taste as an arbiter even if he wanted to, since this changes so rapidly. In 1960, there was a great furore over *Lady Chatterley's lover*, but after a decade the appearance of this book on the shelves of a public library hardly created any stir. One red herring, therefore, has been to to limit the debate to the possible harmful effects of pornography on the unbalanced and on the immature. But, there is no proof at all that unbalanced people are more at risk from pornography than anybody else; and so far as children are concerned, most librarians take the practical step of putting doubtful books on closed access, not principally because they want to keep them out of the hands of children, but because such books are invariably stolen if placed on open shelves. It might appear, therefore, that so long as librarians do not supply material which is proscribed by the government they should not concern themselves with the matter at all.

There is a tradition in public libraries that all points of view should be represented, 'despite the long history of censorship in the world'. It is immaterial to this tradition whether a book be "allegedly anti-semitic, fascist, anti-catholic, full of race-prejudice', or pornograhic. President Eisenhower was speaking the whole truth when he declared : "Don't join the book burners. Don't think you are going to conceal faults by concealing evidence that ever existed. Don't be afraid to go in your library and read every book as long as any document does not offend your own ideas of decency. That should be the only censorship" In this statement, President Eisenhower encapsulated the only valid approach to censorship : the choice and responsibility as to what should or should not be read must always rest with the individual reader himself. The librarian only comes in an entirely pragmatic way : within the inevitable constraints of his budget, he must offer the widest and most balanced selection of books possible. To achieve this goal, he has the responsibility for making it clear to the community that the library represents the democratic ideal of tolerance, that it has the duty to be many-sided, to give service to all of the citizens, and not just those of one particular shade of opinion. That this task will not always be easy, that on occasions it may be impossible, that sometimes it may not be worldly wise, is beyond doubt. The personality, convictions, honesty, and courage of the librarian will influence the course of action taken when groups or individuals outside the library attempt to control its holdings. Keeping his professional responsibility in view, he must defend the principles of the "freedom to read". This requires that the librarian must be his own master, his own man. He must resist all pressures for censorship, in order that the individual reader can find and read in the library whatever he wishes.

In brief, all censorship is futile, ridiculous and wrong. Whatever is permissable according to the standards established by the various courts, from the Supreme Court on down, must not be allowed to be attacked by voluntary groups which claim without basis to represent the community at large. The librarian himself must maintain impartiality when he has his own strong convictions and sees them violated by a book. The document : *How libraries and schools can resist censorship*, promulgated by A.L.A., contains a list of practical suggestions, such as the preparation by every library of a written statement of book selection policy, the establishment of a clearly defined method for handling complaints, and the promotion of good lines of communication with civic, religious, educational and political bodies. Apart from this document, there is a list of other policy statements on censorship issued by A.L.A., viz., *Freedom to read statement*; the *Statement on labeling*; *Library bill of rights* (1948, amended 1961 and 1967); *School library bill of rights* (1955) and *Policies and procedures* for selection of school library material (1961), etc.

While censorship should be challenged (except of proscribed books) by libraries in the maintenance of their responsibility to provide public information and responsibility, the librarians may keep in mind the piece of advice given by Ranganathan :

> While book-selection should not take up the responsibility for censorship, since a public library is a social institution for the betterment of society, book selection in a public library should abstain from including fiction, with anti-social suggestions.

The debate ultimately returns to the phrase "professional responsibility". A librarian's book selection policy is a matter of professional judgement, which is based on a knowledge of books and a knowledge of readers, and on which the only constraint is a financial one. There is no question of libraries being flooded out with pornographic books, because this would not make bibliographic sense, never mind moral sense (James Thompson).

As a responsibility of library service, books and other materials selected should be choosen for values of interest, information, and enlightenment of all the people of the community. In no case should library materials be excluded because of the race or nationality or the social, political, or religious views of the authors. Libraries should provide documents presenting all points of view concerning the problems and issues of our times; no library materials should be proscribed or removed from libraries because of partisan or doctrinal disapproval. Needless to say that library is a "sanctuary" of independent thinking—the one surviving hope of intellectual freedom as also a means of securing and safeguarding it. Whatever else may happen there can be no final abridgement of intellectual freedom so long as individuals, privately and voluntarily, can choose their readings from libraries to seek and grasp the truth in the way they like best. It is essential to encourage dissent which is so vital a factor for a healthy intellectual environment. In fact, the growth and development of knowledge and achievement in action are the products of "both conflict and cooperation, both a struggle among beliefs and a sharing of beliefs".[5] These are the terms on

5. James B. Conan, *The Citadel for learning* (New Haven, Yale Univ. 1956) p. 9.

which those within the democratic society have lived and worked effectively in the past; these are the only terms which will ensure the safety and vitality of the democratic society in the future. Censorship, therefore, should be challanged by libraries in the maintenance of their responsibility to provide public information and enlightenment.

COPYRIGHT

Philosophical Basis

The intellectual excellence and artistic creations determine the quality of the culture of an age. This quality is greatly affected in turn by the appreciation, the protection and the encouragement given to their creators. Literature, whether it be a scientific treatise or belles-letters; art. whether it be a work of Matisse or an advertising poster; music, whether it be a symphony or the latest popular song, may all be copyrighted. The law of copyright is thus the law that helps to shape the cultnre of our modern societies, for it is a vital factor in determining what books we read, what art we enjoy, what music we hear. Without the protection that copyright gives to the creator and the enterpreneur, there would be little incentive to create and disseminate the works that forms the repository of our learning and culture.[5]

Broadly speaking, by copyright is meant an exclusive, legally secured, right to publish and sell the substance and form of a literary, musical, dramatic, and artistic works. Writers and artists contribute immeasurably to man's knowledge and to the quality of human life; their works, therefore, must be protected from infringement. Justice Read of the the United States, Supreme Court, put it like this : "The economic philosophy behind the clause empowering Congress to grant patents and copyrights is the conviction that encouragement of individual effort by personal gain is the best way to advance public welfare through the talents of authors und inventors in 'Science and Useful Arts'. Sacrificial days devoted to such creative activities deserve rewards commensurate with the service rendered". Any person who reproduces the work of the original author without his prior permission violates his right, called copyright. The same principle applies to making of copies of a record or a cinematographic film, whose authors are original producers of musical records.

L.R. Patterson "Copyright and the Public Interest".

Copyright also safeguards the interests of publishers and other processors who transform and package the works of authors so as to present them to the public. It sees that they must be afforded the economic returns that will enable them to perform their functions.

In essence. copyright is a legal device designed to provide the opportunity for economic reward that enables authors to expend their time and talents to creating the works of literature, music and art, and enables publishers to invest their resources and efforts in making the authors' works available to the public. Copyright seeks to achieve this end by giving to authors, who may grant to publishers or other producers, broad rights, of control over the various modes of reproduction of their works, or, at least, the right to exact payment for their reproduction.[6]

The notice of copyright is a great value to the librarians. It serves both as a convenient source of information about the copy-status of the work, and as an indication, given by the year date, of its recency; the year date is said to be particulary useful in works that appear in successive editions. Librarians, because they appreciate the value to society of work of authorship and an important role in the process of disseminating those works, can feel the close kinship of their own role with those of authors and publishers. At the same time, the other visage of copyright perceives that the social value of works of authorship lies in their use by the public for its education, cultural enrichment. and diversion. In the direct view of this visage are the scholar and researcher, the teacher and student, and the mass of people making up the reading, listening, and viewing public.[7]

Looking at these groups of users drives home the fact that it is not enough to have copyrtght stimulate the production of works of authorship; it must also foster the dissemination of those works and their availability for use. The right of control accorded to authors by copyright must, therefore, be tempered accordingly to avoid any undue restrictions on the use of their works. Librarians can readily see their intermediary role between the producers and users of works, and they may well refer to services in making works accessible to users as the end purpose of libraries.[8]

6. Abe A. Golman, "Philosophical Bases of Copyright".
7. Ibid,
8. A.I.R. Manual, 3rd ed. (Nagpur, A.I.R) V. 6.

The fundamental problem of copyright is how best to amalgamate these two aspects : the first, that the creator of intellectual work, who have employed their time for the service of the community, may not be deprived of their just merits, the reward of their ingenuity and labour, and concomitant economic support required by the packagers and distributors of thost works; and secondly, facilitating the public's access to and use of them.

Keeping in view the above two aspects, most countries of the world have copyright laws that seek to stimulate creative authorship and the public availability of intellectual works. In this context the copyright privilege in India is discussed.

Copyright Defined

Under the Copyright Act, 1709 (enacted in the reign of Queen Anne), copyright meant "the sole right and liberty of printing; but under the subsequent Literary Copyright Act, 1842, it was extended to include copying by other means than the press and the right of multiplying copies by printing, including the right to publish and sell. Obviously, "copyright", before the enactment of the Imperial Copyright Act of 1911, meant the sole exclusive right of multiplying copies of a book by printing or otherwise and it extenned throughout the British Dominions. It did not include the performing right in dramatic and musical works.

In 1911, the law of copyright was codified in England and was made applicable to India as well. Under the provision of this Act; the Indian Legislature was empowered to modify or alter its provisions by the requisite legislation. By virtue of this power, the Governor-General of India enacted the Indian Copyright Act of 1914 (Act III of 1914) with certain modifications in the Act of 1911. After India became independent, this Act was suitably revised and became the Copyright Act, 1957.

The Indian Copyright Act 1957

Meaning : 14(i)

For the purposes of this Act, "Copyright" means the exclusive right, by virtue of, and subject to the provisions of this Act,—

(a) In the case of a *literary, dramatic* or *musical work*, to do and authorize the doing of any one of the following act, namely :

—to reproduce the work in any material form :

(i) to publish the work;

(ii) to perform the work in public;

(iii) to produce, reproduce, perform or publish any translation of the work;

(iv) to make any cinematograph film or a record in respect of the work;

(v) to communicate the work by radio-diffusion or to communicate to the public by a loud-speaker or any other similar instrument,

(vi) to make any adaptation of the work:

(vii) to do in relation to a translation or an adaptation of the work any of the acts specified in relation to the clauses (i) to (vi);

(b) in the case of an *artistic* work, to do or authorise the doing of any of the following acts, namely :—

(i) to reproduce the work in any material form

(ii) to publish the work;

(iii) to include the work in any cinematograph film.

(iv) to make any adaptation of the work;

(v) to do in relation to an adaptation of the work any of the acts specified in relation to the work in clauses (i) to (iii)

(c) in the case of a *cinematograph film*, to do or authorise the doing of any of the following acts, namely :—

(i) to make a copy of the film;

(ii) to cause the film, in so far as it consists of visual images, to be seen in public and, in so far as it consists of sounds to be heared in public;

(iii) to make any record embodying the recording in any part of the sound track associated with the film by utilizing such sound track;

(iv) to communicate the film by radio-diffusion

(d) in the case of a *record* to or authorize the doing of any of the following acts by utilizing the record namely .

(i) to make any other record embodying the same recording.

(ii) to cause the recording embodied in the record to be heard in public;

(iii) to communicate the recording embodied in the record by radio-diffusion,

Sec. 14(2)

Any reference in sub-section (1) to the doing of any act in relation to a work or a translation or an adaptation thereof shall include a reference to the doing of that act in relation to a substantial part thereof.[8]

The Indian Copyright Act of 1957 brings into force a new body of copyright law to suit modern and up-to-date conditions prevailing in the world and particularly in India which is developing slowly but steadily. The Act has wroughted radical changes in the law of copyright. It was enacted to protect literary, dramatic, musical and artistic works as the Act of 1914 did, but the language and phraseology derived from the Act of 1914 have not been blindly followed, but mostly discarded, substituting entirely new provisions. Obviously, the Act contains revolutionary changes.

Beside protecting literary, dramatic, musical and artistic works, the novelties of the present Act are manifold, viz., affording protection to films, broadcasting and radio-diffusion, and provision for voluntary registration of copyrights—none of which was the subject of the former Indian copyright enactments.

The other distinguished features are that the Act has established a copyright office. It has also appointed the Registrar of Copyrights, and the Copyright Board with powers akin to the Performing Right Tribunal as established under the U.K. Act of 1956 with powers for settlement of certain disputes or objections concerning the public performance of copyright works with powers to grant compulsory licences, including t e power to grant translation rights of copyrights works under certain conditions and circumstances. It must, however, be noted that copyright does not extend to ideas. plots, dramatic situations and events. Rather it is limited only to the form of their expression.

India is a member of two International Conventions on copyright (1948) and the Univeasal Copyright (1952). Both these conventions were revised in Paris in 1971 whereby special concessions were given to the developing countries to enable them to issue compulsory licences for reproduction/translation of books of foreign origin for educational purposes.

The Indian Copyright Act, 1957 which came into force on January 21, 1958 was amended in August, 1983 with the specific

8. A.I.R. Manual, 3rd ed. (Nagpur, A.I.R.) v. 6.

purposes of (a) incorporating the provisions of the Paris Text of 1971 of the Berene Convention concerning the grant of compulsory licences for translations and reproduction of foreign works for required educational purposes; (b) providing adequate production to author's rights (Sec. 19 A); and (c) removing administrative drawbacks and other lacunae experienced in the administration of the copyright Act, 1957. The copyright (Amendment) Act, 1983 came into force w.e.f. 9 August, 1984.

The Copyright Act was further amended in 1984 in order to check the problem of wide-spread piracy in India. Provisions have been made in it to combat piracy by making punishment for various offences more stringent. Infringement of Copyright has been made a *cognizable offence.* The Act provides for enhanced punishment for the infringement of copyright, namely imprisonment upto 3 years, with a minimum punishment of six months, and a fine upto Rs. 2 lakh, with a minimum of Rs. 50,000. The Act came into force w.e.f., 8th October, 1984.

Copyright and Challanges of Modern Technology

Reprography

How far is the reproduction of documents or parts thereof permissable through reprographic techniques under the Copyright Act. The Indian Copyright Act grants exclusive right over his work to the author during his life-time and 50 years after his death. But under the heading of "fair dealing" and copying by libraries, documentation and information centres under specified conditions, making of photocopies and micro-recording of documents for the purpose of research and private study does not tantamount to be an infringement of the copyright. The specified conditions are that the copy will be used for private study and research and that one copy is supplied to one person. Also, that the cost of copy must be paid by the receipient, who will sign a declaration that the reprographic copy will be used for personal research. No limitations are proposed on the extent of the reprographic copy, and no declaration is required if the receiving institution is a non-profitable body. Finally, the reprographic copies are not for sale, except at cost price.

In this context, one may recall the findings of A.L.A. Copyright Issue Committee report in Jan., 1964.

—That making of a single copy by a library is a direct and natural extension of traditional library service.

—Such service, employing modern copying methods, has become essential.

—That the present demand can be satisfied without inflicting measurable damage on publishers and copyright owners.

—Improved copying processes will not materially affect the demand for single-copy library duplication for research purposes.

Computer

The advent of computer has made remarkable changes in the pattern of information storage and retrieval. Computer enables storage of complete texts of books including encyclopedias, periodicals in the data-base which can be retrieved at the push of a button. Computer programme has been accepted as a "work" in the copyright sense and is eligible for protection under the copyright law of a country as "input" to computer is definitely reproduction of the author's work How can the copyright owner control the use of his work stored in the computer memory is being argued at national and international levels.

Radio/Television

The radio and TV constitute sound and visual-broadcasting by wireless. By and large, the programmes on radio/TV are intended for the national audience of the broadcasting organization. The royalities due to the copyright owners are accordingly determined.

CATV (Community antena) begins when people who can't get TV reception from the other side of the mountain or the tall office building join together to put one high antena and convey the signals to their homes by wire. On the theory that this device constitutes another broadcasting station of a sort, some copyright owners, especially in music, have sought to collect a second series of royalties. Their argument simply is that distribution of their programmes by cable is aimed at an audience different from the one for which the wireless broadcast was intended; and as such their claim for a separate royaly. In litigation carried to the U.S. Supreme Court, it was decided that there was no legal claim for a second royalty on the theory that the copyright Act does not give the copyright owner absolute control over every use of his works and that the CATV broadcast was not a "performance".

Essentially, a CATV system no more than enhances the viewer's capacity to receive the broadcaster's signals; it provides a well located antenna with an efficient connection to the viewer's television set. But at the international convention, the CATV has been defined as communication to the public which rightly belongs to the copyright owner under the copyright laws of many countries.

Setellite Broadcasting

It is a wonder of the twentieth century. Broadcasting transmits signals through the air and these are directly received by the receiving equipment. But the satellites are equipped with receiving and transmiting apparatus. They receive progromme—carrying signals from the broadcasting organisations and beam them back to earth to the ground-stations, established in the territory of the broadcaster. As the satelites are not yet able to regulate the down ward beam so as to confine it to the national territory of the original broadcaster, these can be picked up by the programmes relayed through their own network in their own territory without paying any remuneration to the original broadcaster. An international convention called 'Satellite' convention was adopted at Brussels for providing safeguards to the right of the broadcaster for regulating his broadcast programmes via satellites.[9]

As for the problems posed by modern technology to the rights of copyright owner, it has now become an absolute necessity that :

—national laws on copyright should be updated so that they contain adequate provisions to safeguard the interests of copyright owners in their original creations;

—adequate provisions must effectively be enforced through a well-planned enforcement machinary;

—penalities prescibed in the statute should be enhanced so that these prove effective deterents to the violators of the copyright law[10].

A Critical Appreciation

Copyright is man's property in the fruit of his brains recognized and protected in all civilized legal systems in the modern

9. M L. Chopra, "The challange of technology". *The Hindustan Times*, May 16, 1982.

10. ———"Copyright in India".

world, including the communist countries. The law of copyright was first concerned only with preventing reproduction of copies of books. The subject-matter of projection extended over the centuries to dramatics works and now to literary and graphic works, mo'ion pictures, sound recordings, broadcasts and television performances. It may embrace, in the years to come, many more things (viz., computers' inputs, satellites' broadcastes) and the considerable changes in the rules governing infringements of copyright both in the international and domestic fields as the technique of copying may advance or the forms of human art may vary.

Nonetheless, it is necessary to note that Kalidasa, the great Indian poet and dramatist, could not have written the world-famous play "Abhijnana Shakuntalam" if he had not substantially copied the story from the *Mahabharata* World of literature would have been poorer if the court in England had issued an injunction restraining Shaskespeare from copying and adopting the plots of others !

Readers of modern books are familiar with the symbol © accompanied by the name of the copyright proprietor and the year of first publication followed often with words like "All rights reserved. No part of this book may be reproduced or utilized in any form or by any means, electronic or mechanical, including photo-copying, recording or by any information storage or retrieval system, without permission in writing from the Publishers".

Few questions can be legitimately raised over this claim : Why buy a book if you can't use it ? What is the use if you are not allowed to read it and commit what you read to that most magnificient of all means of storing and retrieving information, he human brain ?

Another notice by the publishers prohibts libraries from putting a permanent binding on a paper back book : "For copyright reasons this book may not be issued to the public on loan or otherwise except in its original soft cover". This prevents the binding of a book.

The problem becomes more acute when a book goes out of print and is not available on sale. A serious scholar may be willing to pay for a photocopy of the whole book. Can a publisher claim copyright if he cannot make copies for sale ? Many librarians,

11. Justice G.N. Vaidya, in his "Foreward" to the *Law of Literary & Dramatic Copyright*...by R.R. Dadachanji, 2nd ed. Bombay, 1957.

therefore, firmly argue that the privilege of copyright should carry with it the responsibility for making copies readily available.[12]

The laws of copyright all over the world tend to balance fairly and reasonably in the public interest the universal temptation to copy what is worth coping with the just necessity to protect whatever is worth protecting, for reasonable periods, in the literary and other works of human brains or talents. The terms of protection and the definitions of infrigement are being re-stated in law to achieve from time to time world uniformity and to preserve and promote the quality and richness of human life and culture. This makes the subject universally dynamic and fascinating.[13]

Closely connected with 'Copyright" is the question of *Legal Deposit* which may be discussed.

Delivery Of Books And Newspapers (Public Libraries) Act 1954

To preserve the literary works of a nation 'Legal Deposit', variously termed as "Legal Deposit Act", "Copyright Deposit" Copytax or Delivery of printed copies has come to stay in most of countries. Of course, this idea owes its origin to the French King, Francis I, who by his ordinance de Montpellier of 1510* made it obligatory on every printer and publisher in the country to send a copy of each newly printed book, free of cost to the Royal Library. With the passage of time, however, the idea has spread throughout the world and has been cultivated by the goverments for developing their legal deposit/national libraries, and India is no exception.

The Delivery of Books (Public Libraries) Act, 1954 was enacted by the Government of India "in order to promote libraries in India and to encourage scholarship, it is considered necessary to build good libraries, and for this purpose, it is desired to acquire not more than four copies of books and publications in India. One set of books so acquired will be deposiled in the National Library, Calcutta, and the remaining three sets will be utilised for important Libraries".

In this Act, the term "book" includes every volume, part or division of a volume in any language and every sheet of music, map, chart or plan separately printed or lithographed.

12. Charles F. Gosnell "Copyright".

13. Vaidya, Loc. cit.

*Some put it as 1514. 1516.

The Act was amended by the Government to include newspapers in 1956 because the newspapers but more so periodicals also contain highly useful nascent information and thought. The public libraries which were granted the privilege of legal deposits by this Act were as under :

—National Library, Calcutta, for the Eastern Region.

—Central Library, Bombay for Western Region.

—Connemara Public Library, Madras for Southern Region.

—(Proposed) National Central Library at Delhi for Northren Region. Since this library has not come into existence, this privilege of "copyright" has been conferred on Delhi Public Library, Delhi,

The enactment of the Act proves the sincerity of the Government of India for the development of libraries to emit knowledge and encourage scholarship.

The privilege of legal deposit, however, raises two problems. First, because "the dust of today may be the gold of tomorrow" no selection of material received under the right of legal deposit can be practiced, and this raises the problem of storage with sufficient ease of access when items are required. Secondly, there is a conflict between preservation and use. Preservation presupposes that use should not cause deterioration and that the legal deposit material should be used for reference not for loan.

In this context, one is constrained to record that the legal deposit libraries in India suffer from both these problems. There is heavy deluge of Indian publications in these libraries creating organizational problems. During his personal visits to two of these centres, the author saw the books lying unclassified, uncatalogued and unsystematically arranged, probably for want of adequate staff. The newspapers have been dumped in an underground hall in one of the centres and being eaten away by vermins. Much of such material is being used for bonfire rather than disseminating information. In National Library of India legal deposit material is being issued. It may entail the loss of an irreplaceable document.

The Act has made it obligatory for every publisher to deliver at his own cost four copies of the publication to four libraries within thirty days of its publications. The Act provides for penalty upto fifty rupees for contravening this provision or the fine may be equal to the value of the book. Only the conscientious publishers may be sending the books. The unscruplous may ignore the Act, particularly in case of the the books of Arts and Science which are highly priced. If noticed, they may like to pay a fine of rupees fifty or the price of the book as decided by the courts— a lengthy and combursome process.

It is, therefore, desired that the provision of the Act be made more stringent so that every publisher may deposit the copies. Lending of legal deposit materials may be discontinued; the alternative is the provision of a photocopy or microfilming service.

25

LIBRARY, COMPUTER AND PAPERLESS SOCIETY

Believe it or not, admit it or not, the computer has come to stay with us. No other single technological development has had the same impact on our lives in such a short time. Forty years ago computets had been heard of as a new and bewildering innovation. Few people had seen one, even fewer used them, and fewest yet understood them; definitely no one envisaged the revolutionary change in the envinronment which they would bring about.

Airlines, hospitals, large commercial organizations, the telephone networks, transport-networks, major cities and governments depend entirely on computer power; and libraries and information centres are no exception in the use of this powerful tool. It is a great aid in collecting, organizing, storing, retrieving, and disseminating the great volume and the varied forms of information and knowledge materials now being produced.

Historical Prologue

Many people are acquainted with punched cards and their use as a means of input data and instruction to the modern digital computer. What is probably less known is that the idea is by no means a modern one. In 1812 Charles Babbage (an English mathematician), began working on a machine designed to calculate and print mathematical tables, using punch c ards to input data. But Babbage had to abandon his work after a decade of experimentation and instead turned his attention to an even more ambitious device, his 'Analytical Engine'. This device was also a failure simply because the engineering knowlegde required to build so complex a machine was lacking and did not come along until the dawn of 20th century.

Nevertheless, despite his failures many writers hail Babbage as the poineer in conceiving the idea of computer. Of course, his ideas lay dormant for more than a century, still the successful dovelopment of the first electronic computer in the 1940s rekindled an interest in his work, and his genius has at last come to be recognized.

Babbage's machine was purely a mechanical device, and even if it had worked perfectly well, it would have appeared uncreditably slow as compared with the modern computer. It was in 1946 that the first machine to calculate at electronic speed was built at the University of Pennsylvania. This was ENIAC (Electronic Numerical Integrator and Computer) which weighed some 30 tons and incorporated 18,000 vaccum tubes in its construction. ENIAC could perform calculations about 1000 times faster than any previous device, and yet its crude switchgear and limited storage capacity made it slow and flexible.

Keeping in view the necessity for increasing the speed of the computer it was necessary to device a method whereby both data and instructions as to what to do with the data could be stored in the computer itself, and both could be proccessed at electronic speeds. Also, the computer would be far more flexible if it could modify its own instructions, taking one course of action rather than another depending upon the results of the current calculations. In 1949, EDSAC (Electronic Delay Storage Automatic Calculation) was invented at the Cambridge University. Simultaneously EDVAC (Electronic Discrete Varible Automatic Computer) was launched by the Pennsyvania University. These two machines contained improvements mentioned above.

Technological advances in solid state physics gave rise to the second generation of computers. Whereas the first generation used vaccum tubes, which were bulky and produced considerable heat, the second generation used transistors, which were smaller, much more reliable and produced less heat. The third generation computers were developed with equipment featuring microminiaturized circuits thin film memory and improved internal core store. These developments reduced the size of computers, increased their capacity and produced operating speeds measured in billitonths of a second (the nano second).

A distinguished advance is the introduction of high level languages to programme languages (viz., ALGOL, FORTRAN,

BASIC, COBOL and Plan) enabling the programmes to communicate wi·· the computer in such a way that the programmes are more or less readable in English as in the case of COBOL, or more or less standard mathematical notation as in the case of ALGOL and FORTRAN. To be more elaborate, FORTRAN and ALGOL are the best known science and technology oriented languages. Basic is a simple programming language designed to be assimilated in a few hours; and COBOL is a language designed for business data processing. PL/1 combines the algebraic features of ALGOL with the business data processing features of COBOL. PL/1 has been relatively popular in library and information systems.

All these developments have led to the production of very powerful machines which, in addition to being able to compute, have two very important characteristics :

—they are able to store large amounts of data;

—they are able to select and present items of information at terrific high speeds.

These two characteristics enable the machine to be used in a large variety of applications, many of which require little if any computing power. They are becoming more and more 'information handlers' rather than calculating machines.

Computers are emerging as revolutionary tools for the processing of data electronically.

In fact, the computer can be taken as an extension of punched card equipment. It can do storing, selecting. merging and performing arithmetic operations as the tab equipment can do, but can do it at much greater speeds, and with great volumes of data. In brief, computer equipment might be thought of as grown up tab equipment.

The computer also has a much larger memory or information storage capacity than tab equipment. Likewise, the computer is able to take in information and write out information much faster. The sequence of machine operations for each step of the job is still established initially by a human. In other words, the use of machinery for the processing of data requires human data formated and analysed for such processing, and requires machinery suited to the task or tasks of a specific installation.

In a strict sense the computer could be defined as a device for manipulating numbers very rapidly; or a device which can accept information, process it, and suppy the results of the processing. This leads us to study types of computers.

TYPES

One recognizes, two types of computer :

(a) ANALOGUE; and
(b) DIGITAL.

(a) Analogue Computer

The Analogue Computer accepts information for processing in physical form, i.e. in terms of weight, volumes, electric current, etc. It can translate temprature, flow, speed, altitude, voltage and other physical varibles into related electrical quantities, and for this purpose it uses electrical equivalent circuits. It performs calculations on the incoming information according to a pre-determined pattern which is usually represented by mechanical, electromechanical or electronic units.

Nevertheless, such a computer is built to satisfy a particular requirement of processing information based on scientific data. This makes it unsuitable for library requirements which necessitate that data be processed and recorded in quite a different way.

(b) Digital Computer

The eletronic digital computer is by for the most powerful and versatile computing tool. It operates at a terrific high speed, making it practical to undertake calculations of much greater scope than ever before possible.

The digital computer processes information in a unitary form, i e. letters, symbols and numbers. All calculations or processing of the incoming data is carried out in digital form, and the results are printed-out in conventional letters, symbols or numbers. The digital computer is, therefore, a general purpose computer particularly suited to libraries.

The digital computer can be catagorised under two main groups keeping in view their mode of operation : (1) Batch Processor; (2) Real-Time Professor.

1. Batch Processor

It has been designed to process data accumulated into groups or batched over a period of time. Seen as a collection of machinery or hardware, such a computer consists in general of four elements each performing a different logical function. These four elements are : (i) Store, or main Memory; (ii) Control Unit; (iii) Arithmetic and Character-Handling Units; and (iv) Input/Output devices.

1. The store or main memory of the computer holds items of information for as long as they are needed. This information may take the form of instructions constituting a programme* to be executed, or data in which that programme is to operate.

   The storage of a computer is not unlimited; it holds some maximum quantity of data. These data may be in the form of characters—usually, the digits 0 to 9, letters A to Z, and a number of special characters, such as*,. —+() $ @ # and %. The capacity of these memories is often used as a measure of the power of the computer. Storage devices are also rated by the speed with which data can be withdrawn from them,

2. The second part of a digital computer is called Control Unit. It examines the instructions contained in the programme, and sends out the electronic signals which instigate the required operations. In other words, the function of the control unit is to interpret the instruction given to it by the operator, and then schedules and directs the activities of all the other electrical circuits and units of equipment in order to get the job done. It acts as the foreman.

3. The arithmetic and character-handling units function as the mill or processor which, under the leadership of the control units, operates on the information given to it and performs all of the logical testing and processing required. It can perform arithmetic operations such as addition and multiplication, as well as many logical operations such as comparisons, and the extractions of selected portions of a string of number or characters.

4. There are a number of input output devices controlled by devices control units, by means of which information

*Programme is a series of instructions which are devised by computer manufacturer or by the computer user. It tells the computer what operations to perform and in what sequence.

is communicated to and from main memory. Instructions can be issued by the programmes to read from or write to these devices.

In batch processing, data is collected in batches, and then the supervisory programme determines the most economic time at which to process it. Batch processing is particularly suitable where regular runs are required, but may have serious drawbacks for a system when it is important to know instantly who has borrowed books.

The output devices may either be in print or in machine readable print—on punched cards, paper tape or magnetic tape.

The input device refers to a coding system for the representation of the data.

(2) Real-time Processor

The main difference between a batch and real-time processor lies in the input and output units used. Real-time processors are intended to handle the large volumes of data associated with the batch method. These units are connected to computer enabling direct entry of data into the processors. Such connection is termed *on line* and the units so connected are called *terminals*. The terminal is often an electric typewriter on which an operator can key an information or a question, within a given format, without the need to present such information on machine readable media such as punched cards. A programme will control the processing of data received from a terminal, adding it to files on backing store* or referring to the data already on file for transmission back to the terminal. As with the batch processor, all calculations take place in the working store. This type of processor provides a quick response to interrogations which may be received from a number of terminals.

Videotext Technology

The Union of Computers and home television has generated a new breed of technology designated as Videotext or Teletext. Videotext combines the use of a here-and-new technology with a universal terminal (a multi-purpose television receiver), simplicity, use of existing widely distributed communication channels and potentially low cost. Videotext systems consist of three components :

(1) The transmission medium;

*The *backing store* ean be regarded as the filing system for the computer. The store comprises a magnetic recording medium such as tape or disc., etc.

(2) The distribution system; and

(3) The terminal/ancilliary devices.

A number of innovative approaches involving various combinations of transmission technologies like telephone cable, TV cable, satellite, optical fibres have been recommended for videotext delivery. Personal computers may become one kind of home terminal device used to approach videotext system. The users could store and interact with the information inexpensively through their home computers. They could get hard copy by using home facsimile or printing devices.

Vedeotext Services

Britain is credited with generating videotext services. There are in operation in Britain three videotext services : (1) CEEFAX (BBC), (2) ORACLE (ITV), and (3) the PRESTEL (formerly known as Viewdata). All these three services have been developed in Britain as a means of disseminating current information with the help of television equipment with special devices incorporated or attached.

CEEFAX and ORACLE are quite similar in nature. They involve selection of information by the user, using buttons on the decoder. Each is intended to offer about 200 pages of information—a page being the amount which can be shown on a television screen (220 characters) Colours are used, as are graphic displays. All the information for all the pages is sent by the same channel as is used for the television programmes, and simultaneously with them. It is transmitted continously[2].

Prestel Service

The heart of the Prestel service is a large computer located in London. It stores information which is available to anyone possessing a telephone and a specially adapted television receiver. The adaptation enables the television receiver to display printed text and simple graphic data conveyed to it from the central computer by means of the telephone lines and already available television service. A.E. Cawkell gives a description of the Prestel system as under :

2. L. Donnelly, 'This is Ceefax' *Assistant Librarian*, V. 69, no. 1, Jan., 1976, p. 2-4.

The system's potential for storing and retrieving information is virtually limitless. To receive specific data the individual subscriber to the service uses a small held push-button device, not unlike a pocket calculator, which is linked to the telephone/ television adaptation, and with it instructs the computer to display required data on his television screen.

The PRESTEL service is different from CEEFAX and ORACLE services in that its signal is carried from the British Post Office to the User's television set via telephone line; and selection of particular pages of information is made by using the buttons on a push-button telephone.

In PRESTEL, by contrast to CEEFAX and ORACLE, only the information demanded by the individual user is transmitted, and it is transmitted only to him and only for the time he wants. Selection is carried out by computer at the transmission end.

The significance of this service is that CEEFAX and ORACLE can make available only as much information as they can send at any one time. PRESTEL, on the other hand, can make a much large amount of information available as it is using a large number of channels—the telephone-lines from all the individual users and also because at any one time it sends only a small part of the information available. It makes wider and deeper selection of information available.

Finally, the PRESTEL service system is interactive. It means that the subscriber can not only receive data from the centre but also respond to it with replies. The individual subscriber, can thus initiate a communication. But CEEFAX and ORACLE are not interactive services, and this fact coupled with the limitations upon the amount of data it is possible to present in any 'magazine', shows that this type of service is best suited to a constantly up-date news, sports, financial information, and current events presentation and public service anouncements. The range of information to be provided by the PRESTEL system included news services, weather reports, current affairs, consumers news, sports coming events information including various games and pastimes[3].

3. Donald Davinson, *Reference Service* (Clive Bingley, 1980).

View Phones

Closely connected is another service known as VIEW PHONES. In enables the people communicating by telephone to see not only each other but also the objects to which they need to refer; and facsimile transmission so that copies of documents can be transmitted immediately to the subsriber.

The British General Post Office is rendering another service known as CONFERAVISION. It enables meetings and conferences to be held by groups of people sitting in their own offices in various parts of the country. This service indicates the revolutionary changes that communication technology is bringing about in all walks of life.[4]

The other videotext services worth mentioning are West Law and LEXIS in U.S.A. for legal information; the application of CATV (USA) etc

Role of Computer Technology in Libraries

According to J.P. Henley the following are some of the features that could be expected of the systems :

1. Elimination of much of the drudge of purely clerical work.

   The computer is expected to reduce, not increase, the work-load involved. It is fast, and ideally suited to the repetitive type of operation involved in following a standard procedure, e g, compiling lists or producing filing cards for catalogues.

2. Elimination of erros in entering the system.

   A computer does not get tired, and should not make mistakes. The detection of errors is crucial to the system, e g., once a book has been misplaced it may be very difficult to retrieve the information it contains.

3. Consistency within the system.

   In dealing with a mass of information, the human element is bound to obtrude, e.g. the same document could be classified in different ways by different people. The machine is accurate and 'remembers' all the details involved.

4. Speed of response to queries.

4. Ibid.

5. A computer should be able to consult files more quickly than a human, and to provide up-to-date information on the latest accessions to the library.

The computer can handle large mass of information in what by human standards is incredibly quick time. In general, the more work that can be given to computer, the more efficient and economic a tool it becomes.

In addition a machine does not get tired, can repeat operations again and again without any reduction in performance and does not commit mistakes. But it requires that the information it receives and the programmes it executes be completely accurate. A system is only as good as the data and the programmes used.

The computer can be applied profitably to the following library works :

(i) Circulation

The entire circulation process can be computerized. The computer based system of circulation performs all the activities related to registration of members; issue of library borrowers cards/tickets; charging and discharging of documents; updating of record file, reminders for overdue documents; maintains statistics and keep record of daily transactions.

The information stored on videodiscs can be transmitted economically; they encourage the library use. Pergamon's "Video Patsearch" enables the users to access the patents displayed on a special screen of the user's terminal within two seconds of the information being given.

Laser scanners for reading barcoded labels are now available that are reliable enough to permit patron self-charging.

The minicomputers and micro processors can be used for automation of circulation, providing the capability for direct use by users and minimizing involvement of library staff in routine enquiry procedures.

Through on-line networks, a user can order document from his terminal and the document can be sent to him electronically. On-line access to libraries' book holdings will be a routine.

The developments in the areas of communication will provide the opportunity to obtain library documents directly in the home or office. Even at present, the request for inter-library loan can be sent on telex service for quick action.

(ii) Acquisition

Acquisition has been defined as the discovery, searching, selecting, ordering, and receiving all kinds of library materials.

The entire acquisition process,—preparation of order cards, sending orders to vendor/s, updating the record file, verification of books with order file and invocies, printouts of received documents and non-supplied documents as well as making payments—, can be automated using computers. Computer quickens acquisition programme.

Swihart and Hefley enumerate the role of computer in the acquisition section under the following heads.

Ordering :

1. Generate order form content, where possible, e.g., if ordering additional copies of a previonsly ordered title.

2. Print purchase orders to suppliers,

3, Print bid list or generate trial title list for the library selection committee.

Receiving :

4. Control items received.
5. Notify requesters that their book has arrived.
6. Control overdue items from suppliers.
7. Generate automatic follow-up notices.

Paying :

8. Print and control payment cheques to suppliers.

9. Determine optimum date to pay suppliers, in accordance with the terms of the purchase order.

Input to Cataloguing :

10. Generate selected input data to the cataloguing department.

Administration :

11. Maintain reurns of the number and type of acquisitions activities performed by the staff.

12. Maintain control of expenses for purchases within the budgets.[5]

The minicomputers and micoprocessors can be used in the library for stock-acquisition process. The minicomputers and micro-processor can also be used for on-line acquisition by utilizing the service of on-line data bases. These computers are well adapted for improvement of on-line data base searching, thus, enhancing the access of wide range of information sources. But with the increase in the on-line networks, there is every possibility of drastic curtailment of physical growth of library collections. The catalogue of the library will not be restricted only to the coverage of documents present within four walls of the library. The library's on-line catalogue also promises access from points located outside library. Library can provide access to an increasing variety of on-line databases, including non-bibliog[h]aphic databases and on-line services, make databases accessible in an on-demand "pay as you go" mode and this cost very much less than the purchase of the hard copy of the entire data-base. This makes databases readily accessible to those libraries which could not afford to purchase the printed equivalents. Libraries can avoid purchasing materials that are rarely used.

The advances made by communication technologies facilitate quick access to large data bases. The ordering of books can be done on-line for acquisition. The impact of electronic mail and the videotext on the acquisition programme can hardly be over-exaggerated.

According to Christopher Evans "Death of the Printed Word," books on chips would be available by late 1980's. The libraries will begin to acquire the electronic books, mostly reference materials, alongwith other forms. Consequently the acquisition of present reference books will decrease.

A videotext system eould greatly enhance a library's information sources by providing access to a large number of databases. The ordering of books or supplies might be performed through videotext systems. The specialized publications like technical journals, abstracts, indexes, reference books, news-papers will be available on videotext forms. Many of the electronic journals

5. Stanley J. Swihart and Beryle F. Hefley *Computer systems in libraries* (Wiley Becker & Hayes, 1973).

will come up out of the specialised conference as setup within computer network. Satellite communications serve to make information sources more internationally accessible than even before.

At the minimum level, the application of computer in the acqisition can result in some of the following advantages :—

Many repetitive jobs are performed at one and the same time, thereby reducing the number of staff members for the acquisition section;

an accurate, up-to-date and automatic information is made availabte about the latest position of each order placed for a book, thereby helping to avoid unnecessary duplicate ordering; and

an accurate, up-to-date and automatic information is made available about the latest position of each head of the book fund.

(iii) *Perodicals*

The acquisition. processing and control of periodicals can be effectively manned with the help of computers. The following works of the periodical section are highly amenable to computerization :

(a) Ordering and receiving of periodicals;
(b) processing of invoices;
(c) classification and cataloguing;
(d) maintenance of a complete holdings list for serials;
(e) a list of current receipts;
(f) various indexes of titles and articles;
(g) lists of periodicals being bound;
(h) non-receipts lists:
(i) expiration of subscription lists;
(j) reminders to vendors/publishers; and
(k) list of new additions.

The fundamental advantages of a computer-based periodical system are :—

(a) Providing a better access to the records of periodicals to the staff;

(b) providing better service to the users, and more accurate records; and

(c) helping in providing Current Awareness Service and SDI service.

Nevertheless, one should not loose sight of the huge expenditure involved for the conservation of the existing manually operated periodicals file into the magnetic tape.

Secondly, development costs of a computer-systems are exhorbitant which are lost over a time.

Thirdly, the cost of continuing operation of computer-based periodical system is not less than that of the manual system. Rather, in some cases, it may be ever double of the latter.

Fourhly, in the computer-based system the time taken for checking a title is not less than that in the manual systems.

However, some developments in the computer application to periodical systems may improve the matter. One may bear in mind the steps taken under the projects to formulate standards for periodicals and formats :—AACR—1967; AACR :—Chapt. 6—1974; International Serials Data System/Canadian National Centre (ISDS/Canada)—1974; International Standard Bibliographic Descriptions—Serials (ISBD-T)—1974; International Standard Serial Number (ISSN)—1973; International Standards Organization Format for Bibliographic Interchange on Magnetic Tape—1973; Library of Congress MARC—Serials—1970, 1974.

The Library of Congress MARC Serials Format serves as a communication format for periodicals between a reporting library and a receiving library in respect of the following :

1. The National Union Catalogue symbol for a reporting library.
2. Information about periodical holdings.
3. Period for which the periodicals would be available.
4. Retention of information.

Periodicals standard format provides guidelines for giving bibliographical description to identify a periodical. It is given in the front cover of the format in the order on the next page :

Title; volume number; issue number in Arabic numerals; date of issue; code number of the issue for the identification of a periodical; and an abbreviated title.

(iv) Reference/Information Services

The potential applications to library and information services of cable television (CATV) are vast. Larry E. Harrelson hails

CATV "as exciting, relatively new communications medium which has great potential." It is apparent, continues Harrelson that cable television offers public libraries the opportunity to expand two of their traditional services—children' work and adult education. As communication professional, librarians have an obligation at least to be aware of developments in this area.

CATV takes the form of a television camera used in the library to transmit a picture of a page of a reference book, illustration on other material over the cable network. Any user who telephones the library with an enquiry and who has a CATV facility can be shown material relating to their enquiry on their own television screen at home. Commenting on CATV service Kenneth E. Dowlin writes :—'The marriage of libraries and television is in an exciting prospect and I hope that libraries will enter into it willingly, rather than in front of a shotgun.' But a sobar analysis comes from B.L. Kenney and R. Esteves who argue that 'Video/Cable technology can help librarians extend their services to groups not adequately served by more traditional means. It can reach those citizens who are not print-oriented and bring information to them by use of a medium with which they are already familiar, the television set. Video-tape is the means for recording and presenting information, cable communication is the means of the transmitting it to clients' homes'. Nevertheless, S. Goldstein is somewhat sceptical about the role of cable television. He writes that doubts have emerged during the past two or three years. The experience of some libraries, especially in the area of cable television, seems to be one of withdrawal or at least caution, as plans have gone awry. In a broader sense, most libraries still do not regard video as relevant to their mission or in some cases as even a legitimate library programme. This warning by Goldstein must be heeded to. But the speed at which the communication technology is advancing it seems obvious that before the dawn of 2000 A.D. communication technology will have advanced to the point that will enable individuals to possess portable miniature communicator/computers giving them the facility to link directly into data banks which if, available or accessible at all at present, are usable only through the agency of a library or other information system.

The impact of PRESTEL service is likely to be great on reference library and information centre. It may be used for some reference enquiries currently brought to the libraries, or telephone to them. The addition of home instructional programmes in the form, as it were, of televised corresoondence courses with instantly recorded responses to questions asked by the use of the interactive terminals is a possibility. When married with coventional video and audio-broadcast programmes for such operations as the open University, PRESTEL is revealed as a powerful information providing medium outside the conventional library networks and information centres.

It can also be maintained that business libraries and the information bureaus of commercial organizations and government departments will need to instal CEEFAX and ORACLE services, if only to obtain up-to-the last minute financial news, and news on current events, which is a ticklish area for the librarians to handle. In short, the advent of such services will supercede the role of traditionally known reference service.[6]

In this age of literature explosion, the computer can store large quantity of up-to-date source matrrial in readable memory and also index and abstract this material. The IBM—3854 mass storage system can contain the text from 2 lacs books. A big computer might keep on-line 40 or more data bases containing over 10 million citations. The OMEX data strip can store large data. This means that in the future not only the citation in the Engineering Index but all of the articles that they represent can be stored and retrieved using computer. The potential of videodisc for information storage and retrieval is simply bewildering. The National Library of Medicine (USA) has been developing videodiscs capable of storing entire data base of MEDLARS. Pergamon's programme "Video Patsearch" service in United States contain 8 lacs U.S.A. patents issued since 1971 are stored in 8 videodiscs and can be retrieved using computer terminals. Some libraries in USA are already using videodiscs for reference service. Short of the push-button library, the really great "promise of automation is to be sought in the projective aspects the opportunity it affords to analyse the reference process and redefine reference service."

(v) Information Storage and Retrieval

The computer based information storage and retrieval system consists of two types of works :

6. Davinson, Loc. cit.

First is the classification and cataloguing of the documents forming the input of the system and transferring the catalogue entries on to the magnetic tape and getting its print-out (if needed.) This catalogue-on-tape can be always updated by adding new entries and correcting the old ones.

The second part consists of :—(i) recording the users' querries and transferring them on to the tape and updating them; (iii) making for a dialogue between the user and the computer through the medium of the language understandable by the computer; (iii) transferring the selected entries on to the magnetic tape, and (iv) getting a print-out of these entries, providing a copy to the user. This job is performed with the help of input and output devices.

A break-through in the development of computer-based information storage and retrieval system emerged from the scientific mind of Ranganathan. In his thought provoking article "Doc-Finder"[7], he outlines the fundamental components and operations of a computer-based document retrieval system in which the basic operations include the classification of subjects of documents and questions according to a freely-faceted classification scheme. The system of document finding using a computer in the experiments in DRTC is an integrated system.

Ranganathan preferred the term 'Doc—Finder' to term 'Computer'. The term "computer" was improvised when electronic machinery was improvised. Since there is no calculation involved in the finding of documents pertinent to a given query, the term computer was not used.

The computer-based information storage and retrieval system has distinctive advantages of :

—facilitating retrospective search and selection of documents as and when needed by a user;

—supplying periodically current awareness service and SDI;

—facilitating the acceptance of user's queries in the language of the system;

—furnishing the users with a documentation list or a retrospective bibliography for his use;

—producing the service in an automatic and expeditious way;

7. S.R. Ranganathan, "Doc-Finder", *Lib. Sc., with a slant to documentation,* v. 5, no. 4, 1968.

The best examples of the success of computer-based information storage and retrieval system are provided by the working of MEDLARS, UNISIST, INIS, AGRIS, CARIS, SPINES, ISORID, DEVSIS, INFORTEM, NISSAt, etc.

(vi) Cataloguing

It is true that no library can boast computerized reference service, the computer has proven an excellent method for high-speed filing and print out information which heretofore had to be laboriously copied from catalogue cards or indexes. This is simply the processing of data or data processing.

MARC (Machine Readable Cataloguing) has been a brilliant example of the application of computer in cataloguing, to library and information professionals for over two decades.

Although the Library of Congress MARC (now US/MARC) was the pioneer in the field, it is now only one of some 20 national or regional MARC formats that have since developed. These range from the Latin American MARCAL in the West to Japan MARC in the East, and the Norwegian format (NORMARC) in North, SAMARC in South Africa. These formats all differ from one another to a greater or lesser extent, despite their Common American Origin[8].

MARC began in the Library of Congress. The pilot project ran from 1966-68; sixteen libraries participated. Distribution of records began in September/October 1966, with a weekly service from November 1966. By June 1968, the L.C. had distributed over 50,000 English Language monographs records. The purpose of MARC I was the automation of cataloguing, indexing, searching and retrieval functions. During this period MARC II was developed (MARC I being the pilot format). It was planned to cover all materials but for ease of handling the system began with books.

MARC II officially began in March 1968. Distribution began for all English language material (not just US imprints as was originally the case) providing a weekly tape of some 1,000 records. Thereafter, other documentation lists began to be issued, including formats for other materials over the period 1970-73. In 1972

8. Anthony Long. U.K. and U.S. MARK : A brief history and compison. *Jour. of Documentation* (V. 40, no.), March, 1984.

films records were distributed, by 1973 records for serials, maps and French books, and by 1975 German Spanish and Portuguese materials.

In 1973 the Library of Congress (L.C.) thought of having Machine Readable Form of Bibliographic Information (MARBI). Guidelines for format changes were formulated, and a two month notification of changes became the norm. Finally, planning began for handling authority records for names in 1974 and subjects in 1976.

In between 1968-69 plans were made for the retrospective conversion of older records. The issues dealt with included the setting of priorities for conversion, the maintenance of current standards, the use of MARC records from other sources and automation of the National Union Catalogue. One of the chief benefits from this was the development of automatic format recognition programmes which began to be used for current cataloguing in 1972. B tween 1972 and 1980 the Library of Congress issued some twenty addenda to books : a MARC format 5th ed. Over the years these changes included extensions to the range of government publications coded, changes in the format of Library of Congress card numbers and the adoption of a character position in the record label to give the descriptive cataloguing form for full, partial or non-ISBD data content. Some changes in format were made in the light of AACR—2.

MARC II is a subscription service. By subscribing to this service, a library can acquire, in machine readable form cataloguing data for American as well foreign publications. In fact it means that the Library of Congress catalogues the documents, records the data on magnetic tape and supplies libraries with copies of the tapes. From the magnetic tape they can then produce printed catalogues of their collections or entries on cards and various kinds of bibliographies by using a computer.

Let it be remembered that the usuability of MARC servies presupposes the existence of a centralized or cooperative classification and cataloguing system on the pattern of the Library of Congress. It also requires that the participating libraries of the programme should instal computers and appoint programmers in their respective libraries.

The British National Bibliography became interested in the possibilities offered by US MARC II. The Fotolist system had been used since 1959 but magnetic tape seemed a more useful method of production.

BNB MARC (now UK MARK) is using a modified format for producing its weekly lists, cummulations and printed cards.

MARC and similar types of machine readable formats provide possibilities for the production of general and special bibliographies. There is a probability that the catalogues of the great libraries of the world might be converted into machine readable form using a MARC type format. A by-product of this could be subject bibliographies, restricted in terms of language, period, country, kind of material and the like. And if the national bibliographies of all the countries were fed into the computer, our dream of having an international biblography might come true.

The following merits of the MARC system have been highlighted by the library scientists :—

(a) A centrally prepared catalogue can be distributed to the receiving libraries in a machine-readable form.

(b) Despite the mounting collections, the catalogue can be kept up-to-date without hiring additional staff.

(c) The production cost of card catalogue on the computer MARC system is lower than that of purchasing the L.C. catalogue cards.

(d) The MARC tapes can be utilized for selecting, ordering and claiming unsupplied books without any additional cost.

(e) The MARC tapes can also be used for producing conventional card catalogue by the subscribing libraries.

(f) The MARC data can further be used for producing book catalogues.

Among the limitations of the Machine-Readble Catalogue the following are worthy of note :

(i) MARC record for any title is almost similar to the conventional bibliographic record, and as a result it has all its limitations.

(ii) MARC format will be limited, at least for some years to come, to the English language books because the character set is awefully limited in respect of special characters and diacritical marks.

(iii) Time gap between the creation of MARC record and a catalogue record copy by the participating library, which is inherent at present in the existing card production methods of the L.C., will not be removed until and unless both the cards and tapes are prepared from the same machine—readable record.

(iv) Expenditure on account of machine time by the participating libraries will go on mounting in light of the weekly shipment of more than 1200 records or about 62,000 records yearly reading about 15,000 ft. of magnetic tape.

Notwithstanding its limitations, the MARC project is a commendable achievement and is likely to revolutionize the field of cataloguing. This service is receiving increasing attention all over the world,

The COMARC (Coorperative Machine Readable Catalogue) project is another venture of the Library of Congress. Under this project the L.C. receives records based on L.C. cataloguing representing those of selected libraries which have converted their catalogues into MARC format. These records are checked with the official catalogue of the L.C. for updating and redistribution through the MARC distribution system.

Catalogue Cards

A computer can perform the following types of clerical work in the preparation of eatalogue cards :

—assembly and arrangement of data in the body of the catalogue cards;

—automatic generation of file points, based upon data in the body of the card;

—printing of one or more copies of a card to go into one (or more) catalogue/s; and

—sorting the finished cards into alphabetical order for later manual interfiling into an existing card catalogue.

Advantages

The computer can print the cards in a correct number of copies in a fraction of the time that would be required under a manual method using typewriters, multiliths or other semi-automatic approaches.

The computer can sort the printed cards into the correct filing sequence in a fraction of the time that would be required to sort by human means.

When cards are lost, it is easy to generate new ones because the master data is still in the computer and can be retrieved whenever new cards need to be prepared.

In library systems where there are several branches or where new branches are being opened, the computer automatically prepares a set of cards for each branch.

The proper filing point is automatically generated at the top of the card (Swihart and Hefley).

Book Catalogues

The book catalogue usually is more than the individual cards in a card catalogue arranged in a bound volume. Thanks to the computer it is now possible to have individual upto-date book catalogues in the division and branch libraries; physical pressures on a massive card catalogue arrangement have been *eased; automated* output eliminates tedious, frequently inadequate filing; and catalogues of all major libraries may be readily accessible to every one. Patrons find the book catalogue easier to work with; the entries, one after another on a printed tape, give a better idea as to the contents of the catalogue, and the book catalogue can be carried to convenient work area. The computer has mostly done away with the demerits of the book catalogue which relegated it into oblivion and made place for card catalogue.

Computerised Indexes

The computer seems particularly suited for indexing and a number of both non-profit institutions and private companies have entered the field. The poineering work in this field is credited to H.P. Luhn of IBM, who based his work on the statistical analysis of words with the idea that the words which occur most frequently in a document are of most significance in subject description. Generation of alphabetical indexes of various kinds, e.g., KWIC, KWAC, KWOC, KWIT and PRECIS on the basis of feature headings is a fine example of automatic indexing.

The subject indexing of documents for providing a subject approach is essentially an intellectual task. But certain phases of indexing such as generation of cross references and display of index entries are amenable to computerization. In this context, the National Library of Medicine, Betheoda (USA) in its indexing system by the use of computer gives a fine example. It employs computer for the preparation of an indexing system known as MEDLARS (Medical Analysis and Retrieval System) used for the retrieval of citations to medical literature.

The MEDLARS system receives, stores, sorts and prints references to medical literature. Trained indexers prepare unit records for input into the computer and each unit record contains among other information, a complete bibliographical information as needed in any standard entry. The machine is fed and programmed by human labour; and the chief benefit of its computerization is the large number of citations that it is capable of manipulation saving much time. MEDLARS system enables the National Library of Medicine to publish the monthly *INDEX MEDICUS* very promptly. MEDLARS was a great break-through in an automated information retrieval. Coblans writes that "August 1964 issue of Index Medicus will probably go down in history as one of the incunabula of the twentieth century". That is a great landmark. It not only aims at bibliographic control based on a complex electronic machine but also combies it with high speed composing and printing devices. But for literature search, this system continues to be as expensive as any other computerized mechanized system. Nevertheless, it has tremendously speeded up the retrieval of citations to medical literature. The device can prrnt 600 pages, with 14,000 citations in 16 hours and the MEDLARS has made it feasible to cut down the total operational time of 22 days to 5 days per month.

In brief, MEDLARS was put into operation in 1964 to produce printed version of INDEX MEDICUS. In 1968, *on line* searching of MEDLARS was achieved. MEDLING (MEDLARS ON-Line) was started. This on-line service includes citations from index medicus and other indexes, e.g., population index; index to dental literature, and international index.

Inter-Library Loan

The use of computers and the latest devices of telecommunication have accelerated the speed providing material demanded on inter-library loan. Such a system includes the use of devices like those of—

1. Tele facsimile transmission
2. LDX (Long Distance Xerox).
3. Tele type
4. Telex
5. INTREX
6. Computers.

1. Facsimile transmission is a speedy transmission of printed pages from one point to another, using electronic devices. Facsimile system will operate over any available communication medium including telephone line, overseas cases, radio, micro-wave and COSMAT satellite. David Heron has emphasized that the telefacsimile should be preferred due to its being faster, less expensive to operate rather than teletype writer manual system.

LDX is certainly more fast and large facsimi e system than telecopier. This system provides 135 lines per inch and electro-static printing on paper. It consists of scanner, transmission link and a printer. The scanner and printer are comparable in size to Xerox 1914. Xerox telecopier works on telephone line and costs less. Only single pages can be transmitted. It is speedy but costly.

Teletype is an equipment being used on a wide scale in library operations specially to solve the problem of inter-library loan. It hardly takes 15 minutes to deliver a book from the branch concerned. This is more famous in U.S.A. and Canada. The message is produced in a visible form.

TELEX is being increasingly used in British libraries to speed up the inter-library loan service. TELEX (teleprinter exchange) transmits the information expeditiously. More than 200 libraries including university libraries have installed TELEX having about eight thousand libraries included in their networks. In brief, it is a teleprinter which speeds the inter-library loan exchange information by instant transmission of the written word. This system has proved highly useful to researchers as it reduces delay in their research works by providing the desired materials promptly on demand. This is being used increasingly by the National Lending Library for Science and Technology (now a division of British library).

INTREX (MIT project) stands for Information transfer Experiment. This device facilitates expeditious fascimile transmission of full texts of journals, books, reports, theses and other research materials requested on inter-library loan.

ULTRAFEX was used to transmit microfilmed text of GONE WITH THE WIND—→from Washington's Wardmen Park Hotel to the Library of Congress in 2 minutes and 21 seconds by microwaves. This system used cathode ray scanner and printer.

Critical Appreciation

One may review the advantages of a computer based system :—

1. Many of the routine and repetitive tasks can be performed by the machine thus saving man's hours.

2. Many of the required tasks can be performed simultaneously as a by-product of the once-for-all accession procedure which has to be performed whatever the system.

3. A measure of control is obtained over the performance of the system, and message to take action can be easily generated.

4. Inter-action with the machine adds a consistency and uniformity, and eliminates the risk of losing information once it has entered the system. This is gained at the expense of an added precision and proficiency needed at the input stage from library staff; and the need to find a suitable retrieval technique and interface medium to communicate with the machine, which is available to library staff and users alike the is source bibliographic information.

One could say in simple words that the application of computers to libraries will mark the dawn of a new era of progress and development by :

—Making everything effortless.

—Disseminating information pin-pointedly, exhaustively and with the speed of light.

—Helping save money.

—Helping in the transfer of computer programes from one place to another without extra expense.

—Economizing in future programming because programmes can be converted to later generation services by sharing computers with others.

As a corollary of above, if several libraries can have computer systems, link-ups between different libraries can be achieved on a computer network. This kind of national utility in computing can provide the kind of time-reducing facility that leads to a more efficient service to library users. Not only can libraries keep in touch with each other and exchange news and ideas, but the whereabouts of an obscure document requested by the user and not available on the premises can be discovered immediately by interrogation, and an order dispatched via the computer link-up. This means that the annoying time-lag while an item is located and 'on order' can be cut to a minimum, and hence the need to stock large quantities of little used material is done away with.

Nevertheless, the meritorious role of computers in information storage and retrieval has not gone unchallanged. The critics like Ellsworth Masan writes : Anyone who computerizes at this point in time is hitching his wagon to a falling star. Computerizing library operations at present and projected costs and with feasible results, is intectually and fiscally irresponsible and managerially incompetent,

However, Ellsworth Mason's criticism of computerization is refuted well by H.D. Avram. She writes that Masan certainly is correct in criticizing much of what has been done in library automation but is wrong to draw the conclusion that all efforts are misdirected and doomed to be failure. A poorly designed project does not prove that library functions cannot be automated : it proves that a disaster is a disaster, It is true that large amount of money have been expended and there have not always been positive or meaningful results.

The basic consideration for mechanizing libraries is the explosion of literature in science and technology and the failure of conventional methods for retrieving information, though, this 'failure' is often assumed without concrete efforts to prove it. But to be a success, the machine should satisfy some eriteria :—

1. It should be able to handle vast amount of information.
2. It should be superior in economies and performance, to existing manual systems.

3. It should be capable of satisfying users' needs as and when they arise.
4. It should be accessible to a number of different users at the same time.
5. It should be capable of being operated by all users without the intervention of the third party unless desired.
6. It should be possible to link the system into other existing systems.

S.R. Ranganathan critically examines the role of the computer. He writes : "The computer is one of the versatile forms in which electronics can help mankind. We must derive all the benefits it is capable of giving us. It can relieve us of much of repetitive routine work and thus it can release man to higher kinds of work-particularly creative work. Its versatility is being increasingly extended year by year". Ranganathan, then, raises the most significant question—whether computer can do classification and cataloguing also, or whether it can, with the Programme Assistant, do all the necessary document search. Can classificationists and classifiers abdicate their function and depend on the computer to take their place ? They cannot. It is because, classification involves judgement—judgement of the subject of the document in all its facets and arrays manifest in it. This cannot be done by the statistical analysis of the words in the document, which alone the machine can do. The computer cannot exercise judgement. Therefore, it will have to be done by humans. It will have to be so until the computer can have the faculty of judgement built into it. Moreover, the computer cannot give its best service unless the "Programme Assistant" has a sound and sufficient knowledge of the latest practice in classification.

Ranganthan further maintains that the computer can give better service in literature searching only if the name of the subject can be fed into its class number, individualizing it on the basis of a Freely-Faceted Scheme for classification, instead of naming the subject in a natural language or even technical terminology. To put it in Ranganathan's own words : "It is only when classified catalogue is constructed on the basis of a well-developed Freely Faceted Classification, and the Computer is developed so as to take into its memory the main entries of such a catalogue, that the relative cost and viability of document retrieval with the classified catalogue and computer, respectively, can be compared on a sound basis. So for as the time required by a reader for document retrieval is concerned, the difference will be negligible." The computer "brain" has yet to catch up with its human counterpart. Veering around Ranganathan, E B. White wryly observes that computers "are deficient in humor, they are not intuitive, and they are not aware of the imponderables."

Notwithstanding its limitations, Computer offers a method of controlling vast amount of information and disseminating it pinponitedly, exhaustively and expeditiously, thus, easing the burden of over-worked librarians, and of quite literally revolutionizing the future patterns of library service. However, computers should be greeted as ready slaves, not as masters. Lawrence Auld in his article "Preventing Failure in Library Automation" commends the following 10 practical ways for making the library automation a success :

1. Motivation based on clearly defined goals.
2. Effective communication between librarians and computer people.
3. Logical and complete analysis of the system; carefully executed programmes, and abundant documentation.
4. Constant feedback of the system's day-to-day operations to the systems' analysts and programmes.
5. Flexible and adaptable programme.
6. A competent computer operator.
7. Computer machinery capable of performing the tasks required.
8. A high priority for computer services to the library.
9. Adequate budgetry support; and
10. Positive long-term commitment by top management, both now and in future.

Electronic Publishing : Paperless Society

The advent of computer has wroughted a revolutionary change in the methods through which recorded information is dissemimated. Ever since the dawn of civilization, it is for the first time that it is possible through computer to disseminate written messages to a scattered audience without reproducing the messages in multiple copies and distributing the copies on vast geographical areas. In a computer-based, electronic information system recorded information is stored in the memory of a computer to which users with their own video display terminals have electronic access. Users of an electronic system who desire to retain a message have the option of transferring it electronically into their personal computer-based files. This is what F.W. Lancaster describes as a "paperless information system".

F.W. Lancaster in a way is a pioneer in the field of electronic publishing. His writings on the future of libraries and paperless information systems have stimulated the librarians to reassess the role of the library as an institution and the role of the librarians as an information specialist. He maintains that in the developments affecting the information profession in the last 3 decades, two major trends can be recognised as predominant. The first is simply the rapid decline of the artifacts-particularly the printed books—as the primary device for storage and transmittal of recorded knowledge, and the replacement of these artifacts derived from many sources and presented in many different formats. Virtually all of these data are now being made accessible electronically. The second trend is increasing diversification in the profession—information specialists no longer need to function within the four walls of library—, the computer terminals, in effect give these professionals access to vast electronic libraries.

In his latest work "Libraries and Librarians in an Age of Electronics" Lancaster attempts to bring together his extensive writings on evolving technology, the paperless society, and the implications of this revlution for libraries. He reviews the technological trends of the last 20 years in telecommunications and computer technology for applications-such as information storage and retrieval, electronic mail, teleconference, inter-active television, and publishing and forecasts that libraries will use microforms, on-line databases, videodiscs, teletext systems or even books or serials on silicon chips to provide their users with the information they need.

From cover to cover Lancaster's book is pure emotionalism, but it is a beacon light to a profession that is losing its way in a slough of despond. Donald King in his rrticle "Electronic Publishing and its implication for Libraries", too, emphasizes the roles of online retrieval system and elecronic processes involving published literature. But King does not believe that a completely electronic and paperless society is going to happen largely because of economic and political considerations as well as the lack of incentive to change on the part of communication participants.

Eugene Garfield in his article "1985 : New Technologies for Libraries" observes that "the role of the librarians will in no way be diminished by these new electronic system and services they offer. Information manager will gather, collate, arrange and make information available. Librarians will guide the information seeker towards its efficient use.

A more balanced analysis comes from the pen of K.E. Dowlin "The Electronic Electric Library" (1980)' in which it is predicted that the future activities of the libraries will revolve around :

(i) Providing access to complicated or seldom used data bases ;

(ii) providing community conferencing and message centre programmes ;

(iii) providing on-line access to information on library resources ;

(iv) providing access to community information locations for referals ;

(v) providing access to the resources in other libraries via networking ;

(vi) providing access to highly demanded information and material viz , computer and videotext; and

(vii) providing access to electronic resources for those who cannot afford to have computers or terminals,

To conclude, the merits of computer based, electronic information systems for certain purposes are real and compelling. One merit is intellectual. Whereas print-based systems freeze data in a particular configuration, computer based systems enhance the malleability of recorded information. Data stored in computer memory can be updated, corrected, rearranged, or otherwise altered practically at will, and new data are interpolated into existing data. Users of such systems can manipulate and interact with recorded data, arranging the data to suit their individual needs. These features give computer-based electronic information systems powerfull capabilities that print-based system can never hope to match. Computer-based electronic information systems appear to be a convenient and potentially economical means of distributing recorded information. Also, capabilities inherent in their technology enable computer-based electronic systems to meet information needs that print-based data systems cannot satisfy.

Nevertheless, the survival of information in an electionic environment becomes an intellectual and technological problem in its own rights. The malleability of information that is one of the major advantage of computer-based electronic systems has its corollary the potential transience of information. Nothing inherent in the technology of computer-based electronic systems ensures that information in the system will survive.

The very fact that recorded information in a print-based system exist in tangible form is a matter of considerable intelectual significance. The very characteristics that make printed books and journals cumbersome for the dissemination of information are a positive advantage when it comes to ensuring the survival of information. The intellectual content of a printed book or journal cannot be erased or altered. It is likely to survive as long as the book or journal itself survives as a physical entity (Gordon B. Neavill). In an electronic environment, we are likely to lose much of the retrospective documented information which we now take for granted.

F.W. Lancaster, in his article "Mission Possible—A Future Information System" creates a scenario for potential furture publication of journals in electronic form, from report writing and text editing at individual terminals to acceptance via electronic mail by publishers, to receipt of journals information at subscribers' terminals. He asserts that the scientist will receive much, if not all, professional mail in electronic form, will communicate with professional colleagues through personal terminals (electronic mail and teleconferencing), and will publish through electronic databases. Electronic journal will be issued by professional societies and commercial publishers will have editors and editiorlal boards, policies and standards for acceptance of contributions, and some form of referring.

Let us not, however, forget that the rate of introduction of electronic publishing will depend on the convergence of telephone, data transmission, and computer technologies. This convergence will in turn depend upon political, social, technological, and commercial factors. The first two will retard the rate of change while the latter two will accelerate the rate. The libraries are in a difficult position to initiate drastically because they are by and large impartial providers of information on demand. It is hard to believe that the modern library will be replaced by the electronic library. However, the advances in technology are likely to affect its operations. Technology will lead to a more complex and more diversified information environment, rather change services and goals in any radical way.

What about the future of the book? Elie Simaour in an article "A Look into the Book of the Future" diagnoses the problems of printing. Paper and labour costs have been rising so steeply as to jeopardize the long-term survival of the book as a major element of modern civilization. But he emphasizes that "the book has attributes of such convenience over every other existing form of information storage and retrieval that it is not likely to be easily superseded." One is quite hesitant to endorse the prediction that the printed book will be replaced by the electronic book or journal. Of course, the electronic book or journal is a practical proposition from a technological point of view and that the economies of electronic publishing will make the electronic book attractive in the market, yet the question arises whether the reading public will purchase electronic books on a scale necessary to make them an attractive purchase. It is too early to predict what will happen but cautions are needed about predicting a premature death for the printed book.

The book remains the best learning tool that the human race possesses; and will remain the best and most effective for decades to come. The book is a very special form of commuuication. It is unique and it will persist. The revolution in the use of printed materials such as paperback books, off-prints of journal articles, facsimile or microfilm copies, and other duplicated materials has received much less publicity, and probably has more long term significance for higher education than television and teaching machines. The programmed textbook may combine some of the advantages of conventional texts with those of teaching machines. The book is "the most nearly perfect learning machine than mankind will ever know, a superb learning instrument which can outpace and outperform any of its so-called new competitors. It will be with us long after they have disappearched[8]. It seems certain that the book—far from being condemned to death by the advent of electronic computer—is likely to be in greater demand than ever before.

In brief, despite the tremendous advances made by the computer, the book cannot become obsolete any more than the poem or the novel can become obsolete, because the book, though in not quite the the same sense as a poem or a novel, is an excellent intellectual construct; it embodies thought and expression beyond a certain indefinite minimum length, and as men think and express themselves in writing, books will be written and published. But one should not forget Gardner who writes that the "future of the book is already being questioned and as a repository of purely factual knowledge is already being superseded by the computer...videotape contains an even greater threat to libraries, as we know them, than the computer, and the videorecord could wipe out the use of whole areas of printed material. The death of the book has been predicted many times and the patient is still healthy. But don't let us close our minds to the possibility that the printed word, as a source of information could be replaced"[10]. The Parry Committee rightly declared that the book" is a wonderfull instrument which can be used almost anywhere". It is hard to conceive of any remotely recognizable system of higher education in which books of some kind did not play the major part, and it is highly doubtful that either the educationtsts or publishers seriously anticipate such a possibility. In the Open University, where radio, television and tapes will be in greater use, the aim is to encourage students to read more books more fruitfully. Since books provide perhaps the best invention yet for becoming educated, it might be that we should put a large share of our creative energy into inventing ways of making books more effective for evoking creative behaviour.

9. D. Melcher. *The Book-seller*, Oct 4, 1969.

10. F.M. Gardener *The Book-Seller*, Oct., 10, 1970, p. 2043.

26

LIBRARY AND MASS MEDIA OF COMMUNICATION

Communication

The word "communication" comes from the Latin verb communicare meaning "to talk together, confer, discourse, and consult, one with another". It is closely related to the Latin word *communitas* which means *community*, *fellowship* as well as justice in men's dealing with one another. Through communication men share knowledge. information and experience, and thus understand, persuade, convert, or control their fellows.

Mass Communication

Mass communication is a specialized profession; it is also a highly developed technology. Their fusion constitutes the modern mass. media. But equally important in Indian context is the informal, society based and non-specialized process of person-to-person communication. Successful use of man communication, in fact, hinges upon the integration of the formal institutions of communication and the social processes of communication to the point that each must respond with sensitivity to the other. Once we reach this conclusion, it is easy to determine the role of mass communication in the dissemination of knowledge and information. Mass communication creates awareness of various aspects of life that are not part of the personal experience of the receipient of the message. It also create knowlegde of desirable things faster than these things themselves can be produced.

Mass Media

Mass media pertain to those instruments of communication which can present identical, one way messages to large number of persons who are often physically separated. The identical messages may be printed in newspapers, books, or magazines. They may be recorded on films, videotapes, or magnetic tapes They may be presented as live television or live radio. Television and motion pictures both represent major mass media.

The mass media instruments are broadly catagorised as under :

1. Audio Materials : Radio, language laboratories, tape and disc recordings, telephone, tele-lecture, sound distribution systems.

2. Visual Materials : Illustrated books and self-instructional materials, pictures, photographs, flash cards, flip books, charts, maps, posters, exhibits, bulletin boards, magnetic boards, models, mock-ups, film-strips, slides, transparencies, silent films, chalk boards, drawings, cartoons, flannel-graphs, diagrams.

3. Audio-Visual Materials : Television, films, videotapes, sound filmstrips, printed materials with recorded sounds, study trips, demonstrations.

Mass media function in relation to actual events, policies and programmes, and in terms of the need and objectives that the nation sets before itself. It is extremely lively subject and has been offered for study to people in various disciplines—engineers, physiologists, psychologists, sociologists, linguists, teachers, librarians. In the following pages, we shall study the role of radio, television and cinema in the dissemination of knowledge and information to masses.

Press

The press means daily newspapers, periodicals, journals, and magazines which are sold by the millions everyday. Press is an integral part of modern civilization. It has rightly been hailed as the Fourth Estate—the very soul of democracy. It not only informs and educates but it is also the inspector of public affairs and the custodian of people's rights. A newspaper gives free expression to the views of the editor on current issues in national life and keeps the people up-to-date of burning problems.

Newspapers do not create a community, but they do much to define its boundries and to maintain its unity. They produce common interests and attitudes. Similarly, a local newspaper helps a town or a district to keep its sense of identity. In the broadest sense, too, newspapers underline the unity of the modern world by reporting complex, light-hearted events that take place thousands of miles away. In earlier ages we should have heard remours of such things only months afterward. But, newspaper should not serve a party but the whole of a nation. It is the beacon light of truth and justice. It is the watch-dog of democracy and a great defender of liberty. It can make and unmake leaders. Through news, views, cartoons and special articles it can change public life.

Although newspaper is the strong sword-arm of justice but the editor is likely to mar its importance as the most objective agency for disseminating information because of wrong intertations. In the communist countries the press is controlled by the governments, it is, in fact, their mouth-piece. In the developing countries, the press sometimes faces censorship when the governments find it hostile to their policies.

The press must enjoy freedom and liberty. It may freely criticize planning, and failures just as it welcomes successes, disseminates information about trade, commerce and helps shape public opinion.

Press is one of the important mass-media for disseminating latest information. But newpapers are a medium for entertainment as well as for information only for the literates; for the illiterates we must seek alternatives.

Electronic Media

The face of the modern society has been tremenously changed by the rapid growth of three novel means of communication—radio, television and films. Today, these three inter-related media, the off-shoots of the technological revolution that began in the nineteenth century command audiences of a size that would astonish our grand-parents and probably surpass the dreams of the individual scientists from whose research they sprang.

Radio, television and films have evolved—and are still evolving—languages of their own. These languages are the means by which moving pictures and the spoken word capture and hold our attention. By-passing the conventional languages of the written word, they use their own language, grammar, punctuation, and figures of speech to make an immediate impact on the audience. They are equally effective as means of communication in highly literate and illiterate societies. And because they reach into all our lives all three media may be instruments of persuasion and change.

The electronic media affects the minds of the people so intimately that through them the people almost sense, as it were, a feeling of actual participation in national affairs. The activities of mass media follow closely the developments in various fields, informing people, reacting to policies and creating the social climate in which development and nation building programme can take place. They cannot operate in a social and political vacuum, nor do they deal with abstruse philosophies. Mass media are everyday dealing with problems that affect the destiny of the nation and, in the wider context, of humanity at large. It will be better to discuss the contributions of each in transmitting knowledge and information.

Radio

By definition, radio is the transmission and reception of signals by means of electric waves without the use of connecting wires. It is one of our most important methods of mass communication. Having been invented by G. Marconi in 1901, radio has grown from a gadget to almost permanent fixture in every home.

Radio has become an important limb of mankind because it has added to the amenities of life by disseminating recreational and inspirational information. Radio can actually override the barriers of time and space by bringing for the masses on-the-spot information from Moscow, Addis Ababa, Hong-Kong, Washington, Ottowa or London. Physically the world has become a unity but mentally and spiritually our minds are not prepared for that unity. Radio can help us bridge the gap.

Radio has a great educative value. If properly conducted, it can serve as a medium of educating the common masses catering to various tastes, news, music, talk. Radio brings dramatic feelings into homes. It has the warmth of drama, the prersonal feelings of actors' presence whose voice or music can inspire deep, poignant emotions. Radio can be used to bring the voice of an authotity to the very door of the poor man. We can intervicw and record the ideas of doctors, engineers, M.P.s., religious leaders, librarians etc. It is, indeed, impossible to estimate the facilities which radio has provided to the common masses in different spheres of life—social, economic, political, cultural, educational, religious and commercial.

Since broadcasting is a hand-maiden of the government in majority of countries, the governments use this agency to impose their policies, programmes on the people. Can a citizen listen to radio broadcasts from anyother country without interference ? Probably not. Security reasons dominate.

Still the radio broadcasting is the most efficient and effective means of disseminating information to all alike. It has become a specialized medium catering to the varied tastes of the educated or illiterates or even the blind, living in metropolitan cities or in the far-flung dwelling places. It has become an inexpensive source of mass recreation, inspiration, information, education and propaganda. If properly used, it is sure to forge unity and educate the teaming millions. It can exert an immeasurable influence on their attitudes, appreciations, social behaviour, and power to develop critical thinking. In addition, radio provides self motivation, creative expression, and even the development of skills and techniques.

Closely connected technique of mass communication which is rather fascinating the minds of people as an agency for disseminating up-to-date knowledge is the television.

Television

Television is the most wonderful means of communication ever devised by man. It has an immediacy that spans time and space and brings to the viewing audience thousands of miles away historical events in the making, still pictures, films,objects, specimen and drama. It is a superb dissemination device. It has revolutionlzed human outlook in educational, social and moral spheres. TV combines the immediacy of radio with the mobility of pictures. It can transmit events as they happen via satellite, and its cameras can reveal new aspects of earth, sea, and and space. TV is unique in its power to capture life and to reproduce it in a hightly realistic way. With the development and acceptance of colour in television, we can expect even greater reality in this medium for the future. Manktnd, therefore, is greatly indebted to John L. Baird of Scotland who invented it, in 1926 and made it possible for the masses to learn sciences, technology, social sciences and humanities on the screen. But TV being a costly affair does not find a place with a common man as radio does for seeking information.

Radio and TV both mirror our day-to-day activities and there is, in fact, no alternative to them as an instrument for the distribution of a live event to millions of viewers.

Cinemas : Motion Pictures

The year 1456 (or 1447) is a great landmark in the history of modern civilization because in that year John Guntenberg took from his press a copy of the Bible (now preserved in BM), the first book ever to be reproduced by the art of printing. Within a short span of time, the printing press came to be looked upon as one of the greatest inventions of mankind. Today, it is impossible even to attempt to evaluate printing in terms of its contributions to modern civilization.

The twentieth century has witnessed the development of another epoch-making invention—the motion picture. This invention in the space of half a century has revolutionized the industry of entertainment throughout the world as it is coming to be recognized as one of the most dynamic of educative aids. Probably, in the years to come, the motion picture may even excel the printing press as a disseminator of information. In fact, cinematograph has helped in making cinema a temple of learning. It has become an important organ of modern civilization. It enables us to project on screen in rapid succession a multitude of pictures—living, moving, talking and breathing. In modern era of science, the great emphasis is given on cinema in educational, social, moral and political spheres. The cinema is a practical teacher and makes it possible for the people to study literature, history, economics, science in a novel way. Thus cinema is a powerful instrument for affecting cognitions, personal feelings, desires, perceptions, motives, values, needs, habits and drives of people by disseminating ideas and facts. People taught with films are better able to apply their learning than people who have no film instruction, is proved by researches.

We may say that Radio, TV and Cinema serve the same purpose—though, in different ways—to inform and to educate people with a view to growth-oriented development and to act as a *catalyst* for social change, and to fight against poverty and illiteracy

The mass media entertain, inform and teach; but they cannot gain—much less inform and teach—a mass audience unless they present their material in an entertaining way. In simple words, they can never afford to neglect their entertainment functions.

The introduction of satellite communication for conveying information will revolutionize the world in more than one way. It will help leaders to exchange ideas speedily on matters of mutual interest This will certainly add to the free flow of information. It is also likely to make more data available on which to base a decision.

Every boon has its limitations and free flow of information is no exception. Communication must be a two-way process and it will fail if the receipient cannot understand the message. It will fail, also, if there is lack of determination by one part or another to pass in or to receive, the information.

Many of the difficulties result from an inappropriate use of language, either oral or written. Many other barriers exist in the attitude held by people communicating or receiving information : attitudes which can include fear, derision, boredom and many other emotional responses that affect human behaiour. Who will share information pertaining to atomic and nuclear energy, the secrets of manufacturing sophisticated arms, supersonic jets. Such "top secret" information only comes out through illegal channels.

Notwithstanding its limitations, mass media is a powerful and forceful agency for the dissemination of ideas. The most vital function of a newspaper is to keep the people up-to-date by printing global news. It presents a picture, continuous and yet constantly changing, of the community it serves.

In India, in particular, radio is very powerful vehicle in eradicating social evils from the society and thereby promoting civil sense among the people. The malpractices in religion and other spheres of life can be eradicated, with its help. Of course, it cannot replace a temple, church or a shrine, but it can broadcast the lessons which have been given a great importance in those scriptures. Therefore, it can play a vital role in the general drama of human life.

It adds variety to class-room teaching. Listening to radio is different from the usual class-room routines and hence brings interesting variety. The participation of students in the broadcasting radio programme provides an outlet for student's ability and talent; develops better speech habits; provides an opportunity for student creativity, and stimulates a spirit of cooperation and responsibility.

Television can bring the world of reality to the class-room either through the immediacy of a "live" broadcast or as mediated through film or videotape. TV, moreover, can become a great equalizer of educational opportunities because programme can be presented over national, state wide or regional networks. Television can bring the versality of TV camera to the teaching process. It lets everyone look through a microscope at the same time; gives all the students of medical profession a good view of surgery; handles films and other changes from straight class-room presentation with a minimum of transitional difficulty. It lests a school or a college share its best teachers, rather than rationing them.

Similarly, motion pictures also educate. People learn from films. Films can be used for a great variety of objectives : increaring factual knowledge, teaching skills, teaching attitudes; in some circumstances, changing motivations and opinions. The use of effective and appropriate films results in more learning in less time and better retention of what is learned.

Films facilitate thinking and problem solving. People taught with films are better able to apply their learning than people who had no film instruction. Films are of greatest influence "when their content reinforces and extends previous knowledge, attitudes, and motivation; they are of least influence when previous knowledge is adequate, and when the film content is antagonistic or contrary to existing attitudes and motivation". Response to a motion picture is most intense, efficient and predictable when the pictorial content is subjective (personally related) to the audience. The closer the veiwer to the film is, the better he will remember and use what he sees on the film.

In brief : it is difficult not to believe that the communication of ideas can be greatly helped by the use of audio-visual aids. A mode of communication which makes both an aural and visual appeal, with the lecturer selecting the aid most helpful to him and his students, promises to be most successful than simple oral communication. Each type of electronic media has a unique contribution to make to the educational process. The new world of educational technology, incorporating as it does new media of communication opens up exciting possibilities for both learning and teaching. Edgar Dale, therefore, aptly said : "Our job is now to integrate these materials into a system of teaching to get balanced communication—speaking and listening, writing and reading, viewing and overt doing, and a balance in the media themselves."

Role of Library

A considerable amount of information is supplied to the public by audio-visual media of communication revolutionizing tradational methods of imparting information. Many libraries have realized the opportunities which new media provide for presenting the library and its services to the user, and allowing him to guide himself through the library at his own pace. There are examples of introductory films, video-tapes, tape-slides and growing cooperation in preparing audio-visual guides to the subject literature for use in library instruction and education programmes.

Radio and TV programmes have been arranged by many libraries (particularly by public libraries in U.S.A.) and with good results; and library use of a good book is often stimulated by local showing of the motion picture made from it.

In the field of information, we must note how audio-visual media function on a world scale. The pictorial method offers as important a means of understanding and expression as does the linguistic method; each is an agent for an understanding of the world; they can exert a decisive influence on the formation of artistic, scientific, philosophic and political values. In addition, they reveal the social problems of a particular time, indicate its underlying psychological trends, and reflect the mentality of a country by the degree to which they satisfy certain expectations on the part of the public[2]. The entry of new media materials into the library emphasizes the importance of the transmission of information in the educational process and of the role of the library in the communication of information needed by its users. A logical extension of the function of the library would, therefore, be to provide readers' access to information in all its various forms. The A.L.A. scunnictly emphasized that the "philosophy of library service that has evolved through the years can readily be applied to audio-visual materials. The librarian's ability to select, organize, aud service materials applies to all types of learning resources. The intelligent application

2. C.M. Iglesias, "Audio-visual materials and libraries", *Unesco Bull for Libraries*, (V. 12, 1969), p. 287.

of this ability will supply him with additional opportunites to influence and support the educational programs of his institutions". The library is the institution's information centre and information should be stored there on tape, film, and microfilm as well as the printed page.

The entry of media materials and methods both emphasizes the library's outward looking operations and adds a powerful dimension to the education it has to offer in the skill of disciplining information. Erickson correctly writes : "when print and audio-visual services are combined in one service organisation, then we have the true instructional media centre"[3]. The media materials and methods cannot only make any formal programme more effective, but can also assist individual users to find out for themselves.

For the foreseable future, books and periodicals will not disappear, they will be extended and supplemented. New technology will modify rather than revolutionize methods of treating information. Librarians are not just the keepers of documents, they must also be the interpreters who match the reader with the document through the handling of words and symbols. By their classifications, by their indexing they must contribute to that synthesis which presents each generation through its books, each culture through its artefacts[4]. The more varieties of information media librarians have in the libraries, the wider the range of experiences offered to their users.

In developing countries like India where an average person cannot afford to purchase a daily newspaper much less having radio, and TV, the presence of electronic media in libraries will enrich the cultural, intellectual, socio-economic life of the people, in addition to making them politically conscious. Unfortunately, our libraries are deplorably poor even in printed materials for want of adequate and stable finances; the provision of electronic media as a source of mass communication is a too distant a dream. But the media is strongly needed for throwing light on the advances made by the governments in the field of science, technology, industry, commerce,

3. C.W. Erickson. *Administering instructional media programmes* (N.Y., McMillan, 1968), p. 247.
4. H. Coblans "Words and documents", *Aslib Proceedings*, V. 23, (July 1971) pp. 348–49.

agriculture, irrigation, foreign policies, secularism, education to woo the people. And there is no better place for disseminating information through mass media than a library. The future belongs to those who prepare for it. and in order for the library to survive as an information source it must be prepared to supply total infomation in any format and to provide the facilities for its utilization[5]. This wiil tremendously change the concept of library as a static repository of books, and the librarian as a "glorified caretaker", and, the definition of the library as "a dry and dusty place where books are kept and which students avoid".

The effect of new media on libraries may be closely linked to that of automation : "A second major impact on libraries will result from radical broadening of the communications spectrum from print to sound to image. ... Because of the nature of libraries, non-print will at first only cause an extension in the variety of packages handled. But, like automation, the seeds for change in basic objectives are built into this process. The culture surrounding non-print media will tend to emphasize a different concept of content, communication and use".[6]

It is too early to emphasize that new media have marked the dawn of a golden era of library service, but they are definitely pregnant with unimaginative potentialities for mass communication. But the inter-relationships between print and non-print materials are so involved, and their futures so closely inter-linked, that librarians have a clear interest in organizing the newe rmaterials in close conjunction with the books with which they have been predominantly concerned in the past. When the story of libraries through the ages is written, the extension of its interest beyond the written or printed word to non-book materials appears to be logical as well as inevitable The new generation of iibrary users (in countries like USA) are strongly oriented towards audio-visual materials : They have been raised on television, radio, films, photographic slides, tape recorders and gramophone records. An entirely print-oriented institution will be alien and unfamiliar. It, therefore, follows that libraries must not be concerned only with books.[7]

5. W.J. Quinly. "Carrels for learning" *Library Trends* (V. 19, 1971), p. 473.
6. R.S. Taylor "Technology and libraries", *Educom* (May, 1970), p. 5 cf B.J. Enright. *New* media and the library education (Lond., Clive Bingley, 1972). It is an excellent work,
7. Ibid.,

27

PRODUCERS, DISTRIBUTORS AND CONSUMERS OF KNOWLEDGE IN MODERN SOCIETY

In the ultimate analysis of any social phenomenon, we are invariably concerned with the three aspects of the producer, the distributor and the consumer. An approach to an analysis of the social function of the library has, therefore, to reckon with the producer of knowledge (i.e. the authors and publishers); the distributor of knowledge (i.e. the library); and the consumer of knowledge (i.e. the reader).

Authors

The Authors are the key entrepreneurs in the industry of knowledge. They are responsible for the creation of intellectual and artistic thought of the document. The authors as producers of thought have had been in existence since times immemorial. Even before the invention of paper and printing, our great sages, philosophers, thinkers, priests and poets imparted learning in respect of religious scriptures, law and administration. They may be called as walking encyclopedias or travelling libraries. The modern author, however, produces knowledge with his own stamp : His ideas and theories are copyrighted and his discoveries and inventions given the government certificates in the shape of patents. The authors also generate knowledge through staging dramas, producing films and through radio and television programme.

Universities

The Universities and institutions of higher learning are the intellectual workshops for the authors to seek and cultivate new knowledge vigorously and fearlessly, The learned deans and academics produce thought. Through the publication of research works, treatises, monographs, hand books, papers, dissertations and organizing as well as attending seminars, conferences and workshops.

Valuable information appears in Ph.D., D.Sc., and D.Litt., theses. But theses are usually neither published nor covered by the regular indexing and abstracting services. Their procurement poses a problem. It is, therefore, necessary for the libraries to know the sources of location and procurement so that the information contained in them is properly utilized.

The papers and proceedings of the conferences, seminars, workshops and institutes organized by the teaching departments are circulated amongst the participants and sent to the libraries on demand. Since such material usually remains unpublished but contains valuable information, the libraries should make earnest efforts for the acquisition, processing and dissemination of information, contained in such unpublished sources.

Book Trade

Book Trade includes producers of materials (viz., printers, binders, and governments) and distributors of materials (viz., publishers, book-sellers, etc). These commercial organizations give physical shape to the thought produced by the authors. They produce materials in the shape of treatises, monographs, text-books, reference books, handbooks, manuals, periodicals, reviews or advances in subjects, indexing and abstracting periodicals, magazines, bulletins and books of aesthetic appreciation, recreation, inspiration and of religious values. And with the fast means of transport and communication at their disposal, the book-traders transmit both macro and micro knowledge (of seminal research, reporting, expository, elementary and informative value) expeditiously, with the sole motive of profit making.

Technical Trade Literature

The Technical Trade Literature is an important source of information for special libraries as it provides accurate technical information about products or material that are offered for sale. Since it describes and illustrates equipment, or goods or processes or services relating to manufactures, special librarians look upon the technical literature as an excellent source of information to be integrated in their collections. Trade literature is available in various forms—periodicals, pamphlets, books, trade catalogues, etc., and is free of cost. The most useful method of securing their procurement should be to find a place on the maling lists of the pertinent industrial organizations.

Industrial House

Big Industrial Houses have been showing an increasing involvement in the research in science and technology leading to inventions and discoveries. They have developed their systems of publication and communication. Patents, standards and specifications are types of materials emanating from these houses.

Another important source of information is said to be provided by 'House Journals' being issued by big business and industrial houses as gestures of good-will, welfare, or public relations, e.g., IBM Journal of Research and Development, Electrical Review, etc.

Governments

The modern welfare *GOVERNMENTS*, too, have now entered the fields for the development of science and technology to abridge the gap between the very rich and the mass of poor people. They have felt the need of setting up permanent teams of research including information service units to ensure a well-balanced and integrated development of the society in scientific, technological, socio-economic, religious and political spheres. It requires continuous research on large scale,—development research, pragmatic research, applied research, and pure or fundamental research. The modern government disseminates the information about its research and welfare activities through the documents issued by its various ministeries, departments, commissions, committees and other organs.

Government publications are authentic, reliable, up-to-date and invaluable sources of information useful for the scholars. Unfortunately, these publications are not available through normal book channels. Therefore, the scholars, the business and industrial organizations, usually remain deprived of this precious mine of information. Hence, steps should be taken for their distribution.

Semi-Government Agencies

Semi-government agencies (viz., universities, research associations, professional societies, research institutes, public authorities, congresses, councils, etc.) produce and transmit nasçent micro thought in the form of reports and proceedings of their meetings and delibrations at their conferences, bulletins, circulars, summary of debates, policy decisions, etc. Most important are periodicals and research reports containing articles of the authoritative, fundamental discovery type, in their specific fields. News journals published by society often include papers of review type (e.g., Specturum). Abstracting and indexing journals are also published by such bodies.

The value of research reports as the most rapid and effective means of disseminating the results of scientific and industrial research and development to the identified audiences cannot be minimized. But research reports are difficult to locate and procure as they contain the results of research which are closely guarded, atleast until all benefits are realized. The main areas of such research are, the large scale organisations who spend millions of rupees for improvment of their products and techniques to meet the cut-throat competition in national and international markets, and the new challanges thrown up by the increasing body of scientific and technical informaion useful for industries. As a rule, large business, industrial organisations possess research and development facilities, well-established libraries and information units. The annual reports of several organizations and those of councils are published for public use.

Taward Summing Up

Library is essentially a response to the total communication patterns of modern society. The traditional concept of a library being a depository for books has been supplanted by the concept of a resource materials centre as a depositry of information in many forms. This changing emphasis is the result of the development of new techniques for storing and retrieving information which have developed concurrently with new instructional procedures incorporating groups of various sizes, and extended use of individualized instructional materials and the availability of numerous communication media. Improved technology in the form of automatic systems for the retrieval of information, instructional television, individualized audio-visual equipment, microforms, and computers mandates, the planning of the information depository of today and the future based on the concept of the resource materials centre if the needs of the public, students, faculty and curriculum, are to be served more effectively and efficiently (R. Fothergill).

Library today is viewed as a "learning resource centre", "instructional materials centre", "educational materials centre", "student self-directed study centre", "unified resource service", or "exemplary individualized learning centres"[1], which accomodates all materials and equipment that contribute to learning. But as J H. Shera has said, the "basic role of the library is not changing; it is the dynamics of that role, its expression in implementation, that is undergoing alteration". However, the successful development of the library as the centre of the community's intellectual attainments, the beating-heart of the educational institutions, and the life-blood of research depends entirely on the knowledge, enthusiasm, and capabilities of the librarians.

Unfortunately, the librarians have actually failed to reflect that "scholarship and service" is their motto. The root of the trouble lies in the tradition of the library as a storehouse and the librarian as a caretaker of books. Many libraries provide both means of self-development and materials for relaxation. But few, if any accept the necessity for fostering, prompting, and encouraging scholarship. Many of the librarians spend much of their time on purely custodial and clerical functions. Many of them are suspicious of intellectual achievement and welcome routine and pedestrian tasks. Little thought is given to finding out why many groups do not use the library and demand reference service Probably all this was in President Roosevelt's mind when he dismissed the claims of librarianship as a profession as bunkum. What was lacking in librarians was imaginative energy and vision, and that such a person should be "a man who knows books, loves books, and makes books. If he has these three qualities, the craftsmanship of the library calling is an easily acquired quality". Even today, it is difficult to contradict Roosevelt's decision.

By concentrating their efforts on the more routine aspects of library operation, by emphasizing institutional goals, and by adopting bureaucratic organizational patterns, the academic librarians have effectively aligned themselves with the non-academic segment of their communities. Even librarians who have most vigorously advocated their acceptance as full-scale academics have recognized the serious defects in the image they present to those who must accept them into partnership[2]. Morrison, too,

1. cf B.J. Enright. New media and the library in education (Lond. Clive Bingley, 1972).
2. Eldred Smith, 'Academic status for college and university librarians; problems and prospects. *College and Research Libraries* (Jan. 1970)

comments that many academic librarians have an outlook on life similar to that of people in clerical, rather than professional, occupations. This may reflect the fact that too many of them are actually doing work on a clerical level[3].

No amount of training in library techniques can make a successful librarian of a person who lacks a good general education that is ordinarily secured now-a-days through a college/university course. Jacques Barzun has rightly emphasized the pre-eminent need for a librarian to be well-read, to "reader-and-teacher, leaving the role of technician to the computer and the apprentice"[4]. Jack Dalton, therefore aptly suggested : "Perhaps the most important job for the library schools these next few years is not teaching students but defining roles and goals". Libraries themselves should provide "richer in-service education for experienced librarians", and library associations should "adopt a more active policy of providing service to improve professional development." James Thompson has strongly argued that librarianship must become an elite profession, of well-educated people who occupy themselves with truly professionally tasks in a democratic set-up, as opposed to the present reality where so many-called librarians are clerical officers bureaucratically organised.

Only when the librarians become worthy of operating libraries entrusted to their care efficiently and effectively will they be able to interpret successfully the role of library in society, education and culture. The librarians are called upon to serve a society in flux poised between annihilation and utopia, torn asunder by great social movements and tremendous political changes and confused by a babble of conflicting traditions[5]. Such a society needs, as never before, an effective access to knowledge "pleasant and unpleasant, approved and disapproved, useful and useless" for its very survival and its provision is the librarian's sacred duty. To achieve its aim of recording, organizing and disseminating knowledge, leaders of the profession will have to be intrinsically superior men. Brilliant men and women must be motivated not only to join the library profession but also to remain in it.

---

3. Perry D. Morrison : The Career of the academic librarian. (A.L.A. 1969).
4. Jacques Barzun. "The New to the rescue" LJ (Nov. 1, 1969)
5. John Wakeman. "The Context of librarianship." *Wilson Library Bulletin* (V. 37, no. 4, 1962), p. 348

28

Library Buildings

Library buildings are a warehouse for books, a workshop for the readers, and business-home for the staff. Each function must be well served, else the structure has failed. A library building is, therefore, a clear, specific, and direct expression of the functions of a library. 'Form every follows function. This is the law... the shape, form, outward expression, design or whatever we may choose, of the....building should in the very nature of things follow the function of the building.'[1]

The successful library building is one which clearly and directly expresses and provides for the functions that are performed within it. Any library building should be able to meet generally the following functions :

1. Effective technical operations of the library ;
2. Effecient and rapid production of information and material on demand ;
3. Provision of quiet, comfortable and attractive areas for Study ;
4. Provision of individual and collective studies for the users doing intensive research work ;
5. Provision of facilities for developing reading habit ;

1. Louis Henri Sullivan, *Kindergarten chats and other writings* (N.Y., writtenborn, Schultz. 1947)

6. Provision to facilitate the contact of the users with the contents of the library ;
7. storage and preservation of reading material ; and accessibility of the reading materials to users without loss of time.[2]

A library building reflects a structure or a plan of service in an institution. The details of the interior of the building should take into considration the under-mentioned activities :

(a) Book-preparation activity ;

(b) Book-storage activity ; and

(c) Book-service activity.

The activities should comprehend the present and the future needs. There are many conflicting needs and internal paradoxes to be faced in each library. The library buildings have naturally to suit the funcuons of different types of libraries.[3]

Difficulties obviously arise in any attempt to set up detailed building requirements which will apply uniformaly to all university libraries. No less than the book-collection or the staff, the physical plant should be adopted to the needs of particular institution. A so-called ''adequate'' library building for one institution will not necessarily serve effectively the purposes of antoher. To state these requirement in detail is clearly the role of the university librarian ; it is a responsibility and prerogative for which his professional education and experence should fit him above all others in the university.

PRINCIPLES OF PLANNING

The most important requisite of a satisfactory library plant is careful planning. Before designing any building for a library, it is

2. P.N. Kaula, *Library buildings, planning and design* (Delhi, Vikas, 1971), p.55.
3. Ibid, 55-56

necessary to understand the principles of planning. The architectural design, nature, and quality of contemporary academic library buildings in the United States, Great Britain, and, to a lesser extent, in western Europe results from a number of factors : historical precedents, customs and fashions ; burgeoning enrolments ; the expansion of the curricula, involving the addition of new specialized courses, teaching departments, institutes, and professional schools; the introduction of new methods of instruction-involving more initiative on the part of students-which have placed new responsibility on the library : increased emphasis on research; explosion of literature : the nature of library's purpose, function, and use ; the state of communication technology : the state of building technology ; environmental factors, including campus plans, site, climate, and degree of air pollution ; the librarian-his ability and freedom ; external controls exercised by attitudes, and ability and freedom ; and finally, the status of the library as a symbol of the measure of man's respect for the power of knowledge and learning.

Nevertheless, the library scientists have advanced a number of set principles for planning a library building. The most usual are :

1. Every library building should be planned especially for the kind of work to be done, and the community to be served.

2. The interior arrangement should be planned before the exterior is considered.

2.1 Convenience of arrangement should neve be sacrificed to mere architectural effect. The building should be highly functional. Architectural beauty must be derived from the usefulness. Achitecture is the science and art of making buildings useful as well as beautiful.

3. The plan should be adapted to probabilities and possibilities of growth and development in future.

4. A library should be planned with a view to economical administration.

5. The rooms for public use should be so arranged as to allow complete supervision with the fewest possible attendants.
6. Modern library plans should provide accommodation for readers near the books they want to use, whatever system of shelving is adopted.[4]
7. The building should provide convenience in proportion to the number and nature of the users. Physical conveniences should include the conveniences for the library personnel responsible for managing the activities of the library.
8. The building should represent simplicity in chararacter.

The renowned British library architect, Henry Faulkner-Brown has enunciated ten commandments for a new library building :

1. Flexible : with a layout, structure and services which are easy to adapt ;
2. Compact : for ease of movement of readers, staff and books ;
3. Accessible : from the exterior into the building and from the entrance to all parts of the building, with an easy comprehensible plan needing minimum supplementary directions.
4. Extendible :to permit future growth with minimum disruption.
5. Varied ; in its provision of book accommodation, users' space, and to give wide freedom of choice.
6. Organized : to impose appropriate confrontation between readers and books.
7 Comfortable : to promote efficiency of use.
8. Constant in environment for the preservation of library materials.
9. Secure : to control users' behaviour and loss of books.

4. Charles G. Soule. 'Points of agreement among librarians as to library architecture''. *Lib Jour.. 16.* 1891 Cf. Gelfand,p.123.

10. Economic : to be built and manintained with minimum resources both in finance and staff.[5]

In a systematic approach to the planning of the university library building based upon the above broad principles, we have to answer in detail the following questions :

1. What has the library to accomodate ? How much material, of what sort, and in what physical conditions ?
2. How many users must it cater for ? How many at peak times, how many at less busy times ? How many will sit, or sit and write ; how many will choose books and leave ? What hours will the library be open, and how many of each category of user can be expected to use it, at what hours of the day and at what times of the year?
3. What physical conditions (heat, light, humidity etc.) must be provided ?
4. How much security is needed, and how much interference with ease of access is acceptable in order to get it ?
5. How much money is available to build the library, and to what extent is absolute economy to be the prime criterion in its proposed operations.

   (we shall take the five questions and sketch out answers a bit later).

Planning of a library building begins at the main entrance, for it is here that public traffic commences and proceeds to lending, reference, periodical and other sections. The general policy determining the location of various elements of the library should be based on the accessibility, utility and efficiency of each element in relation to the overall structure of the library. In this connection the following points are of vital consideration in planning a library building :

1. work-flow to determine the functional basis of each

5. H. Faulkner Brown, "Accademic Library Building", *On Advances in Librarianship*, v. 3, p.117.

activity as put-forth in above questions. In library terminology, it may be stated as under :

(a) Users flow

(b) Material flow

(c) Service flow

(d) Operations flow

(e) Storage flow

(f) Control and supervision flow.

2. Display area to be near the entrance;

3. Circulation counter to be in the central position with easy access to public catalogue, bookstacks and reference ;

4. Main catalogue to be within the easy reach of the users and the reference staff ;

5. Reference area to be near the public catalogue with a central desk ;

6. Main study areas to be near the bookstacks and on the main floor ;

7. Periodicals area to be an integrated area for current periodicals ;

8. Carrels to face the outside wall of the stacks ;

9. Multitier stacks to be as solid blocks ;

10. Processing departments to be interconnected as a consequence of the chain of operation of a book ;

11. Technical staff activity to be on the same floor ; and

12. Modular concept to be used in construction.[6]

The University library building is a complex, highly specialized structure, the planning and equipping of which require a thorough understandig of library functions and requirements.

The importance of careful planning can hardly be overexaggerated. It has received increasing attention of university administrators,

6. Kaula. op. cit., p. 64-65.

librarans, and architects. Functional design has been particularly emphasized. Monumental buildings with architectural beauty are no longer preferred. A number of factors have been responsible for the change in attitude. Probably the most important has been the need for economy both in construction and in administration and the growing realization of the importance of flexibility and compactness in interior arrangement. From an architectural or aesthetic viewpoint, it is considered desirable that the library building should be attractive and in harmony with its surroundings. Its architectural features should be such that it lends charm to the place where its stands. Its outer frame, its silhouette, its door and windows, its arches, should all produce a concordant note.[7] "A building is music in space.[8]"

Library Building Committee

Having formulated the principles of planning, the librarian and an architect may work together-the former describing his needs and the latter expressing them in a design. This is a minimum team. But it is worth while to form a small committee consisting of representatives from the faculty and students, a librarian, an architect, a representative of the university governing body, and the superintendent of university buildings and grounds (if there is any). If the university librarian lacks experience in library buildings, it is desirable to appoint a library consultant to the committee. As a member of the planning team, the library building consultant will be a key factor in interpreting the library's needs to the architect, and structural limitations to the librarian'[9]

K.D. Metcalf is of the opinion that many competent architects do not have on their staff engineer who are capable of designing difficult foundations, heating, air conditioning, plumbing and electric

7. H.D. Sharma, *Library buildings and furniture* (Jullundur, I.B.C., 1972), p.2,

8. Ibid.,

9. R.A. Ulveling "Getting the most for your money." ef. Gelfand, p.132.

lighting installations for a large and complicated library building. If necessitates to include in the library committee, the electrical and mechanical engineers.[10]

Functions of the Building Committee

The function of the building committee is to make a thorough study of the library needs of the institution and to accumulate the data necessary for planning a suitable structure. With the objectives of the library clearly defined, the committee should determine the local needs systematically by consulting the representatives of all departments as to their needs and desires. The future educational plans of the university, so far as they can be ascertained, should be incorporated into the plan. The committee should acquaint itself with the experience of other university libraries with respect to new buildings; if possible, it should visit some of the newly constructed libraries and examine library building plans. With the assistance of the university librarian and the library consultant, if there is one, the committee should make detailed estimates of the requirements of the different library units which will perform their functions in the library building.[11]

Role of the Librarian

The librarian has an important role to play in this preliminary planning. He shold work closely with the buillding committee in preparing specificcations and should pay particular attention to such matters as the functions of the various rooms, the relationships among them, the probable use of the building and its supervision, the flexibility of its interior, provisions for future expansion, and probable costs of operation. He should be prepared to plan each room in detail, determining the desired layout and the appropriate equipment.[12]

To play his heroic role the librarian must have the following

10. Keyes D. Metcalf, Planning academic and research library buildings (N.Y. McGraw Hill, 1965), p. 258.

11. Wilson and Tauber, op. cit., p.487.

12. Ibid., p.487-88.

information :

1. The objectives of the institution and their implications on the library service.
2. The number of potential users in various categories like the following :

   (a) Undergraduates;

   (b) Postgraduates;

   (c) Teaching staff;

   (d) Research staff;
3. Activities of users;
4. Space requirements for;

   (a) Reading materials;

   (b) Users; and staff
5. Hours of the opening of the library;
6. Size of the library personnel;
7. Special access to users;
8. Avoidance of traffic;
9. Entrance and gangways;
10. Exit and control;
11. Treatment of reading materials;
12. Special Storage conditions;
13. Financial resources;
14. Furniture and equipment;
15. Drawings and Sketches of each area;
16. Construction schedule;
17. Revision and rectification at each stage;[13]
18. Interior finishing and decoration;
19. Exterior of the library;
20. Provision of atmospheric control e.g., heat, light, noise, etc.

13. Kaula, op cit., p. 81-82.

21. Provision for communication system through telephone, lift, fire alarms;

22. Special provision for audio-visual equipment, e.g., micro-filming and photo-copying equipments, xerox, and micro-film reading apparatus, etc.; and

23. Site of the library[14] :-

    (a) Location;

    (b) Shape;

    (c) Size;

    (d) Orientation; and

    (e) Access.

To discharge his responsibilities nicely well, the librarian should—

1. Learn as much as he can about library planning, from books and articles in periodicals and from visiting new builds.

2. Learn all the can about the educational programme of his institution and the relation of this to his library.

3. Must formulate his philosophy of service.

4. Should discuss his problems with the administrative officials of the institution.

5. Should learn what he can about architects in general, about methods of selection of an architect for his building, and what his realations with his would be.

6. Should learn about building cost, so as not to expect too much, but to plan realistically.[15]

The College and University Postwar Planning Committee of the A.L.A. made the following recommendations in this regard :

14. Anthony Thomson, *Library building of Britain and Europe* (Butterworth, 1963), p.7.

15. K.D. Metchalf, "Programme of Library Buidling" *In Planning a library building* ed. by H.R. Galvin (A.L.A. 1955).

1. That all professional librarians be conversant with the fundamentals of good library architecture and that they courageously oppose, with facts and figures, all efforts to erect buildings not functionally planned.
2. That more careful study and thought be devoted to new buildings by the librarians concerned than has usually been true in the past and that the plans for each new building be accompanied by a re-evaluation of the library service of the entire institution and a library budget which will permit the complete and effective manning of the building.
3. That in planning, the librarians have the assistance of representatives of the faculty and administration.
4. That special attention be given in new buildings to housing and servicing of those audio-visual aids which are increasingly supplementing the block.
5. That all librarians realize that educational methods change from generation to generation and that they, therefore, as they have occasion to play new buildings, or alter old ones, make them as fluid and adaptable as possible.

Role of the Librarian Consultant

The role of the librarian-consultant is important even if the librarian is competent : when a librarian has to create a new building he has three disadvantages :

1. **He is too busy running his old library to spend enough time planning the new one.**
2. **He has usually had no experience of building a library; and**
3. **For these reasons he does not think out his future requirements sufficiently thoroughly : he tends to use slogans in place of specific requirement.[16]**

16. Godfrey Thomson, "Library Planning and Design". in Library architecture ed. by vidut K.Khandwala (IASLIC. 1982), p.17.

Moreover, librarian has to work with an architect who will usually have some disadvantages :

1. He has never built a library.
2. He has been trained to make his own assessments and judgements and not to take the client too seriously.
3. He does not accept the librarian as a fellow expert.
4. He wants to get on with the job and not discuss it with the librarian.[17]

In such a situation, the functions of the Librarian-consultant assume greater importance. He should know the minds of both the librarian and the architect. He shold make preliminary investigations and should continue till the final details regarding the furniture and equipment are worked out. Among his important functions, the following are worth mentioning :

1. To know precisely the working of the institution for which the building is to be designed.
2. **To use basic formulas and standards applicable to various requirements : These include :**
   (a) Number of books per shelf ;
   (b) Number a periodicals per shelf ;
   (c) Space for a reader ;
   (d) Space for service points ;
   (e) Space for technical operations ;
   (f) Space for gangways ;
   (g) Number of potential users ; and
   (h) Number of nature of seats for study.
3. **To decide the category of reading space like individual study, faculty study, group study, seminar work, etc.,**
4. To consider the special features for the library like

17. Ibid

auditorium, audio-visual areas, technical information area, reprograph area, etc;

5. To decide about the policy of access to the collections;
6. To decide about the physical conveniences of users :
7. To design the work-flow charts for main functions of the library ;
8. To translate into approximate square metres all the space requirements ;
9. To determine the library personnel for the operations and services of the library ;
10. To study the possiblity and advisability of further expansion ;
11. To examine the site in terms of area and size of the building taking into consideration the future expansion ;
12. To state clearly the basic points of design in terms of space and other requirements ;
13. To make definite recommendations on each major point;
14. To prepare a write-up of the basic principloes and primary elements in design for the guidance of the organization and the architect ; and
15. To specify materials, equipments and furniture for each area of the building.[18]

Thus the role of the librarian-consultant is quite significant. He should decide in consultation with the architect the traffic patterns, floor load, floor coverings, lighting, acoustic problems, ventilations and climatic problems. Sketches and drawings of each area as worked out should be a guide for the final design. His advice at the stage of construction and later in the organization of various area in the library according to the functions stated by him should be available.

18. Kaula, op. cit., p.58-59.

Role of the Architect

The librarian should play a major role in choosing the architect and in proposing consultants though the final action is taken by the administration authorities. In the choice of an architect for a major structure, the following criteria should be kept in mind :

1. The firm should be of sufficient size to have a variety of talent and design ability, yet not so large or so exceedingly busy that this commission would receive less than top-echelon attention.
2. The firm should not necessarily be a local organization though for ease of communication it should definitely have an office in the region-or be willing to establish one as a condition of receiving commission.
3. The chief designer should himself be the architect, at least through preliminaries (also called designed development); and the firm should be selected as much for the project chief as for the principal in the firm.
4. The design architect should have proven competence-be a man of demonstrated stature in his profession.
5. The architect should be a craftsman, in that he is attentive to aesthetics, to plannings details, to the economics of construction, and to the niceties of the operation result.
6. **The architect should be imaginative-creative in design but not flashy or monument creating-and his work should not be stereotyped.**
7. **The architect need not have designed a library although academic commissions would be a useful background.**
8. **The architect must be interested in the needs of the owner (rather than be a strong-willed innovator) and willing to create a result exciting chiefly for its brilliance of function expression and purity of form.**
9. **There should be no requirement that a firm traditionally used by the institution be used even if it fails to meet the criteria.[19]**

19. Rutherford D. Rogers and David C.Weber, *University Library Administration*, op. cit., p.330-31.

The architect is a co-ordinator. He is master at blending the paper ideals worked out with architectural features, materials and site. The architect's brief should emphasize the following particulars:

1. The stack area estimated for accomodating (a) the existing collection, (b) the anticipated acquisition of reading material over a period of five decades, and (c) its location and expansion when required;
2. The general reading rooms and research rooms required for the optimum number of readers;
3. The open access to book shelves with adequate safeguards and seating space near the books.
4. Special rooms for current periodicals, display storage till they are bound, and reading accomodation with adequate natural and artificial lighting.
5. Staff work and rest rooms.
6. Ancilliary services—refreshment room and clock room.
7. Janitorial and security staff accommodation at the back corner or the basement.
8. Audio-visual aids storage room and adjoining sound proof room for their use.
9. Air conditioning plant accomodation, if the building is designed as such.

Collaboration Between Librarian and Architect

The ultimate design of a new library building is the result of cooperation between the architect and the librarian. Good cooperation usually results in a building which is both functional and pleasing to the eye. Frank and complete cooperation with the utmost interchange of ideas, should be aimed at, for this without this the complete building will almost certainly fall very far short of perfection. Elaborating the principles of cooperation between the architect and the librarian, it is suggested :

1. That the librarian should be the first to be consulted, if a new library project is envisaged.
2. That the librarian should have a forceful voice in the highest councils of administration on the question of the general architecture of the library.
3. That the librarian should have an equally forceful voice at the same levels in the selection of the architect.
4. That the librarian should be provided with sufficient funds to prepare a thorough-going written programme and to employ outside consultants to assist him in the preparation of such a programme.
5. That the architect should be present at all conferences involving locations, design, cost or any other attributes of the building.
6. That is the librarian and the architect reach an impasse on any question, and as a matter only of last resort, the librarian should be arbiter of all matters, relating to organization of space in the building for working purposes, and the architect the arbiter of specifications of materials, construction, equipment and decor.
7. That since most institutions have a building committee, the librarian should be appointed as its chairman.
8. That the architect and the librarian should approach each other with respect, should welcome conflict if it springs from honest conviction, and should collaborate and not compete. Neither should seek to dominate the other or to appeal from the other courts of higher resort. Both have places to which they can appeal, neither should do so.[20]

The Programme

We have stated that the building committee should be charged with the responsibility for ascertaining the library's needs and for accumulating the necessary planning data. After the committee has

20. Burchard, op. cit., p.126.

completed its survey and planning, it should put in black and white, for the guidance of the architect, a detailed, explicit statement of the requirements of the library. This statement also called programme may be prepared by the librarian or the librarian-consultant, by the architect in consultation with the librarian or by the building committee itself. Of late, the librarians have started playing a vital role in the planning and designing of their new buildings.

A typical building programme should cover the following points in detail :

1. Title page.
2. Table of contents.
3. Programme justification (often in the form of a separate document written by the director and approved by the provost and the trustees).
4. Academic plan or function of the building (an articulate exposition).
5. Location of site and orientation (usually determined by the director, the provost, and the trustees).
6. Architectural compatibility (usually determined by the planning office, president, and the trustees).
7. General building configuration and access (determined by the director).
8 Functional relationships (of the departments).
9. General restraints on spaces and mechanical equipment (inculdes ceiling heights, fenestration, module dermination, wall insulation, and mobility, electric power, lighting, sound control, and ventilation and airconditioning).
10. Memorial name requirements (specified by the director).
11. Architect's scope of work (usually specified by the planning office).
12. Code references and procedures during design and construction (written by the business or planning office).

13. Synopsis of space requirements.
14. Detail of space requirement (each administrative unit to be described in terms of individual spaces and each space to have a statement of (1) desired net assignable square footage ; (2) location in relation to other spaces, when important, and special character ; (3) built-in or attached equipment, e.g, shelving, counter, book conveyor, or washboul ; (4) movable furnishing).[21]

R.R. McLarren and D.E. Thompson have prepared the following "Architectural Checklist" to prepare a building programme :

1. Statement of library history, philosophy and organization.
2. Outline of library and non-library functions and activities to be included in the building.
3. Summary of the study of library's community.
4. Indication of amount of fund available for planning, site acquisition, and construction.
5. Indication of architectural style required.
6. Reference to standards.
7. Indication of space requirements.
8. Complete list of furniture and equipment ; and indication of provision for expansion in future.

M.A. Gelfand also emphasizes that the programme should state at the outset the objectives of the institution and their implications for library service. The clientele should be described briefly and same indication should be given of the needs of the main classes of library users.

This may be followed by a detaild analysis of users' and staff activities. Diagrams illustrating the flow of work, especially in technical service departments, can be very helpful. This can be done by graphic means or listing the main areas by floor.

21. Rogers and Webers, op. cit., p. 334-35.

Space requirements should be given in details under such headings as : space for books; space for users; and space required for other purposes.

A description of the interior should also be given for the guidance of the architect. Here the programme can discuss aesthetics and colour, space dimensions and ceiling heights, lighting fixtures; sun control, noice and traffic control, floor coverings, wall treatments, furniture and furnishings, elevators. stairways and booklifts, security and fire protection, etc.

It will be important for the architect to receive a description of the site, which should be as explicit as possible. Plot plans, master plans and other graphic devices for showing the relationship of the proposed library to existing structure should be provided.[22]

It may be kept in mind that the role of the architect, especially if he has had experience with library buildings, begins after the librarian and university administrators have outlined the basic service needs of the structure. The architect, however is not a draftsman; he will have fundamental contributions to make in regard to arrangement of the several units. If an appropriation has been made for the building it is desirable to mention it in the programme. Architects find lost figures helpful in determining the limitations within which they have to work.

The architect's first task is to prepare a visualization at the requirements in "preliminary plans", showing a tentative layout of the building in floor plans and elevation. In this stage of the planning, it is the function of the architect to provoke discussion, to enable the librarian and the library committee to visualize their ideas from different angles, and to help them arrive at a definite physical expression of the nature and character of the building. The preliminary plans provide an excellent opportunity to the librarian to critically examine the architect's first drawings to determine whether the building as a whole will be sufficiently flexible and expandable. Attention to details at this point in planning will produce a building relatively free from errors.

22. M.A., Gelfand, op. cit., 125.

The architech may begin the process by presenting a sketch of the main floor for disscusion. He will try to interpret the requirements of the building programme in visual terms. The first floor sketch will be discussed by the architect and the librarian and it will probably be followed by many more until agreement has been reached between them. The sketches may also be shown to the consulting architect for architectural designs. With various suggestions, the architect should draw the new plans. Then the same procedure will be applied to the sketches for the other floors. At this point the architect and librarian may find it profitable to visit other libraries, particularly some of similar type and size. But libraries of other types may also be viewed with profit, for their interior arrangements and furnishings may be of great value. Now the architect may well desire to draw the plans and add stairways, shaftways for elevators or booklifts; the position of entrances; rooms, corridors, and other architectural features. This is a point at which the preliminary plans may well be referred to consulting architect and or library consultant if one has not been used previously, and to the supervisory staff of the library. Their first hand knowledge of the library needs can be of great value. Detailed consideration of furniture and equipment will probably arise at about this point. Furniture and equipment will probably arise at about this point. Furniture layout well be made, equipment located, tentative provisions will be indicated for electrical outlets, lighting needs will be considered further. The basic requirements will have been met, the building plans adapted to the site and costs involved.

Final plans, which are also called working drawings, will consist of floor plans, elevations and sections and details of the structure. These will provide graphic illustrations of the building from several physical points of view. The gereral construction plans will be supplemented by separate set of drawings illustrating the design of the heating, ventilating and air-conditioning systems; of electrical work, plumbing, special communication system; and there will be additional drawing illustrating the detailed design and location of many general and special features of the building such as stacks, furniture and built-in shelving along walls. These plans will be supplemented by written specifications which will describe the type and quality of the materials that are to be used, quality of workmanship desired, and such additional information as is necessary to supply the builder with a full description of the building he must construct and the conditions he will have to fulfit. The librarian should always review the architectural floor plans and bring to the notice of the architect any important error or oversights. He should concern himself with the drawings which give details of furniture layout, ceiling treatment, floor treatment, etc., here he can request changes, if they appear necessary. The criticism of final plans and specifications is often the last opportunity the librarian may have to affect the character of the library building; changes are rarely made once the contracts are awarded and construction is under way.[23]

In sum : It is not possible to produce a good building without a good programme. Its basic purpose is to ensure that the librarian and the building committee have grasped the functions of the library with regard to the irrespective departments and the requirements necessary to carry out these functions. The programme should explain the use which will be made of each of the facilities needed and the space requirements of each so that the architect will have a clear idea of the problems he is going to be called upon to solve.

Selecting the site

Where to locate the new building is a vital issue which must be decided before finalizing the plans of the building. Dimensions of the plot and its orientation greatly affect the building.

Major factors should be taken into consideration in selecting of site :

First, is its size adequate ? In these years of burglossing enrollments and publishing, it is hardly conceivable that any library building will be too large. The probability is that expansion space will soon be needed, and care should be given to making this possible. Metcalf has stated that an institution planning a new building should provide space for books sufficients to care for an

23. Ibid., p.125-26.

increase in the book collections for twentyfive years at the present rate, and seating capacity for the anticipated increase in the study body during a similar period.

Second, what is its relation to neighbouring buildings and to the whole population and traffic flow of the institution ? The setting of a main library is dependent on projections of dormitory and classroom usuage and of pedestrian traffic patterns. The library should be conveniently close to classrooms so that students may use reserved books and other collections during free hours. The building should be reasonable convenient to dormitories to encourage evening use. If the library can be located next to the bookstore, each will support the other. If commuters form a sizeable part of the enrollment, proximity to public transportation or parking lot is important. A public road is necessary for delivery trucks and public safety vehicles; and some parking is useful for library delivery trucks, and for cars which transport distinguished visitors, elderly faculty, and physically handicaped readers. These and other factors will have to be weighed.

As a corollary of above, a building should be located in the heart of the university campus. A central location is frequently sought from an architectural, as well as from a functional point of view. The library is usually a building of considerable size. Consequently, it may occupy a central position. While placing the library in a central position may be strategic, it should not be surrounded on all sides by other buildings so that extension becomes impossible. Moreover, the surroundings should be quiet, in order to secure good working conditions in the building.

Third, what orientation is possible for a library building erected on it ? Usually it is recommended that the building should face in such a way that the main reading rooms may have a northern or southern exposure. Since these rooms are often placed in the front, this means that the building should face north or east. Northern light is relatively steady throughout the year and does not expose the readers to the direct rays of the sun.

Fourth, are there advantages or disadvantages in the slope of the land ? It is easier to build a functional building on a rectangular plot of land than on a square or triangular one. Rectangular areas rooms are found to be most suitable for efficient work and they cut down distances to the minimum'.[24] However, this shape of plot need not worry the librarians much as the rectangular buildings can also be built on a square or triangular plot; other factors should also be taken into consideration. Librarian may not have much to do in the selection of the plot but he can be of much help to the authorities in the selection of the plot.

Finally, what complications will arise from the nature of the ground beneath the building ? The tendency to have stack rooms underground should not be imitated for the ground below may turn out damp or marshy.

Designing the building

As soon as the planning team—the library authority, the librarian/librarian consultant, and the architect for a library building has drawn and adopted the programme preliminary plans and the working drawings, as well as choosen the site, the actual construction will begin. The multiple functions carried out in a modern university library will determine the layout, location, floor space, interior decoration and the furniture and equipment of each integral part or department. A satisfactory library building usually contains both reading rooms, and administrative work rooms. The librarian should have acquaintance with the methods of concentation so that he is able to collaborate with the architect in the use of building materials and construction device. Of course, this is field in which an architect should have his final word, but the librarian should never lose the sense of participation and pride on his part of a most imortant operation.

Two types of interior construction have been recognized. These are :

24. Sharma, op. cit., p.20

1. fixed construction ; and

2. modular construction.

Fixed construction is a permanent interior arrangement with more or less clear demarcation of several areas with study area and stack area as completely different parts of the building and not interchangeable. There are fixed partitions for each interior area of the library. Modular constructions, on the other hand, permit flexibility in construction.

Modular Construction

The modular system of construction has been introduced in library building to provide for flexibility. Few contemporary librarians are willing to accept a building which imposes on the future, the past or present pattern of book use and management. Almost every building now being planned seeks flexibility in some way and modular construction permits flexibility in construction. The future needs of a building are difficult to anticipate and, therefore, the specific parts of the university library should be capable of elasticity of use and ease of modification to meet changes in university educational pursuits. Modular construction allows adjustment of space compatible with the changing functions and the new operations of a library.

Modular construction refers to a system of building construction in which the floor area is divided into equal rectangular unit at space defined by structural columns at the corner instead of by overbearing walls.[25] In simple words, this system implies the construction of a building in units or modules.[26] The modules are identical in size; however, sometimes modules of different sizes are used in different parts of a building. There is no unanimity as to the best size for a module, their sizes vary from 3' to 27'.

25. Kaulp, op. cit., p. 182

26. Module ; one of the rectangular units of space in which modular construction is divided.

The assumption has been made that modular construction allows complete flexibility, since modules can be adjusted for any purpose which may arise. The idea beneath the modular system is to keep the building as "open" as possible, so that permanent partitions are kept to the minimum. This system has completely replaced the old concept of "room" or "area". Stack room has been changed to stack area, reading room to reading area and so on. The only spaces enclosed by walls now generally are work rooms, librarian's room, seminar room, lavatories and the like.[27] Where a seperation of areas or services is desired, it is made, whenever possible, with movable doublefaced book cases, display room dividers, screens, planter boxes, dry construction and furniture.

The modular system gives a completely flexible building, the interior arrangement of which may be altered at a very low cost to suit new uses to which they may need to be put. In these days of uncertainty concerning what libraries may be called to do in the future, this is an advantage of considerable importance.

The column spacing of this system provides for :

1. maximum utilization of floor space ;
2. economical ceiling height ; and
3. low construction cost.

The ceiling height is kept uniform to meet every purpose. The weight-bearing capacity of each modules is kept the same so that any part of the building is used for any functions of the library. Movable partitions preferably of glass are used to give greater elements of flexibility. Modular buildings are economical and easy to be maintained and administered.[28]

K.D. Metcalf highlights the following advantages of the modular system :

27. Sharma, op. cit., p. 46.

28. Kaula, op. cit., p. 176.

1. It simplifies the task of estimating costs and makes the result more accurate.
2. It saves time on the site because materials are acquired in suitable sizes, and it largely eliminates cutting, patching, and wastage of materials.
3. It simplifies supervision as much of the work is routine.
4. It should the finished product because more of the work is done under factory control instead of field conditions.
5. It provides more flexible space adopted for any likely purpose.
6. With pre fabrication being put into increasing use, each of these advantages will gain more importance in future.

S.R. Ranganathan also maintains that the use of a single modular unit in library architecture should be put to the maximum possible use by permiting freedom for forming rooms and passages at any point at any time, with sizes made by any desired number of modules. For this purpose there should be no rigid wall other than parapet wall for the building as a whole. There should be only large halls, one on each floor of each of wing of the main building. The formation of the rooms should be with easily removable portable panels of standard dimensions, without the need to break down plastered masonary walls.

However, objections to modular construction include the facts that no module is perfect for all types of use, that a compromise is attained rather than a first-class building, and that the idea of flexibility is so strong that the architect and librarian are likely to plan insufficiently for the future. In K.C. Metcalf's works : Like most innovantions, however, the modular system is not a panacesa; it has its faults and pitfals. The fundamental objection is that no one column spacing or bay size is ideal for all purpose; the module that is almost perfectly adampted to one function, such as book storage, will not be equally well suited to another. The attempt to obtain flexibility entails certain sacrifices; and some inflexible features, such as columns at regular intervals, remain in any case. At best, the modular system represent a series of compromises, with too often mediocore results. He also highlights the acoustics' defects when he writes that modular buildings have sometimes encountered serious accoustical problems because the movable partitions and book cases on which they depend to divide up each floor have not been adequate barriers to sound.[29]

Thus modular construction is not an unmixed blessing as painted out by Metcalf. Those librarians who consider the modular construction a revolutionary idea would do better to keep in mind the evaluative factors projected by Ellsworth. These involve the relation of the modular idea to the plan of library organization, expense of operation, aesthetic considerations, cost of construction, ventilation problems, ceiling heights, size of modules, kinds of movable partitions, lighting, attractiveness of interiors, effects on users and general applicability to libraries.[30] Ellsworth concludes his discussion by writting : He view is satisfied that the concept of modular planning is the ultimate and final basis for library planning is lacking in both hind-right and foreright indeed, because it should be clear to all that the technology of building construction is siill in its infancy in some respects. Building still cost too much, use materials that are too heavy, cannot be moved readily, have not mastered proper ventilation and lighting, or sound proofing, have not provided interior remodelling procedure that are sufficiently inexpensive and have not made sensible use of new materials. He furhter commants that-in library where there is no need for flexibility, where codes do not permit, or where the predominant style of architecture clashes, and where there is no need for economy, other methods are more suitable. Artificial circulation and treatments of air are essential in most climates in a modular building and this costs money.[31]

Weighing both merits and limitations one can conclude that

29. Metcalf, op. cit., p. 49-50.

30. Ralph E. Ellsworth. "Determining factors in the evaluation of the modular plan for libraries". *Coll. and Res. Libs.*. V. 14; 125-28.

31. Ibid., p. 142. See also, Bean and Ellswort. Modular planning for college and small Univ. Libraries, p. 60.

the advantages of this system are greater than disadvantages. In modern times the planning should be modular. This idea of planning a building on a multiple series of basic 'modules' is as ancient as architecture itself, and just as sound. This system of constructing an open structural shell supported at regular intervals (thus forming modules of 'lays') is suitable in modern library buildings. Flexibility is maintained, since interior partitions are not restrictive to the basic structure; also, since book shelving is normally manufactured in standardized sections, a multiple of those section dimentions can be used as a basic for the module. Modular planning will permit of interchangeable use of any area for book stack, reading space or other purpose and thus the future development of the library is facilitated.

Monumental vs Functional Building

Another issue closely related to library designing is one of monumental vs. functional building. So far as the external treatment, the elevation, and the section are concerned, full weight may be given to the monumental. But as regards the inner lay-our and the utilization of the inner space, the expression and dramatization of its functions. The inside of library is a silent intellectual work-shop, into which no sightseers will be permitted. There will be no general traffic of the intellectual workers themselves. Therefore, the inner architectural feature should be designed so as to secure comfort and quiet to the users, without any eye to impress on tourist traffic. The overlook of this principle reduce library service to a mockery in a university library. A big high rotunda with excellent echoing qualitles, the hanging of huge portraits in the inside, and the outlook of the authorities, used to bring in the reading room crowds of sigh-seers with babies in arms.

Massive ornamental staircases occupying the most accessible part of the building, high ceiling with paintings, circular design, square design, and the butter-fly design, which make extension difficult, do not generally go with the functional design of a library building. This does not imply any objection to turrets, towers, and dooms above the roof level—that is, outside the functional part of the buildings-or to any external treatment in order to give the library building, character, dignity, and beauty without any denial to the freedom of a creative architect.[32]

Single Level

Each floor of the library building should be in one single level. There should be no threshold for the internal doors anywhere in any floor. It should be possible to push a loaded book-trolley from any point in a floor to any other point in that floor or any other floor, without any transhipment and the dangers due to the sloping surfaces and Kerbs.

The movement of book-trolley from one tier to another where there are three or more tiers in the stack-room, should be through electric lifts provided within the stack-room with landing at every tier of the stack room and at every floor of the other adjuscent rooms. In large libraries where quick mechanical carriage of books and related materials are required, arrangements may be made for pneumatic tubes and belt conveyors.[33]

Design for Open Access

A library building designed for 'open access system' can also serve a closed system but the converse is not true. Therefore and in view of the world trend toward 'open access system', the design for a library building should be as for 'open access'.

The freedom given within the building of an open access library will tempt abuse, unless safeguards are provided in the design of the library building. Stated in general terms, there should be no opportunity for unauthorized removal of books through windows, door, or other openings in the outer walls of of the building. Other implications are :

1. Only one entrance and one exist should be provided for the public. This should be at the counter so as to be under

32. University and College Libraries, *Report* op. cit., p 91.

33. Ibid.

the control of the circulation staff within the counter enlosure.

2. It should be secured that there is no means for passing of books between the readers in the entrance or exit gangway and those inside the library.

3. Door and windows should be protected with wire fabric for safety of books. All the windows and doors opening out should be fitted with locked or fixed shutters with meshes, each aperture not more than 10 sq cm in area, except for the single door or the two doors used for coming into and going out of the building.

4. The circulation within the building should be designed in such a way that the readers are not distracted by the traffic and that the catalogue room and the stack room are within the closets reach possible from the counter.

5. The height of a unit rack should be such that the books in the top-most shelf-plank can be easily picked out by a person of normal height standing on the floor. The inference is that book-racks should not exceed 2.20 metres in height. This leads to another inference. The ceiling of a tier in stack-room should not be more than 2.35 metres high. Otherwise, much space will be wasted.

6. Each window in the stack-room should have the maximum possible area so as to admit maximum possible natural light in the cross gangway facing it. It will be an additional advantage if the tier-floors are all of glass. The light through the entire height of the top-most tier will then reach the ground floor which will be the one most used by users. For proper lighting during night, the gangway lights should have reflectors which bathe the books with light and save the eyes of the readers from direct light. Moreover, to provide for the comfort of the readers browsing in the stack-room, there should be a minimum of 1.35 metres of widh for gangways between consecutive lines of book-racks.

7. Each window in a reading room should be so placed as to throw sufficient natural light on the reading table of the readers sitting in a line at right angles to it.

8. Provision should be made for research cubicles-one for each reader to have a quiet enclosure, all for himself, in which he can keep his reading materials for several days. It is desirable to have cubicles for not less than 20 per cent of the number of teachers, research fellows, and advanced students.[34]

Sun-Breakers and Sun-Shades

It is necessary to minimize the effect of solar heat on the readers, in order to enable them to do their intellectual work for a long stretch of time. This requires the provision of sun-breakers to all the windows opening out into the east or the west; or in the alternative, verandahs should surround all the eastern and western walls. It is also necessary to provide sun-shades for the south or the north.

The longer axis of the stack-room should run East to West. There will then be no need for windows on the eastern or the western walls. This will prevent direct sun from falling on the books in the forenoons and the afternoons.

To prevent the southern and the northern sun from falling on the backs, books of the stack-room should have a gangway of a metre of width all along the southern and the northern walls.

There is no denying the need for preventing rain water from falling on books. The provision of the gangways along the walls is a help in this matter. But at times of storm and torrential rains, even the gangway may prove insufficient. It is, therefore, desirable to reinforce the protection. This is done by making the glass shutters of the windows turn as a horizontal axis. The shutters can be left at a suitable slope during the rainy season.

By making the walls of the stack-room hollow, a better protection from solar heat may be secured. This can be done easily if the walls of the stack-rook are not load-bearing.[35]

Dry Construction

The modular system leads to dry construction. The use of a

34. Ibid., p. 114-15.

35. Ibid., p. 95-96

single modular unit in library architecture should be put to the maximum possible use by allowing freedom for forming rooms and passages at any point, at any time, with sizes made of any desired number of modules. For this purpose, there should be no rigid wall other than external wall forming the building as a whole. In fact, there should in a sense be only large halls-one in each tier of the stack—room and one in each floor of each of the wings of the main building. The formation of the rooms should be with easily removable, portable panels of standard dimensions. It should be possible to shift them as desired without the need to break down plastered masonary walls and to rebuild them in the conventional way. Traditional construction should give way to dry construction.

Dry construction consists in putting up temporary, thin, easily removable partitioning walls of prefabricated material like pressed plywood, glass, aluminium, etc. wet mortar is not required for such construction; hence the name dry construction. The material used is held of nuts, bolts or wooden frames. Dry construction allows the building to retain its flexibility because the partitions can be easily removed. Also it can be put easily and speedily and the same material can be used time and again. Whenever possible book stacks can also be used to demarcate space for various activites.

Impact of Extension Services on Architecture

Additional rooms are required for carrying on extension services by the librarian. These include :

1. Group—study rooms of small size;
2. Seminar rooms of small size;
3. Conference room of large size with audio-visual and other equipment for all modern methods of communication and demonstration; this can be found in the other buildings of the university;
4. Open air reading room for the day for which enclosed quadrangles should be automatically formed in the layout of the wings of the library building.
5. An exhibition room for bringing to the attention of potential readers from time to time beautiful books and manuscripts, new books, worth-while books, forgotten old books, and books on topical themes, as a means of converting into book-lovers persons without interest in books;

6. Public conveniencies of the cleanest kind at suitable points within the library premises;

7. Canteen within the library premises so that the serious readers need not go out for refreshment and thereby run the risk of losing the mental set-up built during study; and

8. A cooperative stationery and book-shop where the requirements of readers can be had and their urge to own books stimulated. The conference room and the stationary and bookshop may perhaps be provided in some other place within the campus of the university.[36]

Amenities for Library Staff

A modern library has to be kept open for long hours. A library building should, therefore, provide an adequate relaxation room for the staff. It is desirable to have separate rooms for the men and ladies on the staff. A small kitchen to make coffee or tea is found to be of great help. Accomodation for caretaker of the building should also be provided.[37]

Library School

While all the above adjuncts to a library building are necessary for all kings of services—libraries, a university library should also provide adequate accomodation for a library school. For, the university library will have to be used as the observatory as well as the laboratory of the library school. The space for the school should contain.

1. Minimum of two lecture rooms;

36. Ibid., p. 99-100.

37. Ibid..

2. One room for practical work with lockers for the students and space to stack about 3,000 books to be used as practice materials;
3. One reading room cum common room;
4. Separate room for each member of the teaching staff;
5. One common room for the staff;
6. One room for the administrative staff of the school.[38]

SPATIAL RELATIONSHIPS

Stack-room

The stack-room should be palced centrally so that it is easily accessible from every part of the library.

Ctalogue-room

The catalogue room should be like an ante-room to the stack-room, on the way from the general reading room to the stack-room.

General reading room

The entrance to the library should open into the general reading room.

Periodicals reading room

Periodicals reading room may be removed from the general reading room. But independent access to it should be possible when the other rooms in the library are closed.

Special reading room

Special reading room may be still further removed from the general reading room.

38. Ibid., p. 100-101.

Librarian's room

The librarians and the Deputy Librarians should have their rooms in close proximity to the general reading room.

Work-room for the staff

The work-rooms of the technical and administratice staff should be palced in close promimity to the rooms of the Librarians and the Deputy Librarian.

Independent access to stack room

The technical staff should have an independent access to the stack-room.

Cubicles and other rooms

The cubicles, the rooms for group study, the committee room, etc. may be in a separate wing or on a separate floor.

Rooms for department of Library science

The rooms for the department of Library Science may be provided in a separate floor or wing.

Text-book reading room

The text-book reading room may either form part of the general reading room or be a separate room. It should have in it or adjacent to it stack space for about 5,000 books.[39]

Space requirements

A building should be designed to supply adequate and efficient accomodations of materials, readers, and staff. It should provide for the preservation shelving, and storing of books and other library materials; for the convienient use of these materials by the clientele;

39. Ibid., p. 108-109.

and for the work of the library personnel involved in acquiring and processing reading materials for use, and in making them easily available to clientele. A detailed study of the requirements of a particular institution is fundamental to the provision of facilities that will be adequate for effective service.

Standards

How much space is needed for accomodating materials, readers and library staff is difficult to answer. As E.M. Broome so rightly said in an article in the Library Association Record (Dec. 1963), "there are now an almost bewildering number of standards to help, or confuse, the would-be library planer".

At the suggestion of the chairman of the Library Committee of the U.G.C., The Indian Standards Institution established a Sectional Committee on Library Buildings, Fittings, and Furniture (BDC 127). S.R. Ranganathan was also the Chairman of BDC 127. The following space estimates were worked out by it.

Sizes of rooms and Gangways

Generally speaking, dimensions of rooms, gangways, etc, may be based upon a planning module of one metre. Dimensions of furniture and fittings may be based upon a module of 10 cm.

Stack-room

The dimensions of stack-room should be as under :

1. Clear length—1.80m plus 3.15 metres where n is the rows of books racks.

Note 1 : The centre to centre distance between consecutive racks is 1.80 m (on the basis of 0.45m of rack-depth plus 1.35m of cross-gangway width).

Note 2 : The distance from an end wall of the stack-room to the centre of the nearest row of racks is 1.575m (on the basis of 1.35m of the end cross gangway width plus 0.225 of half the rack depth).

2. Clear width : 3m (on the basis of one books rack 2m long plus one side—gangway of one metre) close to longitudinal wall; or

5m (on the basis of 2 book racks each 2m long plus one side gangway of one metre) close to a longitudinal wall; or

8m (on the basis of 3 book racks each 2m each of the longitudinal walls) or

10m (on the basis of 4 books racks each 2m long plus two sides-gangways of one metre width) close to each of the longitudinal walls.

Note : Three metres and five metres width are generally only in the case of stack spaces, as the stack room and the reading room may be combined into a single room in such cases.

3. Clear height—Floor to ceiling 2.35m.

Note : 1 : The height of the book rack is 2.20, and allowance for bary guides is 0.15m.

Note : 2 : Each unit book-rack 2m. long may be assumed to house 700 to 750 volumes and one square metre of stack-room area may be assumed to house 150 volumes.

Note : 3 : In a university library the number of tiers may be four.

Provisions for Bay Guides

Suitable provision should be made for suspending bay guides from the ceiling of each tier of the stack-room.

For example, a depth of about 5 cm from the ceiling of each tier of the stack-room and at a distance of about 5 cm from either side of a row of book racks, a rod may be run from wall to wall of the stack-rooms, so that frames holding the bay guides may be suspended and slide along.

Reading room

The size of a reading room should be as follows :

1. Length—1.5 m (excluding the control region where n is the number of rows of reading tables).
2. Width—5 m (on the basis of three tables each 2 m long plus central gangway 1 m wide); or

   7.5 m (on the basis of three tables each 2 m long plus central gangway 1.5 m wide); or

   10 m (on the basis of four tables each 2 m long plus central gangway 2 m wide).

Note : The size of the reading table is 2 × 0.70 m. The centre to centre distance between two consecuitve rows of reading room tables is 1.5 m with seating arrangement on one side of the table only.[40]

OTHER ROOMS

The sizes of the other rooms may normally be as follows :

	For use of	*Area in Sq. M.*
1.	Librarian and Deputy Librarian	30 per person
2.	Professor and other Teachers	15 per person
3.	Classifier, cataloguer, Accession Librarian and Maintenance Librarian	9 per person
4.	Secretary to the Librarian	9
5.	Secretariat of the Library School	30
6.	Visitor's room	15

40. Ibid., p. 110-111.

7.	Administrative and Professional Staff not at service points and other than those mentioned in (3)	5 per person
8.	Class room	5 per person
9.	Practical room	3 per student
10.	Group discussion room	15
11.	Seminar room	20
12.	Cubicle	7
13.	Committee room	20
14.	Other room	according to level need.[41]

Strangely enough, no standards have been provided for issue counters, reference section, public catalogue, periodical section and room for accomodating audio-visual equipment and other such sections. Moreover, while calculating the space for readers it has accounted for the number of rows in which reading tables are to be arranged in the reading room, the dimensions of the tables and an adequate provision for gangways. We may now take into account the space estimates given by western writers on the subject. The following figures have been suggested for making rough estimates of floor area requirements :

Books : 1 square foot per 15 volumes

Non-Book Materials may occupy from 2 per cent to 6 per cent of the sapce occupied by books and journals. In specialized baranch libraries the percentage may be much higher.

Seating sapce : 25 sq. feet for each undergraduate, 35 sq. feet for each graduate student, 75 sq. feet for each faculty member.

For staff, counting present and anticipated size : 100 sq. feet per person. A figure of 160 sq. feet for salaried person in technical processing and 135 sq. feet in public services will allow for card

41. Ibid., p. 111-112.

files, shelves materials in process, sorting areas, counters, file cabinets, book trucks, and other equipment and furniture associated with the staff.

Space for other purposes : Under this heading there may be included the space required for stairways, lobbies, corridors, ductwork for ventilating or air-conditioning, building service and other accomodations. For rough estimating purposes, Metcalf suggests adding 40 per cent of the total floor space requirements for books, readers and staff, to permit for other purposes.[42] Thus, if 100,000 sq. feet fo space are required for books, readers and staff, 40,000 square feet should be added for all other purposes.

P. Harvard—Williams in his article "Standards for Surface Needed for University Libraries" has suggested the following standards :

1. That of library buildings should preferably be planned for about 25 years and must normally be capable of extension.
2. That the library buildings should be planned with a minimum of pillars and partition walls, and a minimum floor loading of 125 lbs. per square foot or 600 kgs. per square metre.
3. That for each reader a place of 25 square feet or two to three square meters should be allowed. For graduate readers, 30 sq. feet or 2.8 sq. meters; for professors 40 sq. feet or 3.7 sq. meters should be provided.
4. That the stacks areas should be also to accomodate 160 volumes per sq. meter or 10,000 volumes per 60 square meters. An allowance for futher development of the collections must be included for a minimum of 10 years from opening and preferably for a period of 25 years to allow for unforseen expansion.
5. That an allowance of 120 square feet or 11 square meter per member of library staff should be made, including an

42. M.A. Galfand, op. cit., p. 127-28. Also, Rogers and Weber, op. cit., p. 339.

area for an appropriate number of staff envisaged as necessary for the development of the library during the period for which the building planned; and

6. That non-assignable space or balance area should be not less than $33^{1/3}$ of the area devoted to library accomodation.

As regards the number of seats, it is suggested that 50-75 per cent of undergraduates and 40-50 per cent of the faculty members should be provided accomodation for seating in the library.

The recommendations of the working committee of the U.G.C. (U.K.), 1964, and that the total number of reader and study places should not normally exceed[43] :

One seat for every three arts undergraduate students.

One seat for every five science undergraduate students.

One seat for each arts post-graduate students.

One seat for every three science post-graduate students.

Provision for number of staff, micro reproductions and specialist reading places is included in this total. Where there is evidence of extensive use be extramural departments an additional allowance may be made of approximately ten percent. Further provisions for external users may be made where records of visits exist.

F.N. Whithers, "Standards for Library Service" suggests that the seating accomodation should be based on anticipated growth for over two decades. Seats for at least one-third of the student enrolment is essential.

The U.G.C. Library committee (India) has suggested that in the Indian conditions 1/5 (20%) of the total number of students and 1/10 (10%) of the number of teachers be provided reading seats in the university library.

Equipment and furniture

Once of general layout and different types of accomodation for books, readers, and staff have been decided, the question of

43. Cf. H. Faukner Brown, op. cit., p. 112.

equipment and furniture should be seriously taken-up. In a building as specialized as a university library, adequate equipment is especially important; and task of planning is one that calls for expert judgement.

It is convenient to consider the equipment of a library as falling into several broad categories determined by the function it will perform. Basically, these categories are concerned with the following considerations :

1. Equipment which is special to libraries and is used largely in direct face-to-face service to the readers. This includes book shelving, display equipment, control counters, enquiry desks and public catalogues, as well as the machinery used for the recording of library transactions such as photocharges and computer-issue devices. Some furniture such as atlas cases, A-V storage cabinets are especially designed for any library. In choosing the most efficient and economical item for each purpose, the librarian must also bear in mind the effect it will have on the appearance of the library.

2. Storage shelving, together with the equipment necessory for the swift retrieval of books stored away from public areas. In this category are book conveyors, book hoists, communication equipment, and air-conditioning.

3. Equipment and fittings which, while certainly not peculiar to libraries, have to be chosen judiciously for their suitability to library service. These include tables, chairs, carpets, curtains and furniture for relaxation. The choice of decor too falls into this group.

4. Equipment for the office function of the library; this includes desks for the staff, typewriters, (electric and manual), duplicators and copying machines, (photographic, xerographic or dye-line processes).

5. Recreational, kitchen, store room, rest room and toilet funiture, fittings and equipment. The choice of individual

items will be a matter for the architect; the librarian's task is to say in general what is needed.[44]

In short, the librarian must be competent to choose the most efficient and economical item for each purpose; he must bear in mind the effect it will have on the appearance of the library; the must be aware of the possibilities of items being available from outside the normal library suppliers, for example shelving and book convenors or hoist from the materials—handling manufactures. He will also need to consider carefully the general office equipment suppliers, with particular reference to filing cabinets, type writers and copying equipment. In all these things he should draw on experience of other libraries, keeping in view the local needs, the finance available and the type of library service to be achieved. The librarian must profit by the technical knowledge of the architect and his team who, for example better know the strength of beams to support heavy loads and materials available in the market. Some of these need further elucidation.

Heating, Cooling and Ventilaiion : Air Conditioning

Air-conditioning is a series of independent energy processes so connected that the over-all effect is to transfer thermal energy from one place to another. In winter the purpose is to distribute heat uniformly in the controlled space; in summer the object is to remove heat from the controlled space and to dispose in it a thermal reservoir.[45] But air-conditioning is something more than keeping the library hot or cool. In the strictest sense it means the simultaneous control of eight factors, viz., temperature, humidity, air motion, air distribution, dust, bacteria, odors, and toxic gases as well as ionization, most of which affect in greater or less degree human health and comfort.

The important advantages which a library may derive from air-conditiong are :

44. Godfrey Thomson, "Furniture and equipment", op. cit.,

45. Mc Graw-Hill Ency. of Science and Techonogy, v. 3.

J.E. Burchard, et. al. *Planning the university library building* (Princeton Univ. Press, 1949).

1. It protects the materials and equipment from the dust which is a serious problem in most places.

2. It makes it possible to maintain the temperature and the humidity of the stack-room at an optimum which minimize the breeding of insects and the fungi, injurious to books.

3. Paper and covering material of the binding will also preserve better if there is at least dehumidifying. The uneven contraction and extension of the paste used in binding will be minimized; and the cracking and warping of the binding will be eliminated.

4. Provides ideal working conditions for the library staff and readers.

5. Eliminates the cost and noise of electric fans.[46]

In brief, the sunlight, extreme heat, dryness, dampness, solid particles of dirt and liquid, and gaseous forms of acids in the air are injurious to papers, binding, vellum and leather. It is, therefore, essential that for the best preservation of books, the atmosphere should be free from dirt and acidity in gas or liquid form and that temperature and humidity should be controlled. This necessitates the installation of full air-conditioning plant.

Limitations

Air-conditioning, however, is too costly; and electric heating dries the air in wet season. While the ratio of people to floor areas in libraries with open stacks is quiet low, still comparatively large quantities of air must be circulated to keep the books "conditioned" as well as the people.

Cooling load due to heat given off by people will vary avidely. For instance, conference and seminar rooms may have an occupancy load of 10 sq. ft. per person, while the stack area will average 80 to 100 sq. ft. per person. The areas with differing occupancies thus have to be carefully zoned.

46. U.G.C. Report, op. cit., p. 97-98.

Clean air is not only desirable, but necessary so that the books will not become soiled.

The sound level of the air-conditioning system must be low enough to prevent distraction, but cannot be so low that normal sound will be obtrusive.

A university library often operates sixteen hours a day. This means that heavy duty, long life equipment must be used.[47]

K.D. Metcalf in his oft quoted work "Planning Academic and Research Library Buildings" has focused attention on the following acoustic limitations of air-conditioning plant :

1. Compressors or transformers be immediately above, below, or beside a reading or work room area.
2. Fan noise transmitted through walls or duct work.
3. Air movement at too rapid a pace through supply or exhaust duct work.
4. Meter noise, particularly through walls or duct work.
5. Cooling tower fans, a noise usually more disturbing outside than inside the building and a serious matter when the building in near dormitories or residences particularly at night when the noise seems to be amplified by the quiet prevailing elsewhere.[48]

Expert technical advice be sought to overcome ocoustic limitations. But adequate funds will be necessary for the installation and working of an air-conditioning plant, as it requires high power to run the refrigerators, pumps, fans, and a continuous supply of water for cooling. It is only the big university libraries, with plenty of finances which can afford to have air-conditioning plant. Keeping this in view, the U.G.C. Library Committee has recommended that air-conditioning may be confined to the small area containing the rare books and manuscripts.

47. Ian Grad and Alfred Greenberg, "Air Conditioning for Books and People".

48. Planning academic and research libraries, op. cit., p.198-199.

Prevention of Noise

The prevention of excessive noise in libraries is of utmost importance as an aid to effective use by students and as a prerequisite to the comfort and conservation of the energy of staff members. Outside, or background, noices can be controlled by double glazing which involves air-conditioning. But noices which originate within the building owing to conversation electirc fans and ventilators, walking, and the use of telephones, typewriters, and other types of equipment should be kept to a minimum. A variety of insulting materials and devices is available.

To avoid noise created by walking consideration should be given to the selection of proper flooring materials. Long wearing quality, ease in keeping clean, resistance to stain, low cost of maintenance, good appearance, comfort and resilence are the factors in selecting the required reading materials. Flooring of title, of ground cork, of asphalt, or of rubber are some of the more satisfying flooring materials used in libraries. Choice between rubber, corks and tiles may be made on the basis of heavy traffic and use.

To prevent noice acoustical materials are used for walls and ceilings in corridors, reading rooms, and work rooms. It includes sound proofing materials for the walls of the bindry of other rooms in which heavy machinery is in operation; of padding which contains insultaing materials for door; of carefully selected floor coverings.[49]

"R.M. Pierson in his article "Two Aspects of Readers' Services Areas; Recommendations to Library Planners" has made the following valuable suggestions for reducing the noise. The noise-quantum, according to Pierson can be reduced to a great extent by—

1. So planning auditorium, class—rooms, and the like that traffic in and out of them does not enter library service areas.

2. Arranging the various units so that the least frequented will be the most remote.

49. Wilson and Jauber, op. cit., p. 517-18.

3 Avoiding traffic lanes that cross the reading areas.

4. Erecting banks of room—offices, rest rooms, stairs, in ceilings, walls, book's and partitioning surfaces.[50]

All legs of movable furniture should be provided with rubber shoes. The book trolleys should also have rubber tyres.

In this venture, the librarian should proceed in full consultation of the engineer.

Lighting

Adequate lights is of such paramount importance that the librarian must make every effort to obtain the best possible illumination for his building. The problem of lighting should be considered early in the planning programme and expert advice should be sought for the design of the lighting system.

How much lighting is necessary for a library building has been a controversial matter. While experts suggest that library lighting might be 30 foot-candles, others have recommended 40 to 50 foot-candles for library reading. Krachenbuehl in his work "Modern Library Illumination" has recommended foot-candles ranging from 5 foot-candles for hallways and corridors to 25 foot-candles for all reading purposes.

While there is no unanimity on the amount of light that is required for library purposes, there appears to be some agreement on the following points :

1. Lighting should be uniformly distributed.
2. Sharp brightness contrasts should be avoided in the treatment of walls, ceilings, floors, table tops and other reflective surfaces;
3. Lighting fixures should provide maximum diffusion of light and should be installed so as to avoid high brightness contrasts with their surroundings.

50. *In College and research libraries*, v. 23, 1962.

4. Daylight cannot be relied upon as an exclusive source of light, nor should its use influence the design of the artificial lighting system (windows, contrary to some views, are not the least expensive nor the most efficient souces of light, the cost of windows is often greater than a corresponding area of wall).

5. Stacks shoulds be lighted to provide adequate light for the lowest as well as the highest bookshelves.

6. The relative merits of incondescent versus fluorescent lighting needs.[51] Problem faced by the Librarian in deciding on a lighting system include the effects of ceiling heights, the nature of the fixtures, and the kind of lighting needed for specific areas in the building, corridors, aisle space, entrance and such area require general lighting of lesser intensity than in the rooms set apart as reading, reference, stack and carrels. Lighting of reading tables and book stacks should be local and spread evenly over the surface.

7. Illumination experts agree that the best kind of lighting in a library is glare-free and shadowless, because it eliminates eye-strain and fatigue to a great extent. In this respect, flouorescent lighting of the book stacks is found more successful than incandescent lamps, because the luminous tubes are glarefree and throw light evenly on the bottom and top shelves. Fluorescent lamps consume less current but their initial installation costs are heavy than ordinary incandescent lamps.

Finally, in a country like India where power/breakdowns are not infrequent, an emergency lighting system, supplied by batteries, must be provided in the library. Moreover, in addition to individual switches at each light point, there should be a single control switch to put off at the closing time.

In breif, adequate and proper kind of lighting is 'a must', in order that reading is done with all pleasantness and spontaneity.

51. Gelfand, op. cit., p. 130.

Unfortunately, proper and satisfactory lighting has been achieved less frequently than almost any other feature of the library erected in twentieth century. The librarians should, therefore, seek the advice of illumination experts to create cheering, exciting, sustaining, and warming environments for study.

Communication and transportation

To increase operational efficiency, to reduce errors, and to release the professional staff from pedestrian tasks, librarians have installed a number of machines and special types of equipment, depending upon the size of library services. Among these communication devices are : teletypewriters, teleprinters, fire alarms, electirc book lifts and pnuematic book conveyors, which eliminate drudgery to the staff and save time. More advanced libraries install "Telex" service, similar to teleprinters, to receive and record biblioraphical information for the use of readers. Unless labour is cheaper than the operating costs of these machinery, it is certainly worth-while to make provision for their installation at the time of planning a library building.

Fumigation Equipment

In warm climates particularly, where fungi and insects attack materials repidly and devastatingly, it becomes necessary to provide fumigation equipment. This equipment should also be used for the processing of incoming materials and handling manuscripts and archival documents which are likely to be infested with pests. The new Singapur National Library Building contains a fumigation chamber "at the top of the stock tower with a capacity of about 1,647 cubic feet. This has book shelves for the materials to be fumigated, extracting and intake fans and an coscillating fan".

Maintenance

Adequate facilities should be provided for the janitorial and other category of maintenance staff. Janitors' rooms containing slope sinks and storage space for cleasning equipment and supplies should be located on each floor of a large building, and space should be provided for machinery and minor building repair and maitenance of functions.

Furniture

The interior planning of a library building must take into account the layout of furniture shelving and other movable equipment in order to ensure maximum efficiency in the functioning of the various sections of the library. Although the librarian is not a technical expert in the desigining and construction of furniture and movable equipment, yet he needs a distinct and well founded idea of what he wants in furnishing a library to maintain harmony with the building and collour of the floor, walls, and ceiling.

While undertaking the selection of furniture and equipment the librarian should bear in mind the following factors :

1. Flexibility of arrangement is desirable; built-in furniture and equipment such as catalogue cabinets, exhibition cases and loan desks should be avoided as these are not easily moved or expanded in furture.

2. Wherever it is possible book shelving should be standardized so that the parts easily interchangeable as furniture should also be purchased in groups of uniform sizes. Tables, chairs, counters and desks lend themselves to such treatment.

3. Comfort, durability and variety should be sought in furniture especially although the quality of durability should apply generally to equipment as well.

4. Economy and ease of maintenance.

5. Colours and materials should be coordinated so as to provide an attractive and inviting atmosphere in harmony with the prupose of the library.[52]

52. Lyie. op. cit., 386-90.

In sum, library furniture must be functional, durable, beautiful, easy to clean and maintain.

Basic equipment and funiture may include shelving, card catalogue cabinets, tables, chairs, counters and desks, filing cabinets, exhibition cases for the public areas; office machines, work tables, files, desks, chairs, shelving, book trucks, etc. for staff work roooms, tape recorders, motion picture machines and photographic equipment for realized services.

Chairs

Three items require exceptional care because of quantity and expense : The chairs, the tables, and the book-shelving. The chairs should be selected with the participation of several members of the staff, the faculty, and the student body. What is comfortable for one person may be uncomfortable for others. Depending on whether it is a table chair or lounge chair, points to watch for are distance from floor to front of seat, width of seat, depth of seat, sculpture of the seat (or structural support of unholstered seat), incline of the seat, width of arm, flatness of arm, length of arm, height of arm on an armchair (to be sure that the table of carrel at which it is to be used with easily clear it), incline of the back (does it hold one up to the table ?), "boniness" of the back, aility to glide, and aility tip on its back legs—as well as rigidity of fabrication, attractiveness of design, durability of fiinish, ease of maintenance, and cost.[53] It will be wise for the librarian to have discussions with the representatives of library supply houses and manufactures. The librarian should carefully inspect samples of all chairs proposed, preferably on the type of floor on which they will be used. The chairs should be comfortable, light, portable and graceful.

A Reader's chari for a library shall, among other things, have the following special characteristics :

1. The chair shall be fitted with noise prevention rubber studs or tips in the legs. It also avoids marks on the floor coverings.

53. Rogers and Weber, op. cit., p. 350.

2. The chairs' seat shall not be hard or upholstered but be preferably of woven material to ensure ventilation and slight yielding when in use :[54]

3. The arm shall be 215 mm high from the seat and set back 75 mm from the front edge of seat; and

4. The back rest shall be curved in plan and shall be not more than 180 mm in height measured from the arm rest.[55]

Tables

Library tables come in various sizes and shapes. For simple note taking, a surface providing six square feet is normal. For use in consulting government documents, manuscripts, conductor's scores, and similar materials, a surface of light to ten square feet is needed, and this is the minimum desirable for assignment to students undertaking research papers or thesis. For use in consulting art books, atlases, other folio's or portfolio's, and most microtest reading equipment, a surface of twelve to fifteen square feet is needed. Just as a microtext carrel should have space for the machine plus six square feet for books and papers, so should type and disc positons provide such space in addition to the equipment.

ISI has recommended different standards : the size of the reading room table should be 900 mm× 600 mm (or 3'× 2') for single and 2400 mm× 600 mm (or 8'× 2') for three readers. The height of the table top should be 750 mm (2'.6"). The minimum knee-hole space per reader should be 750 mm deep; 650 (or 2'.2") high and 600 mm (2') wide. The foot-rest, either in the form of a fixed rod or as a sqparate pipe should be provided at the height of 150 mm (6") from the floor.

Gelfand writes that it is customary for tables to be 29-30 inches high. (The standard library tables are 36" wide. This width can

54. Gelfand writes that for sustained, use upnostered arm-chairs are more comfortable than those without arms.

55. *Report,*

admit two readers to use it at a time. A doublesided table should be 42 to 48 inches wide. Individual study tables may be 2 by 3 feet in area; some are equipped with book shelves, and side drawers with locking arrangement.

Reading tables can take the shape of individual carrels with full or partial dividers and individual desks with or without railings. In turn these may be nested in a variety of ways. Carrels may be constructed in banks of two to eight. Individual reading stations may also be at tables for four, six, or eight persons, and these tables may have 8-inch or 15-inch dividers or 22-inch dividers with shelves. Desks and carrels may have lockers in which to keep personal notes, books, and even type writers. The reading position may be wired for use of a microtext machine, tape recorder, slide projector, or type-writer, and may have a bulletin board and a light fixure. Since students have a wide deversity of attitudes and feelings, a variety of reading accomodations should be provided.[56]

Tables should have linoleum or plastic tops as they will be subjected to heavy wear. Modern illumination design calls for light coloured table surfaces to reduce brightness contrast for readers. Square, rectangular and circular tables can be used according to the shape of the room. The gangway between reading room tables should be 5 feet allowing for movement of chairs.

Book Shelving

Shelving is the most important ingredient. In the planning of furniture and euqipment of a library, shelving must be given the top-most consideration, as it is a basic need and a major item of expenditure connected with the internal equipment. University libraries acquire a variety of reading material—books including encyclopedias, periodicals, pamphlets, news papers, maps, audio-visual aids and manuscripts. The shelving required to store these materials will depend on their physical size, shape and weight.

The chief material with which book shelves are manufactured are basically two; steel and wood. But substitutes are emerging in

56. Rogers, op. cit., p. 351; Also Report; p. 132.

synthetic products, vinyl, rigid and unbreakable plastic polyster, and alkathene, etc.[57]

Metal and wooden shelving

The choice between metal or wodeen shelving is largely one of atmosphere, humidity in atmosphere has little effect on it. Metal feels harder and because of its tensile strength thinner shelves can be used and book storage capacity increased to the maximum. The risk of fire is largely eliminated. Metal shelves look more business-like; it can be produced in large quantity and preserved for future use. The parts can be manufactured to such exactly accurate dimensions that interchageability is at all times possible. It usually allows greater degrees of flexibility in height because fully adjustable shelfs clamps can be fitted. The range of colours offered is very wide indeed, and in some libraries this has produced a revolutionary appearance which can be described as 'exciting' or 'garish' according to taste. Metal shelving is free from the ravage of termites and other insects.

The only limitation of steel shelving is that the investment costs are very heavy in comparison to wooden shelves and it lacks the pleasing finish and appearance of grained wood. But metal shelving of today need not look cold, and it is just as easy to guide and to keep clean as wooden shelving.

Two types of shelving may be recognized : (1) Bracket type, and the (2) slotted type, including the perforated type.

The bracket of shelving is the simplest form of library shelving and is mostly used in libraries. The shelves are supported on barackets having two books which fit into the slots in the pressed steel uprights which are placed at three feet intervals. The shelves may be adjusted to the required height. The advantage of this type of shelving is that any standard width shelf can he used and can be substituted by shelving of other wideths, if required, without altering the position of book stacks.

57. C.G. Vishwanath, *Public Library Organization,* Today & Tommorrow, 3rd ed. 1978.

The slotted type shelving is made of one piece of sheet steel and the shelves slip into the slots cut at one inch intervals in the uprights, which are of double construction. The shelves can easily be raised or lowered. The disadvantage however, is that the shelves must be of some width as that of the upright supporting panels. If at future date shelves of a larger width were required, the uprights also will have to be manufactured of that width and the existing shelf space will remain unused.

The standard dimensions of steel shelving are the height of 7 feet 6 inches. Shelf length should be 3 feet and its depth should be 8 inches; 8 inches shelves will accomodate 97 per cent of the usual university collections. Some shelves will, however, be needed for quartos and a few for folio's and postfolios. Folios and postfolios' may be placed on roller shelves or bracket-type shelves 20 inches deep or 10 inches deep with the volumes shelved through the double face, or on 20-inch cantilevered underbracketed shelves so that volumes may be shelved across the space where two shelves meet side by side and thus save space. Each arrangement has advantages, and each library must calculate its needs.[58]

Wooden shelving is as functional as steel shelving and the initial investment will be within the reach of every library. Hardwood shelving gives the advantage of a more mature and restrained atmosphere; softwood is seldom satisfactory for public areas. Wooden shelving is usually 6 feet 10 inches high. The average weight per foot run of books on 7 inches shelving is calculated at 18 pound, and on 9 inches shelving at 20/ pound. The capacity of book-stacks is calculated at on average of 8 volumes of lending and 6 volumes of reference to a foot run of shelving.

Both steel and wooden shelving have their merits and limitations. A common compromise is to have metal frames with wooden shelves and end panels. For storage purposes money can be saved by using the racks produced by materials-handling firms, with shelves made of compressed fibre. The librarians should decide whether bookshelves are to be open or with centre partitions. The

58. Ibid., p. 352.

trend in recent years has been towards the open type, particular with metal book shelves, but the only way-to make a decision is to study examples of both types. Cases with centre partitions certainly form more efficient screens and can be used to produce study alcoves. Book supporters are needed to keep the books standing in vertical position. These can be of metal, wood or plastic and can stand independently on the shelves being bent on the sides of books. These should be at least half inch thick and rounded. Metal supporters are in vogue in the libraries today. Their basic purpose is to prevent books sliding about on shelves, tries and cases.

Catalogue Cabinet

Unless the library is using a loose-leaf shelf catalogue, the card catalogue becomes an important tool for both staff and readers. It will require card catalogue cabinets for the public catalogue, the shelf list and the official catalogue as well if one is maintained.

Card catalogue cabinets are made of wood or metal. But metal is not widely used, as metal trays are noisy to handle. It cannot be over-emphasized that the present-day wooden card-catalogue cabinet is the result of decades of experience. The designing and construction of a card catalogue cabinet is a highly skillful job, for its component parts should be precisely accurate in their dimensions as well as in their size, shape and colour; local carpenters should never be allowed to make one 'just as good'. It is a time and labour saving device for readers and library staff. It is subject to continuous use. In order to withstand the heavy wear and tear, it must be built of the best hard wood which should be seasoned to prevent building and warping in humid weather.

The Cabinet shall consist of the two parts; (1) The cabinet; and (2) the table stand on which the cabinet rests. The cabinet shall consist of 24 trays each. The bottom of the cabinet should be 750 mm (92 feet 6 inches) from the floor so that stopping down in referring to the bottom row is avoided; while the top row of trays in the cabinet should not be more than 1400 mm (5 ft.) from the ground level, enabling a person of average height to use them with ease and comfort. The width of drawer should be 6 inches (150 mm); height of drawer should be 4 inches (100 mm); lenght of dramer 15 inches and depth of dramer 18 inches (450 mm). Such a tray can accomodate 1500 to 1800 cards of 7.5x 12.5 cm (3x 5 inches). Each tray is fitted with a non-corrosive metal rod in the cente bottom running along its depth to secure the cards in position by passign through the punched holes of the cards. The rod is better fastened by a release catch near the Knob.

Counter

Often known as the issue-and-return desk, this occupies a key position in most lending libraries, and its layout and design are crucial to the success of the library. It must be planned so that its known functions can be efficiently carried out; efficient means permitting both the smooth progress of users and economy of staff time on the desks which must be carried out many hundred of times daily.

Many of the well-known library furniture manufactures now offer counter units of different types but of standard sizes which can be bolted together in a particular combination to suit the needs of the library. Like standard shelving units and catalogue cabinets, these counters can be added to if need arises' or they can be unbolted and reassembled in new shapes to meet changed requirements.

The detailed design of a counter is a matter of great importance to the librarian. There is only one way to produce an effective design: the work which needs to be done at the counter, minute by minute and hour by hour, must be stimulated. The various spaces necessary for books, issue records, registration of readers, space for trolleys to stand for the removal of books, space for cash transactions and so on must be calculated carefully.

The ISI recommendations are that the counter shall have three shelves all round except at a place occupied by the circulation staff.

At a height of 130 cm from the ground there shall be a transparent plate glass shelf all round. This glass shelf shall be contilivered and there shall be no verticle support near the working edge of the counter so that an un-interrupted space is available on the counter-deck for free movement of trays. The vertical barrier between the counter deck and the glass shelf at the further edge shall also be made of glass. If the counter is to be aginst a wall, the side which touches the wall need not be provided with the shelf.

Control gates

The control gates may consist of either a single leaf door with a gravity hinge or any other similar device or a turnstile. The gate shall be fitted in such a way that it can be foot-operated by the staff inside the counter and the device inside shall be so located in relation to the foot rest of the operator that he can operate it with minimum of the leg. The clear passage when the control gate is open shall be 0.5 cm.

Over-flow enclosure

The over-flow enclosure should be fully panelled and the barrier for the over-flow should be continuous.

The over-flow enclosure shall be so constructed that is does not allow passing of books from the inside to the outside of the library.

The height of the over-flow enclosure shall be 105 cm and it may have an enterance and exit door located preferably diagonally opposite to each other.

The counter controlled area shall not be less than 3m× 3m and should preferably be 4m× 4m.

Counter Chair

For the counter chair the following special requirements are necessary :

1. The seat be 760 mm high from the floor level and the chair shall not have arms, and
2. There shall be a foot rest in the chair.

Book trolleys of book trucks

These are made of wood or steel. The trolley may have two pairs of sloping shelf planks and one flat plank or for books of larger size. The trolley may be fitted with four wheels—one of the swivelling type at each end and two of the fixed type in the centre. The wheels should be covered with rubber bumpers so as to prevent noise in movement and scarring of walls and shelf upriths. The book trolleys relieve the assistants much of the tedium of book load transport from place to place in the library and also will enable a larger number of books to be carried at a time than by hand and in an order of arrangement, ready for shelfing. Trolleys can be used to transport books quickly through elevators of lifts from one floor to another provided they are properly designed to accomodate the book trolley.

The height of the trolley may be the same as that of the tables that is 750 mm. Standard sizes of book trolley are (1) 2 feet 2 1/2 inches wide, 2 feet 6 inches long and 3 feet high; and (2) 2 feet 2 1/2 inches wide, 3 feet 4 inches long and 3 feet 6 1/2 inches high. Inclined shelves in the book trolley will be more advantageous as visibility of cal numbers on books arranged by them adds to the convenience of the staff in location of books. The trolley may be provided with two numbers 10 or 12 mm thick longitudinal ite—rods at the levels of the upper shelves.

In the light of the importance of equipment and furniture for the efficient and effective running of library and dissemination of service, librarians need a distinct and well-founded idea of what they want in furnishing a library, and this cannot-result from hasty, last-minute discussion with the representative of library supply houses and manufactures. It is unwise for the librarian and the architect to spend all their time and available money and building plan and its construction. Construction of the building should be carried on in a planned and phased manner, and in each phase provision for sufficient furniture should be made, It must be selected for its durability, comfort and variety.

Costs

Costs of construction vary among countries and within countries. Rough estimates are usually based upon the type of building (institutional or educational, in the case of the library), its size in terms of total floor area in square feet, or volume in terms of cubic feet; and construction costs per sqaure of cubic feet. R.E. Ellsworth in his book "Planning Manual for Academic Library Building", suggests that while arriving at tentative costs of construction, the following factors may be taken into consideration :

1. Usual site conditions and requirements will raise costs but in most cases this will be known in advance.

2. The level of quality of materials, the lighting, ventilation and accoustical systems, as well as the furniture and equipments, are all measurable and predictable elements, of costs which are well with the control of the client.

3. Regional costs differences do exist but these too can be measured.

4. Timing, i.e. the state of construction economy at the time plans are put out to bid, can be a significnat factor, which is usually not within the control of the client.

5. Costs of construction have been enhancing 12 to 15% annually for several past years. Since it is frequently two to four years between the time the planning starts and a building is completed, allowance has to be made for this rate of increase. Shortening the time lag by such procedures as fast-track planning can help, but if this precludes the possibility of careful planning the saving may not be worth-while.

Construction cost figures are frequently kept by architects and builders to a particular region or country; recent figures can be helpful. Some of the figures are given in architectural journals and library periodicals. In cost calculations, the librarian is most unlikely to be able to decide how he would like to spend; he may, however, be able to assert his priorities and to state that, if money will not allow two desirable feature, then a certain one is nore important than the other. The architect is in a position to make an estimate of the probable cost of building suitable to serve the purposes and to meet the detailed requirements of the librarian. he will do this by carrying out a 'feasibility study'. But the following data will be supplied by the librarians to enable the architect to estimate the capital expenditure :

I. Different sections to be housed in the library buildings based on their respective functions.

II. Approximate size of the collections, it means the number of volumes and the number of current periodicals for display.

III. Approximate number of reader's seats to be provided.

IV. Different types of rooms required.

V. The strength of the staff.

VI. Other general controls and conveniences to be provided.

VII. Basic dimension for each of the rooms, fitting and furniture.[59]

Conclusion

The physical facilities of the library have a great deal to do with its usefulness. To enable people to do their best, they must be provided pleasant surroundings, ample light without glare, colours that are pleasing, ventilation that is adequate, temperatures that are comfortable; acoustics that protect the reader from undue distraction, and seating and work surfaces that are conducive to intensive concentration. Not only must the building provide the maximum in physical attractiveness and adequate space for readers and books, it must also provide for a variety of uses—consulting general reference tools or working alone at a private desk or carrel, typing

59. R.S. Begum and M.A. gopinath "Capital Expenditure on Buildings and Equipment". Lib. Se... . ..Doc., V. 1. 1964. p. 353.

without disturbing others, talking over one's library problems with fellow-students or faculty members, smoking, listening to records, browsing among new books, reading a comfortable lounge—type chairs, or examining exhibits designed to exploit library resources.

Seen in this light, it is not surprising that many university library buildings in India have proved inadequate, Among the more serious shortcomings of these building have been the lack of sufficient space for books, readers and staff; unsatisfactory location; inadequate ventilation, heating, and lighting; the absence of easy traffic channels; inadequacy in size to carry on all function; inappropriate relations of space for related functions; the lack of flexibility; the used of space for vested, non-library activities; and the lack of provision for expansion. Failure to anticipate the rapid growth of universities, insufficient preliminary planning, lack of financies, the inexperience of librarians and faculty members, or the desire of an architect or donor (like Roychand Premchand) to create a monument rather than a functionally useful building have been the principal causes of these inadequacies.

It is true that the U.G.C. Library Committee and ISI : BDC Committee provided code of practice relating to primary elements in the design of library building in 1960 followed by the development of code of practice for lighting (1966), specifications for library furniture and fitting (steel and timber, 1976, 1977), etc. But, unfortunately, the ISI standards have mostly been ignored by librarians, library authorities, architects, and engineers—eigher intentionally or their ignorance about their very existence. It is higly important that the library buildings are constructed and designed keeping in view the ISI standards prepared meticulously.

Finnally, the increasing use of automation, micro-reproductions, information explosion and revolution in communication technology applying mechanical and electronic processes for the handling and operation of documents are likely to affect the design of the library buildings. The planning of a new building should contain a re-examination of such services, as special architectural and constructional provisions are necessary for them; adaptability will be the watch-words of such buildings.

INDEX